Strangers
and
Sojourners

Wayne State University Press   Detroit

ARTHUR W. THURNER

Strangers and Sojourners

A HISTORY OF

MICHIGAN'S

KEWEENAW

PENINSULA

Library of Congress Cataloging-in-Publication Data

THURNER, ARTHUR W.
   STRANGERS AND SOJOURNERS : A HISTORY OF MICHIGAN'S
KEWEENAW PENINSULA / ARTHUR W. THURNER.
      P.   CM. — (GREAT LAKES BOOKS)
   INCLUDES BIBLIOGRAPHICAL REFERENCES AND INDEX.
   ISBN 0-8143-2395-2 (ALK. PAPER). — ISBN 0-8143-2396-0
(PBK. : ALK. PAPER)
      1. KEWEENAW PENINSULA (MICH.)—HISTORY.   I. TITLE.
II. SERIES.
F572.K43T49   1994
977.4'99–dc20   93-49673

Designer: S. R. Tenenbaum

GREAT LAKES BOOKS

*A complete listing of the books in this series can be found at the back
of this volume.*

Philip P. Mason, Editor
Department of History, Wayne State University

Dr. Charles K. Hyde, Associate Editor
Department of History, Wayne State University

In memory of my beloved wife,

VIRGINIA PETERSON THURNER

Contents

Acknowledgments

AS A NATIVE OF CALUMET, MICHIGAN, I AM IN-
debted for my early interest in Michigan's Keweenaw Peninsula to
my parents, sisters, brothers, and friends. All accepted the Keweenaw
as unique—a place with a distinguished past, a precarious present,
and an uncertain future. Much of their interest, combined with stories
told me by descendants of earlier residents, aroused at an early age my
fascination with life in the Copper Country. An intellectual interest
served as counterpart to growing up in years of despair like the
1930s when people scanned the daily stock quotations to see how the
price of copper was faring. The uncertainty of the future of copper
mining in the Keweenaw paralleled the vicissitudes of childhood and
adolescence. But the people I knew believed that good days lay
ahead. The people of the Keweenaw Peninsula today continue that
optimism. They taught me much of the history found in this book,
some corrected in time by later more formal training and research.

In attempting to reconstruct ways of life long since gone, journals,
letters, diaries, memoirs, historical society papers, account books,
photographs, minutes of workingmen's meetings, newspapers, and
fragments found in various archives constitute the basic sources used.
I am grateful to archivists and their staffs at various centers in
Michigan.

I wish to thank, especially, the staff at the Walter P. Reuther
Library, Detroit, where Wayne State University's Archives of Labor
and Urban Affairs provides valuable material for Copper Country

9

Acknowledgments labor history from 1938 to 1970. Philip P. Mason, director, led me to materials not only here but elsewhere, resources I either did not know existed or had ignored earlier. A Henry J. Kaiser Family Foundation Research grant enabled me to complete an important phase of my work in spring 1991. I also thank Raymond Boryczka, research archivist, Marjorie Long of the library's staff, and Alberta Asmar for helpful information.

At Lansing, David Johnson and his staff at the State Archives helped considerably. Here, LeRoy Barnett, research archivist, and John Curry, curator of photographs, helped me considerably, as did the staff of the Michigan Library and Historical Center.

Theresa Sanderson Spence, archivist, and Kay Masters at the Michigan Technological Archives, Houghton, assisted ably in a search for materials written by pioneer residents. David T. Halkola, professor emeritus, Michigan Technological University, came to the rescue several times with needed information, especially on political history. I owe a very big debt to E. Chris Dancisak, whom I never met but who suggested that I peruse the papers of the Upper Peninsula Travel and Recreation Association in the state archives. What I found there greatly enhanced the story of tourism in the Upper Peninsula.

Nancy Bartlett and the staff at the University of Michigan's Bentley Historical Library, Ann Arbor, helped much. Evelyn Leasher at Central Michigan University's Clarke Historical Library, assisted in my study of the Reverend John Pitezel papers. Lorraine Uitto Richards of the Finnish–American Heritage Center, Suomi College, Hancock, Michigan, enabled me to find material in its Oral History Project.

Martha M. Saari answered questions regarding her husband Gene A. Saari's work as a Copper Country labor leader. Charles Stetter of Laurium, Michigan, supplied the correct quotation from a Central Mine reunion address that corroborated a basic theme used in this book.

Arthur B. Evans, director of Wayne State University Press, and his staff have helped me shape the manuscript. Their careful reading of an early version of the manuscript and constructive criticisms helped immensely.

The late Virginia Peterson Thurner read and criticized the manuscript at all stages. I am grateful for her vital assistance in bringing this story to life.

Any factual errors are mine. Not everyone will accept my interpretation of life in the Keweenaw Peninsula, but I believe it comes as close to "what really happened" as is possible in these times of rampant historical relativism. History is neither chronology nor meaningless chaos. History is more than record and subjective interpretation. I agree with the conclusions of Alexis de Tocqueville (1840) and

Charles A. Beard (1933), who recognized a worldwide movement to democracy. What happened in the Keweenaw Peninsula between 1650 and the present is part of that larger story.

Arthur W. Thurner
Professor Emeritus
DePaul University

Introduction

AT THE NORTHWEST CORNER OF MICHIGAN'S UP-
per Peninsula, the Keweenaw Peninsula extends into Lake Superior.
Seventy-five miles long and fifty miles wide, the Keweenaw Peninsula
is divided about midway by a waterway some twenty miles long. In
ancient times, portions of the journey through the waterway were
made over a portage, especially at the northwest end. Native Americans denoted the portage as "the place where one crosses" from one
part of Lake Superior to another, avoiding a longer, often stormy,
journey around the tip of the peninsula. Explorers, missionaries, and
voyageurs, hearing the Ojibwa pronunciation of their name for the
portage, derived from that the phonetic Kee-wai-wo-nan or Kakiweo-
nan. Henry Rowe Schoolcraft, explorer and linguist, used Keweena;
and eventually, the term was spelled Keweenaw.

Unknown peoples mined copper some three to four thousand years
ago at scattered sites running southwest to northeast from Ontonagon to Eagle Harbor and on Isle Royale, seventy miles northwest
of Houghton. In the nineteenth century, Americans extracted vast
copper riches at sites of the ancient diggings and nearby places. Much
of the copper was found in large masses. The Keweenaw Peninsula
became world famous for its production of native copper of a purity
rarely found elsewhere. The Michigan mines produced about 95
percent of the nation's copper in 1848 and for another thirty-five
years produced about 80 percent of this country's copper. Thousands
of Americans and Europeans migrated to the Keweenaw in search of

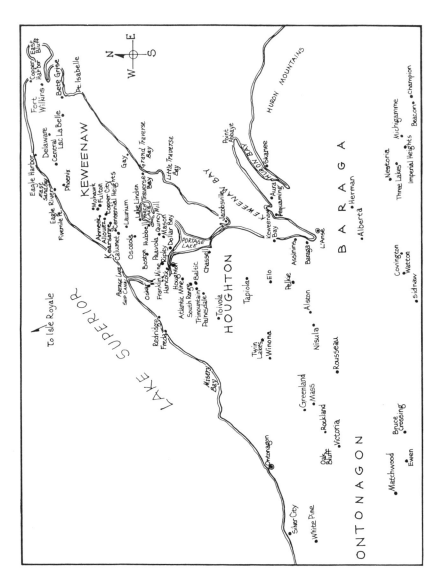

The Keweenaw Peninsula.

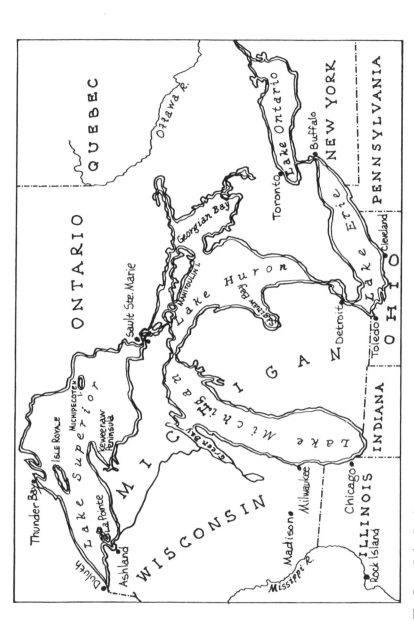

The Great Lakes Region.

the good life, and their story as they developed communities that enriched many lives is the subject of this book.

Much has been written about the Keweenaw Peninsula—of its mineral wealth and productive companies, its boom times, and also its decline as copper deposits became increasingly meager, the deeper miners delved. Others found fascinating the varieties of people who came from every continent to work and live on this northern frontier. Some authors found scenery rivaling the best of New England and California and extolled the natural beauty. Pioneer explorers delighted in the salubrious summer climate, starry nights, sandy beaches, silent pine forests, pure air, long twilights, the lapping of Lake Superior waves, and the aurora borealis, whose pale green or soft pink shimmerings illuminated the night skies. Glorious autumns gave way to Keweenaw winters with hundreds of inches of snow; but the people who stayed learned to cope with all of nature's tempests, fog, rain, snow, thaws, stifling heat, and bitter cold. When all seemed most bleak, spring came rapidly, forest streams rushed joyously, and the sun warmed ponds and swamps. God created the region. The people created a unique peninsular society.

The Keweenaw story is one of incredible successes and grim tragedies. Waves of people came to fish, hunt, explore, mine, and trade and to open stores, shops, schools, and churches—strangers from different cultures who clung together clannishly in groups but who gradually mingled and intermarried. Men and women brought varied concepts of civilization to this wilderness land, missionaries taught the Christian gospel, teachers and antiquarians saw the Keweenaw as something special. They preserved much of its early history. We are indebted to them for their accounts. Reading these now we gain insights into the human condition as we enter their world of joys and sorrows.

Americans, Cornish, Finns, African Americans, Germans, Italians, Irish, Poles, Croatians, Slovenians, Scandinavians, Scots, Syrians, Jews, French Canadians, Native Americans, English, Armenians, and Chinese—patricians and populists—mingled and mixed. Today one can find fifth and sixth generations descended from people attracted by economic opportunities over many decades. Others stayed only temporarily, leaving as the economy plummeted. Always, the Keweenaw served as a challenge for migrants from different parts of the United States. Mobility was central to their lives as many moved from one part to another of the Keweenaw Peninsula. Many believed they were most at home in the Copper Country, a term used synonymously here with Keweenaw Peninsula to connote its four counties: Baraga, Houghton, Keweenaw, and Ontonagon. Thousands who left the area not only for other parts of Michigan but throughout the United States contributed talents and values learned in vital, often simple, Keweenaw homes, thus enriching American democratic society.

This coming and going of many people of different backgrounds over so many years amid the eternal Keweenaw of forests, lakes, rocks, hills, meadows, and skies evoked the title for this book, expressed in the Hebrew Scriptures: "For we are strangers before thee, and sojourners, as were all our fathers: our days on the earth are as a shadow, and there is none abiding" (I Chronicles 29:15, King James Version).

1

Beginnings

1650 – 1840

OVER A BILLION YEARS AGO IN MICHIGAN'S KE-
weenaw Peninsula, copper lay in a soluble state deep below the earth's
surface in extremely hot waters mixed with molten rock, as volcanic
disturbances continued. Eventually, the copper was deposited in cav-
ities in various rock structures in the process of cooling. In fairly
modern times, scientists called such copper deposits "lodes" and
reasoned, further, that centuries of advancing and retreating glaciers
in Michigan exposed some of the copper and that curious, ingenious
Native Americans made use of the red metal they found lying on
sandy shores of Lake Superior or in river beds long after Earth's
convulsions ended.[1]

Who these people were is a mystery. Strangers to the Keweenaw
Peninsula, they lived in areas surrounding the great lake, their habitats
extending far north into Canada and south into eastern Wisconsin.
These prehistoric peoples mined copper, making tools and weapons
some three thousand and more years ago. Archaeologists, using ra-
diocarbon dating, found charred wood samples from 1400 B.C.E.
at ancient mining sites on Isle Royale amid evidence of primitive
mining. They concluded that the ancients who first mined copper in
the Keweenaw and on Isle Royale were allied socially to other native
groups. The pottery and tools they left at the sites indicate an identification with cultural patterns common throughout the northern Great
Lakes region. While Europe experienced its medieval period, Native

19

Americans worked industriously at pits on the Keweenaw Peninsula (sometime between 1200 and 1500 C.E.). Much of the copper mined found its way, via trade, south, west, and to eastern regions of what is now the United States.[2]

The unknown miners employed primitive technology advantageously to extract copper from rock by using fire, water, and hammers fashioned from huge boulders found on Lake Superior's shores. They built fires, heated the rock surrounding the pure copper, then cracked it by dousing it with cold water and pounded out the copper with hammers, prying out some of it with wooden levers. They did not know how to smelt and cast copper, but they procured enough copper for tools and weapons and perhaps for ornamentation. They made axes, adzes, fishhooks, harpoon points, chisels, awls, drills, and needles. Tens of thousands of artifacts made of copper have been discovered in village and campsites in all of eastern North America. Archaeologist John Halsey concluded that nearly all of the copper used by prehistoric Native Americans in the east probably came from Michigan's Keweenaw Peninsula.[3]

The softness and malleability of the Lake Superior copper also led to the decline of the prehistoric copper "industry," for a copper knife would not last long. When the French missionaries and entrepreneurs encountered the Ojibwa people living on both the north and south shores of Lake Superior about 1650, the Ojibwa told them that their ancestors had no tradition of copper mining. After "almost five thousand years, Lake Superior copper . . . and its many roles [were forgotten, and only] the subliminal memory remained that once it had been the symbol of honor, prestige and glory."[4]

The French encountered a people they called Salteaux in the eastern Upper Peninsula, agricultural people who had been driven west along with various Algonquian Winnebago, Cree, and Potawatomi peoples by the Iroquois, who in turn had been affected by the presence of the French along the St. Lawrence River since 1608. The term Salteaux gave way eventually to the name of one of its components— Outchibous or Ojibwa. By 1650, the Ojibwa had moved west to rich fur-trapping grounds and had reached Chequamegon Bay in present-day Wisconsin as the French bartered goods for furs and Sault Sainte Marie became a logical depot for Native Americans who gladly exchanged furs for tools, blankets, axes, knives, kettles, needles, and guns. The term Chippewa is a corruption of Otchipway, or Odjibway, anglicized as Ojibway or Ojibwa.[5]

Thomas McKenney, United States government agent for Native American affairs, said of the Ojibwa in 1826 that their treasures were in forests and rivers and that they knew how to draw upon both: for they "lacked neither food nor shelter, and lived in their uncontrolled

and native grandeur . . . their wants few."[6] The Ojibwa people themselves were fairly recent arrivals to the Keweenaw Peninsula when
the first French missionaries encountered them there in 1660. The
unchanging land of the Keweenaw was marked by rocky cliffs, out-
croppings, sand dunes, endless lines of pointed firs, cedar swamps,
ranges of hills and knobs, forested mountains, capacious harbors and
bays, inland lakes and ponds. Bela Hubbard, explorer, described Lake
Superior as "sublime beyond description," with whitecaps dancing
upon edges of dark blue waves and majestic roaring waves rushing to
shore and receding, spewing foam and spray.[7]

The Ojibwa, as well as the prehistoric peoples, had discovered that
the seventy-five-mile-long peninsula could be crossed about halfway
along its length by river, lake, and a two-mile trek on sandy, swampy
soil. A woodland people, the Ojibwa plied the waters of Lake Superior for subsistence, fishing and wandering into bays and harbors,
investigating islands, and camping near mouths of rivers like the Ontonagon and Pilgrim. Very important to them was Wikwetong, "the
bay." Here they camped, fished, and hunted, using the place as an
important base for their travels through and about the peninsula. The
French called the location L'Anse ("handle of a pitcher" or "bay").
Keweenaw Bay, as it is called today, thus became the most prized
location of the Ojibwa, who had no settlements north of Portage
Lake although they traversed and camped there.[8]

To the Native Americans, the land was inseparable from nature,
which gave sustenance to all who lived upon the earth. To sell and
transfer land among individuals was a concept entirely foreign. In
concert with the Ottawa and Potawatomi, who shared customs with
them, the Ojibwa by the early 1700s drove out the Fox, Sac, Out-
agames, and the Missasaugas into what is now Wisconsin. Competition between French and English for furs in the east drew the Ojibwa
into an economic network that stretched from Chequamegon Bay to
Quebec and Albany, New York. Peoples of very different cultures
thus mixed in an economic contest that disrupted all their lives. The
Upper Peninsula became a buffer zone, even before the coming of
the Europeans, a sort of last outpost of Algonquian-speaking peoples
forming a barrier to Dakota or Sioux enemies who had threatened
them by their eastward migration to the Mississippi.[9]

In the mid-1660s, Hurons arrived at the easternmost village of the
Ojibwa, Pequakquawahming (Round Point, present-day Pequaming).
Here, at Keweenaw Bay, Hurons, with faces painted black connoting sorrow and distress, related stories of Iroquois atrocities; and
although the great Ojibwa warrior Wahboogeeg in council angrily reminded the Huron of past hostilities, he said compassion now caused
his people to receive the Hurons cordially. The Ojibwa assigned the

Lake Superior Ojibwa, early nineteenth century.

Hurons a place to live near Ojibwa villages, adjacent to what is still known as Huron Bay, some fifteen miles east of L'Anse and along the river still named Huron.[10]

The fisheries of Lake Superior initially attracted the Ojibwa to the Keweenaw Bay area. Fishing and hunting in a virgin wilderness and trapping beaver and other animals for their pelts, the Ojibwa entered upon a "golden age" from 1690 to 1720. By 1699, a Jesuit priest reported to France that Chequamegon was the great center, the "metropolis" for all the northwestern native peoples. L'Anse and Ontonagon remained permanent trading and fishing villages. In the late seventeenth century, beaver abounded at Keweenaw Bay. Here the Native American population fluctuated from 150 to 400 depending on the season and consequent economic activity. In winter, twelve or more winter settlements scattered through the Keweenaw Peninsula sheltered Ojibwa family groups during their hunts for deer and other animals. L'Anse, halfway between Sault Sainte Marie and Chequamegon, served as an important stopping place for French fur traders and missionaries from Quebec.[11]

For the Ojibwa, the nation was the tribe, ruled by a chief in hereditary fashion. Should he die before the eldest son could accede, his brother ruled as regent. Only a chief could convene a council, where younger men kept silent, deferring to the elders.

Written laws did not exist. Custom followed for centuries with few modifications predominated. To disobey brought censure of the community, something feared worse than death. The community of human beings living through cooperation was absolute. The Ojibwa had no poor house, no prison. Communality was the keystone of Ojibwa social philosophy. A descendant summarized the moral code, saying, "Fear of the Nation's censure acted as a mighty band, binding all in one social, honorable compact." His people were not brutes needing whips to perform duties, he said: "They would . . . be persuaded to the right. . . . Whatever we had was shared alike. In times of gladness all partook of joy; and when suffering came all alike suffered."[12]

Death was sorrowful but was accepted as part of the cycle of human existence. The rabbit (*wabos*) and fish (*gigo*) were intimates; yet one helped clothe, and the other fed, humans in nature's eternal round. A dream was something significant, to which attention had to be paid. Names they assigned to months combined aesthetics with economic survival: February was "snow-crusted month," June, "strawberry month," August, "rice month," the time to harvest wild rice. September was "shining leaf month," splendor before November, the "month when it freezes," when winter hunting began. The Ojibwa fished, hunted, and gathered berries and nuts throughout the Keweenaw Peninsula but settled only at its base—at Keweenaw Bay and at Ontonagon.[13]

Their lives did not consist of pastoral isolation. Enemies to the south; the hated Sioux to the west; and their inveterate opponents, the Iroquois, far to the east—as well as dissensions within clans and tribes—appeared periodically. Treachery to an ally was "perfectly consistent" with Ojibwa ethics. Mutilation and torture formed part of the pattern of warfare, but at times captives were adopted into tribes.[14] The legend of "the Long Chase" illustrates some of this. Once, Iroquois runners left Keweenaw Bay to spy on Ojibwa living on the island they had named Moonequahnakaungning (present-day Madeline Island, Wisconsin). A young woman discovered the stealthy invaders, told her grandmother (who first disbelieved), and then notified the warriors. The Ojibwa appealed to the Great Spirit for control of Lake Superior and gathered near the Porcupine Mountains to meet the oncoming enemy. They caught two spies and released one, who ran into the wooded mountains; then they burnt the other to death, as they struggled mentally "between their love of revenge and their love of glory." They believed that ever since that time, frequent thunderstorms disturbed the Porcupine Mountains. The legend concludes that among "the greenest of the graves" on Madeline Island was that of the young woman who gave the warning.[15]

The Ojibwa linked religion and medicine, indulging in prayers, songs, and ecstasies. They practiced soothsaying, the laying-on of hands, fasting, and feasting; used baths, sweats, massage, physicks, narcotics, and fermented drinks; and conducted rituals and observed taboos. Using plants for pharmaceutical purposes, they theorized that a part strengthens a part. Thus, hearts, brains, and other parts of animals were eaten to make up for some alleged deficiency or ailment in their bodies. Scores of plants prepared in various ways helped the Ojibwa cope with aches, pains, stomach and intestinal disorders, urinary problems, eye diseases, snakebite, neurotic disorders, and assorted afflictions.[16]

These Native Americans concluded that nature was engulfed in mystery with many spirits ever present, advancing the good and holding back evil. Spirits linked earth to the other world in a mysterious wonder. An awe of things spiritual led to the Ojibwa reluctance to reveal their religious beliefs and rites. Religion and society formed another link. The totem descended along the male line. No intermarriages occurred between persons of the same symbol, even if they belonged to distinct tribes. Five original totems were extended until, by 1850, William W. Warren listed twenty-one clans, among them Loon, Bear, Wolf, Pike, Eagle, Moose, Sturgeon, Whitefish, Beaver, Gull, and Hawk. By that time, Bear and Marten were considered the most aristocratic of the animal clans, and Crane and Eagle ranked likewise among the bird clans.[17]

By the middle of the seventeenth century, Ojibwa and Roman Catholic cultures met in the Great Lakes region with consequences that reverberate to the present. Among the guests at a great Algonquian "feast of the dead" near Lake Huron were Ojibwa from the Sault. There they met soft-spoken Jesuits whom they invited to come visit them. The priests Isaac Jogues and Charles Raymbault, already well versed in the Algonquian language and customs, accepted and preached the Christian faith to two thousand Ojibwa and Algonquian people at the rapids separating Lake Huron from Lake Superior. Raymbault died before he could establish a mission, but Father Jacques Marquette established one firmly in 1668.[18]

Part of the missionary effort involved the elderly Father Ménard, who left Montreal in 1660, paddled in canoes, plodded over portages, and suffered physical privation, eating sometimes only berries and edible moss but who moved ever westward until he found Native Americans who led him to a rendezvous of their people on the shores of a great bay. Arriving on the feast day of Saint Teresa, October 15, Ménard named the great body of water Baie de Sainte Terèse. Today it is known as Keweenaw Bay; and from this "large bay on the south shore of Lake Superior" the priest reported to his superiors that here he "had the consolation of saying Mass, which repaid me bountifully for all my past hardships [and] also I opened a temporary church of Christian Indians, occasional visitors from . . . our French settlements [on the St. Lawrence River], and of such others as the mercy of God has gathered in from this place."

One source indicated that Ménard's mission was at present-day Pequaming, about seven miles north of L'Anse. Ménard stayed eight months, baptized about fifty adults and many children, experienced much hostility from the Native Americans, and (disturbed by the slow progress) decided to visit Chequamegon. Accompanied by only one companion, the priest was lost in the forest while his fellow traveler made "what is called the Keweena Portage." The western Lake Superior region remained forbidding and remote but continued to arouse curiosity.[19]

By 1670 Jean Baptiste Talon, intendant of Canada, had sent Louis Joliet to discover and explore "copper mines" that the French had heard about from Native Americans at Quebec and Montreal—hills of copper and other mineral wealth at the site of the great fresh water "sea" to the west. Joliet was unsuccessful in his quest. The search for riches loomed large in the minds of the French. When Jesuit Father Claude Allouez first saw Lake Superior in 1665, he noticed deep in the lake "pieces of pure copper, of ten and twenty livres' weight." The natives had recovered and treasured many such pieces, often cherishing them "as household gods." Allouez also heard of *un gros rocher tout de cuivre* but did not see this famed immense boulder of copper upstream from the mouth of the Ontonagon River.[20]

Arriving at Keweenaw Bay in September 1665, Allouez and his party found few signs of the mission work conducted by Father Ménard only five years before. Two women had kept the faith and Allouez reported to France that the women were *brilloient comme deux astres au milieu de nuit de cette infidelite*. The phrase expresses well the frustration missionaries often experienced. Allouez was grateful at finding two whose retention of the faith shone like brilliant stars in the midnight of that infidelity.[21] The *Jesuit Relation* (annual report) of 1667–68 listed the apostolic functions as (1) baptizing children, (2) teaching adults, (3) comforting the sick and preparing them for Heaven, (4) overthrowing idolatry, and (5) making the Gospel message "resound to the extremities of this end of the world." The report continued:[22]

> We must follow [the natives encountered] to their homes, [accommodate] ourselves to their ways, ridiculous as they may seem to us, in order to draw them to our ways. And as God became human so that humans could become Gods, a missionary

does not fear to make himself one with the native peoples in order to make them Christians. *Omnibus omnia factus sum.*

But to bring all together in one whole was not easy, as Father Allouez found during his sojourn at Chequamegon. An economic web was developed, however, for the priest noted that the natives dispersed from Chequamegon to other parts of Lake Superior to fish, some journeying to Keweenaw Bay and the mouth of the Ontonagon, using the Keweenaw portage, with others traveling by canoe to Montreal, Quebec, and Isle Royale. The deeply spiritual Claude Allouez also valued the material life, reporting that during his cruise along the north shore of Lake Superior in May 1667, his party saw Minong, the island where "are found pieces of copper . . . true red copper" according to his French compatriots. The French renamed the island Isle Royale.[23] Allouez also had high praise for Monsieur Jean Baptiste Talon, engaged in developing trade in 1666–67, sending "fresh and dried codfish . . . fish-oil, staves [from Quebec] to the Islands of the Antilles." Furthermore, Talon was "directing a careful search for Mines, which appear to be numerous and rich." Allouez found Lake Superior fish "abundant [and] of excellent quality" and concluded that the natives revered the lake as a divinity—offering sacrifices— either because of its size or for its fish. Allouez looked forward to seeing the forests recede and change "into Towns and Provinces which may some day be not unlike those of France." All of this sums up well not only French designs for this new world but also those of many who came to the Keweenaw Peninsula over the next three hundred years.[24]

The Lake Superior region was filled with fur-bearing animals. In Europe, beaver hats became extremely fashionable "and the international market for prime north country otter, marten, beaver, fox, mink, wolf, and bear pelts seemed unlimited." Traders wanted beaver not for the pelts but for the fur-wool, the layer of "soft, curly hair growing next to the skin," which had to be separated from the pelt. For Europeans and later Americans, the beaver hat became not only comfortable headgear but a symbol of high status.[25] The "hat" became fashionable, while the "cap" denoted the lower classes. The impact on the Ojibwa and others was momentous. Historian Edmund J. Danziger summed up succinctly: "For two hundred years after the arrival of the Europeans the Chippewa [Ojibwa] economy depended upon the fur trade."[26] Their entire culture was gradually modified. The fur trade was an international phenomenon. Furs procured by Native Americans all over the northern reaches of the North American continent were shipped to England, France, and Holland and then sent to Baltic Sea monarchies and Russia. This international network with its reshipping helped prevent gluts in European markets and kept prices steady.[27]

Native Americans of the Great Lakes region annually brought furs to Quebec and Montreal, mainly by water, passing through the Sault and using the portage northeast to Lake Nipissing from which a rough, rocky path connected with tributaries of the Ottawa River. Once on the Ottawa, the way to Montreal was relatively smooth. Often, French traders and merchants followed the natives back into the upper country of the Great Lakes. They followed the "ancient Indian route of travel from time immemorial."[28] European settlers and Americans later developed roads in the Keweenaw Peninsula using trails established by natives. The Ojibwa, long accustomed to trapping and using furs of various animals for their own uses, learned from whites the commercial value of furs, resulting in a tremendous slaughter and exchange of pelts for commodities the Ojibwa valued highly; tools of iron and woolen blankets helped them change their ways of living. After a time, natives curtailed the long journeys to Canada and took their furs to posts at Chequamegon, Michilimackinac, and Sault Sainte Marie. As the English competed increasingly with the French for economic supremacy in this part of the world, Michilimackinac and Detroit played important roles as objectives of commercial enterprise, diplomacy, and war. From 1689 to 1763, almost constant warfare raged between England and France and their North American colonies for mastery of the Saint Lawrence Valley and the Great Lakes.[29]

During the 1670s and 1680s, the Lake Superior regions "became an integral part of the French Empire," with natives "confederated with the government." French geographers drew maps, explored tributaries of the great lake, and tapped natural resources. The French rapidly transformed the southern and western shores of Lake Superior as "mission stations and trading posts proliferated."[30] The French fur trade reached its height about 1750. The navigator Louis Antoine de Bougainville estimated that Michilimackinac yielded 600 to 700 packs of furs per year, and Detroit, 800 to 1,000.[31]

The Ojibwa and other Native Americans now became totally dependent on the new economic network, desiring weapons, cooking utensils, blankets, tools, and even clothing. A careful student of the fur trade summarized the situation: "Any interruption of the trade was likely to be accompanied by starvation and ruin [for the natives]. At the same time, they had acquired an unquenchable thirst for the trader's brandy and rum."[32] Dependency had limits. The Ojibwa maintained their sociopolitical autonomy, but the family structure underwent modification as intermarriage between Ojibwa females and French males began. A psychological dependency arose partly from economic patterns. Ojibwa bands camped near French trading posts, creating a center for community activities. When the French moved, natives followed them.[33] Anthropologist Victor Barnouw discerned that the Ojibwa often used French fur traders as authority figures, addressing them as "Father." This led to Ojibwa inhibition of aggressive feelings toward Europeans generally. Barnouw argued that such relationships became the model for later Ojibwa dealings with American agents, "to whom they likewise looked for fatherly leadership, political advice, and economic support."[34]

Coureurs de bois, French woodsmen, defiant of social control that authoritarian Quebec attempted to impose, loved the wilderness life of the Lake Superior region. Scorned as "forest outlaws" by the French monarchical administrators, hundreds of them "had vanished from sight in the immensity of a boundless wilderness," according to the report of one intendant. From their chief resort at Michilimackinac, they set out "to roam for hundreds of miles through the endless meshwork of interlocking lakes and rivers which seams the northern wilderness." They and the Ojibwa shared certain traits that drew them together, according to one scholar: both were "isolated, crafty, adaptable, and present-minded."[35]

Voyageurs comprised another important group, French Canadians who paddled canoes and bateaux in service of fur traders and sometimes worked as subordinates to clerks and proprietors at trading posts. They helped establish cordial relations between natives and French traders.[36] Their most important contribution to the development of the Keweenaw Peninsula and the Lake Superior country generally was their knowledge of the wilderness and survival there. This they passed on to explorers, geologists, mapmakers, surveyors, scholars, traders, and incipient capitalists. Unlettered, unknown, the *voyageurs* helped many discover the Keweenaw's rich resources.[37]

The *voyageurs* also intermarried with Native American women, creating a subculture hardly known to many of their contemporaries. Had their ways prevailed, the impact of the fur trade on Native American culture would have been less destructive. Greed, especially the love of inordinate profits along with the human inclination to evil, produced calamitous circumstances for many Native Americans. Anthropologist Eric Wolf concluded that the trade "deranged accustomed social relations [and] cultural habits" and prompted the "formation of new responses—both internally, in the daily life of various human populations, and externally, in relations among them." Communal ways, as in sharing hunting territory, now fell prey to European conceptions of individualized ownership.[38]

The Jesuit presence helped restrain some illegal activities. Priests helped mitigate some of the traders' excesses, but their paternalism

had sometimes deleterious impact on Native Americans. They fought
the abuse of brandy, but merchants outnumbered them. After 1763,
when the Lake Superior region passed into the hands of the English,
a Catholic bishop visiting Mackinac Island wrote: "The trade here
is principally in liquors, and as long as this state of things exists
there can be no prospects of making [the natives] Christians. . . . God
only knows how many evils flow from this traffic. . . . English rum
has destroyed more Indians than ever did the Spanish sword." The
debauching of the Ojibwa in Michigan's Upper Peninsula continued
as a most pressing social evil in the early nineteenth century. Thomas
McKenney said in 1827 that no United States policy could succeed
in the Upper Peninsula unless it included the "*absolute exclusion* of
spirituous liquors of all sorts."[39]

Most Ojibwa, however, worked diligently at trapping and dressing furs before trading them. They had become specialists in an
international market, as exemplified in the Ontonagon fur trade and
that at Keweenaw Bay, carried on with the French from the 1670s
until 1759, then with the British from 1759 to 1814 and with the
Americans from 1814 to 1840. The basic patterns for trapping, treat-
ing, and trading furs, fixed by the French, remained. Some trade
continued after 1840; but prior to that, the loci of trading centers
in the wilderness shifted constantly due to world market conditions.
Organizational changes under British aegis resulted in companies'
seeking greater control by sending traders directly into the hinterland
to tap the supply of furs at the source.[40]

By 1814, no permanent settlements of Europeans or Americans
existed in the Keweenaw Peninsula. The arrival at Ontonagon of
Alexander Henry, Canadian explorer and fur trader, portended the
future of the Keweenaw. On August 19, 1765, Henry reached the
mouth of the Ontonagon River, where he found an Ojibwa village
and, three leagues above, a waterfall with sturgeon at its foot so
abundant "that a month's subsistence for a regiment could have
been taken in a few hours." He found Ojibwa women with agreeable
features, carefully plaited hair, and cheeks colored "by liberal use of
vermilion." He found the males exotic, faces and bodies painted with
charcoal or white ochre, all trying to appear as "unlike as possible to
anything human." But when he sold his merchandise in exchange for
beaver skins, the deerskin-clad men and women "were scarcely to be
known," because the same people that he first observed now haggled
and traded like the most ardent capitalists in Montreal or Edinburgh
markets.[41]

Henry found Ontonagon "chiefly remarkable for the abundance
of virgin copper, which is on its banks and in its neighborhood" and
not at all well known by Europeans. The natives exhibited masses

of copper of various weights, one of twenty pounds. He recalled later that "the perfect state in which they found it, required nothing [more] but to beat [it] into shape." He noticed copper spoons and bracelets made by natives for themselves. He became curious about possible mineral exploitation in the area.[42]

West of Ontonagon, he came to Pi-wâ-tic, or the Iron River, emptying into Lake Superior. Here he met more natives whom he furnished with merchandise on credit. Ten beaver skins fetched a stroud (coarse heavy wool) blanket; eight bought a white blanket. A pound of gunpowder was exchanged for two skins, a pound of shot or of ball, for one skin. Twenty beaver skins changed hands for one gun, two for an axe, and one for a knife. Such was the market there in 1765. Traveling southwest, Henry arrived at Chequamegon, the metropolis of the "Chipeways," whose "true name [is] O'chibbuoy," where he found fifty lodges with natives in reduced circumstances, their trade having been interrupted by the English invasion of Canada during the French and Indian War (1754–63) and by Pontiac's revolt of various Native American tribes against the British that followed the long war. The Ojibwa chiefs told him of the continued hostility of their enemies to the west, the Sioux.[43]

Led always by Native American guides, Henry, on his way back to Mackinac Island in spring 1766, had them take him ten miles north of the Ontonagon River's mouth so he could see the great mass of copper that so many had talked of for years. He conjectured that this mass of no less than five tons had previously rolled from a lofty hill rising from the river. He marveled at the copper's purity and malleability. With an axe, Henry hacked off a portion weighing 100 pounds. During their occupation of the Ontonagon country, the British made futile efforts to raise the boulder from the river. At an 1823 conference at Fond du Lac (present-day Duluth, Minnesota), an Ojibwa chief negotiating with Americans who wished to purchase their lands said of the boulder that it was "the property of no one man. It belongs alike to us. It was put there by the Great Spirit, and it is ours." More than a decade later, American geologists, surveyors, and entrepreneurs all sought to see the great wonder, the Ontonagon boulder whose weight in 1843 was finally estimated at between six and seven thousand pounds. It was 95 percent pure copper. Eventually, the prized object was removed to the Smithsonian Institution in Washington, D.C.[44]

Henry, like others, continued an interest in the lands round about Ontonagon, distributing maize seed among the Ojibwa, who grew good crops between 1772 and 1774. The British were far more interested in mineral wealth. Alexander Baxter, a mining expert, was sent to the Keweenaw by a group of English nobles who had petitioned

King George II for a "grant of all the mineral rights on Lake Superior." Alexander Henry was part of the consortium representing
the nobility who sought wealth from mineral riches they expected to
find in the faraway Lake Superior country. Miners dug forty feet into
a hill at the Ontonagon River in spring 1772; but when a cave-
in occurred, they told Henry that to begin again was much too
arduous. More men were needed to sink an airshaft, they concluded;
and the best idea was to abandon the entire project. Henry said the
metal was within reach but that the expense of transporting it to
Montreal would exceed the marketable value. More important, his
company sought silver, not copper. He concluded: "The copper ores
of Lake Superior can never be profitably sought for [except] for local
consumption. The country must be cultivated and peopled, before
[the ores] can deserve notice."[45]

Thus, the Keweenaw, as well as most of the Michigan Upper
Peninsula, continued as a fertile field for natives and whites who fished
and traded much of their catch and who trapped, dressed, and traded
furs. In 1808, a German who had already succeeded as a trader,
John Jacob Astor, incorporated the American Fur Company with
President Thomas Jefferson's approval. This signified the beginning
of a far-ranging empire, with Astor scheming, speculating, selling,
and buying in a fashion widely imitated by American capitalists in the
nineteenth century. The American Fur Company displaced the older
remaining French companies over a vast region in Canada and the
United States and competed successfully with Canadian companies
until it went bankrupt in 1842.[46]

From New York City, Astor exported furs from the Great Lakes
territory to London and brought in cloth, tools, utensils, blankets,
and guns, shipping them west each spring to Ramsay Crooks and
Robert Stuart, traders directing the company's field operations from
Mackinac Island. By 1818, the company's posts covered most of the
country where the Ojibwa remained. In the Keweenaw Peninsula,
John Holliday traded six thousand dollars' worth of merchandise each
year during the early 1820s. Catches of Lake Superior fish brought
in during the off-season were packed in barrels for export. Part of
that trading network was the company's post on Keweenaw Bay at
Ance-Ke-We-Naw—today's L'Anse. Representatives and employees
of the American Fur Company fought until the early 1840s to preserve the south shore wilderness sanctuary so they could continue to
make profits.[47]

Chequamegon, now referred to generally as LaPointe, enjoyed a
renaissance. The American Fur Company dominated the scene, with
two large buildings painted bright red (one, a store, the other a long
storehouse for dried fish) and a row of frame houses, clapboarded

and painted white. Here lived six or more families employed by the company. Nearby lived "tenements" of French and some descendants of marriages between French and Native Americans. A half-mile distant, a Protestant mission consisted of a two-story "mansion" and adjoining school with thirty scholars. At the Catholic mission, French and Native Americans lived in some fifty lodges of the Ojibwa. A sizable town, LaPointe impressed traveler Bela Hubbard. He recalled that this picturesque settlement was the oldest, most remote of missions begun by Jesuits led by Father Allouez 175 years before. Here, Ojibwa from Lake Superior's north and south shores gathered, along with other peoples—Americans and Europeans—from what are now Canada, Wisconsin, and Minnesota to trade and relax.[48]

The Keweenaw Peninsula was part of a nexus linking it with La-Pointe, from which the Ojibwa traveled to the Keweenaw portage and then paddled south to their beloved Keweenaw Bay, where they had firmly established themselves. At L'Anse, an economic center on a smaller scale than LaPointe prevailed. But the American Fur Company had changed the economic balance with pernicious results. Lieutenant James Allen of the Fifth U.S. Infantry, commanding the military escort on an 1832 expedition led by Henry Schoolcraft, observed how dangerously dependent on American fur traders the Ojibwa had become. In the Keweenaw, the natives lived well in summer by eating plentiful whitefish, herring, and trout taken from Keweenaw Bay with gill nets and spears; but in winter, a scarcity of food for families due to the depletion of bear, deer, and other large game caused hardships. The Ojibwa procured provisions from trader Holliday but seemed unaware of the economic disaster toward which they veered. Allen believed that the natives must be convinced to resort to agriculture to support themselves. He wrote that the Lake Superior region could sustain ten times the present population if the Ojibwa would only turn to farming and abandon their "established and peculiar habits of living."[49]

From 1823 to 1844, the fur trade suffered extremely rough times. Astor sold the LaPointe complex and other company holdings in 1834 to a New York firm headed by Ramsay Crooks but the economic depression of the late 1830s combined with cutthroat competition in the new craze for raccoon furs and the collapse of the international market in other furs led to the bankruptcy of the American Fur Company. The Native Americans in the Great Lakes regions fell upon hard times not unique to them as bank failures, unemployment, and all the ills of capitalism's periodic dips prevailed over the entire United States.[50]

All was not bleak. Historian Edmund Danziger concluded that in the period from 1650 to 1830, the Ojibwa underwent a technological

*Ojibwa Chief
Shingabawossin.
(State Archives
of Michigan.)*

rebirth; for they had been isolated Stone Age people who had their standard of living raised by trading furs for tools, trinkets, utensils, and other goods.[51] Schoolcraft, visiting the mouth of the Ontonagon River in 1831, found sixty-four natives in the village, where they lived continuously except for trips to LaPointe to collect their annual payments for land sold to the Americans under treaty. Hunting in winter took younger, abler families away for weeks at a time. They lived now mostly as fishers; for no finer fishing grounds were said to exist than those of the Ontonagon country, surpassing even those of Keweenaw Bay.[52]

Five years earlier, Schoolcraft talked with an old chief named the Plover, who told the linguist of a dream he had had during a visit to the Sault. A tall, handsome messenger from God came from the west and told him that the end of the world was near. The Plover told the messenger that he could not overcome his enemies, nor was he willing to fight.[53] This was a variation of a story told by the Ojibwa "long before they became aware of the white man's presence on this continent," wrote a descendant in the 1860s. An old man, sanctified by fasts, had prophesied that white spirits would come in "numbers like sand on the lake shore, and would sweep the red race from the hunting grounds which the Great Spirit had given them as an inheritance." The consequence would be an "ending of the world."[54]

The year 1840 marked a watershed, ending the native–trader–
voyageur symbiosis. Laissez-faire capitalism triumphed as Jacksonian
democracy flourished despite economic woes and greed run rampant.
Michigan had been a state since 1837. This also was the year—1840—
in which Douglass Houghton, with a party of surveyors, geologists,
and mapmakers, examined deposits of copper in the Keweenaw Peninsula, foreshadowing the copper "rush" of the mid-1840s. Writing to
a Michigan congressman in December 1840, Houghton mentioned
finding "nearly two tons of ore, and with this . . . many masses of
native copper." He said, "There can scarcely be a shadow of a doubt
[that the Keweenaw Peninsula] will eventually prove of great value
to our citizens and to the nation."[55]

2

Great Expectations

1840 – 1860

COLONEL THOMAS MCKENNEY, ON HIS WAY TO rendezvous with Lewis Cass, governor of Michigan Territory, on a July morning in 1826, described the southeastern shore of the Keweenaw Peninsula: "Not a bird warbles to cheer us. Not a living thing presents itself to vary the solitude. Nothing is heard but the roar of the waves on the shore, nor seen, but the forests that line it, the lake, and the sky. Whether stormy or calm, the roll of the wave is heard. It never ceases. This is the music of these shores." Occasionally, a loon called mournfully; otherwise, only a stray songbird and buzzing of mosquitoes could be heard, and a few ducks paddled near shore. McKenney and his party saw "no Indians—no human beings—no animals—no horses, or cattle, and not even a snake." Such was the Keweenaw of the early nineteenth century before hordes of prospectors and speculators, lured by talk of mineral wealth, invaded the land.[1]

McKenney and his *voyageurs*, supplied with flour, whiskey, beef tongue, cheese, dried venison, and crackers, rowed round the tip of the peninsula. Native Americans who had accompanied them refused to do so, using, instead, the portage cutting through the peninsula. They had a tradition that some of their people had visited the island off the tip about a hundred years earlier only to find the apparition of a woman growing in size. Believing her to have dominion over all the beaver on Keweenaw Point and fearing her wrath, they fled and never after disturbed the beaver there. Rounding Keweenaw Point, McKenney marveled at the "grandeur, and a barrenness equal to any thing of the kind I have seen": solid rock, massive boulders, shores cut by small bays, and—five miles round the point—a cascade of water flowing foaming out of the mountainous heights into Lake Superior. Nearby, wild roses grew near the remains of two Native American lodges. On rocks in the lake, hundreds of gulls postured and cried. Moving southwest along the shore, McKenney and companions halted periodically to examine specimens of cornelian, chalcedony, and crystallized quartz.[2]

At the west end of the portage, "the carrying place for all the trade of this lake [Superior], except such as goes up in barges," McKenney and his group joined Cass and his party. As governor of a vast territory, Cass had spent much time in the woods and on the lakes "always studying how he might open up all the vast region for peaceful settlement." In cooperation with the federal government, Cass had, in 1820, made, with Schoolcraft, an extended tour of Lake Superior's south shore to investigate various Native American tribes, induce them not to rely on Canada for presents, and examine the mineral resources of the region.[3]

On this 1826 trip—Cass representing local territorial interests, McKenney, those of the federal government—joined forces to make a treaty with the natives near present-day Duluth, Minnesota, hoping to enforce American claims. The recent opening of the Erie Canal in New York State meant migration to Michigan from the settled East. Stories of mineral riches in the Upper Peninsula were rife. As early as April 1800, the U.S. Congress had passed a resolution calling for the appointment of an agent "who shall be instructed to collect all material information relative to the copper mines on the south side of Lake Superior."[4]

In February, 1823, Senator Thomas Hart Benton of Missouri reported a bill whose aim was "extinguishment of the title of the Indians to certain lands on or near the Ontonagon River . . . supposed to contain valuable mines of copper." The *Detroit Gazette* waxed ecstatic over Benton's proposal:[5] "Connected with the fur trade and fisheries, the working of these mines will create an active and profitable commerce on Lake Superior, in which this Peninsula, being washed by three seas, and having almost unparalleled facilities for interior navigation through its numerous rivers, must largely participate." The Cass–McKenney visit to Fond du Lac (Duluth) ended in negotiations with the Ojibwa to ensure peace with other tribes and American promises of assistance so that the Ojibwa could "lead civilized lives." Money for a school was promised. From this time until 1842, when the Ojibwa ceded the last of their lands in the

Upper Peninsula, federal and local American forces were determined to introduce American civilization to the region, to find and exploit the rumored mineral wealth.[6]

Henry Schoolcraft, geologist with the 1820 Cass expedition, made another tour in 1822. Appointed Native American agent for the Northwest, he began his investigations of Native American culture and folklore. He worried about the impact of one culture upon another:[7] "What under the sun do people suppose the Indian is made of? A man spending his time painfully to catch a beaver, with nothing often to eat, and nothing to put on but tatters and rags, and, withal, the whole Anglo–Saxon race treading on his toes and burning out his vitals with ardent spirits. Such is the Indian." Governor Cass also asked Schoolcraft to attempt a settlement between the Ojibwa and the Sioux west of the Great Lakes in 1831, to help end the bitter warfare between the two peoples. Provision was also made for the Schoolcraft expedition to include someone "who would make notes on the nature of the soil and the geology, mineralogy, and natural history of the region to be visited." The person chosen was Douglass Houghton, only twenty-one years old.[8]

Douglass Houghton, born at Troy, New York, in 1809, had migrated recently to Michigan Territory. His work with the 1831 expedition that discovered the source of the Mississippi River prepared him for his important work later in the Keweenaw. As Michigan Territory moved toward statehood, most citizens did not want the Upper Peninsula. They carried on a fierce dispute with Ohio over land that both Michigan and Ohio wanted. The "Toledo strip" controversy raged until the Michigan disputants, encouraged to accept the Upper Peninsula in place of the disputed territory, finally approved of the U.S. Senate Judiciary Committee's March 1, 1836, bill for establishment of boundaries giving the peninsula to Michigan. In one of its first acts, the Michigan state legislature in 1837 appropriated three thousand dollars to establish a state geological survey and appointed Houghton as state geologist. He embarked upon several surveys of both the Lower and Upper Peninsulas, accompanied by experts in geology, zoology, botany, and mapmaking. In the three years that followed, larger amounts granted indicated that many had high expectations of finding wealth in the north.[9]

In a December 16, 1840, letter to Governor William Woodbridge, Houghton described the mineral district as long and narrow, at times approaching the lake shore but sometimes stretching into the interior for twenty-five to thirty miles. Much work needed doing, he reported. Up to this time, almost nothing was really known about the mineral district. Neither natives nor whites had detected veins of ore, although loose pieces of copper found occasionally had fostered a general belief that copper existed in quantities. His reports abounded in descriptions—timber varying from scrubby pine to "beautifully timbered tracts of sugar maple," white cedar and spruce in abundance, white pine, some lands favorable to agriculture, few streams of considerable size but much sandstone, varying in color from light gray to brick red.

Houghton found no fossils embedded in rock. He found innumerable creeks in forests, "remarkably transparent and pure, with brisk currents and numerous cascades, and . . . an abundance of the brook trout," a fish rarely found in streams of the Lower Peninsula. He portrayed the Porcupine Mountains as rising abruptly from Lake Superior's coast and stretching inland for thirty miles, with altitudes of nearly 950 feet while some knobs rose from 1,000 to 1,300 feet. Heavily timbered valleys of beech and maple lay near small lakes that served as sources for the mighty Ontonagon River, with its two principal branches joining to rush on to Lake Superior. The river abounded in both rapids and comparatively still reaches. This rugged country was rarely visited; for in 1840, he found, near the Ontonagon boulder, chisels where he had left them in 1831.[10]

Was agriculture possible here? The rugged hills and low mountains of the Keweenaw were punctuated by "intervening valley sometimes of considerable width"; and the soil was of superior quality, well adapted for agriculture, "with a climate far less rigorous than is

Carp Lake (now Lake of the Clouds), Porcupine Mountains. (Foster and Whitney Report, 1850).

commonly supposed." He knew of Lower Peninsula opinion that the Upper Peninsula was not fit for farming because of its cold climate; but such opinions, he stated, were "almost wholly founded in error." Isle Royale, almost destitute of soil, was nevertheless "of immense value for its fisheries, which are as yet scarcely appreciated." Like most Americans of his day, Douglass Houghton had an eye for expected wealth, especially that gained by introducing science and technology.[11]

The metal in the Keweenaw was elusive. Houghton found that one came upon "considerable masses of native copper," sufficient to excite minds and raise expectations, only to find veins that became so narrow it was "useless to pursue them." His journeys through "a complete wilderness" with no one visible except "savages" convinced him that the natives had no knowledge "of the true sources from which the transported masses of copper had their origin." Masses of copper found lying here and there had originated in the interior, he speculated; for conglomerate and trap rock, instead of continuing parallel to the shoreline, receded rapidly from the coast, so that copper riches lay in the depths of forests.[12]

Above all, Houghton believed that there was not much native copper in the Keweenaw. Still, he had seen enough to set off an "invasion." He wrote: "While I am fully satisfied that the mineral district of our state will prove a source of eventual and steadily increasing wealth to our people, I cannot fail to have before me the fear that it may prove the ruin of hundreds of adventurers, who will visit it with expectations never to be realized." Most of all, much capital was needed. Although he had no desire to "throw obstacles in the way of those who might wish to engage in the business of mining this ore" whenever the federal government would permit, Houghton wished to caution "those persons who would engage in this business in the hope of accumulating wealth suddenly and without patient industry and capital" that they had better take care before rushing into ventures that "will most certainly end in disappointment and ruin."[13]

By 1842, Houghton reported copper ores in the western portion of the range to be "more extensive than was originally supposed." By 1844, his seventh annual report spoke of the geologic complexity and interesting topography of Michigan south of Lake Superior "not only in a scientific point of view, but also in consequence of the intrinsic value of its mineral resources."[14] His assistant geologist, Bela Hubbard, expected much from the territories surveyed not only in the Keweenaw but in both peninsulas:[15]

> With lands [in Michigan] among the richest in the world, well watered and advantageously situated for market, with water

power abundant . . . and facilities for water transportation un-equalled by any other inland state, and added to this, a population possessed of a large share of that character for enterprise which distinguishes their countrymen, nothing will tend more to give full efficiency and permanency to these advantages than to make more perfectly known the value of our mineral resources.

Houghton and his party of Americans spent part of the Fourth of July, 1840, mining at Copper Harbor. They proudly displayed the ton of copper rock they had blasted out of a hill. By four in the afternoon, they had fitted up a large tent and decorated it with pine boughs. Then they formed a procession and, with music and standards, marched about the wilderness settlement. A band played "Hail Columbia," Houghton read the Declaration of Independence to assembled guests, Bela Hubbard orated, someone sang, and Columbus C. Douglass pronounced the benediction. Then, all dined in a large tent where J. Labille, Esq., "chief butler," offered varieties of duck, pigeons, partridges, three kinds of the choicest fish, and pickled oysters. The diners washed down this epicurean feast with generous draughts of wine as they toasted the great day of independence. Hubbard noted that the menu also included corn and bean soup, pork, shortcake, hardtack, and port wine, "truly a sumptuous repast for a party of wilderness vagrants."[16]

Douglass had no doubts that someday, Copper Harbor would become important because of the mineral district. His special assistant Frederick Hubbard, after surveying the harbor, wrote, "A mere glance at the map is sufficient to show how little is left for art to do, to render this harbor one of the most secure places of refuge from storms, to be found in any part of the lake."[17] Expectations ranked high for American civilization to sprout in the Keweenaw; but before that could commence, the invaders had to do something about the natives. Patterns of Ojibwa life had changed little. Natives used Chequamegon as their base, then traveled via birchbark canoes to the Keweenaw portage, Keweenaw Bay, and the upper reaches of Keweenaw Point. They also frequented Ontonagon; and here Houghton and his geologists, surveyors, and mapmakers experienced an encounter that heralded the future relationships of natives and whites.

When Houghton's party reached the mouth of the Ontonagon River on July 10, 1840, natives emerged from eight lodges, shook hands and said *bo jou* (bon jour) all around. The whites offered tobacco and bread. Half a dozen boys, six to fifteen years of age, accompanied men whose black-painted faces Bela Hubbard found

abhorrent. "Grotesque" and of "savage appearance"—such terms
filtered through his mind as he appraised the situation. The natives
belonged to the Buffalo band, whose chief was far to the east of
Tahquamenon River. That leader's son, chief at Ontonagon, his face
painted red, his chest bearing a medal with the likeness of former
president John Quincy Adams, allowed the Houghton party to pro-
ceed up river and, with his men, finally confronted the whites.

The latter were told, "You must wait . . . at the mouth until the
Buffalo [father] comes up or else I and my band shall go with you
to see that you take away nothing. The Buffalo must see all that
you take." Houghton countered: "I have been here several times
before and shall go now as I am ordered by your great father. I
know the country and do not need any of you for a guide." The son
declared, "This country belongs to us," to which Houghton replied
that the 1826 treaty allowed American citizens to visit anywhere in
the country, that he need not ask the consent of the son, that he
was acquainted with the Buffalo and had no objection to showing
him what he brought away. Now another canoe hove into sight. A
native said, "We are determined that you shall not go beyond [the
next bend in the river] tonight." Houghton declared that nothing
would stop the Americans from moving upriver. When the natives demanded pork and flour, the whites haggled with them and Houghton
scribbled an order for those provisions, plus some tobacco to end
the confrontation. Hubbard recalled having seen these men ten days
earlier at L'Anse. He wrote that they expected to meet the natives
again upon the return trip and were ready to dare them "to an assault
& whip them if we could." When the whites returned to the mouth
of the Ontonagon, however, all was silent, the lodges were deserted,
and two lingering natives told the Americans that the son had gone
to Lac du Flambeau in Wisconsin Territory to join a war party against
the Sioux.[18]

At LaPointe the party relaxed, and Hubbard and others found
Native Americans amiable enough and joined them in dancing. In his
journal, Hubbard noted families with intermixture of Native American blood, "which detracts little even from the fairness of the daughters." He found these people "intelligent and highly educated," busy
with the fur trade. A colleague concluded, "The Indians are a mirth
loving race."[19] Fifty years later, Hubbard wrote that the natives were
not wild, solitary, simple, and hospitable men and women of melo-
dious language. He argued that their virtues were few, their cruelty
and vindictiveness pronounced; they were lovers of war and seekers of
revenge—the males itinerant, the women drudges.[20] A half-century
of American exploitation of the wilderness and the arrival of their
civilization had caused denigration of the natives.

The Americans acquired the copper-bearing lands of the Keweenaw and other lands of the Lake Superior region primarily through
three treaties.[21] The first, with the Ottawa and Ojibwa, concluded
March 28 and ratified May 27, 1836, ceded lands bounded by Lake
Superior on the North, Saint Marys River on the east, Lake Michigan
on the south, and the Escanaba River and Chocolate River on the
west. The second, concluded September 3, 1836, with the Menomonee and ratified February 1837, resulted in the cession of the tract
bounded on the east by the Escanaba River, on the south by Green
Bay, on the west by the Menomonee River, and on the north by an
irregular line extending from the mouth of the Brule River to the
headwaters of the Escanaba River. The third, concluded October 4,
1842, with the Ojibwa of Lake Superior and the Mississippi River and
ratified March 23, 1843, ceded the remainder of the area washed by
Lake Superior on the north and extending west to the Montreal River
from the Chocolate River, and south to the Michigan–Wisconsin
boundary. Isle Royale was included in the 1842–43 cession. Each
treaty included lands other than those described. For years following,
arguments ensued as to what had been ceded.

     With Native American land claims exterminated, the federal gov-
ernment continued its survey, dividing land into townships subdi-
vided into sections. Prominent in this was William A. Burt, born in
Massachusetts, a war veteran who after 1815 worked as a merchant
in New York State, then wandered as far southwest as Saint Louis and
finally succeeded in Michigan, teaching himself elements of geology,
engineering, and surveying. By 1840, the forty-eight-year-old Burt
masterfully surveyed the Upper Peninsula for the federal government.
A historian has concluded that Burt, "[more,] perhaps, than any of
the other Upper Peninsula pioneers, . . . fits the pattern of the early
American great men, laboring hard all day, studying at night by a
guttering lamp."[22]

     The way was now open for seekers of copper to move into the
Keweenaw wilderness. The copper boom was set to begin. Men with
and without money, ambitious and filled with keen expectations,
invaded the Keweenaw Peninsula. LaPointe and Sault Sainte Marie
served as assembly points for prospectors arriving from afar by water.
The federal government established Fort Wilkins on May 28, 1844,
adjoining Copper Harbor, where companies A and B of the United
States Fifth Infantry were stationed to protect the anticipated copper-
mining industry against resentful natives and to assist in the removal
of any remaining Ojibwa. Situated on high ground between the
elliptoid harbor and Lake Fanny Hooe, the fort in 1845 consisted
of neat buildings painted white, housing soldiers, a parade ground,
storehouses, and a guard house. A visitor that year described the

Stars and Stripes spreading gracefully from the tall staff in "the soft morning breeze . . . a guarantee that order and protection [were] established in this wilderness of lakes and mountains."[23]

Douglass Houghton continued Burt's work and became a familiar figure. He was well liked—a small man who dressed without much care, talked fast, and endeared himself to prospectors and miners by avoiding excess gentility. Whenever he landed at tent settlements at Eagle River, Eagle Harbor, Copper Harbor, and Ontonagon, Houghton was "immediately hailed and surrounded by the characteristically noisy miners."[24] On October 13, 1845, three miles off the shore of Eagle River, Houghton's boat capsized, and he perished along with two of his four colleagues. Seventy years later, on October 10, 1914, Keweenaw people dedicated a monument to this man whose explorations figured largely in setting off the original Keweenaw copper boom. To honor him, designers chose a rough and rugged cenotaph with rock from every lode traversing the district: conglomerate, amygdaloid, whitneyite, mass copper, and sandstone, as well as bits from the iron country to the south and marble from Escanaba quarries. A bronze tablet, designed locally but cast in New York, paid tribute to Michigan's first state geologist. The Keweenaw Historical Society, the Fortnightly Club, and women's and other clubs of Houghton and Keweenaw counties erected the monument, dominated by a huge, greenstone fifteen-ton boulder of traprock from the bed of Eagle River.[25]

Fort Wilkins, established 1844, near Copper Harbor. (Foster and Whitney Report, 1850).

Houghton's work was continued by the erratic and testy professor, Charles T. Jackson, appointed by the U.S. secretary of the treasury to study Upper Peninsula lands, classifying them as either mineral or agricultural. Ably assisted by John W. Foster, Josiah D. Whitney, William F. Channing, and Dr. Wolcott Gibbs, Jackson's 1848 report provided much information about mining operations, as well as geology and flora and fauna of the peninsula. Jackson credited to his own astute observations the startling realization that in the Keweenaw something existed that had no parallel anywhere in the world, that is, native copper in large quantities—copper in an almost pure state and often containing bits of pure silver.[26]

An early arrival in the search for copper was James Paul from Virginia. Hearing of the Ontonagon boulder, he made his way to the river's mouth in 1843, accompanied by Nick Minclergue, of Ojibwa and French parentage. They journeyed up the river, Paul hoping "to get rich quickly and depart;" but he remained to found the town of Ontonagon and die there in relative poverty.[27] Others followed. Whitney's field notes for 1847 mention companies that had been formed: the Delavan, Hope, Croton, and Isle Royale. He added, "In regard to all [these] locations on the Porcupine mountains, there can be no hesitation in saying that there is no promise of a sufficient yield of copper in any one of them." As for Boyd's location, six miles from the trail leading from Iron River to Lake Gogebic, some native copper was found, but prospects of a rich lode were nil. The Charter Oak Mining Company had two small cabins and a large clearing on the north shore of Lake Gogebic and preparations to build a commodious house, "but the locality was deserted before the completion of it."[28] A year passed before the discovery of the fabulous Minesota Lode. The first great bonanza occurred at the Cliff Lode, not far from Eagle River, in the winter of 1845–46.

Here explorers struck a great chunk of native copper, far bigger than anything found up to this time. Scholar David J. Krause wrote recently that this "discovery was, without any doubt, one of the truly significant moments in the long history of the Keweenaw copper district." John Hays, Pittsburgh druggist, seeking improved health, as well as copper, is credited with being the "moving force" behind the opening of the extremely successful Cliff Mine.[29] In October, 1847, Jackson visited the Cliff, operated by the Pittsburg and Boston Company, and found 120 men at work, 70 of them regular miners, most from Cornwall, England. Near the mine, seventeen houses served as harbinger for "a village [that] will soon spring up there." The company retained a regular physician at the Cliff, and he worked also for other companies in the vicinity. A clergyman came periodically "to perform Divine services" and a school was planned for children of miners and laborers.[30]

In his 1849 report, Jackson said that the Cliff was producing 860 to 900 tons of copper annually, averaging 65 percent pure metal. The pure copper required only fusion to cast it into forms required for manufacturers. He said the mix of copper and silver found at the Cliff and at the nearby Copper Falls Mine had been "used in Boston for making church bells, and has proved to be of excellent quality."[31] So began the widespread use of copper from Michigan in the developing industrialism of the late nineteenth century. Thousands from all over the country, as well as from Europe were attracted to the Keweenaw. The Lake Superior Copper Company, formed principally by Boston capital, had been the idea of Colonel Charles H. Gratiot and John Bernard; but important in its formation had been a former mayor of Detroit, De Garmo Jones, and also David Henshaw, former secretary of the Navy and onetime kingpin of the Massachusetts Democratic political organization.[32]

Exploration continued, all searching for a strike similar to, or greater than, that at Cliff Mine. The explorers, men of "energy, courage and vim," braved storms, heat, and mosquitoes in their search. Wearing flannel shirts, moccasins, and slouch hats that hid unkempt hair, they were "eager, determined, impressible fellows, many of them indifferent to heat, wet, cold, hunger and toil, and with plenty of wild oats to sow." Rough and rude prospectors hunted for the red metal in constant competition, fearful that someone would strike it rich before they did. Such was the description given by John H. Forster, a private surveyor who accompanied some explorers.[33]

Advice by word of mouth, brochures, and books issued from the first explorers for copper. The prospector was told to carry hardtack, beans, salt pork, tea, coffee, sugar, hatchets, tin cups, knives, forks, and spoons. For every two men, a camp kettle and frying pan could be added. Pocket compasses were imperative. Matches, flint, and steel to make fires were to be prized. Knapsacks, heavy cotton ticking trousers, pea jackets and flannel shirts, and a heavy mackinaw blanket were recommended. Charles P. Whittlesey, who had experienced it all, said prospectors would encounter summer rain, winter sleet, snow, wind, insects, swamps, and marshes and would have to cross ravines and gullies as they sought surveyors' marks. The search would sometimes prove fruitless. No minerals would be found; or if they were, the surveys would later prove the land already belonged to someone else![34]

Other, smaller mines opened. Forster wrote that "everywhere on the Trap Range, for one hundred and fifty miles, one could hear the click of hammer and drill, and the explosion of power in the primeval forests, during the busy season of 1846."[35] Word traveled quickly. A blacksmith at Keweenaw Bay, Daniel D. Brockway, wrote his family and friends downstate on December 10, 1844, that "now is the time for farmers, as well as miners, to make money in this country, as there will be a ready market in the mines for vegetables, hay, etc." He reported selling twenty-five dollars' worth of produce to miners: potatoes brought one dollar a bushel, and turnips, seventy-five cents a bushel. His wife requested a box of medicines sent up: bitters, tincture of nerve powder, tansy, sage, "and such herbs as you think we may need."[36]

Forster said that all along the mineral range, "one found every few miles a notch in the woods from which ascended the smoke from a few log cabins," which meant a mine nearby being opened. "Not one in twenty or fifty of these new concerns ever became permanent, profitable mines," he noted many years later. The birch woods near Fort Wilkins had undergone transformation by summer 1846 "and a lively town of white tents gleamed out of the green groves." This was Copper Harbor, now "an improvised metropolitan city," where men of several nations gathered: politicians, scientists, speculators, surveyors, engineers, packers, and *voyageurs*—all involved in the search for copper. Forster watched expeditions making ready for the tramp into the wilds of the Keweenaw. Sailboats, canoes, and mackinaw boats "gliding to and fro" in the rockbound harbor symbolized the action transforming the peninsula.[37]

In slack times, social amusements consisted of card games and drinking; and there was "some good fighting with fist and pistol." At the west end of Copper Harbor, Daniel Brockway, who only eighteen months before labored at L'Anse, now operated a hotel that did a thriving business.[38] In April 1846, John R. Stockton, superintendent of mineral lands, said that the terra incognita of the Upper Peninsula, believed to be "desolate and unprofitable," was destined to be "one of the richest mining countries in the world and a source of national aggrandizement."[39] Forster at Sault Sainte Marie noted on April 22, 1846, that the place was in "a perfect whirlwind of excitement" about the Keweenaw copper mines. On streets, in barrooms and reading rooms—everywhere men congregated—they jabbered about copper, which astonished Forster "exceedingly, and I am much inclined to put it down as humbug."[40] Talk was cheap, and hopes, high. Jacob Houghton, writing in 1846, said "thousands visited the country, . . . companies were daily organized, and the results of the Grand Rush are yet to be realized." He hoped that all would ultimately succeed but feared "that the visionary hopes of some will meet with a glooming disappointment."[41]

Charles Lanman traversing the area in 1846 recalled that "conglomerate" was the word on everyone's lips: "You stand upon a commanding hill-top, and while lost in the enjoyment of a fine landscape, a Copper Harbor 'bear' or 'bull', recently returned from Wall-street, will slap you on the shoulder and startle the surrounding air with the following yell: 'That whole region, sir, is *conglomerate*, and exceedingly rich in copper and silver'." Should you ask your landlady for some milk for the coffee, she will tell you that her husband had traded "the old red cow for a conglomerate location somewhere in the interior." Lanman saw a child playing with rock specimens in a homemade doll house. He believed that "all the men, women and children residing in the copper cities, have been crystallized into finished geologists." The "bright red copper" was their favorite theme.[42]

A second bonanza occurred in 1848 at the other end of the mineral range, when Samuel O. Knapp discovered the Minesota Lode near the Ontonagon River. Here was mass copper and plenty of it. Stockholders invested $366,000; and by 1867, the Minesota Mine had paid them $1,760,000 in dividends. By the 1850s, the Ontonagon area led in Michigan's copper production.[43]

The federal government, proceeding in orderly fashion, leased the mineral lands for three years in areas of one or three square miles. Renewable, the leases provided that the lessee pay the federal government a share of every hundred pounds of metal procured. In the first year, 892 permits were granted, only 65 of them for pieces of land three-miles square. The government also stipulated that the land could not be used for agriculture. The lessee had to mark corners of his tract and transmit to the proper department a description and plat of same. Certain conditions prevailed: the lessee had to work such mines with "due diligence and skill, and render to the United States six per cent of all the ores raised." Lessees lived in Maine, New Hampshire, Vermont, Massachusetts, Connecticut, New York, Pennsylvania, Delaware, Maryland, the District of Columbia, Virginia, Louisiana, Tennessee, Kentucky, Missouri, Illinois, Indiana, Ohio, Wisconsin, Iowa, and Michigan. A slight majority of them claimed residence in the northeast, particularly in New York City, Boston, Baltimore, Philadelphia, and Portsmouth, Maine.[44]

The American East was bursting with Democratic and Whig ideas and enthusiasm: one's freedom included freedom to become rich, take risks, while laissez-faire was touted and scorn heaped on the paternalistic policies of the Federalist founders of the nation. Although the Whigs descended ideologically from the Federalists, they caught the fever of "free enterprise" also. As Alexis de Tocqueville had noted, by the early nineteenth century, many Americans had made "material well-being the main object of [their] existence" and their eagerness to "possess things goes beyond the ordinary limits of human cupidity." Their greed produced torment, for they desired wealth and followed "every path to fortune that [was] open." Tocqueville, startled by the phenomenon of American democracy, acknowledging its inexorability, concluded that "there is something wonderful in [American] resourcefulness and a sort of heroism in [the] greed for gain."[45]

The laissez-faire conflagration of the 1830s and 1840s resulted in changes for leasing the mineral lands. After 1847, agents at Sault Sainte Marie with assistants at Copper Harbor and Ontonagon were to *sell* the lands and keep records of their disposal. As was true everywhere in the young United States, speculators and companies bought up huge areas, thus shunting aside democracy and setting the stage for enormous landholdings of big copper companies and corporations that rose in the late nineteenth and early twentieth centuries. At Sault Sainte Marie, by 1845, men launched sailing ships above the rapids. Until then, small craft had been towed across a portage there. In the early 1840s, a few vessels sailed on Lake Superior: *Algonquin*, the *Merchant*, and the *Swallow*. The American Fur Company's ship *John Jacob Astor* was wrecked in 1844 during a storm, on the rocks of Copper Harbor.[46]

In 1845, a French–Ojibwa cook operated a log house at Copper Harbor, where one slept under one's own blanket on bags of oats for twenty-five cents. For an additional sum, one dined on baked trout, pork and beans, bread, butter, applesauce, and coffee or tea. George W. Thayer, who worked the summer of 1845 helping explorers, remembered the comment of the African American waiter on board the *Independence* on his way south from Sault Sainte Marie at the end of the season. A passenger in the dining room complained of old and new butter mixed in a jar, unappetizing streaks clearly visible, and asked, "Do you call that butter?" The waiter replied instantly, "Yes, sir, that is conglomerate butter with spar veins in it." The Keweenaw had become an obsession. Thayer in his old age wrote that after fifty-seven years, he longed to take a second and final look—"to again cast my eyes upon the hills and mountains I climbed," at swamps he tramped, and icy streams he waded. The Keweenaw had been his "school, my education in the great university of nature, whose mentor no men hath seen."[47]

John Forster made a forty-five-mile round-trip on snowshoes for a Christmas dinner at Fort Wilkins. Pioneers visited each other at various locations. Forster realized that "by some mysterious providence," there was never a lack of wine and other liquors. He summed up the socializing: "Good cheer, hearty enjoyment, roaring laughter, filled the snow covered cabins. Let the winds howl, let Jack Frost do his worst outside, inside all were warm and jolly." After the last boat in autumn, pioneers waited until late April or early May for the first ship with supplies, mail, newspapers, and packages from "down below." Native American or French Canadian packers brought mail from Green Bay, Wisconsin, sometimes once a month but usually less frequently. In summer, Native Americans worked as guides; one named "the Admiral" won admiration from all for guiding a boat through wind as high waves threatened while another native bailed constantly.[48]

Forster, noting the absence of women, found the Keweenaw forlorn in that respect: "The sight of a bit of calico in those days was more thrilling than the flashing of banners." But there *were* women who worked in developing the country. Deep in the woods, some sixteen miles from Eagle River, Forster supervised a mine location where a few rough German miners and some Frenchmen constituted the work force. They ate potatoes, salted fish, and sometimes pork. All were Catholics; and Madame C., who cooked, saved the pork by announcing on Ash Wednesday that all must live on fish and potatoes for the next forty days. Forster observed that she sometimes had to "whip in all the malcontents." He marveled at her genius in serving fish chowder, fish balls, fish stews (with potatoes and without), boiled fish, broiled fish, and, her chef d'oeuvre, salt fish pie, baked in a tasty crust, the sampling of which drew men from miles about. Only once did miners and workers at Forster's location enjoy fresh beef in winter, via the accidental death of a neighbor's ox![49]

The Brockway Mountain Drive, in the northern part of the Keweenaw Peninsula, today pays tribute to pioneer Daniel Brockway. His wife, Lucena Harris Brockway, who came as a young mother to the Keweenaw Peninsula in the mid-1840s and spent the rest of her life (nearly five decades) in fledgling communities in the northern forests, also deserves tribute. A woman of many skills, provider of hospitality that could hardly be surpassed, midwife, comforter and helper to many, Lucena spent her Keweenaw years affirmatively, despite an awesome loneliness that at times almost overcame her. In diaries that spanned more than twenty years, she recorded the joys and trials of life in north-woods communities.[50]

She had come north with Daniel from the Lower Peninsula, living first at L'Anse where her husband worked as blacksmith under government contract among the Native Americans and raised crops that he sold at the Cliff and other mines. When the copper excitement further ignited aspirations, the Brockways went by boat to Copper Harbor. Lucena raised five children and ably assisted her husband in his hotel and mercantile establishments at Copper Harbor, Eagle River, Cliff Mine, and Phoenix. A host of those

*Daniel D. Brockway. (Michigan Historical Collections, Bentley Historical
Library, The University of Michigan.)*

helped by their generosity called them affectionately "Ma and Pa
Brockway."[51]

Lucena worked at household chores, sewing, tatting, harvesting
and preserving fruits and vegetables, raising poultry, selling eggs,
and nursing the sick and comforting mourners among them. For
diversion, she played her piano. She was hostess to an almost constant stream of family members, friends, acquaintances, and sojourners returning to visit the Keweenaw. Reviewing the year 1843–44,
she recalled that mine manager Simon Mandelbaum had come from
Copper Harbor to visit the Brockways at L'Anse: he stayed for two
months.[52] Of old New York State stock, the Brockway and Harris
families had joined the westward migration to Michigan. Lucena and
Daniel had followed Daniel's brother William north. William had
been appointed in 1838 to serve at the Keweenaw Bay Methodist
Mission. He had initial misgivings, for he had worked as blacksmith
and thought it somewhat improper "to spoil a good blacksmith for
the sake of making a poor preacher." Daniel replaced him as smith.
William served a year as pastor, and the Ojibwa called him Pewabic

(Iron Man), grateful for all he had taught them about agriculture. He left to serve nine years as superintendent of the missions in the Upper Peninsula.[53]

Daniel prided himself on his agricultural pursuits. He boasted to relatives downstate, "I have raised here in this country where you thought nothing would grow, on a piece of ground ten rods square, 110 bushels of potatoes" of as fine a quality as one ever cultivated anywhere, twenty bushels of turnips from seed in three months—big turnips almost nine inches wide—twelve quarts of peas, cabbages, beets, carrots, and parsnips. His corn did not ripen; but he harvested melons, cucumbers, and a half-acre of luxuriant oats and cultivated flowers. Native Americans helped him transport the produce by boat to the mining camps, and so successful was he that he offered to loan a downstate relative three hundred dollars the next season. "Why don't you come visit?," Brockway asked his kin in 1844.[54] In 1845, Lucena wrote from L'Anse that the greatest trial she experienced was that her family did not write more often. She was twenty-eight years old, mother of two. Her daughter Sarah, born in July 1844, was one of the first two white children born in the Lake Superior country. Lucena nursed children ill with scarlet fever at L'Anse in 1844.[55] Four years later, at Copper Harbor, she helped deliver the firstborn son of Abby and the Reverend John Pitezel. A "fine Lake Superior boy—a missionary of course," the father bragged. No doctor was available, he wrote his mother; but no one could have done better at delivering than "the landlady of the house where we now stop," Lucena Brockway.[56]

Earnest, God-loving Pitezel, aware of material rewards for those willing to work in the Keweenaw wilderness, wrote his brother Joshua in 1848, telling him he could sign on for a job in the mines and earn twenty dollars per month, from which he would have to pay board. "You could also chop cord wood at 62½¢ per cord," he advised, and save one hundred dollars a year. Mine work was hard, true, but not harder than the farming Joshua did in Ohio. The fare from there to the Keweenaw was twenty-five dollars—less if he took deck passage. The steamboat *Detroit* left every Tuesday at 9:00 A.M. for the Sault from Detroit where Joshua could first rest and look up Chilton Barney who kept the Temperance Tavern there. Earlier, he related that one could make up to thirty dollars a month clear; but "it is a hard country viewed in every respect and people who are doing well in other places had better stay [there]."[57]

Horace Greeley of the *New York Tribune* uttered similar ambivalent advice. He visited the Keweenaw Peninsula during the summer of 1847. His accounts, published later in his newspaper, served as advertising for the promotion of mining. Many today believe that his advice, "Go West, young man!" meant that youth should head for the Keweenaw. At the Cliff and other mines, the editor found hardwood timber impressive, the stony soil adapted to growing of potatoes and root crops, miners earning thirty dollars per month for eight hours work a day, and labor commanding fifteen to twenty dollars a month for ordinary work. But living was expensive, with potatoes selling for $1.12 per bushel and hay and feed for horses and cattle, all imported by ship, thirty to forty dollars per ton.[58]

Slowly, the wilderness gave way to axe and construction. By 1846, John Saint John noted that a road had been completed connecting Copper Harbor with Agate Harbor, nine miles distant with work in progress on its extension to Eagle River. Public houses appeared at Copper Harbor and Eagle River. There was talk of a daily stage-coach running between the two settlements. Fledgling companies were responsible. Mr. Stoutenburg, agent (manager) of the North-west Company, by 1847 had built the six-mile road from his mine to Eagle Harbor and a five-mile road from Grand Marais to Agate Harbor and had also cut a four-mile trail from Grand Marais to his mines. Not for another decade would local and state governments involve themselves in road building.[59]

The times shouted for individual economic enterprise. Charles T. Jackson argued against reserving mineral lands, a "great evil to the country," seriously embarrassing "the settlement of the newly acquired territory." Robert J. Hybels, historian, concluded: "The copper rush helped reverse the traditional policy of public ownership of mineral lands. The sale of the copper lands was one of the first indications that Americans would no more husband their metals than their other land resources." Dishonest speculators and inexperienced adventurers proliferated, observed Charles Lanman; but he had no doubt that "all those [people] who are prudent and industrious would accumulate fortunes."[60] Foster and Whitney reported that in Ontonagon country, before 1848 ended, "nearly all of the companies in Township 51, range 43 had abandoned their locations, regarding them as worthless." At the end of the next season, geologists said "there was not, to our knowledge, a white man left."[61] Enterprise accompanied by flux brought sudden upheavals. In 1845, the Lake Superior Copper Company at Eagle River had six shafts, thirty buildings, 140 men and women, "and children in numbers" and was producing small quantities of copper and silver.[62] By 1850, mining operations had ended there as they also had, temporarily, at the Copper Falls, Northwestern, and Phoenix Companies. That year Foster and Whitney listed twenty existing mines extending from the very productive Minesota up to and beyond the Cliff. Two mining companies also operated on Isle Royale.[63]

By 1847, the initial intensity of the copper boom had evaporated. Forster discerned that spring brought new stock and supplies but not many adventurers. In 1848, the California gold rush thinned the ranks even more. Great expectations of many had collapsed. Few remained to populate the rudimentary communities that had been developed.[64] In the quieter period that followed, missionaries who had arrived earlier and located mostly at Keweenaw Bay continued efforts to make the Native Americans Christians.

Difficulty in interpreting the 1842 treaty led to the reservation of lands between Keweenaw Bay and Huron Bay by the LaPointe Treaty of 1854. Native Americans claimed they had not ceded Isle Royale, but none lived there. Jackson, in 1847, found on the island a fishing station at Siskowit Bay operated by the American Fur Company. Four men packed siskowit and lake trout and noted that in the season previous they had caught, salted, and packed sixty barrels of fish between July and November and hoped to do five hundred in 1847. Bela Hubbard estimated that about a thousand natives inhabited the entire south shore of Lake Superior. L'Anse was a focal point. There the American Fur Company's trading post (actually three miles from the head of Keweenaw Bay) in 1840 engaged natives, paying them four dollars a barrel for putting up fish; it supplied the barrels and salt. The company also paid twelve shillings each for marten skins and four dollars a pound for beaver skins. The company paid in produce. Flour ranged from ten to twenty dollars a barrel; powder, two dollars per pound, with three shillings for shot. Blankets and dry goods were also traded. Not far from the company's "factory," where natives packed fish, the Methodist mission's officers attempted to teach them the settled ways of agriculture. The economic depression of 1842 forced the Ojibwa to sell their lands via treaty. When Hubbard visited the Methodist mission in 1840, he found a dozen neat huts of log and bark but no natives, as they had gone fishing at Point Gros Maul (Big Mallet), present-day Pequaming Point.[65]

In 1844, Daniel Brockway wrote of natives returning to L'Anse from spring sugar camps. They made the "finest sugar" he wrote. He traded one-and-one-half pounds of flour for one pound of sugar— "an excellent bargain," he told relatives, "and we are both satisfied."[66] Brockway helped shape the United States government's plan for acculturation. Mrs. W. A. Childs, his niece by marriage, related many years later that the purpose of the whites was "not simply to teach the Indians how to work, but also to instruct them how to live as white people."[67] Methodists and Catholics assisted in this.

Interestingly, one of the first preachers of the Gospel at Keweenaw Bay was John Sunday, a Native American who was convinced of the truth of Christianity. He left the Wesleyan mission in Canada and, after visiting the Sault, made his way, in 1834, to what was then known as Kewawenon. The Reverend John Clark followed, built the log mission house, a schoolhouse, and huts for the natives. Two youths assisted, one of them Daniel Meeker Chandler, a New Yorker who decided in 1834, while living at Rutland, Vermont, to become a missionary among Native Americans in the Northwest. The last missionary at Keweenaw Bay had been Father Ménard, 174 years before. When Chandler, after inclement weather and physical privation,finally completed building his cabin, he met with as much opposition as had his Catholic predecessor long ago. On Christmas Eve, 1834, Ojibwa visited him. All had been away on a hunting trip when Chandler arrived at the bay. Now they filled his house. The chief, his face painted black, and his followers seated themselves and remained silent for half an hour. Then the chief spoke: "Where did you come from? Who gave you a right to build a house on my land?" Chandler answered that while the Ojibwa hunted as winter approached, he needed shelter. "Then pay me," said the chief: "I will not sell [the land], but every year, I must have a barrel of flour, one bag of corn, and some tobacco, for the land your house covers, and the wood you burn." To preserve peace, Chandler yielded—at least for a year, he noted in his journal. Chandler procured provisions from the trader while his assistant exhorted the natives, urging them to flee from the wrath of God, to which they replied "that they never would embrace the Christian religion while they lived."

The Methodists began proselytizing, organizing prayer meetings, opposing the "satanical exploits" of the Ojibwa medicine man, opening a school for the children, and teaching them to read. Chandler rose at four and by nine each morning was teaching youngsters gathered in his kitchen. He taught until four in the afternoon, then made the rounds of Ojibwa lodges until nine at night. One Christmas, a French fur trader asked him to preach to the hired men, French Canadian Catholics. When John Clark joined him in June, 1835, they set to work building the village that continues to this day. After much opposition, many of the Ojibwa accepted the new life. By 1842, Chandler died, having suffered much fatigue and pain; but he had been instrumental in pacifying much of the opposition.[68]

His most notable successor, the Reverend John Pitezel, arrived at L'Anse in October 1844 from the Sault, where he had bought a large canoe, hired three man, and then, with wife and daughter and a winter's provisions—flour, pork, sugar, butter, cheese, tea, coffee, spices, candles, bedding, and clothing—embarked on the 250-mile trip. He had missed sailing on the *John Jacob Astor*, and he thought canoe travel safer because the canoe would "ride almost any wave." Rowing always near the coast, one could go ashore when stormy weather approached. The family, forced to leave their personal belongings at the Sault, longed for spring, when they could retrieve them.[69]

Pitezel labored four years at Keweenaw Bay and was then appointed district superintendent for Methodist missions after some missionary work at Cliff Mine. Despite the work of predecessors, Pitezel found the Keweenaw Bay Ojibwa reluctant to abandon "superstition and old habits." He wrote his mother that they seemed, at times, not to advance at all; but "if their condition is lamentable with all the means used to Christianize and civilize them, what would be their fate if left to themselves?" Visiting LaPointe, he wondered why Catholic missionaries seemed more successful. He reasoned that Catholic ritual and superstitious forms attracted natives; but, more important, priests "go and stay for a year in the Indian country, learn the language, [and] preach in it." Pitezel, like Chandler before him, had always to rely on slow, laborious communication through interpreters. He wrote that although he preferred to labor among white people, at L'Anse, he worked in a spirit of self-sacrifice.[70]

Pitezel raised one hundred bushels of potatoes and twenty of turnips and sold almost forty-five dollars' worth of the surplus to support the mission. Winter supplies, shipped from Copper Harbor, arrived in autumn. In October 1845, the ship *Fur Trader* arrived with a package that Pitezel's mother had sent the previous spring! Peaches in it were mostly well preserved, the dried tomatoes, musty, the apples, "condemned" except for skin and cores, and the peach butter, nearly spoiled. He thanked his mother for long underwear that would be "very good this winter." His wife gratefully acknowledged the yarn, as she had "[k]nit herself out." They lacked for no good thing and, since living "in this country [had] enjoyed almost uninterrupted health." By this time, Catholics under Father Frederic Baraga had set up their mission across the bay. Pitezel assured his mother that he and his family were in no danger from "Indians and Catholics. . . . We feel safe [at L'Anse] as we should in your own [Ohio] neighborhood."[71]

An assistant, Brother Holt, in November 1846, preached to the natives in the morning, while Pitezel told the afternoon congregation, citing Hebrews 13:12–14, "Here we have no continuing city." Constantly, he felt that "ungodly" natives and some whites used all their malevolence against missionaries. He fought the liquor traffic and once had "plain talk" with a trader who sold natives eight gallons of liquor for thirty dollars. The trader had circulated rumors that the Methodists had appropriated funds for their private use. Pitezel said the truth was that all goods sent were given free to the natives except for some exchanged for fish or berries. Also, to encourage industry, at times missionaries asked "a moderate price in labour," as such work done by natives was good for the natives.[72]

John H. Pitezel.
(Clarke Historical
Library, Central
Michigan
University.)

Rising daily at 5:00 A.M., Pitezel read when not building a new church edifice, planting, weeding, harvesting, or visiting the sick. By 9:00 P.M., fatigued, he fell asleep. The natives enjoyed the preaching of a visiting Canadian, one J. Muskrat, one of their own race. Pitezel recorded in his journal that when "J. M." preached "with the Holy Spirit accompanying," the natives, much affected, "cried aloud before he concluded." Difficulties always loomed. Pitezel conducted an inquiry into an "unpleasant affair" when one of the women was suspected of killing her baby. The congregation had trouble with a man and wife who had to be expelled. Preaching one September morning to the natives on I Corinthians 6:9–11, he noted that some parishioners had lately fallen into some of the sins enumerated by Saint Paul: fornication, theft, idolatry, adultery, and effeminacy. Fast days, days of prayer, preaching, organizing a Bible study class, and traveling to the Cliff, where he conducted services—in good and in foul weather—the missionary carried on. The Ojibwa puzzled him. On January 14, 1847, he noted in his journal: "This morning another little child died among the Indians. It seems as if they were destined to extinction."[73]

His people at Keweenaw Bay, employees at the trading station and their families, did not consider themselves parochial; but often, the Native Americans surpassed them in generosity. On June 27, 1847, a collection for the suffering poor in Ireland garnered $8.50 and $5.00 worth of jewelry, nearly all contributed by Native Americans and missionaries. Pitezel stated that one of the white men, as in the past, raised impertinent questions as he "strove to damp the charity of others" toward starving people as the potato famine gripped a nation thousands of miles distant. Delinquency and backsliding among the natives continued, as they often complained about Methodist rules. Pitezel and associates worked diligently, pleased that eventually many natives accepted Anglo–American concepts of property and agriculture. By 1849, whites and natives discussed land purchased and how it should be divided among them. When, two years after he was transferred, Pitezel returned to L'Anse to visit and preach, the natives rejoiced; and when he departed, they crowded the dock and bade "an affectionate farewell." Pitezel considered this leave-taking much warmer than some elsewhere, particularly one at Wisconsin's Fond du Lac, where only one native sat cold and speechless while missionaries accompanied Pitezel to his boat.[74]

While stationed at Keweenaw Bay, Pitezel also conducted missions among copper miners and their families at the Cliff and in settlements north of the rich mine. His first mission lasted three weeks and two days, time spent at mines and locations where he met "with a very warm reception," some backsliders, a few who professed religion, and "a good many Roman Catholics." He traveled mostly on foot, preaching eleven times during this trip in November 1846. Proudly, he wrote that his was the first Protestant preaching in these parts.

His trip home through forest trails blazed by Native Americans was harrowing. Reaching the head of Torch Lake safely on November 30, he rowed across the lake, then walked with four companions where the lake narrowed and was blocked with ice. He set off alone through the woods for the remaining eight-and-one-half miles to Keweenaw Bay. He could not find the surveyor's line; thick snow fell on his pocket compass unprotected by glass; and he became lost, veering west toward Portage Lake, supposing all the time he was approaching Keweenaw Bay. Suffering from dampness and great fatigue, he found himself in an almost impenetrable cedar swamp. With a small hatchet, he cut wood, made a fire, and fashioned a shelter of balsam branches, in which he spread other pine boughs, to serve as bed while the wind howled and Portage Lake's waves roared.

Rain fell most of the night. He had only a few biscuits and slept little, as he had to keep the fire going. In the morning, he found the bank of Portage River about three miles from its entrance into

Keweenaw Bay. James and Mrs. Tanner and their children, rowing upon the river as they searched for wood, rescued him; and he spent a night in their bark-covered cabin while a new storm raged. After breakfast next day, Tanner put Pitezel on the trail leading to the Catholic mission on the west side of Keweenaw Bay. After a twelve-mile walk, Pitezel reached the Catholic mission about four in the afternoon, where he obtained "conveyance" across the bay to his home. This saga was typical of travel in the pioneer days of the Keweenaw Peninsula.[75]

Transferred to the Cliff location in 1848, Pitezel and his wife settled there after a disastrous stay at the mine itself, where the Jones family from Cornwall displeased them with sloppy housekeeping and neglected religious duties. As for the miners, they listened and made generous contributions to the temperance cause (thirty signed pledges of total abstinence) but were given to profanity, drink, and various excesses. Many were single, and a horrified Pitezel saw them "ramble about" on the Sabbath, like "spirits seeking rest." How few then took the Holy Sacrament of the Lord's Body and Blood, he mused one weekend. Instead, the mine workers climbed the steep cliff that rose up from the mine and, with instruments, "made music enough to charm the ear." When they climbed down, they stood in idle groups and gossiped, much to the chagrin of Pitezel.

He was appalled by sleighs filled with drunken men returning from Lake Superior, the men "bawling and singing" as they passed through the streets. He was increasingly disenchanted. He believed that temperance could make no headway: "This is as barren a moral field as it is physically." Only four received the sacrament of communion at Fort Wilkins on a spring day. After preaching at the Brockways' house at Copper Harbor, he thought the prospect "for doing good here rather dark." Mine managers encouraged his work, donated small sums of cash: temperance would serve them well. In his peregrinations, Pitezel often encountered the Catholic priest, who came to hear confessions and say mass the following morning, catering to increasing numbers of Irish, German, and French Canadian laborers.[76]

In February 1848, the Cliff community was so disturbed by a fight involving intoxicated men—one receiving a near-fatal wound from a "dirk knife about a foot long"—that Pitezel held no worship services next day. By August, living at Eagle River but working at the Cliff, he said he had preached little elsewhere: "Every other door has been closed." In October, at Copper Harbor, where masons, carpenters, and boatmen worked building a lighthouse on Hays' Point, Pitezel was rebuffed when he came to preach. Men offered excuses: distance from home, lateness of the season, recent bad weather. He preached that afternoon to "a little few," writing later that he longed for the time when he would be "in my appropriate sphere." But the seeds had been planted, and he had often exulted in the sacrificial work he had done, given God thanks for the bracing climate and good fellowship amid hardships. The men he later superintended succeeded in the Keweenaw Peninsula, and the Methodist way of life became vital for many. Pitezel deserves much of the credit.[77]

Father Frederic Baraga founded the Catholic mission in autumn 1843. Born June 29, 1797, in Slovenia and left an orphan at twelve, he had entered the seminary at Ljubljana in 1821 and two years later was ordained to the priesthood. European intellectuals, including Goethe, thought America "had it better," and Madame de Staël wrote that the United States was the "future of the world"—while others like Baraga believed the great American wilderness needed the saving gospel of Christianity. When he was thirty-two, Baraga asked permission to apply for the American missions; and he was first sent to Arbe Croche in Michigan's Lower Peninsula. He was fascinated with the Native Americans he encountered there and by 1832 had published a prayer book, *Otawa Anamie-Masinaigan Wawiyatanong* in their language. By December of that year, he expressed a wish to go to the Lake Superior country. Eventually, he was sent to LaPointe, where he labored eight years (1835–43), during which time he made a trip to Europe to raise funds and collect religious articles. With LaPointe as base, the priest visited Minnesota, Canada, and Michigan, recruiting lay persons to assist; people like Margaret and Pierre Cotte used Baraga's Native American prayer book at Fond du Lac. Nancy and Pierre (Peter) Crebassa collaborated with Baraga, Crebassa advising that L'Anse would be a fertile field for converts, saying some natives there had begged for missionaries to come help them in their plight.[78]

Baraga visited L'Anse early in 1843, where he heard of the Methodist missionary activity from Crebassa who now lived there. Baraga used part of Crebassa's house for a chapel and school and, in a three-week visit, baptized thirty, leaving others curious and "receptive." In October, the priest returned to found a permanent mission on the west side of Keweenaw Bay, opposite the Protestants. The original mission was about two miles from the present village of Baraga. As of 1900, the post office of that mission was called Assinins, after a native chief who had helped Father Baraga compile some of his celebrated works in the Ojibwa language.[79]

Hoping to create a "reduction" (collecting natives in one village near the church building), similar to Jesuit enterprises in Paraguay, Baraga wrote to European aristocrats, begging for money. He told them that the natives could never be civilized living scattered in forests, that he had already been advanced the materials needed for erecting mission buildings, and that he estimated the cost of building log structures with board floors as between four and five hundred dollars. Expensive, yes; but he added: "What a gain if once this mission be established! How many poor, barbarian savages, who live in huts, which are to be compared to *bear-lairs*, and whose habits correspond to their surroundings, will become civilized and be transformed into good, God-serving Christians!" Left to themselves, the natives succumbed to pagan dances and feasts, Baraga told prospective donors and, when ill, called in the medicine man to "perform his diabolical incantations." The Leopoldine Society in the Austrian Empire sent him generous funds, including two thousand florins in 1843–44, so Baraga could repay money previously provided by the fur company.[80]

The priest rose in the middle of the night, prayed, read the Scriptures, said mass at dawn, then taught, visited, tended the ill, and advocated temperance. Complete abstinence from hard liquor was the only solution, he was convinced. He wrote a famous dictionary of the Ojibwa language, prayer books (including one for children), instruction manuals for his fellow and succeeding Catholic missionaries. He wrote a life of Jesus in the form of a prayer book. His diaries and journals provide graphic pictures of his sincerity and zeal. At first dismayed, he wrote: "L'Anse is an unpleasant, sad, sterile place, in no comparison with LaPointe. Solely the wish to help these poor Indians attain eternal happiness keeps me here."[81] But he became fond of the place; for he loved the Ojibwa and truly wished to assist even if he could not always accept that they *were* civilized in that they had retained remnants of their vital culture which had suffered from debilitating influences of fur traders. Baraga had only contempt for purveyors of liquor and had several acrimonious encounters with such men.[82]

The natives appreciated whites who spoke their language. When Baraga opened his school, he had, as students, nineteen girls, nine women, three men, and twenty boys. He instructed them in Christian doctrine, reading, writing, and arithmetic. The economic and social upheavals endured among the Ojibwa over almost two hundred years led to their desperate plight, and many now looked to the European–American culture to ameliorate conditions. Many took up farming and no longer relied on hunting and fishing as sole means of subsistence. Others resisted, despising Christianity and its appurtenances. But the mission flourished. More log houses appeared. Dominating everything was the church structure that Baraga dedicated to the Holy Name of Jesus on September 29, 1844.[83]

By midsummer 1845, Reverend Pitezel wrote his mother that across the bay, the priest laboured for the promotion of his religion with "zeal worthy of a better cause" and that this should make

Protestants blush. Admiring Baraga's spirit, he abhorred Catholicism's "tyrannical power, the false and idolatrous worship and the erroneous doctrines." He reported that the priest slept no more than five hours and dined simply on fish and potatoes. Pitezel wrote his brother in 1846 about the "old Priest" across the bay (Baraga was forty-nine), stating: "We have neither spiked our cannons nor smoked as yet the pipe of peace [with him]. I trust I have waged an eternal war with Popish superstition and idolatry."[84]

Actions are more telling than bigotry, however; and when Pitezel worked on his church building the last summer he spent at Keweenaw Bay, Father Baraga supplied the Methodists with a bell. Late in life, Pitezel recalled that despite differences, he and Baraga were "neighbors, and freely exchanged the amenities of social life." Pitezel described Baraga as temperate, devout, dignified, and "universally respected by the Indians and mining community, and affectionately loved by those in closer fellowship."[85]

Baraga traveled hundreds of miles from L'Anse, serving men and women of the mines to the north, plodding on snowshoes in dead of winter, on "very laborious journeys . . . full of peril and unlimited hardship," walking sixty miles to baptize a dying child or to cater to the sick. He sometimes slept in a rude shelter of pine branches in cold weather, disturbed that the short day prevented him from reading his breviary.[86] In the Keweenaw, snow commenced falling in mid-October but rarely exceeded a depth of four feet. The Keweenaw winter, dreaded even today, was often one of dry cold with the mercury sinking below zero occasionally. Wind and prolonged exposure gave the season its bad name; and in some areas, the cold was more intense than in others.[87]

One night, while Baraga was traveling with a guide from Fond du Lac (Minnesota) to LaPointe, twelve inches of snow fell, and they had to burn wood for sixteen hours. Upon returning to L'Anse on December 17, 1847, Baraga found all in good order, the natives during his absence having assembled on Sundays and on the holy day of Mary's Immaculate Conception, praying and singing. The priest wrote, "I live here satisfied and grateful, loving and beloved as a father amongst his children, for which I thank God in the Name of Jesus." The following month, having to travel again, he wrote, "It was with difficulty and a heavy heart that I could tear myself away from my dear children at L'Anse."[88]

Always, he had one goal to bring as many as possible to Christ and the new way of life.[89] He was a fanatic, in the sense that fanaticism is great enthusiasm. His expectations remained high as he rejoiced in the rich harvest of souls possible at all the mining locations from Ontonagon to Copper Harbor. Here Irish, Germans, French

Bishop Frederic Baraga, 1854.
(Bishop Baraga Archives,
Marquette, Michigan.)

Canadians, and others responded eagerly to the scriptures, mass, and sacraments. When Methodists and Catholics at Keweenaw Bay joined forces in buying land on which their missions were located, they deeded them to the Native Americans so that the latter need not be forced west. Such was the nucleus of the Keweenaw Bay Reservation, which continues to the present. The *Catholic Almanac* for 1848 said that after three years, more than thirty-three Ojibwa families lived industrious lives and in "decent houses," each with thirty acres for tillage. The agent for the U.S. government's Indian Affairs reported that Methodists and Catholics had realized their expectations of helping the Ojibwa "become like white people."[90]

3

Mines and Towns

1850 – 1870

NEW ENGLAND POET JOHN GREENLEAF WHITTIER
wrote of the Lake Superior country in 1848 and predicted:

> By forest, lake and water-fall,
> I see . . .
> The lofty with the low. . . .
> I hear the tread of pioneers
> Of nations yet to be;
> The first low wash of waves where soon
> Shall roll a human sea

The Cliff Mine's riches, Minesota Mine's abundance of copper, and the spectacular deposits unearthed later at Quincy, Calumet, and Hecla transformed the Keweenaw Peninsula between 1850 and 1870, as development there helped usher in the nation's Industrial Revolution.[1] United States population census takers confirmed the poet's prophecy (see Table 3.1; Houghton County included present-day Keweenaw County).[2]

The Michigan census of May 1854 showed an increase in four years of 2,000 people in Houghton County (from 708 to 2,873).[3] In 1850, its population consisted of 515 white males, 1 black male, and 192 females. They were young: 348 of the 516 males and 93 of the 192 females ranged in age from twenty to forty. Among the total population, there were 150 children, ages one to fifteen. In

Table 3.1. Keweenaw Peninsula, Population 1850–1870

County	1850	1860	1870
Houghton	708	9,234	13,879
Keweenaw	—	—	4,205
Ontonagon	383	4,568	2,845

1860, sixty-two African Americans and over 1,000 Native Americans accounted for 10.5 percent of Houghton County's population. The federal census of 1860 indicated that 4,544 whites and twenty-four African Americans lived in Ontonagon County, but Native Americans were not counted.[4]

The earliest settlements in the Keweenaw Peninsula had developed where most boats made landfall, particularly at Copper Harbor and Eagle Harbor—both providing excellent havens for ships—and at Eagle River and Ontonagon. As the peninsula's population grew after the initial copper rush, mines, instead of harbors, determined location of settlements and towns. Another factor influencing the shaping of peninsular society as miners, entrepreneurs, merchants, farmers, and town builders poured in was the desire to have Native Americans removed or concentrated at Keweenaw Bay.[5]

By 1857, John Forster remarked on the decline in population at the Sault, as many had migrated to the western end of the Upper Peninsula to exploit mineral wealth. Sault Sainte Marie had become "a very dull village, with grass-grown streets and rotting wharves and warehouses," with few Anglo–Saxons, a place given up to "lounging Indians and contented Frenchmen, who could laugh and grow fat on a diet of fish and potatoes; [enjoying] their evenings with the violin and dancing."[6] The new focus in Michigan was on the four counties of the Copper Country organized as follows: Houghton (1846), Ontonagon (1855), Keweenaw (1861), and Baraga (1875).

Alexander Ramsey, reporting to the federal government in 1849, waxed enthusiastic about ships, canals, and copper wealth and connecting links east and west, north and south. Like many, he wanted the Ojibwa moved west of the Mississippi, out of the way of Yankee progress. Charles Penny earlier had sounded a warning heard with increasing frequency: "Let an Indian show his head and it will soon be scalpless. . . . Three or four of them are as vicious looking a set of devils as live this side of tophet." Do not give Native Americans money, warned Orlando Brown, commissioner of Indian affairs, in

1849; in future treaties, he advised, give them tools, utensils for agriculture, and provisions. Experience, he continued, has taught that "there can be no civilization without a rigid exclusion of ardent spirits" among the Ojibwa. He advised keeping traders away from the natives; for though most were honorable, a few by selling liquor devastated the native population.[7]

Two German visitors to the Ontonagon country found their Native American guide exotic. At rest stops he squatted in the bottom of the canoe, occasionally smoking "kinni kinick," a substitute for tobacco made from the inner rind of the red osier dogwood. The aroma was not unpleasant; and this tobacco substitute far less injurious, said the Germans, than "vile compounds" used by the "half-civilized" whites they had encountered earlier in the Far West.[8] John S. Livermore, subagent for Native American affairs, wearied of demands for Isle Royale, which the Native Americans insisted they had not given up in treaties. Livermore explained to his superiors in Washington, that the natives with "an extravagant opinion of its mineral wealth, [demanded] a large sum in compensation." He told them he thought "they had nothing to expect" but that he would forward their views.[9]

By the eve of the 1854 LaPointe Treaty council, the six hundred-member band of Ojibwa at Keweenaw Bay dressed like whites and farmed. Six years before they had produced three thousand bushels of potatoes and five hundred of turnips, salted five hundred barrels of fish, and sold furs worth twenty-five hundred dollars. Article II of the 1854 treaty designated reservation lands to be set apart there. Michigan's 1850 constitution allowed voting rights for "every civilized male inhabitant of Indian descent, not a member of any tribe." It provided, as for white males, that such a man be twenty-one and that he live in Michigan for three months and in his election district for ten days immediately before the election. Despite this, the compilers of the *Michigan State Gazetteer* declared in 1862 that it was impossible to induce the Native American "to conform to the usages of civilized life, and except in the manufacture of a few baskets and the supply of a few furs, . . . no evidences of his industry" are to be seen. The natives simply sank into vice, the editors stated, the more they mingled with whites, and "it would be of immense advantage to us [in Michigan], if not to themselves, if the negro and Indian could both be removed to some more genial clime."[10]

Fort Wilkins, as protection against Native Americans, had been useless; there was simply no threat from them. When the United States invaded Mexico in 1846, troops at the fort were withdrawn, and the facility fell into comparative neglect. Soldiers reoccupied the fort in 1867 and remained until August 1870. Although he loved the

Native Americans, Baraga—by 1863 a bishop—wrote: "It requires
much patience and heroic self-sacrifice to spend one's life with the
poor, simple, and naughty Indians." He had spent twenty-three years
among them and wrote, "I am not yet entirely free of the Indian
and never will be as long as I live." Such comments were unusual
in his diaries and letters. He sometimes grew frustrated with the
indolence, mendacity, and dependence of some Native Americans—
characteristics fostered, in part, by white-native contact.[11]

Now, the Keweenaw was to be developed along Anglo–American
economic concepts, using the labor of Cornish, Irish, Germans, and
French Canadians who would be joined eventually by Finns, Slavs,
and Italians. By 1870, copper was "king" and the Lake Superior
region became nationally and internationally renowned.

The news from the Cliff Mine until 1870 continued to amaze.
Refined copper production reached 2,363,860 pounds in 1857. In
Boston's market, financiers quoted Cliff's stock at $175 in 1857 and
$300 in 1858. After that, production fell but hopes continued high.
Work stopped in 1870 and in 1871. The mine was sold—a pattern
repeated often in the Keweenaw until the 1960s. From 1848 to
1870, the Cliff, after paying expenses, disbursed $2,627,000 among
stockholders (slightly over 2,000 percent on the paid-in capital).

An observer in 1863 watched miners placing drills and hammer in
buckets, Cornish pasties in their pockets, fuse in other pockets, and
descending quickly by ladders some twenty feet, then another descent
until finally they reached bottom. They were "singing all the time."
It sounded "fine" through the drifts. Forster, astonished at the size
and purity of copper hoisted in 1860—masses weighing four to eight
tons—watched four to six yoke of oxen pull "great groaning" wagons
"slowly down the smooth road to shipping docks at Eagle River."

Clifton was, in the 1860s, a large village of 1,443 residents. It
nestled "under the picturesque cliffs." Broad, cultivated fields under
strong summer sun yielded hay, oats, potatoes, turnips, beans, and
other vegetables. The Cliff Mine Store had a large supply of cheap
salted meat, some of it sold to Eagle River boardinghouses. People
dined on fresh fish, pigeons, berries, and nuts—sumptuous fare in
contrast to the salted beef, "wormy beans, indifferent bread, and
a little rice occasionally" that Joseph Rawlings remembered from
the 1850s.[12]

Rawlings, who arrived to work as engineer in 1850, found Clifton
a village of five hundred Cornish, Irish, and French Canadians, an
ethnic composite that changed little over the years. In his old age,
Rawlings recalled stories of Cliff silver having bought "a good many
farms." Miners appropriated for themselves the largest share of the
native silver often found with copper. Boys employed to sort the two

metals at the Cliff's crude mill pocketed silver from the apron in front
of the stamps. Cliff copper and silver also provided work for children
employed at Pittsburgh, Pennsylvania, where Keweenaw copper was
carried for refinement and manufacture.

Fashion had no virtue at Clifton. Women, few in number, observed Sunday dandies in the 1850s clad in "pepper and salt" pants,
high boots or moccasins, red or blue flannel shirts with silk sashes
or scarves twisted around waists. Vests or coats were rarely seen.
Grace Episcopal Church, the oldest Episcopal edifice in the Upper
Peninsula, built largely through efforts of Hervey Parke, later founder
of Parke, Davis, and Company but then chief clerk at the Cliff Mine,
provided solace and visiting clergy in 1859. The larger, more vigorous
Methodist establishment that John Pitezel founded imposed strict social standards. It led the temperance movement and allowed Cornish
miners to preach sermons. Rawlings recalled that no ball playing was
allowed in public on Sundays, and "woe to the transgressor, for the
'good people' were very 'goody, goody.' "[13]

Henry Hobart, only twenty-one when he left Vermont to come
teach 224 students ages five to twenty at Clifton in 1863–64, considered parents "very indifferent to the education of their children."
They hoarded their money, instead, or wasted it by drinking; for "all
the evils of intemperance in its worst stages are seen [at Clifton]."
He found the Cornish coarse, dirty, and rough, the Germans only
somewhat better, and the short-tempered Irish, males and females,
only too eager to join in holiday fights, "pulling hair, . . . swearing,
kicking." Hobart, happy to hear these "Paddies" received twenty-
dollar fines later, thought that good but preferred that "the grog
shops in the vicinity were burnt to the ground." He could not comprehend miners who considered gin and beer necessities.

Hot, sultry July days, cool, cloudy October mornings with some
pleasant sunny Indian summer alternating, May days with atmo-
spheres one could never find in dusty streets of great American cities,
and January storms that deposited four feet of snow and left 150
warehouse barrels of apples frozen solid were part of the Keweenaw
cycle that the young schoolmaster depicted so graphically in his diary.
Given much to philosophic reflection, often homesick as he recalled
his Vermont home, Hobart found the Lake Superior country eminently healthy, "the air . . . pure and bracing" with some March
mornings so beautiful he had never experienced their like. Typhoid
raged in 1863 in the Portage Lake area; but Clifton, like Ontonagon,
remained a healthy site.[14]

The earlier lakeside communities continued as small settlements.
Joseph Austrian, born near Dinkelsbühl, Bavaria, Germany, came to
the United States when he was only seventeen, attracted by brother

Julius' LaPointe fur trading and general store. At age nineteen, Joseph worked as clerk and bookkeeper for Henry Leopold at Eagle River and boarded with Leopold and his wife Ida (Joseph's sister). They lived in unheated rooms above the store that sold flour, coffee, meats, hardware, and clothing. Joseph made daily rounds to the Cliff Mine and others nearby, boardinghouses, and miners' homes, soliciting orders and collecting accounts due. Every season, Samuel F. Leopold, another brother-in-law, traveled to New York City to buy clothing, dry goods, boots, shoes, and men's furnishings. Business was so good that a hostler with horses and wagons eventually assisted the enterprise. Henry was unable to read and write English, so Joseph Austrian handled all business correspondence and accounts. No fire insurance company dared risk insuring the eighteen-by-twenty-four-foot frame store perched atop a hill facing the lake and heated by a boxwood stove with a huge pipe running the length of the store. Joseph recalled working as watchman and sitting there evenings in winter "shivering, wrapped up in a blanket waiting for Mr. Leopold" to return from playing cards at one of the boardinghouses.[15]

Eagle River with about one hundred inhabitants in 1852, depended on the Cliff, North American, Lake Superior Copper, and Garden City Mines. A few log houses stood side by side with taverns. Drinking seemed to be "the principal business transacted" at Eagle River, wrote one commentator. In summer, the shipping of copper rock and laying in supplies for the coming winter enlivened the settlement. By 1862, its population of nearly three hundred included three physicians who treated injured miners, a lawyer, insurance agent, and three justices of the peace. When Keweenaw County was formed out of Houghton County in 1861, Eagle River became the seat of government.

Steamers from Great Lakes cities stopped here with mail, supplies, and passengers. In 1862, the town, three miles distant from Cliff Mine, had a brewery, three saloons, blacksmiths, a lumber dealer, and boardinghouses. Shifting fortunes of mining companies affected stores, society, and professions. Joseph Austrian, disappointed when the brothers Leopold sold out to a Mr. Mandelbaum, moved with the Leopolds to a richer future at Portage Lake.[16]

Economic flux brought social change. Amid the sternest realities of copper production's attracting varied characters, a fervent idealism flourished also. Justus H. Rathbone came from upstate New York in 1858 to visit his friend Thomas W. Shapely, who worked at Central Mine (opened in 1854) but lived at Eagle Harbor. For awhile, they walked the five miles to the Central. Later, Shapely worked for his father in the forwarding and commission business at Eagle Harbor; and Rathbone taught school there. Talented, musical, fond of the theater, Rathbone helped form a drama group. Once, reading a play on Damon and Pythias, he conceived the idea of a fraternal order with worldwide influence promoting friendship and peace. Shapely thought him a visionary, but Rathbone wrote the ritual for his Knights of Pythias in the little Eagle Harbor schoolhouse during the winter of 1859–60. Rathbone was a big man, nearly six feet tall, weighing over two hundred pounds, spirited, witty, generous, "the life of any party or gathering of young people." His ideas of friendship, conjured up as he whiled away winter evenings at Eagle Harbor, had repercussions. He left after a year and organized the fraternity in Washington, D.C., in 1864. The Knights of Pythias enjoyed national success, with nearly a million members by 1921.

Nostalgic pioneers half a century later spoke of how as children in one-room schoolhouses, they dreamed of careers as business and social successes. Perhaps the idealism and kindness of a Rathbone and a Hobart influenced many. The records of school inspectors indicate that students in Eagle Harbor Township, in 1865, attended school five months out of a possible ten. The children used McGuffey's readers and spellers in a few of the five district schools. At the Eagle Harbor School in 1868, boys and girls named Paull, Smith, White, Downey, Mertz, Swartz, Kaiser, Schnider, and Pastorale knew their village of five hundred as still an important port for shipping copper rock, a center for grocers and general stores, with a carriage maker, a carpenter, hotels, smiths, boot makers, a milliner, and daguerreotypist. Fathers of the children worked at mines including the Copper Falls, Petherick, Central, Amygdaloid, and Pennsylvania.[17]

Copper Harbor was a hub of activity in summer and isolated in winter. With four hotels in 1862, a general store, and a church, Copper Harbor remained the base for men who still sought hidden mineral treasures at the northernmost part of the peninsula. Tourists found the scenery enchanting, one commenting on the "very pretty lake just back of the Fort [Wilkins], where speckled trout abound to a considerable extent."[18]

Daniel Brockway dabbled in the search for copper at Medora Lake. He took home a specimen of thirty-nine pounds and entertained hopes that the "mine may pay its own way." He hoped that the nearby Bluff Mine could be opened "for a trifling Sum of Money." He was happy to direct explorations, he told George S. Swartz, as he had a "deep interest in seeing the country improved." He advanced three hundred dollars of Swartz's money to six men who had worked twelve hours ridding the Medora shaft of water. The men had reached a depth of eighty-one feet and Brockway expected they would dig another twelve feet once the spring "break-up" had been completed.

Each spring, Brockway sailed off on a steamer to settle bills in Detroit for clover and timothy seed, coffee, sugar, and other provisions. He enticed acquaintances to come north, saying he could set them up in business. In 1861, he had "a nice little trade," had made $1,400 the previous season, and expected to surpass that in the succeeding year. Bring cattle, he urged one man, whom he called "Friend Mack," and join in a partnership. Beef had sold "by the carcass" for ten cents per pound the past winter. Brockway served as a middleman for men raising milch cows and complained to S. P. Brady of Detroit about stock that had not arrived or was of poor quality: One cow was too thin. "How the dickens is it that all the cattle from Wisconsin are so perfect [in some respects] and in every other respect inferior to the stock from other States?," he queried. Brockway asked a brother in Washington, D.C., to use his influence so that Daniel could lease Fort Wilkins, which had been occupied since 1855 by Dr. John S. Livermore on a lease for one cent per annum![19]

At the south end of the mineral range, the celebrated Minesota Mine, located fourteen miles from the mouth of the Ontonagon River at a place where ancient miners once worked, turned the Ontonagon district into a busy center "alive with [a] variegated collection of people" from all over the United States, "as well as wandering Indians, . . . consumptive New Yorkers come to regain health by inhaling the breath of pines," entrepreneurs, speculators, Native Americans to guide strangers, families, farmers, preachers, merchants, and a young lady from the West Indies who taught girls in public school French and embroidery.

From 1850 to 1860, Ontonagon was the biggest, most prosperous town on Lake Superior. By 1860, four sawmills annually produced 1,850,000 feet of lumber so that log cabins gave place to frame houses. Mines, mills, and other manufactures employed 1,419 persons, who produced yearly products valued at almost one million dollars. From Ontonagon's docks most of the copper from the surrounding area found its way onto ships bound for Detroit, Cleveland, or the East. By 1862, steamers from Cleveland, Detroit, and Chicago touched there each trip. Fare from Detroit was then fourteen dollars, and sixteen dollars bought a ticket from Chicago—each city a thousand miles away by ship.[20]

Besides the Minesota, the principal mines operating in the Ontonagon area by 1862—the National, Rockland, Evergreen Bluff, and Bohemian—provided work for Americans, Irish, Germans, Cornish, English, and French Canadian settlers. Only one of these mines ever paid a dividend. Still, laborers believed in a bright future. A plank road built to the mines from the river's mouth was followed with a better road, usable even in winter, from Ontonagon to Houghton

Ontonagon, c. 1860. (State Archives of Michigan.)

at Portage Lake. Some called this one Finnegan's Road, honoring Michael Finnegan, who had been given the contract. Most of the improvement was defrayed by a Houghton County bond issue. French Canadians from Wisconsin drove cattle and brought poultry north from Green Bay, Wisconsin, to Rockland and mining settlements, with Ontonagon the terminus. They stamped out a well-defined pony trail. By 1864, this trail, widened and fitted out with post stations, allowed faster travel; mail flowed over this route, day and night, reaching Ontonagon from Green Bay in just forty hours.

At Ontonagon, docks, warehouses, and ships lined the river. Stores, saloons, and boardinghouses rose along the main street. By 1862, the grand Bigelow House (Peter Mitchell, proprietor) catered to people such as wealthy Pittsburgh man of affairs, Jason Hanna; James Close, a partner in a docking and warehouse business; James Mercer, who became a state senator; William Condon, who ran one of the town's six general stores; and Jay Hubbell, a lawyer who became a congressman and later a prominent citizen of Houghton. Besides the Bigelow—"one of the most comfortable hotels" in all of Michigan—one could lodge at James Rough's Exchange Hotel or Lothrop Johnson's Johnson House. The "neat weekly quarto" *Lake Superior Miner*, Ontonagon's sprightly newspaper, cost two dollars a year. Already, by the early 1860s, summer attracted tourists from downstate and the Great Lakes region generally. They came to enjoy "beautiful scenery and [a] healthful location." Some visited Carp Lake (present-day Lake of the Clouds) in the Porcupine Mountains, where prospectors still moseyed about.

Steamers from late April to late October brought mails two to five times during the week. Ontonagon, lively with saloons and smelters, boasted of attorneys, dentists, and generally law-abiding citizens, although there were also riots, fights, and intemperance. Dr. Samuel S. Walbank, in 1862, served as physician, druggist, and bookseller. A Mrs. Schneider and Lewis Webber operated bakeries. A brewery and two tanneries prospered. The Ontonagon Mining District Association held meetings once a week, presaging later chambers of commerce.[21] Such was Ontonagon and vicinity—"the harbor alive with boats, . . . long lines of teams rumbling loads of copper down over plank roads, grain ripening in the August sun on the Cash farm across the river and on farms along the Miners and Rockland roads."[22]

By 1850, a Philharmonic Society, its membership almost exclusively German, added cultural refinement fostered also by a Methodist meetinghouse, Episcopal and Presbyterian churches, and Saint Patrick's Catholic Church. The Odd Fellows, Masons, and Good Templars flourished. Baptists and Bible Christians also built churches. Bishop Baraga visited the Minesota Mine in 1858 and found the Reverend Martin Fox, a Prussian, laboring to build churches. Fox spoke German, English, and French. On August 17, 1856, Baraga dedicated a church at the Minesota, naming it Saint Mary's. Although the largest in the diocese, the edifice was already inadequate, as only two-thirds of the congregation could be accommodated; many stood at three doors to participate at mass.[23]

German visitors to Ontonagon in 1852 found stores and saloons open on Sundays, as on weekdays. A Methodist from the mines, preaching at a schoolhouse, launched into a political diatribe against the French for their "godlessness," emanating from the 1789 revolution. General Daniel Pittman, influential in founding the Episcopalian Ascension Church in 1854, had come from Detroit in 1851 to manage a mine named for Douglass Houghton. Pittman donated both his residence, which later became the rectory, and the lot next door. James Burtenshaw, born near Brighton on the south coast of England, assisted him. He came to Ontonagon in spring 1851 and, with Augustus Coburn, engaged in the mercantile business. In 1855, a Detroit architect arrived to complete the work on the church. All materials had been shipped from Detroit except window frames made in Ontonagon. They had been sent to Detroit for fitting with stained glass. Mrs. Sarah Boardman of Ohio donated a marble baptismal font, and Cornelia Boardman of Connecticut, an Oxford red-covered Bible and prayer book for the pulpit and reading desk. Both women were relatives of Mrs. Burtenshaw. In such ways, employees, merchants, and mine managers combined services, talent, and wealth to carry on long-established patterns of culture. This practice, repeated in other towns that sprang from the mines, became an indelible mark of life in the Keweenaw Peninsula.[24]

Only seven years before, in 1848, Dr. Wolcott Gibbs, in field notes for a United States government survey, wrote of "several good cabins on this location [Minesota Mine]," with others a-building, and twelve miners, mostly Cornish, "at work, and all, as usual, very sanguine." Twenty-five years earlier, the entire region exhibited rugged, elevated hills, dark hemlock forests, yawning gulfs—a dreary and forbidding region unfavorable for animal and vegetable kingdoms in the words of Henry Schoolcraft, who in 1823 shrank from "this frightful region" of the Ontonagon country. Now, underground mining, filled with danger, beckoned men who saw the region as a bonanza benefiting them and their families. Cornish miners told visitors they wanted to work only underground. A party of miners walking to work stopped and observed the place where a man engaged in building a fence on the surface had been killed by a rolling log. One said, "Damme, I wouldn't work on the bloody surface. Man killed here building a fence."[25]

Children at school learned that Ontonagon was known to the natives as Nintonaganing (The Place of My Dish); for, according to legend, a woman washing a dish or bowl dropped it into the river and, as the current carried it away, cried *Nia! Nind onagan! Nind Onagan!* ("Oh, my dish, my dish!"). They learned, too, that as early as 1843, the great Ontonagon copper boulder had been removed to the shores of Lake Superior, where General Walter Cunningham claimed the treasure for the United States. Twenty white men and some Native Americans had helped Julius Eldred and his sons Francis, Elisha, and Anson move the copper rock after paying $150 for it to Okondókon, "head chief of the Ontonagon band" of the Ojibwa. Cunningham reported to his superiors that removal of the rock had involved "very great risk as well as expense, and is one of the most extraordinary performances of the age." Thousands of visitors to the nation's capital viewed this Keweenaw treasure in the Smithsonian Institution. In 1987, the Ontonagon boulder returned for a brief visit to Michigan Technological University's A. E. Seaman Mineralogical Museum when Michigan celebrated its sesquicentennial.[26]

Sixty miles northeast of Ontonagon, along the mineral range, men discovered, in the mid-1850s, the main body of the immense Pewabic amygdaloid lode, which spurred community building in the Portage Lake district. Minor portions of the lode had been worked since the early 1850s; but William Frue, prospector and miner, with a party investigating ancient pits once worked by Native Americans, stumbled across the Pewabic riches. Here lay beds of amygdaloid rock with 2–4 percent copper finely distributed—low-content rock, but geologists and entrepreneurs recognized that here was an immense deposit to be mined. How different from the mass copper at northern and southern reaches of the long mineral range! Many men scoffed, believing that the amygdaloid of Portage Lake would never pay![27]

The lode adjoined Quincy Mine, established in 1846 with patient investors from Detroit and Marshall, Michigan, who sank forty-two thousand dollars in the enterprise, interrupted by suspension of operations at times, before being pleasantly rewarded. Quincy became one of the truly great mines of the Keweenaw; its company "ultimately rewarded investors handsomely." Quincy's success spawned the city of Hancock and numerous locations.[28]

Success of Portage Lake mines and mills belonged partially to eastern men who invented, improved, and managed brilliantly, although some of their "previous pursuits had been of a widely different character."[29] Samuel S. Robinson was typical. He came west from New Hampshire in 1853, having worked as schoolteacher, stonemason, and bridge builder. He learned mining through experience in the present Gogebic County before managing the Quincy Mine between 1860 and 1865. Later, he operated silver mines in Nevada, Colorado, and New Mexico and built bridges in Chicago, Indiana, and Missouri.[30]

The Keweenaw was a great place, Robinson exclaimed late in 1863 to J. P. Brewer in New Hampshire: "I want a half dozen or more of our steady and wide-awake—energetic—practical Yankee Boys—I can give such young men places worth from five to six hundred dollars a year and if they are the right kind of stuff can keep them growing right along, but they must not be too nice or afraid of hard work." He would train them as foremen. He currently employed some fifteen men at salaries from six hundred to two thousand dollars. Robinson earned over three thousand dollars per year. He lived with his wife Eliza in a rent-free house and was provided with fuel, some cows, horses, and even servants. Robinson went downstate to buy powder for blasting; other trips took him to Chicago and Canada. All his work was hard, and he worked till he was "pretty well used up."

His estimates of supplies required before winter set in reveal much about life at the Quincy Mine in 1865–66: twenty-four hundred barrels of flour, two hundred of pork, three hundred and fifty of beef, fifty of herring, and five hundred barrels of smoking tobacco. He wanted ten thousand pounds of lard and of dried apples twelve thousand, butter forty-eight thousand, sugar sixty-five thousand, tea forty-five hundred, coffee, six thousand, rice twenty-five hundred, and twelve thousand pounds of soap. Quincy must have ten thousand kegs of powder, three hundred thousand feet of fuse, sixty thousand pounds of tallow, and eight hundred pounds of candles for miners to wear in helmets underground. He wanted 120 axes, seventy-five tons of coal, and blacking, bluing, needles, clothespins, baking powder, condensed milk, and snuff. Everything was sent in ships.

He wanted no "green stuff" (vegetables), as local farmers sold produce; the company itself raised thousands of bushels of potatoes. Local beef had been killed and salted. The health of miners the previous year had been remarkably good; some laborers had helped construct a good cellar for storing provisions under a new office building. Quincy had its wharf down the hill, where hay and grain lay in storage until needed. A company store operated until Hancock produced stores in abundance (management closed it September 1, 1866).[31]

Young men lived in boardinghouses, and some of the more fastidious quartered at homes of mine officials. The company, before 1866, built houses for valuable men who might have left for larger salaries elsewhere. Robinson did not live in luxury. He recalled nights when he arose to set about pots and pans to catch "water beating through the roof and dripping all through the house." Some mine workers lived in Quincy houses but worked at other mines. They did this "to be with their friends." Men worked ten hours per day, averaging $41.50 per month since January 1862. The Civil War made labor scarce and wages higher. Robinson wrote a mine agent at the Minesota that he thought these wages lower than those paid in the district. Other men worked on contract. Workers paid twelve dollars board per month. Men who broke rocks or filled cars made thirty to thirty-five dollars. Robinson told a man in Whitewater Falls, Minnesota, to come to Quincy if his business was dull, for he could employ a good mason (brick and stone) at fifty dollars per month.[32]

The Quincy Mine and others hatched towns that included the two facing each other across Portage Lake—Hancock and Houghton. Ransom Shelden and Columbus C. Douglass served as energetic pioneers and founders of the Portage Lake communities. Douglass, living in a log house at the site of an early mineral claim halfway up the steep hills rising on the north side of Portage Lake, served as agent (manager) for the Quincy Mining Company, off and on, between 1851 and 1858. He and Shelden operated a store at Portage Entry as early as the spring of 1847. Shelden had married Douglass's sister Theresa eight years earlier. When Shelden joined Douglass in managing at Quincy in 1851, they moved their store to the Quincy Mine location. Shelden had prospected, lived with his family on fish and game for years, and suffered privations. He had visited the large village of Native Americans at Pilgrim River and the one at Portage Entry, where he bartered goods for game as his fortunes improved. An 1854, holograph notice indicated he hired four men to sink a mine shaft and to timber it, paying them twenty dollars a foot and expending fourteen hundred dollars in the effort. Mining at Portage Lake prospered. By 1865, Houghton County's copper production exceeded the combined production of Keweenaw and Ontonagon counties by ten tons. The towns that developed at Portage Lake soon dwarfed any to the north.[33]

Hancock had been platted in 1859 by Samuel W. Hill, agent for the Quincy Mining Company, on "a most unpromising spot . . . [the] terrain extremely rugged," with a steep slope running down to the lake. A heavy growth of hemlock trees then covered the area; some trees in the virgin forest measured seven feet in diameter. The nucleus thus platted extended only from present-day Reservation to Montezuma Streets. From this locus, Hancock expanded west and east, as well as north, and became an important city.[34]

Hancock rose on land that once belonged to Columbus Douglass, who had sold it to Quincy. The village of Hancock was not really organized until 1863; but five years before, the Leopold brothers and Joseph Austrian opened a store there, 25 by 150 feet, two stories high, with stone foundation and cellar. Their success at Eagle River had produced the capital to start the new mercantile establishment, at the corner of Reservation and Water Streets, near the Quincy stamp mills, where one car loaded with copper ore running down the hill to Portage Lake via a pulley allowed an empty to rise on an adjoining track.

Austrian remembered Hancock as "mostly woods" as of 1860. By 1862, Hancock had a population of seventeen hundred, three hotels, six saloons, three general stores, three grocery stores, a hardware store and harness maker, plus a few doctors, lawyers, insurance agents, and jewelers. Hancock Township, containing a tannery, ashery, schoolhouse, four stamp mills, and smelter, was described as being mostly in "an uninhabited wilderness, . . . a considerable portion of it . . . covered with swamps."[35]

In 1852, Shelden and Douglass had purchased the land where Houghton now stands and built its first building, known as Shelden's Store, at the foot of present Isle Royale Street. The Huron Mining Company organized in 1853, the prospects of other mines opening, and the concentration of miners and their families across the lake helped create Houghton. Benjamin Wright of the Huron Mine commented: "Laborers are crowding in to Houghton by every steamer and the mystery is, where they find a place to rest their weary bodies at night. Every house is crammed with humanity."[36]

Houghton was incorporated as a village November 1, 1861, with a population of 854 persons. An election in December found 185 citizens casting votes for William Rainey as president, John Atwood as clerk, and William Harris as treasurer.

Both Bishop Baraga and an assistant from L'Anse, the Reverend Father Edward Jacker, preached at the Portage Lake mission—the bishop in English, French, and German. Very quickly, Baraga collected one hundred thirty dollars for building Saint Ignatius Loyola Church in Houghton; and the bishop presided at the dedication on July 31, 1859. At Hancock, Methodists opened their church in 1860; Congregational and Catholic churches appeared in 1861 and 1862, a Lutheran church in 1866. By 1854, the Methodists established themselves at their present location on Montezuma Street in Houghton. Trinity Episcopal Church, partially built in Hancock then ferried across the lake, was moved to its present site at the corner of Montezuma and Pewabic Streets in 1861. Father Dennis O'Neil served as Saint Ignatius' first pastor. Houghton was a hive of activity, situated strategically between Ontonagon, Keweenaw Bay, the Cliff, and Copper Harbor. Mails arrived frequently. The village had contact with Detroit and Chicago via lake steamers.[37]

Benjamin Wright pictured Houghton as of mid-May, 1860: "Nature is putting on her gayest attire and the trees are green enough; the cows find good pasturage and the birds . . . delight us with their sweet carols; the frogs set up their nightly croaking. . . . Pretty soon musketos [sic] will come, and then for a lively time." Wright, in a semimanagerial position, considered himself fortunate at the Huron Mine for he received fifty dollars per month for about ten days' work and the remainder of the time "is my own." The area reminded him of his native Springfield, Massachusetts, except he missed the bob-o-links' sweet songs. He sent home a specimen of leaf copper procured at the Huron.[38]

In the 1860s, John H. Forster saw Hancock and Houghton as "two hamlets . . . struggling into life, while back from the lake, on the elevated plateaus, were . . . seen the rude mining camps half hidden in the primeval woods." The Portage Lake area at the time, with saloons open night and day including Sundays, drinking, blasphemy, fights, Cornish-hating Irish who viewed all English as inveterate enemies, and law officers few and powerless, seemed to Forster "a veritable pandemonium, where all the bad passions of embruted and lawless human nature had full swing." But refinement struggled to assert itself.[39]

Described as the largest and "most important village of the upper peninsula," Houghton, in 1862, had a population of nearly two thousand. Boosters claimed that the "prospect for the future [was] better than ever," with plans to build a county courthouse and jail for $18,000, to erect new hotels and more churches, and to improve the school system. The Douglass House guest register testified to large numbers of "health and pleasure tourists" arriving during the warm summers. A large frame structure three stories high, the Douglass House, completed in 1861, had been built partially by a subscription of $9,500 by stockholders who surrendered all claims upon the property to private hands. Mrs. J. W. Van Anden managed the hostel described by the *Michigan State Gazetteer, 1863–1864* as "the best hotel in the upper peninsula." Besides this commodious place, Houghton had also the Lake Superior House, operated by Francis Mayworm, and the Peninsular House (Caspar Shulte, proprietor).

Four general stores (one of them owned by Columbus Douglass, Ransom Shelden, and his son Carlos), five saloons, tailors' shops, four carpentry shops, a sawmill, a tinware manufactory, and two mills for stamping and washing copper, lay amid many small boardinghouses and shops. The Haas Brewery, begun in 1859, produced five hundred barrels of beer per year. Masonic Lodge, Mesnard, No. 79, helped some men enjoy social life; and women formed various church societies. Samuel Robinson, across the lake, lamented the scarcity of lawyers in Houghton County; Jay Hubbell served as Houghton's attorney. By 1865, the First National Bank had organized, with a capital of $160,000; Ransom Shelden served as first president and worked with John Chassell, cashier. A weekly newspaper, the *Portage Lake Mining Gazette*, begun in June 1859, became a daily by the end of the century, when William Gardner Rice wished his paper to be "an institution for the betterment of the community . . . to serve [and be] helpful to the industries and business institutions of the district." As elsewhere in the Keweenaw, industry, business interests, schools, churches, and people of all classes merged to create their peculiar societies. Like many others, Shelden and Douglass had their hands in half a dozen local enterprises.[40]

M. Van Orden, who began with a lime kiln, engaged in a lucrative coal business eventually. James R. Dee managed Western Union after the telegraph arrived in 1866, subsidized in part by the Quincy Mining Company and Houghton boosters. R. R. Goddell represented the Saint Mary's Ship Canal and Mineral Land Company, vital in improving local transportation. James Edwards, civil engineer, was instrumental in building the iron bridge connecting Hancock and Houghton. Houghton's main street was named for Ransom Shelden. The Keweenaw was a land of opportunity, where businessmen had a free field as energetic industrialists exploited rich copper mines.[41]

The enthusiastic Americans in the Portage Lake towns introduced bourgeois civilization. They scheduled lectures and read books but abandoned some of the exacting formalities and etiquette that their families practiced in such places as New England, Ohio, or New York. The few families met "like brothers and sisters" in small, rudely built houses. Women abandoned silks and laces to appear at soirées in muslin or calico gowns. Men, dressed in "all the glory of moccasins, red sashes and flowing shirtsleeves of blue or red flannel," joined in square dances or danced a hornpipe before "appreciative lady judges." Forster recalled that during "long, dark, dreary winter evenings of that north land, dancing and card playing were the only recreations," with folks coming from miles about to Hancock and Houghton, wading through snow drifts and intense cold "for the sake of society."[42]

Women, family life, churches, and schools brought civilizing influences, as did men championing their peculiar form of democracy: free individuals were masters of their destinies and at the same time worked out God's providential will. In this mid-nineteenth-century America, progress was inevitable and free trade, natural; and equality meant that men should have opportunities to work and accumulate and, with their families, devise for themselves the good life. That is what American democracy consisted of, and they worked diligently at its realization.[43]

They were practical men. Like Friedrich List, exile from Germany, economist, farmer, editor, and promoter, they argued that the best book on economics one could read in the United States was "actual life;" for only here "one may see wilderness grow into rich and mighty states." Like Abraham Lincoln, they conceived of local, state, and federal governments as instruments "in the hands of the people which they could use for the protection of the ideal of the free individual."[44] They saw no conflict between their laissez-faire ideology and their later demand for national tariffs to protect Keweenaw copper from foreign competition. Robinson wrote William Warner in 1864 that what was wanted from the Michigan legislature was judicious management in construction of a road from Copper Harbor to Wisconsin and no interference with harbor and river improvements.[45] One's politics was very much linked to one's economic interests.

Robinson felt that he owed his success to Providence and his moderate share of merit. "Blessed by Providence," he said of himself, his merit was "a careful attention to details, a diligent attention to the interests and business of [his] employers and a religious regard for the rights—health—and comfort of the men under his control." No man could be a good manager, he wrote, unless he believed that labor had rights and "that the common good should be the mutual interest and glorious result of the combination of both [labor and capital]."[46]

Problems of slow communication and transportation to the outside world plagued the Copper Country, but important steps were taken to resolve them after 1860. Samuel Robinson was awarded the contract for carrying mails by stagecoach from Green Bay to Hancock in 1864. He was determined to remove "inconvenience, perplexity, and damage" and provide "regular and comfortable means of conveyance" over this route: "Our population is increasing rapidly. Business interests would seem to insure a fair passenger traffic here, and there is little room for doubt that it would grow with all other developments of the country."[47] So the stage was instituted and played its role; from Hancock, regular stages soon ran to the tip of the peninsula, as well as to Ontonagon. As so often in American life, industry's needs provided improvements benefiting towns and their people. George N. Sanders, assistant to a general in 1844, came north and recommended an eight-hundred-mile chain of mule trails, eight feet wide, from Copper Harbor to Green Bay, Wisconsin, to make supplies available by land during winter and to accelerate travel generally—only one of several schemes proposed to link the Keweenaw with the regions "below."[48]

For a time, Shelden and Douglass managed a small side-wheel steamer the *Princess* running daily from Houghton to Portage Entry, bringing mail and passengers. This was before the dredging of the channel allowed large craft to enter Portage Lake direct from Lake Superior. At the entry, two Lake Superior steamers usually arrived daily during the season. One spring Sunday in 1860, five appeared. Benjamin Wright declared that the beginning of navigation "makes us all feel smarter and take a livelier step, . . . All mankind in this region is jubilant."[49]

In 1859, Captain John Hoar built a tramway—rails of wood with an iron band fastened on top—two miles long, from the Isle Royale Mine to Portage Lake. There, at Houghton, two large wharves and warehouses stood, in addition to the wharf and warehouse of the Isle Royale Mining Company. At these, 230 vessels arrived during the 1861 season; and for the month ending July 16, 1862, fifty-three vessels arrived.

Crude roads of logs laced part of the Keweenaw; but usually, the only avenues through forests for long distances in the 1860s were footpaths and bridle trails. From Portage Lake one followed old Native American trails along the water to the head of Torch Lake, then connected with the meandering Trap Rock River. This took one close to the northern regions, where one followed a woodland trail to the Cliff Mine and Eagle River before the macadamized road connected the two locations. Spring was disagreeable, as melting snow, mud, water, and cold caused difficulties. Sleighs proved useful in winter only in and around the numerous villages that sprang up near mines.[50]

Samuel Robinson wrote New Hampshire relatives that he had gone "below"—to the Lower Peninsula and Wisconsin—on November 8, 1863, by ship but came home "by the overland route footing it some 130 miles through the woods, [making] about 30 miles a day."

He had not liked "that kind of travelling especially in Winter"; for cold and ice opposed him and no road "over which a team can be driven for 150 miles" existed between Green Bay, Wisconsin, and the Keweenaw.[51]

Lucena Brockway, in January 1867, spoke of snow so heavy that next day "all hands [were] out breaking roads [and] gone all day" shoveling the eighteen inches that had fallen. On May 6, 1867, at five in the afternoon, she sighted the first boat of the season at Copper Harbor. Inhabitants cheered at the sight of the propeller *Union*. The cabin fever of the long winter produced near-hallucinations. In her loneliness, Mrs. Brockway recalled that she observed her fifty-first birthday the day before and the Empress Eugénie in faraway France her forty-first. Daniel Brockway was not home to help celebrate. The first day of May had been "such a lonely day . . . in this room month after month" that it seemed at times that she could "almost take wing and fly away."[52]

Bishop Baraga and others had had to rely for winter travel on snow-shoes, four to five feet long, a foot wide, tied to one's feet. They were useful but contributed to fatigue. Years later, residents spoke of "the ungovernable prey of Lake Superior storms. . . . Nothing could stand the fury of a Superior gale." In 1845, Daniel Brockway and Native American rowers barely escaped death when delivering a boatload of potatoes.[53]

Travel by water was impossible from November to late April or early May each year. In 1848, geologists from Boston came to Copper Harbor via Northampton, Albany, Buffalo, Detroit, and the Sault in a trip lasting from June 20 to July 8, with stops overnight at Buffalo and Detroit and a week at the Sault. This was a remarkably short time, considering the distance. Summer travel on the Great Lakes was generally pleasant; but in spring or autumn, a wild storm drove many passengers to nausea or prayers.[54]

Lands appropriated by Congress and Michigan (1865) resulted in the twenty-two-mile Portage Lake and Lake Superior Ship Canal, built between 1868 and 1873 through the Keweenaw Peninsula at a cost of $2,500,000. By that time, the copper industry and the iron industry farther south in the Upper Peninsula produced ten million dollars of minerals annually. The canal sped the development of the mineral regions and assisted the agricultural, commercial, and railroad interests not only of Michigan but also of Wisconsin and Minnesota.[55]

The canal built at the west end of the old Keweenaw portage was the final step of a move begun in 1859. Then, ten mining companies, including the Quincy, Franklin, and Huron, had joined the Houghton firm of Ransom Shelden and Company to improve Portage River, the outlet of the lake into Keweenaw Bay. Done quickly, this improvement cut a channel 1,400 feet long, one hundred feet wide, and twelve feet deep from the bay to Portage River. Large enough to admit the "heaviest ships" on the Great Lakes, the project cost fifty-five thousand dollars and aroused much excitement and pride, when on May 17, 1860, the propeller *General Taylor*, drawing eight-and-one-half feet of water, made its way to the dock at Houghton.[56] Steamboats had entered Portage Lake as early as 1855; and Captain Sam Eales, "a very irascible old English sailor," who came to the district about 1852, operated a public ferry, charging passengers two shillings for the half-hour trip on his yawl. If one was the sole passenger, one paid four shillings or waited for another passenger to arrive. This was not an excessive hardship; for Eales's waiting room, in his home, was cozy, and one could get a drop of "half and half" or "Triple X pike"—hard liquors—if one had the price. Later, John T. Martin and his "Dutch wife" operated the ferry; and by 1863, many competitors sought passengers, many of them impressed by the Martins's introduction of the *Niagara*, a "magnificent side wheel streamer," which hauled teams of horses and wagons, as well as men and women, between Houghton and Hancock. So great was the traffic as mines and towns flourished that a toll bridge of wood was erected in 1870, eventually to be replaced by one of iron.[57]

Between 1848 and 1860, twenty-nine copper companies operated in the district. Seven had business offices in Boston, seven in Pittsburgh, and seven in New York City; six had two offices each in Philadelphia, Cleveland, and Detroit; one had headquarters at Eagle Harbor, and one, at Rockland in Ontonagon County. Mines opened, and some closed. By 1862, among the discontinued companies in Houghton County alone were the Columbian, Montezuma, Dacotah, South Side, Mesnard, Pontiac, and the Albany and Boston.[58]

For a long time, Lake Superior copper rock was shipped in vessels to the Sault, landed and transported one mile across the portage there in wagons, then shipped through the lower Great Lakes to the Erie Canal and thence east to the seacoast; or else it was taken by ship to Ohio and sent to Pittsburgh via canals and the Ohio River. The cost of delivering copper to Atlantic coast cities in 1848 was about fifteen dollars a ton. At the Cliff Mine in the 1850s, copper rock was broken up, pieces barreled for shipment east (barrel work), and the balance sent to local mills for stamping, crushing, and washing. Some twenty-five tons of rock were stamped daily. In 1845, the first shipment of copper had gone from the Cliff to Boston via the Sault and Buffalo, New York. By September 1851, a typical shipment resembled that of general agent John Senter, who sent on board the propeller *Napoleon* from Eagle Harbor, via the Sault, to Detroit Smelting Works, nine barrels of copper rock marked "kiln" and sixteen masses of copper weighing between 261 and 3,360 pounds each, taken from the Northwest Mine.

The *Northern Light* took copper rock from Eagle Harbor to Cleveland in 1865 and stopped another time at Ontonagon to pick up copper bound for Detroit from the Lake Superior, Rockland, Superior, Minesota, Flint Steel, Ridge, and Evergreen Bluff mining companies. Transportation was a great obstacle to profitable mining. Eastern capitalists, interested in both copper and in the iron in regions south of the Keweenaw, accomplished in 1852 what the Michigan legislature had failed to procure—an appropriation of 750,000 acres of public land for building a ship canal at the Sault. The canal, when completed in the spring of 1855, opened a new era for the Upper Peninsula.[59]

Two weeks after the rebels bombarded Fort Sumter in Charleston Harbor, South Carolina, the news reached Copper Harbor, where Brockway said lovers of the Union would respond crying "No, No, to King Cotton." The Civil War produced a demand for copper, and the price went from seventeen to fifty cents a pound by 1865. Hancock soon outranked Houghton in population and business. Mining companies cooperated to raise ninety thousand dollars and sent agents to Norway and Sweden to procure miners. Some of these potential miners, after one look at the mines, refused to work, while others enlisted to fight in the Union army for a bounty of three hundred dollars. Mines worked at capacity. Samuel Robinson and John Forster, plagued by miners demanding higher wages, feared financial chaos and ruin at Quincy and Franklin–Pewabic, respectively. At Quincy, miners' wages averaged $41.23 per month in 1862 and rose to $65.45 in 1864; Forster's salary rose from two thousand dollars—with house, office, and wood for fuel provided—to thirty-five hundred dollars in 1863.[60]

Forster wrote his brother-in-law, Colonel John Harris, in 1862 that he was "ready to shoulder a musket when the time comes"; but he paid fifty dollars to receive an exemption from the draft in October 1863, citing the need for his remaining at the helm of an industry vital to the war. Thirteen mine managers, including Forster, approved his exemption! Though far removed from battle, the Keweenaw felt the impact of war. By 1863, Bishop Baraga wrote of "this terrible war"—a horror bringing ruin, destruction, the maiming of men, and huge debts. Prices rose to two and three times prewar levels.[61]

Robinson had opposed the draft, writing Governor Austin Blair that Houghton County had furnished more than its share of volunteers and had also given liberally of money. The district had struggled for eighteen years and was now short some two thousand miners, he added; and those at work, nine-tenths of them of foreign birth, feared the draft, expressed hostility, and were ready to join in a "stampede" to dodge the draft. The labor shortage could "seriously cripple" the copper mines. Robinson told Blair that arrangements could be made for lawful substitutes should the draft become a reality. The war brought forth in the Keweenaw a blend of caustic hostility and patriotism.[62]

William Heywood of Boston, official of the Pewabic Mining Company, wrote Forster that as of October 1861, after six months of war, "the government is weak, the effort being made to make this a war of Emancipation is dividing the north, and the country or the republican party must go to the devil." Forster deplored politicians' handling of the war.[63] Some 833 peninsula men served in the war: 460 from Houghton County, 119 from Keweenaw County, and 254 from Ontonagon County. Of the volunteers, thirty-eight from Ontonagon County, nine from Keweenaw, and fifty-eight from Houghton died. Of the sixty-five commissioned officers from the Upper Peninsula, thirty-one were from Hancock, Houghton, Ontonagon, Copper Harbor, and Eagle Harbor. Most were first or second lieutenants; but some became captains, majors, or colonels. Two African Americans were listed on the Keweenaw County enrollment lists, which totaled 1,157. At Ontonagon, almost 100 percent of the volunteers were of German descent; but the draft brought in Cornish, Irish, and French Canadians. Of all its soldiers in the Civil War, Ontonagon provided the youngest, John Death, Jr., age sixteen; the oldest was Mathias Brambert, age forty-five.[64]

In early February 1861, Forster took a dim view of the "foreign portion of our mining populace," who rioted at the Franklin Mine as war approached. Miners, bucket fillers, wheelers, and others struck for higher wages and compelled all surface workers to stop operations. Men at the Cliff had struck on the previous Saturday. Forster wrote that if management then gave in to demands, the men would demand again. He and his colleagues remained adamant, and the strike ended after one week. The incident, in retrospect, serves as portent for the singular labor relations that shaped much of the Keweenaw Peninsula's history.[65]

By October 1863, Robinson wondered whether Congress hoped to promote immigration "from northern or central Europe." He thought the effort should be encouraged. Why not "turn a few thousand loose in these woods," given the severe scarcity of workers due to war? By January 1864, he feared that "capital will [soon] be at the mercy of labor," given the scarcity of workers and their demands for higher wages. Why not cut production by half, thus ensuring a greater profit? He added, "drowning men catch at straws [and] no one more so than mine agents!"[66]

By May 1865, however, with the Civil War ended, conditions were such that men at the Ridge Mine in Ontonagon County constituted surplus labor. Robinson advised a colleague there that perhaps the best thing to do was to pay off all of the men, then hire only one-half at old wages. He admitted the contradictions of the capitalistic business cycle: "It goes against the grain to work so hard for years to try and get a stable population into the country and then turn around and drive them away but it is the course that the capitalists are bound to pursue and remonstrance is useless." This theme would be sounded again in the history of mining in the Keweenaw Peninsula. Give family men preference, Robinson concluded; and advise as many as possible "to turn farmers."[67]

After the war, Robinson urged his nephew, Captain O. D. Robinson, to come to Quincy; for though economic stagnation now prevailed in the United States, he did not know of a better way for a man to be "a more efficient missionary or do better service to his Maker or his country than by an upright and straightforward manly course as a business man in one of our western towns." All such men were needed "to give a proper tone and shape to mixed chaotic elements that mingle in our new towns on the frontier." Jane Masters, married to a carpenter, raised seventeen children and brought beauty to their Copper Harbor home: pewter, candlesticks, a shawl of bright colors, and richly bound books—all brought from Cornwall. She, like many who followed, live among rude, ignorant, and dirty neighbors but, with her husband, taught the children proper speech and good manners, inspiring them to do well in a rough world.[68]

Once mines were organized and their satellite communities began to grow, efforts were made to provide schools and libraries to educate the young. Mine managers encouraged the establishment of schools to induce workers to bring their families into the district. Only a thorough Anglo–American education, stressing fundamentals, produced good citizens and able workers, according to the prevailing ethos. A common complaint was that the children often attended school for only a small portion of the term. School inspectors blamed parents for much apathy and neglect. Emigrants from other states ignorant of Michigan laws respecting school attendance were blamed, as well, for not seeing that their children spent the full term in school.[69]

Of 229 children age five to twenty at Clifton in 1865, 143 attended school an average of just over three months, although the ungraded school had a session of six months. In Ontonagon Township in 1865, each student attended but slightly more than five months of a ten-month school year. Of seven hundred young people between the ages of five and twenty in Portage Township, 616 attended school an average of only three-and-a-half months out of a nine-and-a-half-month school year. Salaries for male teachers throughout the district were well above those for females. Clifton Township paid a male teacher $398 plus $66.37 for board, while a woman teacher received $165 and $27.56 for board. A male teacher at Houghton earned $709.65 plus board, while six females were paid a total of $1,719.96 and board.[70]

Attempts were made to provide libraries at schools. In 1865, the Clifton school had 336 books; but the inspector reported, "They were not much read." Only one school in Franklin Township had a library in 1865, and it had only forty-four volumes. In Ontonagon Township, students had access to a much larger library that year—864 books. In the spring election, citizens had voted one hundred dollars for the library's upkeep.[71]

Franklin Township's ungraded schools had playgrounds offering "great inducements to the innocent amusements of Hide and Go Seek as the stumps of trees [were] numerous." At an ungraded school in Pewabic Township, an inexperienced woman teacher had the inspectors concluding that they did not know how she compared to a male teacher but that she seemed "to give entire satisfaction, as is plainly evidenced by the progress of the children . . . and their conduct both in and out of school."[72]

Where Shelden and Franklin Streets now meet in Houghton, twenty students attended an ungraded school conducted by F. G. Sewell. By January 1859, they moved, with others, into a new building at the corner of Portage and South Streets, a school in use until the Rock School was built in 1864 to accommodate more students. This school, which existed until 1899, boasted of steam heat. A private school, with James Pryor as teacher, was conducted in 1862 at Houghton in a log building erected in 1854 by Columbus Douglass. In December 1864, a Miss Cummings operated a private school above the Huron Mine office for small children, "where they would be free from the older boisterous ones." Professor S. E. Adams that same winter conducted a "Select Private High School," where he taught the "Common and Higher English branches, French, Latin, and Drawing." Earnest citizens constantly reformed the curriculum, expanded the public schools, and weeded out teachers who were not "first class," as they sought only the best instruction for the communities' children.[73]

While war at its worst raged in Virginia and Georgia in 1864, Edwin James Hulbert, a civil engineer, had an excavation made where he had found indications of a copper lode earlier in 1858, while surveying for a road. The location was thirty-six miles south of Copper Harbor and twelve miles north of Hancock. In a few days, his men uncovered in the swampy ground the copper-bearing conglomerate that became the richest of all the Keweenaw Peninsula companies—the Calumet and Hecla. Few in the area realized that these mines would transform the Keweenaw Peninsula as they did. War and peace occupied most minds.[74]

On February 22, 1865, only six months after the fabulous discovery, a benefit ball for Union soldiers in Ontonagon's Bigelow House attracted guests from every mining location. Some came on snowshoes from Eagle River and Eagle Harbor, one hundred miles away. On this Washington's Birthday, wine and punch flowed freely as, amid candle and oil-lamp light, men and women dined on the best game and preserved foods. Fiddlers played cotillion after cotillion in the five-story grand hotel for Copper Country men and women, who knew that the long and bloody war, instead of bringing ruin, had brought prosperity and a more rapid development of the entire Keweenaw.[75]

4

Community Builders

1870 – 1890

LEXINGTON AND CONCORD AND CALUMET AND Hecla, a reporter once wrote, were the four most famous names in New England. The first two made its history, and Calumet and Hecla dividends enriched Yankee families and cultural institutions.[1] Harvard University's Museum of Comparative Zoology and the Boston Symphony Orchestra (to name only two) were developed, in large part, by the labor of thousands of mine workers and fabulous dividends. Twenty years after the discovery of the enormously rich Calumet conglomerate lode, the *Boston Sunday Globe* declared that "Calumet and Hecla is likely to prove, if it has not already proved, the richest mine ever opened on this continent and one of the richest in the world."[2] The *Globe* concluded: "Within seven years after the consolidation [1871,] the Calumet and Hecla paid its stockholders over $8,000,000, and since then, . . . it has been dumping fortunes into the laps of its happy stockholders." John H. Forster hailed the mine as "the wonder of the world," marveled at the enormous production and admired fortunate stockholders who need only receive quarterly dividends and "lie down and sleep in peace."

The Calumet and Hecla success story was not typical. Millions in capital investment and laborious efforts of miners and managers elsewhere failed to yield profits. Forster believed, however, that even these efforts were seed sown for good purposes as they "introduced civilization into the wilderness of the upper peninsula."[3]

Population increased rapidly. Men came in droves from Cliff Mine and the Ontonagon country to work at Calumet and Hecla. Men from Quincy and Pewabic mines brought their families to try their luck at what came to be called Calumet—the locations, towns, and settlements surrounding the great Calumet and Hecla mines. The pattern of migration, already old, continued for years—workers deserting older mines to apply their skills and seek their livelihood at those opened later.

In the great times of the Copper Country between 1870 and 1920, few paid attention to a reality expressed by a Bostonian as early as 1876. Calumet and Hecla had stamped 239,000 tons of rock in the year ending April 1875, more in one year than England's most famous copper mine, the Devon Consuls; but any "mining man will see at a glance that a rapid exhaustion must be going on. . . . Everything is well while the bottom continues good, but what are more changeable than mines?"[4] Most residents either accepted realistically the unpredictability of sustained mining or spent little time waxing philosophic about a dire future. Many believed about Calumet and Hecla (or a new mine that might be discovered and prove even richer!) what the Boston newspaper had stated in 1885: "Only recently a far-sighted seer has foretold that the Calumet and Hecla is to continue this sort of thing [providing work and enormous dividends] for a century to come." Few heeded Forster's historical jottings that of some 220 organized mining companies that had opened and operated mines, only ten were alive or working in 1888. He could count the total number paying dividends on one hand if he included his thumb, he told his readers.[5]

Michigan's mine commissioner wrote in 1886 that the enormity of Calumet and Hecla landholdings, its equipment, technology, and continuing development left only one future question—"how best to reach the copper."[6] Edwin Hulbert, the man who had begun the already fabled success, was born at Sault Sainte Marie, April 30, 1829, to pioneer settlers from Connecticut. His father, John, worked for a time as sutler at Fort Brady at the Sault. His mother was Maria Eliza Schoolcraft, sister of Henry. Edwin came to the Keweenaw when he was twenty-three years old and was employed as surveyor–engineer for several mining companies before working on a survey from Copper Harbor to Ontonagon via Eagle Harbor, the Cliff Mine, and Houghton. Earlier, he had labored at the Sault in the U.S. Land Office, where he copied maps in plat books and became familiar with surface formations of mineral regions.[7]

Only by accident, while working on the survey of a wagon road authorized by the Michigan legislature, did Hulbert happen upon an enormous boulder deep in the forest on the site of what became

No. 4, Calumet shaft. Near the boulder was a pit, circular and bowl-shaped, described by Hulbert as a "depression, the chord of which was about fourteen feet, the versed sine less than two feet," with a burrow supporting "an enormous hemlock tree on the northeast and an old black-birch tree on the southwest." The birch had nearly two hundred wood rings, and the entire pit was covered with "a floor of leaves and humus." Hulbert deplored later mythology describing this find as an ancient mining pit.[8]

It was nothing of the kind, said he; for he and his companions never discovered any tools or utensils used for extraction of copper. What they had come upon was a cache, where ancient Native Americans had stored copper mined elsewhere. He figured the early miners had filled and emptied the cache in successive years or periods. The green carbonate of copper Hulbert exhumed from the pit along with nuggets of native copper convinced him that the ancient miners had "*not known . . . or even suspected*" the existence of the great Calumet conglomerate. Had they, one could reasonably conclude, they would have left pits to the northeast or the southwest. They had not. Thus, by sheerest accident, Hulbert had stumbled upon a hiding place or temporary storage pit on the *border* of what came to be one of the world's richest mines producing native copper of the purest kind.[9]

Hulbert, his brother John, and explorer Amos H. Scott, in the last weeks of August and the first ten days of September 1864 made the original opening that revealed the Calumet conglomerate. Hulbert organized the Hulbert Mining Company covering lands he had previously purchased from the United States government. He had organized this company, which owned 1,920 acres, with men from Boston and money they had raised. Hulbert owned one-fourth (5,000 shares). In Boston, Hulbert borrowed at least $16,800 from Quincy A. Shaw for which Shaw received for security an assignment of Hulbert's Huron Mine stock along with a power of attorney to dispose of the stock should Shaw's financial situation warrant that.[10]

According to his critics, Hulbert as mine superintendent lacked the "capable management" required. As early as March 13, 1865, Shaw became secretary–treasurer of the Calumet. He resigned on October 5, 1866, to be replaced by his brother-in-law Alexander Agassiz. Shaw became president; and in July 1867, Agassiz was given full power to act at the mine. The Calumet and Hecla consolidated with the Portland and Scott Mining companies May 1, 1871; and by August 1, Shaw stepped aside as president in favor of Agassiz.[11]

Alexander Agassiz, born in Switzerland in 1835, the son of Harvard's famous Louis Agassiz, came to Boston when he was thirteen and graduated from Harvard before he was sixteen. His mother, the gentle, artistic Cécilie Braun, illustrated Louis's scientific articles until the couple slowly grew estranged from one another. The father's work absorbed him; he paid little attention to domestic matters. He was more concerned with his future as scientist. Louis Agassiz—geologist, botanist, and scientific theorist—left Europe on a scientific expedition and ended by becoming professor of natural history at Harvard.[12]

Cécilie "lavished care and affection" on Alexander but died of tuberculosis when the boy was thirteen. The boy was sent to America, where, at Cambridge, his father was famous for scintillating lectures and for abandoning distance from students and supercilious demeanor, endearing him to many.[13]

Alexander Agassiz hoped to become as famous a scientist as his father. His ambition to make Calumet and Hecla a "going" proposition would ensure the enormous profits needed for his worldwide expeditions to study oceanography and to promote the zoological museum Louis had planned at Harvard. As a youth, Alexander was indebted to the woman Louis married, Elizabeth Cary. Years later he wrote that she was his "mother, . . . sister, my companion and friend, all in one." When his own wife, Anna Russell, died one week after the death of Louis in 1873, the three sons of Anna and Alexander were raised by Elizabeth.[14]

The deaths of both wife and father within days of each other stunned Alexander Agassiz. All who encountered him after 1873 found him reserved, with few intimates. He could be brutally dominant, at times seething with anger. He brooked no interference at Calumet in his management of the mines. Their profits enabled him to pursue a notable career in oceanography. His son wrote of Alexander's death in 1910 "fittingly upon the ocean, in whose mysteries he had so deeply delved."[15] A year after his wife's death, Alexander wrote his stepmother about his attempts to overcome his grief: "I feel as if I were acting a constant lie, but it is a harmless one which I must make up my mind to keep up for many a weary year."[16]

His work in helping make Calumet and environs an almost model community, with pronounced social controls, can be understood, in part, as a lifelong search for order and control after an adolescence and young manhood troubled by a distant father, his mother's death, and his wife's sudden death in the prime of life. While he was noted for benevolence, Agassiz was often irascible, hurling scorn at enemies, namely, anyone who attempted to interfere with his supervision at Calumet and Hecla. He was not, however, the selfish autocrat determined to stifle thousands of workers and their families. Agassiz was a community builder influenced by Teutonic orderliness, Bostonian noblesse oblige, and psychological wounds inflicted by personal grief. Determined to provide for his family and work diligently at

oceanography, Agassiz concerned himself also with working conditions and housing for his "extended family" who labored in the mines
and communities of the Keweenaw Peninsula.

In early 1867, he had told Charles W. Eliot, then a young professor at the Massachusetts Institute of Technology: "I am going to
Michigan for some years as superintendent of the Calumet and Hecla
Mines. I want to make money; it is impossible to be a productive
naturalist in this country without money. I am going to get some
money if I can and then I will be a naturalist." He was only thirty-
one years of age; and after working efficiently, often at great odds,
he placed the mines on a secure footing. Late in 1868, he wrote a
colleague, "Thank Heaven I am now done with copper mines, and
have returned with all my heart to my studies;" but until his death,
he kept strict watch over the mines and community he helped create,
visiting at least twice each year.[17]

The first years at the mines proved arduous. Hecla called for
assessments of eight dollars a share in 1866 and twenty-five dollars a
share in 1868. Shaw disposed of the Hulbert stock he held; and this
allowed Shaw, Agassiz, and the board of directors to inform Hulbert
on April 1, 1867, that they would accept his resignations as director
of both the Hecla and Calumet mines. To the end of his life, Hulbert
claimed that Shaw had treacherously and fraudulently deprived him
of his stockholdings. In 1874, he sued; but the case was settled out
of court, the Calumet and Hecla directors making a generous lifetime
settlement for Hulbert, who left, often writing tendentious articles
decrying the underhanded tactics of Shaw and Agassiz. Eventually,
he lived in Rome, Italy, where he died in October 1910. Although
Calumet paid its first dividend in August 1870—Hecla having paid
its first dividend of five dollars, the previous December—assessments
averaging fifteen dollars a share had been called by Calumet from
1866 until 1871. The consolidation of the two companies in 1871
and Agassiz' assumption of the presidency marked the beginning of
a flourishing community at the mines.[18]

By May 31, 1897, Calumet and Hecla had produced 1,176,276,471
pounds of refined copper. Its output for 1896 accounted for 63
percent of the entire Lake Superior region's production. Between
1870 and 1880, the giant company produced from 50 to 55 percent
of United States output, with the exception of one year, when its
production was about 48 percent. In 1865, its stock was held at one
dollar per share, then advanced rapidly until it reached thirty dollars a
share. By 1879, the number of shares was increased to one hundred
thousand, with a capital stock of $2,500,000, the limit allowed by
Michigan's mining laws. In 1866, when Calumet stock could be
had for twenty dollars a share Samuel Robinson said he would not

Alexander Agassiz, c. 1860 (Museum of Comparative Zoology, Harvard University.)

Alexander Agassiz
about 1860

"touch any stock so fixed except at very low prices." Henry D'Aligny, French engineer and resident agent of the Saint Mary's Ship Canal and Mineral Land Company, when asked in 1868 about the prospects for Calumet, told friends not to hang on to their shares. Many sold out at from one to five dollars a share—"a common error" said one newspaper in Boston later but the kind that lost "more fortunes than are ever destroyed by war, famine or pestilence." One of the discouraged stockholders had sold his thousand shares at one dollar each to Quincy A. Shaw.[19]

Though communities including Red Jacket, Laurium, Tamarack, and Centennial Heights and locations such as Osceola, Raymbaultown, Blue Jacket, Yellow Jacket, and Red Jacket Shaft would never have arisen were it not for the Calumet and Hecla mines, they along with the rapidly growing Portage Lake communities of Hancock and Houghton, and the towns of Baraga, L'Anse, Ontonagon, Rockland, Greenland, Mass City, and Silver City and the earliest settlements at Clifton, Eagle River, Eagle Harbor, and Copper Harbor owed their building to those who came as strangers to work, raise families, and create rich cultural institutions. The miners, trammers, timbermen, wives, mothers, school teachers, principals, and superintendents—along with merchants, liverymen, doctors, forwarding agents, wholesale dealers, farmers, longshoremen, railroad workers, and clergy—built vital and energetic communities. Much of the mystique of the Keweenaw to the present day lies in the memories of pleasant experiences fashioned by men and women amid harsh and demanding labor and environments. By 1890, the Keweenaw had developed communities with schools, churches, and literary societies; and lively boosters were advocating even more improvement. By 1900, the village of Red Jacket, the business center of the Calumet complex, vied with Hancock and Houghton in erecting banks, churches, stores, and public buildings of stone, much of it the red sandstone from Portage and Torch Lake quarries.

In 1866, when a sixteen-year-old Welsh girl came with her parents to Calumet, she saw only boardinghouses built of logs as the forest gave way to shafthouses and mining equipment. Daily, people arrived in oxen-drawn wagons, on horseback, or "on foot with bundles on their backs." Families of English and Scots came from the Ontonagon region or from the Bruce Mines of Canada. From the Cliff and such northernmost settlements as Delaware, Copper Falls, and Copper Harbor came Cornish, Irish, Germans, French Canadians, and Yankees. The sixteen-year-old remembered that everyone "was happy with expectation and heady with the excitement of growing up [at] a rich copper mine;" and all were young, for "there were no gray heads in Calumet for the first few years."

She remembered the forest and shrubbery surrounding Calumet, the berries and wild fruits, streams "alive with trout," and Lake Superior whitefish and herring. Wild pigeons in great flocks sometimes darkened the sky. She worked in a boardinghouse where she tended a cookstove, whose huge iron, brass, and copper kettles, filled with beans, potatoes, pork, rice, and cornmeal mush, sat "forever stewing, day and night" on twelve lids, providing food for up to sixty men. At first, most were single men; but when families of married men came in, single and double log houses appeared. Deep wells sunk by the miners provided pure water.

Nearby, stood Halfway House, built by William Royal, whose pigs, according to a growing legend, had actually discovered the Calumet conglomerate before Hulbert. An African American family named Jones provided food and drink at this house at the time of Hulbert's discovery. In winter, sleighs carrying mail stopped here, as did many a traveler between Portage Lake and Eagle River. The Welsh woman at the boardinghouse thought Longfellow described Calumet winters when he wrote in *Hiawatha*:

Anna Russell Agassiz (Museum of Comparative Zoology, Harvard University.)

O the long and dreary Winter!
O the cold and cruel Winter!
Ever thicker, thicker, thicker
Froze the ice on lake and river,
Ever deeper, deeper, deeper
Fell the snow o'er all the landscape,
Fell the covering snow, and drifted
Through the forest, round the village.[20]

Agassiz wrote December 7, 1867, from Calumet, "The railroad is blocked entirely by snow and we cannot use locomotive until snowplow is finished." Work on a trestle for a company railroad to connect the mines with mills at Torch Lake was impossible, as "men cannot work out of doors in such a gale as has been blowing; thermometer five below zero, a regular hurricane most of the time, and about 15″ of snow badly drifting."[21]

Despite everything, the civilizing process continued. Anna Russell Agassiz, who joined her husband at Calumet, at first walked about with a revolver strapped to her waist. She gave the Methodist Sunday School much attention. Organized the year of her arrival (1867) along with the church, the school had 150 members. The company contributed five hundred dollars for the church structure built two years later. Only one other church, the Congregational, existed in Calumet; organized in 1873, with only twenty-five members, it had built an edifice by 1874 and by 1882 had raised its membership to 132. Cornish miners spurred the creation of the Calumet and Hecla Hospital in 1870; it accommodated up to twenty persons. The Cornish also approved the idea of the company aid fund (1877), with each employee contributing fifty cents a month and the company, an equal amount. If disabled, a man received twenty-five dollars per month for eight consecutive months. If permanently disabled, he received three hundred dollars; in case of death, his survivors received five hundred dollars. As other ethnic groups arrived, each created insurance and disability programs and funeral funds, as well as social institutions.[22]

Much was made of the last moose in the Copper Country, killed near the Calumet Mine by Native Americans and "half-breed" Peter Marksman. He skinned the animal and sold the flesh in Calumet for fifty cents per pound and made three hundred dollars. Mrs. Brockway, in 1867, mentioned her nephew's traveling to Calumet to help butcher cattle brought there by her husband and his partner. As early as 1866, a good road was under construction to connect Calumet with Hancock.[23]

In the beginning, four stores (two carrying general merchandise), privately owned, operated at Calumet. Agassiz had no desire for company stores, and even these privately owned establishments soon moved west of the mines to the commercial and residential village of Red Jacket. To the southeast, the village of Calumet began about 1889 but changed its name in 1895 to Laurium and became a handsome village with moderate, as well as palatial, houses and a business district along its Hecla Street.[24]

Red Jacket rose rapidly. Merchant prince Edward Ryan arrived from Hancock to open a store and wrote M. Freud and Company at Eagle Harbor on March 14, 1871, asking for all the butter, coffee, and sugar that concern could spare, two barrels of currants, "all the smoking tobacco you can give—and all the family soap you have to spare." North and Briggs asked Freud for two cartons of codfish to be sent immediately by stage for a particular customer. A fire that originated one noon in mid-May 1870 in the vicinity of what is now Tamarack swept through forest and undergrowth, destroying everything thirteen families owned except the clothes they wore; in half an hour, with "a dearth of water," no systematic attempt to halt the blaze, and no fire company, two blocks of Fifth Street in Red Jacket between Elm and Portland streets lay in charred ruins. Merchants like Ryan, Ruppe, Idenberg, Northrup and Kurbin, and others suffered losses; and men and women ran here and there with "bedding, clothing, furniture and children in their arms." A half dozen buildings, McDonald's Drug Store, and Streeter and Brothers Bank escaped harm. Within days, Ruppe, "with his usual energy, was the first one to drive a nail" and had "a shanty opposite his old store and [was] selling." Fitzgerald, Davey, Hirsch, and Shea followed suit.[25]

By 1875, Calumet Township had five frame schoolhouses, seating 816 (though 1,225 attended), and graded schools (Calumet, Red Jacket, Hecla, Osceola, Schoolcraft), where four males and eleven females taught all the basics, including natural philosophy (science) but no bookkeeping, geometry, chemistry, or drawing. Bookkeeping came later; for by the early 1880s, so many left school before age fifteen that educators paid attention to studies needed to prepare young people for business.

Libraries grew. In 1875, some 105 new volumes added to the Calumet school library made a total of 536. The Rockland Township library had nine hundred volumes, a Quincy Township library had 290 volumes, the Hancock Township district 400.[26]

Throughout the mining district, getting youngsters to attend a full school year continued to be a problem, although schools proliferated and in some areas there was improvement in attendance. Children were sent to work or kept at home to help with chores. Portage Township reported that attendance of most students averaged six months out of ten. In Hancock Township in 1875, about 44 percent of eligible scholars attended seven months of the ten-month school term. In Grant Township at the Penn Mine in Keweenaw County, attendance averaged only two and one-half months in a six-month term. Few parents visited schools. The Quincy Mining Company owned a building housing a graded school, where 192 out of 423 eligible scholars, ages 5 to 20, in 1875 attended school only an average of 4.4 months out of a possible ten. Houghton boasted of the Union School, built of stone and two stories high, with living accommodations for a janitor's family, as well as eating and waiting rooms for students who arrived early. In Ontonagon County, teachers sometimes raced through texts, so that youngsters often complained, "I've *been through* the book three or four times." Critics said the youngsters grasped little from dashing through books.[27]

Sources of entertainment were quick to appear in and around the mining communities. Baseball teams grew in the early 1870s, the German Socks (1870) eager to engage neighboring clubs, the Calumet Aztecs battling the Hancock Athletics (1872). Some of the Brockway offspring enjoyed the play *Queen Esther* at a Calumet theater. The Calumet Cornet Band, organized in 1872, entertained; its members, all employed by Calumet and Hecla, claimed to speak thirteen different languages among them, including Swedish, Norwegian, German, and Italian.[28]

Businesses multiplied. Sili Lenzi, who worked six years in the company mines after arriving in 1872, opened his own Red Jacket business selling wines, liquors, and cigars and enjoyed a prospering business in 1882. Many, like Lenzi, worked awhile in the mines, then started a business. As early as 1867, the company built the imposing Calumet Hotel, to accommodate fifty people, on ample grounds; it had rooms that were "large, airy" and "wide halls [and] modern conveniences" and was patronized by summer tourists, as well as businessmen. Before long, numerous hotels emerged in Red Jacket to handle its visiting salesmen as the Calumet region became an important marketplace.

In 1870, Calumet Township had 3,182 inhabitants (1,131 native-born and 2,051 foreign-born, including two African Americans and five Native Americans). By 1880, the township had more than doubled its population: 8,299 lived there, 2,140 of them in crowded Red Jacket. The twelve-mile trip from Hancock to Calumet proved popular after October 13, 1873, when the Mineral Range Railroad began running freight and passenger trains regularly. The train climbed the steep hill from Hancock "leading around back of the range of bluffs extending high up from the lake." The cost of $328,235.86 seemed high; but the line had four locomotives, two passenger coaches, two baggage-and-passenger cars combined, twenty-two flatcars, thirteen boxcars, and forty rock cars. Gross earnings in 1881 amounted to $117,956.24. The line hauled much of the all-important freight to accommodate Calumet's growth.[29]

Hancock had 1,835 people in 1884 and seemed unconcerned about rival Red Jacket. Connected, by 1875, to Houghton via a toll bridge standing sixteen feet above Portage Lake to permit all local craft to pass, Hancock concerned itself more with rival Houghton. James Edwards recalled that one reason for the bridge was that Houghton citizens felt that Hancock was "reaping all the benefit of being the port of entry" now that the Mineral Range Railroad existed. The bridge was wooden; and double-team wagons were charged forty cents, carriages and buggies, thirty, and foot passengers, five cents. Some idea of the quasi-rural environment may be gleaned from the five-cent charge for sheep, ten for hogs, and fifteen for cattle and mules. Not until 1895 was an iron structure built, partly to accommodate the Mineral Range Railroad, which would connect with lines to Detroit, Milwaukee, and Chicago. For a time, passengers could, alternatively, cross on the passenger tug *Lizzie Sutton*, named for its owner's daughter. The fare was five cents each way, and the tug made trips every half-hour.[30]

The productive Quincy Mine contributed much to Hancock's growth, which was only slightly disturbed by a disastrous fire, April 11, 1869, which wiped out the Leopold Store, as well as those of Edward Ryan, James A. Close, M. H. Mandlebaum, Baer's Meat Market, hardware, liquor, jewelry, millinery, and drug stores. Fire broke out at eight in the morning; and by two that afternoon, over one hundred houses were destroyed. No lives were lost, but village citizens said the loss amounted to about half a million dollars. The pious deplored the fire's having started in a Quincy Street saloon near where the present post office stands. No organized fire department existed until 1871; once formed, the organization prided itself on its equipment and its cupola-topped building.[31]

The fire convinced Leopold and Joseph Austrian that they should not continue their business. With growing competition among mercantile firms, they figured (rightly) that a lucrative field lay in purchasing and shipping supplies to Hancock—a practice Leopold had begun even before the fire. The Leopolds shipped cattle, hogs, and sheep from Chicago to Hancock. This paid well; but Joseph Austrian found such freight most disagreeable, with the greatest difficulty the bringing of the animals to the steamers at Chicago River wharves. The firm did well. The work was arduous and fraught with anxiety. Captains sometimes collapsed under stress navigating in late autumnal Lake Superior and Portage Lake storms. Austrian recalled his plight in Chicago procuring deck hands "who did not fancy shipping for Lake Superior, on account of the severe weather" late one season, so he hired an entire crew of African Americans who had worked as hotel waiters and supervised their loading of the ship, a chore for which they had no experience; but the job was done.[32]

Nothing deterred the Hancock entrepreneurs. Although two years passed before Hancock was rebuilt, J. Scott, son-in-law of the Brockways, sold James Close two corner lots for fourteen hundred dollars only four days after the fire. Fred Kausler remembered arriving in 1855 to help clear the land where Hancock stood. There was nothing but timber then until "old man Udich" knocked together a shack for a boardinghouse. There was not a house on the Hancock side of Portage Lake then. The Quincy Stamps stood down by the lake. Kausler helped grade streets, worked at the mine, operated a tavern, and watched Hancock's rapid growth. Once, an opera troupe scheduled to appear at Saint Patrick's Hall found themselves stalled in Houghton; but Kausler brought them and their five trunks across the ice for fifteen dollars.[33]

Although the Quincy Mining Company built housing for employees, not enough existed; and Hancock expanded, filling with mine workers. One of the most notable developments was East Hancock, where between 1880 and 1900, some of the most comfortable and charming houses appeared. Wooden sidewalks, some over ravines running north and south, added a civilized note; and tidy housekeepers prided themselves on new frame structures. Besides the mines on hills high above Hancock, the town benefited commercially from productive industries; prominent by 1882 were the Sturgeon River Lumber Company (organized 1872), Matt M. Morallee's sawmill and lumberyard (established 1860 and rebuilt in 1881), the Hancock Ashery (turning out a hundred barrels of potash annually), and at neighboring Ripley, a wagon manufactory, blacksmithery, ironworks, and a foundry. Two or three livery stables, wagon, paint, boot-and-shoe, and tailor shops "equal to the necessities of people," along with boardinghouses and saloons, rounded out thriving Hancock.[34]

Hancock, c. 1890. (Michigan Technological University Archives and Copper Country Historical Collections, Michigan Technological University.)

Banks offered loans, and mercantile houses, everything one needed from work clothes to the finest in dresses and haberdashery. No longer was it necessary for a man to order a suit made in Detroit, as Samuel Robinson did in 1862: "Have him [the tailor-cutter] stick to the big style of last summer and he'll fit me every time." No longer need the women of Hancock and Houghton depend on *Godey's Lady's Book*, as they did in 1862. John E. Hocking, who had millinery shops in Hancock and Red Jacket, advertised the latest styles of hats, bonnets, trimmings, and laces at reasonable prices, stating that "none but first-class hands are employed in the millinery department."

Hancock had two newspapers as of 1884: the *Northwestern Mining Journal* and the *Evening Copper Journal*, which began that year and continued until 1938. By 1882, Hancock prided itself on the Lake View House, Northwestern Hotel, Pacific House, and Hancock Hotel; but there was not a full-fledged practicing lawyer. Four physicians practiced. Vice existed in houses of ill fame; and citizens heard of saloon fights in Frenchtown, up the hill from Hancock. Churches, benevolent societies, and watchful citizens did their best to overwhelm the evil. Curbed in one area, dens and dives sprouted elsewhere.

The *Ivanhoe*, a mail steamer, made daily trips (except Sunday) between Hancock and L'Anse, carrying express and some passengers. In May and June 1882, the steamer brought *up* 1,521 passengers and took *down* 1,543. Some bragged of its engine, originally built for New York's William Marcy "Boss" Tweed for the river police there. As early as 1876, lake steamers like *Cuyahoga* and *Missouri* carried pleasure seekers from Chicago to Duluth, calling at Hancock, Houghton, and the northern harbors, as well as Ontonagon to the southwest. Ships including the *Pacific, Arctic, Winslow* and *Saint Louis* reached Portage Lake, where one could then connect with the *Manistee* for Eagle River, Eagle Harbor, and Ontonagon. Adults and children delighted in watching the numerous stately steamers come and go. Flags and pennants fluttered. Whistles blew, and bells rang, during the busy spring and summer.[35]

Social life and intellectual pursuits developed. The Emerald Literary Society began in Hancock as a debating and lecture association in 1874; by 1882, members enjoyed a three-hundred-volume library. The Congregational Church supported the Young Men's Literary Association, established in March 1875 with reading room and lectures, and five years later presented Gilbert and Sullivan's HMS *Pinafore*. It sold at auction, from its reading room, back numbers of *Harper's Monthly*, the *North American Review*, and *Frank Leslie's Weekly*. Shops in Hancock carried dime novels for lighter reading. Catherine Mullett Hall, sister of Martha Forster, wrote in the early 1860s of how impressed she was by members of Saint Patrick's Society turning out "in full regalia," marching in the rain, their umbrellas held high, in a long funeral procession at Hancock. Organized in 1860, this society had its own hall and 180 members by 1874. Saint Patrick's was one of three organizations catering to Irish folk and preserving remnants of their heritage, the others being the Ancient Order of Hibernians (1876) and the Robert Emmet

Young Men's Benevolent Society. Germans had three: Saint Joseph's
Society (1877); the Order of Hermann's Sons (1865), with branches
at Calumet and Lake Linden; and the German Benevolent Society
(1860). English and Americans swelled the ranks of lodges such as the
Masons, Odd Fellows, and the Ancient Order of Foresters. The post–
Civil War era produced the Soldiers' and Sailors' Association. Women
belonged to various church societies and sewing circles. Some conducted businesses. Hannah Hoffenbacher operated a confectionery
shop, as did Agnes Washburn, in 1889. Elizabeth W. White, Mrs. W.
McLauren, Mary Dwyer, and Catherine Flynn worked as dressmakers,
while Mrs. J. P. Steichen sold notions in her shop and Mrs. T. A.
Flynn competed with Mr. Hocking in millinery.[36]

Rivalry between Hancock and Houghton was intense. A common expression in Hancock was "Well, Houghton tried to do this
and that," while in Houghton, some complained, "Didn't Hancock
stick in her oar and want . . . to run the machine?" Such mixing
of metaphors to produce unique statements and petty antagonism
developed among all the copper range towns. As late as the 1930s,
some people at Calumet used "Go to Hancock!" when they meant
"Go to Hell!" Rivalries exist to the present day.[37]

By 1890, Houghton, the county seat, assumed superior airs. But in
1871, a night watchman still walked the streets; and a bookseller said
standard authors like Dickens and Thackeray took second place to
such best-selling novels as *Absolute Jane Ann.* City officials worried
about girls and boys coasting down Houghton's hills on sleds at
Christmas time but took pride in Houghton County's being the only
one of three copper counties that had increased steadily in population
since first being settled. A Houghton editor, probably thinking of
upstarts Hancock and Calumet, wondered in 1872 why men and
boys at Houghton did not organize a baseball club. Hogs still roamed
about, and he wondered if strychnine "taken by a nice little piggy in
his grub" would affect the sausage made from him!

Houghton County had an assessed valuation of $7,000,000 in
1881 and $24,500,000 in 1882. Much of the 1881 tax revenue of
$105,000 was used for schools.[38] By 1880, Houghton County had
a total population of 22,473, including 24 Native Americans and
"half-breeds."

By 1889, Houghton was described as "one of the most wealthy
and substantial villages on the peninsula"; and its population was
2,500. It had "the finest court house and jail in the upper peninsula," costing seventy-five thousand dollars and a city hall costing
fifteen thousand dollars. Docks, warehouses, and tugs lined its shores.
The Hoar Brothers had two large stores, one on either side of the
main street, in competition with those of Louis and Joseph Hennes,

Graham Pope, and many others. Like Hancock, Houghton had its share of groceries, drugstores, jewelry establishments, "and [in 1882] an exceedingly healthy number of small boardinghouses and saloons." Here five lawyers found much work, along with four doctors. There were three breweries and the Lake Superior Native Copper Works (smelters). Numerous small industrial shops and factories existed, including the Houghton Candle Factory, established 1865, which turned out three hundred tons of candles for use by miners underground. The Houghton Cigar Factory, established in 1861, employed, in 1882, eight men; and they made 360,000 cigars annually. Shops to repair wagons, shoe horses, manufacture safety fuses, and house lime kilns made Houghton an industrial center. By July 1882, about one hundred persons subscribed to the newly introduced telephone, in Houghton, Hancock, Calumet, and Lake Linden.[39]

Houghton also prided itself on the Michigan Mining School (it went through several name changes but since 1963 has been the Michigan Technological University), established by act of the Michigan legislature in 1885. Opened in September 1886, the school occupied part of the former town hall and a large building across the street that had once served as a roller-skating rink. Its purpose was to enable students "to obtain a full knowledge of the science, art and practice of mining and the application of machinery thereto." By 1889, the Michigan Mining School had thirty-five students, taught by five instructors and was managed by a board of six appointed by the governor for a term of six years.[40]

People "down below" often thought of the Upper Peninsula as a lawless area or a remote backwater. As late as 1891, an arriving graduate student at Houghton wrote of Houghton as "this Godforsaken hamlet." There was no resident judge until 1865; and mining seemed to attract drinkers, braggarts aching for fights, whores, and many seeking to get rich fast. But the eastern and New England emigrants joined European social conservative elements, who outnumbered the rogues and helped make the Keweenaw Peninsula a most law-abiding place after the Civil War.[41] Houghton had impressive Catholic, Congregational, and Methodist Episcopal churches and an energetic moral citizenry determined that their village would remain a good place to live. But they also enjoyed life. Later, a more militant Puritanism permeated the Copper Country. The vote by counties in 1875 on the temperance amendment is revealing (see Table 4.1).[42]

Houghton, like other Copper Country communities, was a font of entertainment. In 1885, W. W. Cole's "New Colossal Shows" with four circuses, two menageries, twenty clowns, an Arab troupe, a Mexican show, a museum, and skating artists attracted many. When, some three weeks earlier, Abbey's Uncle Tom's Cabin Company,

Table 4.1. 1875 Temperance Amendment Vote by County

County	Yes	No
Baraga	151	371
Houghton	1,166	2,684
Keweenaw	153	285
Ontonagon	250	2,627

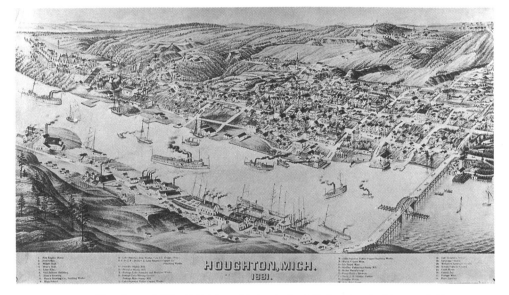

*Houghton, 1881. (Michigan Technological University Archives and Copper
Country Historical Collections, Michigan Technological University.)*

direct from New York City, gave a performance at Miller's Hall, with
"Topsys, South Carolina Jubilee singers and the smallest of Shetland
ponies," few customers showed up. The newspaper commented that
the company did not do well and would report Houghton a "poor
show town." Their failure was an exception to numerous successes
enjoyed by scores of traveling shows.

Miller's, built in 1863 and enlarged in 1867, provided much popular fare in its large public hall. Located on Shelden Street in west
Houghton, Miller's annual Mardi Gras party attracted hundreds and
in 1884 offered twenty-five dollars in prizes for the best character
in costume. Houghton attracted the elite of the Copper Country to

the fancy dress ball at the Douglass House. Some came from as far
as Champion and Marquette, in the iron country. Meat merchant
Henry Baer of Hancock appeared as Hamlet, and Mrs. Henry Brett
of Opechee [Osceola] as Queen Elizabeth, while C. A. Wright, Mineral Range Railroad executive, wore English court dress of the early
nineteenth century. Governor John J. Bagley of Michigan and party
stayed at the Douglass House when they visited the ship canal in
August 1873, and hordes of tourists came as early as 1861. In August
of that year, a wag wrote in the margin of the hotel's register,

> From Adams fall to the end of time,
> There will be no end of making rhyme,
> But the pointed end of these four lines:
> Is—strangers all, keep clear of the mines!

—to which a wit appended, "*Or else—get back to the Boat in time.*"
Numerous lively soirées held in the hotel's ballroom delighted the
cream of Copper Country society. Schoolmaster Hobart said of the
Douglass House in 1863, "It is a fine hotel . . . and will compare with
many in Detroit."[43]

Houghton residents in the 1880s pointed out the two-story frame
courthouse high on the hill facing north over the lake, noting that
only one man had ever escaped from its jail nearby. No one could miss
the dominant sandstone courthouse with tower, constructed later
with a mansard roof in 1887. In the early 1880s, a poorhouse and
farm in Hancock Township held thirty-eight people. An observer then
found the institution decent enough but deplored the lack of ample
bathing rooms. Six hundred and fifty people of the county received
assistance (.017 percent), and 150 of them were permanent paupers
maintained outside the poorhouse. Taxpayers in 1881 spent about
fourteen thousand dollars caring for the poor. They no longer had
to concern themselves with the Native Americans living at Keweenaw
Bay; for in 1875, Baraga County had been formed out of Houghton
County, so that now most Native Americans lived in Baraga County.[44]

Along beautiful Keweenaw Bay, Methodists, Catholics, and Native Americans had built functioning communities; and here Native
Americans, despite hardships, enjoyed lake and forest. Now their
descendants and a host of strangers arrived to help construct new,
quite different, communities. Slate quarries and logging, along with
suitable locations for advancing railroads coming from east and south,
helped to develop what came to be known as Baraga–L'Anse in the
local patois. Baraga County had its county seat at L'Anse village,
the western terminus of the railroad from Marquette. Platted in
1871–72, L'Anse seemed destined for greatness. With the coming

of the railway, hundreds poured in; lots sold on the main street for one thousand dollars. Samuel Lloyd operated the first hotel, L'Anse House, brought to the village by scow, thirty miles from Houghton, where the enterprising Gloucestershire (England) emigrant had hosted traveling strangers for a decade.[45]

L'Anse, it was anticipated, would be the port from which would pass copper from the north and iron ore from the south and east. An enthusiastic booster wrote from Lansing, "I expect to hear, within the next eighteen months, the whistle of the locomotive of a regular passenger train at L'Anse, and the shout—'All aboard for the East and South'." He expected blast furnaces to "darken the air all along the shore [soon] from L'Anse to the head of Portage Lake." White sails of an iron fleet were envisioned on the blue waters of the great bay. The north country legislators could leave Lansing in style via the railroad, instead of having to stay downstate, where they lived subject to downstate hauteur.[46]

A large slate formation ran in a wide belt west from the Huron Mountains for many miles. In 1872, the Clinton Quarry and the Huron Bay Slate Quarry began operations, producing considerable quantities of a jet black or very dark blue-black slate; operations were suspended five years later but resumed under a new management and name, Michigan Slate Company. The panic of 1873, which hit the entire United States, ruined much of L'Anse. Lumbering helped in the slow economic recovery, but the entire town suffered devastation by fire in 1896 and twenty years later was still recovering from the double blow.[47]

A great ore dock that had been constructed with such high hopes lay dormant. The bright, happy summer of 1871 evaporated in grim realities of financial recklessness, along with L'Anse's general stores, hardware, paint, and tobacco shops, iron warehouse, bank, dance hall, hairdressing salon, and three bakeries. A bustling community was ruined. Logging and lumbering followed slowly and built a new economic complex; by 1889, the population was eight hundred, and iron ore, slate, fish, and lumber were shipped from the two docks that once connoted L'Anse as an important lake port.[48]

In 1880, Baraga County's four townships and L'Anse village had a total population of 1,804. Native Americans and offspring of whites and natives numbered 528 of that total. The land was rich; but of the county's 576,000 acres, only 852 had been turned to agricultural pursuits. Forty-one farms existed. An observer speculated that if the total acreage had been equally divided, each man, woman, and child in the county would possess some 319 acres. Four miles by road—and two directly across the bay—from L'Anse, Baraga Village rose just southwest of the old Catholic mission. English-born Captain

James Bendry became Baraga Township's first supervisor. He saw population increase from 160 in 1870 to 400 in 1880 in what became Baraga Village. Population leaped to 1,090 by 1890. In 1891, the village was incorporated. All this was indicative of the fluctuating fortunes of the two villages of Keweenaw Bay.

Bendry had settled in the United States in 1841 and by 1846 found his way to the Sault while serving as sailor on the Great Lakes. He and his wife Charlotte Contoui—part French, part Native American—produced six daughters and five sons. A building of Bendry's at L'Anse became the first courthouse. Charlotte and James died within two years of each other (1892 and 1894), pioneer community builders deeply mourned.[49]

Native Americans also built community. The LaPointe Treaty of September 30, 1854, set up the L'Anse Reservation consisting of lands surrounding the missions. Although ratified in 1855, no allotments of land (eighty acres for each head of family or single person) materialized until 1875, because no U.S. president saw fit to allot the land. Sectional rivalry and the Civil War were often brought forth as excuses for the tardiness. Congress, on June 22, 1874, resolved a long-standing dispute about some lands claimed by Native Americans but not included in the government's decisions. These 18,427 acres should be sold for $1.25 per acre to farmers and settlers, mostly white, and the proceeds (some twenty-three thousand dollars) allocated for educational or other beneficial purposes as directed by the president of the United States.[50]

To protect the Native Americans' allotments, the federal government stipulated restrictions on their selling the land. By the end of 1875, 300 allotments had been made. Between 1875 and 1930, a total of 679 allotments—83 percent of them between 1874 and 1894—helped change the configuration of life for the new owners. As early as 1854, government officials spoke of the acculturation of the Keweenaw Bay bands: they dressed like whites, had been educated, and spoke well; and many of them had turned to Christianity. Now they should prosper as owners of land in fee simple.

The U.S. Department of the Interior, in 1885, allowed allotees to cut and sell stumpage; and many owners allowed whites who were interested in cutting trees to buy acreage after approval by the federal government. But not many buyers were found. Those who bought secured ten or forty acres, rarely buying the entire allotment of eighty acres. Baraga County slowly developed agriculture and lumbering.[51]

An 1870 editorial in Ontonagon's *Lake Superior Miner*, recalling the Cliff, Minesota, and National Mines' experiences, stated the case succinctly: in the Lake Superior country, "the lodes, instead of increasing in richness became impoverished the deeper they [were] penetrated." In 1852, Michigan's contribution to the building of the Washington Monument had been a massive block of copper, weighing a ton, containing some silver, from the Cliff Mine. In 1870, that mine was twelve hundred feet deep; but the 1873 product of 120,000 pounds dwindled, by the early 1880s, to about twenty-three thousand pounds. Diminishing returns was the order of the day.[52]

The 4,270 inhabitants of Keweenaw County in 1880 continued to work at whatever was available. Of that number, 1,966 were foreign-born; and of those one-half were from various parts of the United Kingdom. Of the native-born, most hailed from Michigan, but many, from New York, Ohio, Pennsylvania, and New England—all adding regional characteristics to the developing mix of Anglo–American culture. While Houghton County's population increased by 8,594 from 1870 to 1880, Keweenaw County's remained almost stationary. In 1850, nineteen mines had operated there; thirty years later, only nine operated. Several had exhausted financial resources and found decreasing copper content in the ore extracted. In 1874, Houghton County produced 79 percent of Michigan copper, Keweenaw, 18 percent, and Ontonagon, 3 percent. By 1880, Ontonagon produced only 2 percent, and Keweenaw, 9 percent. Central Mine, near the Cliff, by 1882, distinguished itself as the most important producer outside Houghton County with an output of about 1,250,000 pounds.[53]

Although Julius Freud and Company sometimes garnisheed wages of former Keweenaw miners who had relocated in Houghton County, some mine workers remained conscientious. Several working at the Hecla Mine wrote Freud that they had moved but added, "You need not be doubtful about your money." One man wrote that he had left Phoenix "some little in your debt [and] I feel it my duty to inform you of my whereabouts." Much courtesy prevailed amid mobility.[54] In 1868, Daniel Brockway was back at Copper Harbor, a partner in a general store and as peripatetic as ever—off to purchase supplies and arrange financial transactions at Bay City, Saginaw, Albion, and Marshall. He borrowed, loaned, consulted experts on taxes, sold land, took apples for exhibition at Detroit's State Fair, and took time off to attend there the Republican state convention.[55]

The Brockways opened a store at Cliff Mine in 1872, with the assistance of son Albert. Daniel also served as mine agent at the Cliff and prided himself on the ownership of the Atlas Mine. They lived at Phoenix. Mrs. Brockway served breakfast to "boys" from the store and others (including Samuel Leopold) on New Year's Day, 1874, then served roast goose and roast turkey with all the trimmings for dinner. Her diary reveals an active woman, at times stricken with severe arthritic pains. She lamented over daughter Sarah's loss of a twelve-dollar shawl on the road to Eagle Harbor. She joined her husband on a trip to Calumet where they attended the funeral of Captain Hoatson, then dined in town at a friend's and later called on acquaintances, as well as nephew Will Childs.[56]

Lucena Brockway was acutely ill in March 1866, and her case was pronounced by a physician as "a slight shock of paralysis and general prostration of the nervous system." She could not understand husband Daniel's going off a month later to Portage Lake: "Started at 5 o'clock A.M. Went unbeknown to me, the cruelest thing he could do when I was so sick." Her illness came with intensity, at times, and at others temporarily disappeared. She ended her days in a wheelchair. Her illnesses may have been accompanied by unconscious psychosomatic protest. When her beloved husband "Pa" Brockway again left early in the morning of March 16, 1874, with Judge Platt, by stage, for Houghton and L'Anse, she recalled, "Five minutes after, I was taken sick . . . pretty sick all day [with] symptoms of Paralysis again."

On July 8, she took her crutch and chair and managed to get out "into the door yard" and back; but "Pa" did not come home, as promised, from Copper Harbor. He was gone for four days and returned late just "before we eat dinner." On August 21, she "put up" forty quarts of whortleberries and was very tired. On October 27, she wrote: "I feel lonely enough I can tell you."[57]

Her house was deluged with women and men who came for tea and often stayed for dinner. A good businesswoman, Lucena Brockway sold milk, eggs, butter, and berries in season. In July 1878, she picked strawberries each day from the seventh through the sixteenth, thirty-two quarts in four days alone at the Cliff, gave away some, then sent son-in-law Scott to Calumet with forty quarts for the market there. She and the family picked some 531 quarts by July 19. She tended her large garden with care and followed advice culled from journals, noting in the rear of the 1878 diary: "For white worms in plants put 10 drops of Carbolic acid to one quart of water." The homely, as well as the scientific, delighted Lucena Brockway, who noted that daughter Sally and her son Dunbar saw "the comet to night the first time."[58]

Lucena and Daniel Brockway spent the last part of their lives in Lake Linden, where their son Albert established himself; but they were forever identified with Keweenaw County and pioneer days of the peninsula. They died within two months of each other in spring 1899. By that time, about twenty-six hundred people lived at Lake Linden on the west shore of Torch Lake, five miles southeast of Calumet and connected with it by Calumet and Hecla's Hecla and Torch Lake Railroad, which transported rock from mines to stamp mills and smelters. The Tamarack and Osceola companies, as well as the Quincy, had—or were building—mills nearby, a favorable location

Lucena Harris Brockway. (Michigan Historical Collections, Bentley Historical Library, The University of Michigan.)

due to the flatness of the land; the lake absorbed tailings that the companies would recover fifty years later.

Lake Linden was also a stop on the Hancock and Calumet Railroad. The town, in addition, welcomed large steamers; for Torch Lake was navigable for them after Calumet and Hecla dredged Torch River, two miles long, so ships could pass through Bootjack Bay, an arm of Portage Lake. A memorable Fourth of July occurred in 1883, when Reverend John Pitezel aboard the *Nyack* and distinguished passenger General William Tecumseh Sherman, accompanied by his chief of staff and justices from federal and Massachusetts courts, arrived at Lake Linden. Hundreds of people on the wharf waved flags, and banners flapped in the wind as two brass bands enlivened the festivities; a gun salute was fired for the irascible Union savior "and cheer after cheer rent the air from the multitude on shore."[59]

Agassiz had found this area perfect for the milling of his mines' ore. Down a long sloping bluff from Calumet, Lake Linden served well, situated on the water. Many persons can still recall the copper ingots piled on its docks awaiting shipment, as well as the coal steamers unloading Calumet and Hecla's voluminous supply. The earliest settlement was that of Alfred Beasley in 1851, a residence later used as a schoolhouse. Alfred and James Beasley, two years later, opened the first house for the public's entertainment—a tavern serving light meals—at the north end of Torch Lake. It was called the Halfway House but should not be confused with the identically named house closer to Calumet of William Royal.

Lake Linden, organized in 1868 a year after the Hecla Stamp Mill was built, expanded with the fortunes of Calumet and Hecla. Smaller industries, peripherally connected with the company, provided work for many. Joseph Gregory and Company constructed a sawmill in 1867 and after 1872 developed this with a large door, sash, and blind factory. Gregory and Company owned some twenty-five thousand acres of pine land and forty thousand of hardwood timber lands. Their steam tug *Mentor* plied Torch and Portage Lakes in connection with their extensive business. Joseph Bosch and Son filled a thousand barrels of beer for export annually. The elder Bosch, born in Baden, Germany, worked four years in the stamp mill before opening his brewery in the early 1870s. French, English, and German immigrants opened mercantile and various other establishments. In the decades that followed, with new immigration, Lake Linden filled with French and French Canadians, so that its initial cultural milieu was transformed into one dominated by Francophiles.[60]

The entire town was liquidated in May 1887 by a fire that burned from noon until three in the afternoon. Mrs. Brockway recalled that friends came from Eagle River to Cliff "to hear about the burning of Lake Linden town." The business district was gone—several blocks along the main street—and many residents lost all except "what they had on their backs." Forty acres were gone in three hours, but Lake Linden rebuilt quickly. Within a year, a business area was constructed of solid brick, "as fine buildings as any city north of Milwaukee," said the *Michigan State Gazetteer*.

By 1890, Frederick Sargent managed the imposing stone Hotel Duquette, the *Torch Lakes Times* was published weekly, and the Holy Cross Sisters taught in their private school and tended their convent; a public school, graded, with room for seven hundred, flourished, as did Saint Joseph's (Catholic) and the Methodist and Congregational churches. Confectioners, dressmakers, barbers, photographers, bakers and butchers, grocers, saloonkeepers, doctors, and lawyers populated the thriving village.

Typical of Lake Linden success stories was that of Henry Fisher, Jr., born in Cleveland, Ohio, in 1846, son of a German immigrant who lived first in New York City, then Cleveland, then Keweenaw County for awhile, and finally Ontonagon, where he was educated in night schools and "the dear school of experience." At age ten, he worked driving a team hauling ore from the Rockland Mine to its mill. Then he learned the mechanic's trade in his father's shop and labored there four years before migrating to Houghton, where he worked in several

mining machine shops. In autumn 1868, he came to Lake Linden as it
was born and followed the mechanic's trade for two years, after which
Calumet and Hecla made him foreman of their mill department. By
1895, not yet fifty years of age, Fisher was still in charge as foreman,
as well as director of a Hancock building-and-loan association, a
member of Lake Linden's school board (Schoolcraft Township) for
eighteen years, and married to Elizabeth Paul of Hancock. The couple
had three children. Fisher's was not an extraordinary case.[61]

Adjoining Lake Linden, the village of Grover—named for President Cleveland and sometimes listed as Groverton, the home of
Calumet and Hecla smelters, with a post office since January 1887—
evolved into a community with a distinct life of its own by 1890. On
August 21, 1889, Grover changed its name to South Lake Linden.
Rumor had it that hidebound Republicans there wanted nothing to
remind them of a Democratic president! In 1903, the village was
incorporated with a new name, Hubbell, in honor of Jay Hubbell,
who had served as Republican representative in Congress before his
death in 1900.[62]

Some seventy miles southwest a visitor dining at the Paul House in
Ontonagon in 1880 noted the changes "civilization" had wrought.
The twenty-year-old Ojibwa woman in charge of the dining room
and who waited on his table was "bright, fair-looking, polite and
intelligent," a high school graduate who spoke English plainly, as
well as her native tongue—typical of her people, about thirty of
whom lived in the village, "quiet, civil people." This was a change
from times past: in 1852, German travelers had cringed to see in the
Ontonagon country human beings "so profaned and distorted . . .
laughed and sneered at by the white people" on a Monday morning
when fifty poverty-stricken Native Americans performed a "Beggar-
Dance" to secure provisions and liquor prior to setting off to the
West. Who, they wondered, was to blame for this depravity? Ignorant
Native Americans or whites who gave them, "poison" instead of
bread? The LaPointe Treaty of 1854 helped ameliorate part of the
problem. Some Native Americans remained within the white man's
communities. "Indian mail-carriers" brought the mail from Green
Bay in 1855, sometimes leaving bags hanging in the woods, for the
later delivery.[63]

In Ontonagon County, the white men's successful mines sired
more villages as settlements rose near areas where ancient pit miners once toiled. Rockland became the post office name of an important village encompassing the mining settlements of Rosendale,
Williamsburg, Webster, Minesota Mine, and others. It had a pleasant
location, encircled by high ranges of rocky heights. Old-timers there
recalled 1858, when 6,000 people lived in the vicinity and there were

seventy-odd saloons "to supply their thirst." Rockland's Methodist Episcopal Church built by the Minesota Company was closed for a time but reopened in 1870 with a gala cake-and-ice-cream social, choral singing, solo numbers, and a declamation on "Woman's Rights." Rockland's population grew in one decade to 1,844 in 1860 (40 percent of Ontonagon County's), due to the successful Minesota, then declined by 1870 to 1,479 and by 1880 to 877. As elsewhere, the fortunes of corporations decided the fate of communities.[64]

The population of Carp Lake Township rose from 336 in 1860 to 825 in 1870, then remained stable. By 1882, the visitor could find no villages within its limits "save a mining hamlet or more." Just west of the Minesota, the National Mining Company produced mass copper and the village of Webster, where most of its 273 miners lived in the early 1860s. The company also cultivated hay, oats, potatoes, and turnips on three hundred acres of land by offering contracts to farmers. Men earned, in 1862, an average of twenty-five dollars a month, and skilled workers, such as blacksmiths, up to forty dollars. A peak of 692 tons of copper was mined in 1862, and five thousand tons during the mine's lifetime. The National was the sole operating mine in the 1880s. In the Rockland–Greenland–Mass area, companies explored, a few succeeded, and many failed. Some fifty-eight began operations between 1843 and 1895; an additional five began between 1900 and 1910. For decades, before Ontonagon County found new life in lumbering, miners and their families depended, at times, upon the Rockland, Michigan, Lake Superior, Superior, West Minesota, Algonquin, Toltec, Bohemian, Great Western, Ridge, Ogima, Evergreen Bluff, the Farm, Merrimac, Hazard, Flint Steel, Nebraska–Caledonia, Indiana, Victoria, Algomah, What Cheer, King Philip, Mass, and Adventure mining companies, and many more.[65]

A mine agent wrote a superior that by 1865, fifteen years after its founding, the Adventure Mine had fallen upon hard times, with wages reduced, men dismissed, and management unable to help them. The practice prevailed of hiring without reason in favorable times and discharging men in wholesale panic in hard times. For years, the Adventure utilized the "tribute system," whereby miners worked at assigned places and received a percentage of what they mined. Settlement day ("payday") occurred once each year. Miners and families enjoyed picnic lunches, contests, drinking, and dancing as agents negotiated the next year's contracts and men divided the proceeds for the past year's work.

Greenland emerged as a company-controlled town after the Adventure was reorganized in 1898 (after nearly closing in 1880); four new shafts were sunk, a stamp mill erected, and a flow of millions of dollars from shareholders attempted to inaugurate profit and prosperity. But deficits, ranging from nineteen thousand to ninety thousand dollars annually, prevailed. By 1917, the mine closed, and Greenland faced dire times.[66]

Mass City was the last of the larger Ontonagon area towns to be developed; it was platted in 1899, its streets named after previous mine ventures. Noel Johnson, an African American, a slave who escaped from Missouri to Ohio, discovered copper deposits near Mass and sold the land to the Mass Mining Company (organized 1855), its name denoting the kind of copper found there. Johnson was brought to Ontonagon in 1848 by prospector Cyrus Mendenhall, who paid $250 to the estate of William Pemberton of Missouri for Johnson's freedom. The Mass Mine ran erratically until 1886. Then, at the end of the century, after a reorganization, Mass City emerged with fifty new dwellings on Ridge location; and the future looked bright. The company produced over twenty-five thousand tons of copper, about 28.5 percent of all that was mined in the Rockland–Greenland–Mass area. The Mass Mining Company had paid Johnson ten thousand dollars for rights to the land. Johnson died before the company organized, leaving a widow and children.[67]

Ontonagon County's prominent mine officials, merchants, professional men, and clergy came from the United Kingdom, Germany, Canada, New England, and eastern states. Its workers emigrated from Cornwall, Ireland, Germany, and French Canada. This configuration changed with the arrival of Scandinavians, Finns, and others after 1890. Ontonagon harbor in 1881 saw 136 ships, sail or steam, in its waters. Exports consisted of 627 tons of copper, 82 of general merchandise, hides, fish, timber, railroad ties, corn, and oats. Imports brought 760 barrels of apples, 3,800 of flour, 520 of port wine, and 31 of whiskey; 110 head of cattle; and 1,146 tons of general merchandise.

An 1870 problem was too many boys lazing in public, drinking, and playing cards and billiards. Civic fathers fretted about the county's lack of plows for snow removal. Still, Ontonagon's intellectual activity remained lively, with editors refusing to spare individuals and corporations that warranted criticism. Civic boosters supported federal assistance for harbor improvement loudly and clearly. Bankers hailed the county's liquidation, by 1868, of a huge indebtedness incurred paying bounties during the Civil War. They beamed with approval at the county's healthy financial condition in 1881.

A debating club met weekly for many years. In 1870, men and women met to discuss whether "more information can be obtained by traveling than by reading" and, a week later, "the propriety of the federal government granting public lands to railroads." The *Lake*

Superior Miner expected "ladies in great numbers" for the January 27, 1870, debate on woman suffrage. When this had been announced, one irate man rose and fulminated about females in areas they did not belong; but the newspaper's editor said that "if a woman does her work as well as a man could or would do it, the woman is entitled to as fair compensation." Ontonagon village had changed. The 1870 Fourth of July celebrated with firecrackers, torpedoes, drums, cannon, footraces, and a reading of the Declaration of Independence saw no drunkenness and no fights—quite a change from the old days. The editor concluded, "Long live the nation."[68]

The Keweenaw Peninsula remained basically a frontier area until the 1890s. Contrary to much that has been supposed, it was not entirely a "man's world." Single women from "down below" or Canada who came to teach influenced generations of young people. Women who married mine agents replicated the life and society they knew in eastern states or southern Michigan. Their insistence on high moral tone offset much of the disruptive spirit of the frontier. Maids born in Ireland or in Michigan of English parents worked long hours serving mistresses and masters. Mrs. Senderson, who did housework for Sarah Scott, received one dollar a day and probably her meals, in 1876. When Mrs. Scott was appointed postmistress at Phoenix in 1884, her parents went over to "fix up" the place. After her mother, Lucena Brockway, worked all forenoon "fixing" the garden, made chicken coops, and took fifty chickens off to market one day in May 1878, mother and daughter spent the afternoon having tea after a man had come to tune the piano. Women made petticoats of down, sent to Chicago or Boston for fancy trimmings for their homemade dresses, washed, ironed, baked, cooked, sewed, scrubbed, and cleaned silver— "a little of everything" wrote Mrs. Brockway before she departed in 1869 with her daughter Sarah for a Canadian excursion.

With their families, women attended weddings, the bedsides of sick neighbors, and social events. Women washed and prepared the dead for burial and thought nothing of having ten friends stop in for refreshments during the day or sending to Boston's Faneuil Hall Market for tripe.[69] Maria Pantera, born in New York, was married to Italian-born shoemaker Joseph and lived at Franklin Mine. She sent daughter Mary, age 11, to school with sons Charles and Frank, ages 17 and 15, and took care of William, age 8, Frederick, age 5, and Catherine, age 4, at home. Maria, age 45, had a servant, Elizabeth Dorrity, born in Michigan of Irish parents. The household also consisted of Maria's son by a former marriage, Eugene Brewer, mine laborer, age 24, born in New York; brother-in-law Rafaello, age 28, a shoemaker; and five Italian-born mine laborers, ranging in age from 22 to 55. Such households of from sixteen to twenty—often the rule, rather than the exception—mixed the foreign-born, the assimilating generation, and the children who would often abandon their ethnic heritage.[70]

Life was hard, work strenuous—often dangerous—strangers grim, and accidents frequent. The irascible John Slawson berated women shopping at the Cliff's Leopold store. He was said to have forced workmen at the mine to eat cornmeal when the last boat failed to bring flour and called in the sheriff when his men went on strike; but few knew that his heart had been broken long before, in 1849, when his wife Priscilla died at age twenty-four, three months after their four-and-one-half-month-old son Willie had died. Eventually, Slawson left to prospect and was killed fighting Native Americans in Arizona. By 1916, none of the Slawson family remained in the Copper Country; and Priscilla's gravestone had fallen over.[71]

Anna Smith at Houghton had been private secretary to Columbus Douglass for many years, and he left her one-third of his estate and made her administrator. John H. Forster praised his sister-in-law as "a sunbeam in the house"; she lived for a time, in the 1860s, with the Forsters at the Pewabic Mine. When Martha Forster was on a visit downstate, Catharine ("Kate") Mullett Hall wrote frequently, reporting all the news from weather conditions to ship arrivals, telling her sister how anxious she was about her safety in traveling by boat to the Lower Peninsula. She wrote of whortleberry pies, the berries just purchased from "an Indian who came by," and doughnuts made just before writing.

Forster, in 1861, described to his absent wife, the peregrinations of a widow they both knew. The woman, "a great *toast*," stopping at the Douglass House, was "pretty and her widows weeds are put on with artistic taste." He had not taken his wife's advice to "call on the ladies." He expressed his extreme loneliness and that he missed their little daughter. A decade later, when he returned to the Copper Country to work on the Portage Lake Ship Canal, he wrote her every evening and told her that the Lord had been very good to them and gave him "the best of earthly treasures, a kind loving wife."

In 1859, when a mine agent at Ontonagon ran off to Eagle River with a "school Madam" and after six months returned repentant, his wife "told him to wait awhile"—after which time he "might have a chance"—then departed with the children for "below."[72]

Mrs. Brockway, at the end of November 1874, recorded that she had made "969 meals this year this far." A week later, she cooked a Sunday turkey for Henry Leopold's fifty-fourth birthday, invited guests, and did not get to bed until midnight. She was proud in 1882 of her thirty hens, who hatched at least a hundred chickens. In eight months, her chickens laid 2,532 eggs. Her meticulous attention to details seems, in part, an antidote to her loneliness despite her busy days:

> July 27, 1884: I got up before seven o'clock, built a fire, fed my chickens & hens & pigs, skimmed milk and chored around generally, made a pot pie for dinner—and read 12 chapters in the bible, and when I got ready to write Mr. Ed Daniel came, then pretty soon after, Rev. Mr. Johnson came who was once Rector of this Episcopal church at Cliff. Then Mrs. Senter and children came and then we got Ed D. a lunch and then I done my chores and it was dark.[73]

When her husband sold a favorite horse of hers, she wrote: "I had a big cry over it and I shall never feel right about it. I think it was about as shabby a thing as he could well do and I do not get over it as easy as he imagines." Although he took her to Chicago and, late in life, to a spa in Tennessee and although she traveled by stage or horse and buggy to Calumet, where she bought books for grandchildren, had her picture taken, and visited, often staying overnight, nevertheless, his predilection for enterprise and financial speculation often separated them. Her frugality and sense of propriety never left her. At age sixty-six, she wrote: "September 13, 1882, I bought a pail of blue berries for fifty cents of some Indians. Were large but been picked some time."

In May 1884, she recalled how, at age eighteen, she had come with her family from Richfield, New York, to Galesburg (Kalamazoo County), Michigan. She reflected: "And now not one left to see this day but me. A solemn thought is it not?"[74] So much had changed. The Copper Country through the work of pioneers had brought forth lively, thriving communities. Houghton County, reputed now to be the wealthiest county in the state and linked to the "outside" world by rail and road, promised even better days. John Forster wrote about 1885 that the legislators at Lansing finally came to see that the Upper Peninsula was "not an out-of-the-way province too near the north pole to be of any political or social importance."[75]

One could now ride a train from Chicago to Houghton at the speed of twenty-one miles per hour. Ontonagon boosters in 1870 called a railroad "an absolute necessity"; and by 1882, a line ran the twenty miles to Rockland. In another decade, Ontonagon was connected to the nation's railways, as were Houghton, Hancock, and Calumet. The Duluth, South Shore and Atlantic (DSS&A), by 1888, and the Chicago, Milwaukee, and Saint Paul (CMSP) railroads changed life for everyone. Federal land grants helped enormously. By early winter 1883, one could leave Houghton daily at 7:30 A.M., arrive at Marquette at a quarter to one in the afternoon, and make connections for downstate. The two railroads, with much prodding from editors and civil boosters, rearranged hours and schedules until most folks found such travel satisfactory. As late as the mid-1930s, however, some still argued that DSS&A stood for "damn slow service and abuse."

By 1884, morning, afternoon, and early evening trains traveled between Hancock and Calumet—three northbound, three southbound. For those who only twenty years before snowshoed between the Keweenaw and Green Bay in snow, cold, and sleet and plunged into swamps and thickets, railway travel seemed the greatest of delights. All who had pioneered in the Keweenaw rejoiced in the daily receipt of letters, business papers, and newspapers from "down below." The rock road connecting the cluster of mines at Calumet with the Portage Lake region was transformed into a smooth macadamized thoroughfare. The once-projected military road to connect Fort Wilkins with Fort Howard at Green Bay had, by 1890, taken other forms; and despite severe winter weather at times, one traveled comfortably by stage, train, or wagon between these two places, as well as from Houghton to Ontonagon. The Ontonagon and Brule railroad connecting the port with Rockland ran its first train on the Fourth of July, 1882. Passengers traveled for five cents per mile— expensive, compared with the two-cent-per-mile fares that eventually prevailed.[76]

Summertime was a delight in the Copper Country; for one could board the iron mail steamer *Ivanhoe* at Portage Lake at 5:00 A.M. and enjoy the leisurely ride to Eagle River, visit with friends, and ride on to Eagle Harbor and Copper Harbor. In 1885, all kinds of excursions existed. For twenty-five cents, one could travel round-trip from Houghton to L'Anse on a Sunday, leaving at 11:00 A.M. and returning at 5:00 P.M. via the Marquette, Houghton, and Ontonagon Railroad, a perfect way to indulge in a picnic "on the beautiful shore of Keweenaw Bay." Such trips—sometimes unfortunately spoiled by drunken louts aboard—attracted many. Short and long excursions became part of life at Portage Lake.[77]

African American deckhands aboard Captain E. B. Ward's ships hauling copper ingots from Houghton to Detroit related their troubles in work songs:

> De Capt'ns in de pilot house a'ringin' de bell,
> An' de mate's down a'tween decks givin' de niggahs hell!
>   Who's on de way, boys,
>   Who's on de way?

. . . . It's wo'k all night an' wo'k all day,
An' all we get am not half pay

Men who worked aboard barges carrying copper to Detroit sang "The Old Mont Line," narrating voyages of the barges *Montmorency*, *Montcalm*, *Montpelier*, *Monticello*, and *Republic*, some of the lyrics being:

> There's one 'Mont', two 'Monts', four 'Monts' in a row,
> and you come to the old *Republic*, the end of the rotten tow.
> . . . .
> And when we got to Houghton, near nine o'clock one night,
> The men put up a hell of a kick and damn near had a fight,
> 'Twas all about our shoveling dirt, we wanted some extra pay,
> The Old Man said, "you can go to Hell, I'll pay you off today."
> We spent our dough at all the bars and in port there came
> Another vessel from below, and we shipped right out again.[78]

Joseph Austrian recalled a rescue mission he undertook when his line's Captain Hardy cracked mentally under stress when the *Norman* arrived at Houghton on its way, late in the season, for Isle Royale but became trapped in the Portage Lake ice floes. The *Norman*, which had left Chicago November 10, finally made its way to Duluth, arriving December 6, after first reaching Isle Royale. Austrian remembered the "fresh" meat that arrived in the 1850s at Eagle River as "anything but tempting" and the strong vinegar used by boardinghouse cooks to hide the "flavor." But refrigeration, railroads, faster ships, the ship canal, telephone, telegraph, and hosts of militant community leaders had transformed the Keweenaw Peninsula.[79]

The Civil War changed the political allegiances of many who had been Democratic in their prewar allegiances. Ransom Shelden, at first Whig, then Republican, found himself in a "hopeless minority" at Houghton prior to 1865. By 1882, an early annalist recalled Shelden's work in organizing the Republican party, "now the dominant party of [Houghton] county, State and nation." Ontonagon voters cast their ballots for Democrats in the presidential elections from 1860 to 1880, except 1872, when Ulysses S. Grant beat Horace Greeley, 218 to 161 and in 1880, when Republican James

Garfield won over the Democratic candidate, General Winfield S. Hancock. From 1854 to 1880, Ontonagon County voters cast ballots for Democratic governors, with few exceptions; the Republican won in 1858 by only ten votes![80]

John H. Forster, in August 1860, was vice-president of the Democratic Club he had helped establish. He ended one letter, "Hurrah for the Little Giant," indicating his enthusiasm for Stephen A. Douglas of Illinois in his race against Abraham Lincoln for the U.S. presidency. One finds in his letters—and in those of Samuel Robinson—much dissatisfaction with the Republicans' management of the Civil War; but once peace came, followed by Republican ascendancy favoring business, industry, and their growth, political affiliations changed. At Calumet, by 1870, men who guided the fortunes of Calumet and Hecla, including John Duncan, John Hoatson, and W. A. Childs, worked ardently for the Republicans. The local newspaper said of an October 1870 caucus at the Calumet Mine's reading room: "The proceedings were altogether novel and evidence the fact that republicans out this way, regard time as money, and don't propose to fritter it away by too much red tape." One example explains almost everything about Republican ascendancy in the Copper Country. In an 1869 diary entry, John Scott, Sarah Brockway's husband, wrote: "January 19. . . . News came this P.M. of the passage of the Copper Tariff bill— great rejoicing among the people [at Hancock–Houghton]. Stamp mills whistle and Bells Ring out the glad tidings." Only some faithful Irish and Germans adhered to "the Democracy."[81]

John H. Forster—by 1888, a gentleman farmer living downstate— toured the range from Copper Harbor to Ontonagon and found enormous change since the 1840s. The picturesque scenery and beauty of the Keweenaw remained. He found the landscape charming and the "pure air exhilarating." Now many macadamized roads allowed one to travel swiftly. From them, dirt roads from the past extended into tangled brushwood, where old shafthouses, adits, decaying log houses, and abandoned mine buildings met the eye. He observed that the "owl and porcupine are the only denizens of the place." Such were the scenes near Copper Harbor, where second-growth timber covered clearings. At Lac La Belle, much of the denuded land looked absolutely deserted. A few guards moved about idly, without aim. "A melancholy stillness pervades the scene," he noted.

Once busy, attractive Copper Harbor was now "a deserted village." Eagle Harbor lay in half-ruined condition. Nearby, one or two mines still worked feebly. Central Mine looked good; but between it and the Cliff, Forster saw many abandoned mines. The Cliff was silent, for water filled its shafts and drifts. The center of work and

John H. Forster, mine manager, explorer, engineer, historian. (Michigan Historical Collections, Bentley Historical Library, The University of Michigan.)

prosperity was Houghton County, where the Quincy, Calumet and Hecla, Osceola, and Tamarack Mines continued with phenomenal yields. In Ontonagon County, miners had taken to farming; for here the same lamentable conditions prevailed, with ruin and decay everywhere among mines like the great Mendota, whose "glory had departed." In once-vital villages and locations, only "a seedy, dejected look" remained which made Forster wonder whether "life is worth living" here.[82]

The fiftieth wedding anniversary celebration of Lucena and Daniel J. Brockway at Calumet's Armory on January 21, 1886, symbolized the past great work of pioneers and hopes for an even better future. Over three hundred guests attended, many writing the year of their arrival in the Keweenaw in the homemade guest book. The Brockways, seated under a bell of gilt and flowers ordered specially from Chicago, welcomed the pioneer elite: the Vivians, Hoatsons, Van Ordens, Duncans, Daniels, Dymocks, Coopers, Urens, people from Copper Harbor, Hancock, Houghton, Laurium, Lake Linden, Ontonagon, and Calumet. Daughter Sally (Sarah), born at L'Anse and the oldest living white person born at Lake Superior, joined sister Anna, now a physician, two other sisters (the younger attired in her mother's dress of fifty years before), and their brother Albert. The twelve grandchildren enjoyed the music by the Calumet Cornet Band; and after a banquet held in sections of over one hundred each, dancing continued until four the next morning.

One of Daniel Brockway's extended journeys (in this case six months) took him to the Dakota Black Hills, when he caught the "gold fever" in 1879. Now he and Lucena received gifts of gold: candleholders, "salts," ice cream spoons, cups and saucers, a card receiver, a thimble, a golden toothpick, and fifteen hundred dollars in gold coins. Guests admired an oil painting, *The Old Copper Harbor Home* presented by one daughter and her husband; and many recalled the arduous but adventurous past. The gala occasion made all reflect upon what had been done and the great things yet to come in the Michigan Copper Country.[83]

5

Ethnicity and Singularity

AMERICANS, CORNISH, CANADIAN FRENCH, IRISH, Germans, Scots, Scandinavians, a "sprinkling" of Italians, "half-breeds," and others—drifters "from the old kingdoms of Europe" in many cases—drawn by economic opportunities offered by copper: such were the people of the Keweenaw as viewed by a historian in 1887. People with "a diversity of languages, habits and customs," retaining many ethnic characteristics but fusing harmoniously, they were an ethnic conglomerate homologous to the "variety of minerals, the wreck of older formations . . . connected and tied together by the shining native copper."[1]

Americans from northeastern states promoted an aggressive capitalism linked with a democratic republicanism led by an Anglo-American Protestant elite. European immigrants, most of them strangers to political participation in their homelands, succumbed gradually to the novel idea that American individualism in the developing society demanded that they participate and abandon much of their past. Communal life, respect for authority, and a lingering dependence on social welfare in continental European villages boded well for the growth of "a remarkably well-conducted" paternalism by copper companies at various communities along the mineral range.

The dominance of Cornish miners initially led to their insistence on medical treatment, physicians, and hospitals between 1845 and 1890. From this evolved fairly elaborate policies whereby employers displayed concern for employees who contributed small, fixed amounts from monthly pay for personal and family assistance such as disability benefits, low-rent housing, pensions, and various services, including fire fighting and garbage collection. Emigrants from Slavic hamlets, Finnish socialists, Germans, Italians, French Canadians, and others accustomed to a lingering feudal heritage espousing the organic community accepted much of the "benevolent paternalism." Ironically, schools promoted by copper companies and the powerful currents of nineteenth-century American republicanism championed by the ruling Anglo-American citizenry worked diametrically against forms of social cohesion and dependency.

The federal government's numerous attempts to acculturate Native Americans corresponded with the Copper Country's public and parochial schools' insistence on allegiance to the new country. Books such as *McGuffey's New Sixth Eclectic Reader* introduced pupils to English political liberalism and American love of liberty, equality, and union. Girls and boys reciting Fitz-Greene Halleck's "Red Jacket, the Indian Chief" expressed the great man's love for the land, hatred of missionaries, pride in martial prowess, hope that the Great Spirit would right wrongs done by whites, and the author's sorrow over the natives' loss of liberty. The entire poem, along with odes to Pulaski and Poland's suppression by Russia, simply reinforced American ideals of liberty.[2] Various ethnic groups helped transform the Copper Country, while its dominant institutions and Anglo-American ethos worked on them and their children.

Migrants scrambled for advantage in the Keweenaw Peninsula's economic hurly-burly. Here one might, with one's spouse, shape a life superior to one in the East, where often "the pay of a common laborer was insufficient to enable [a man] to support his family without outside assistance."[3] To work in the copper mines or the contiguous service industries meant helping create the United States as an economic power.

Samuel Robinson, writing in 1864 from Quincy Mine, thanked the directors for promoting immigration and hoped the first arrivals constituted precursors of many needed " to develop and work all of the country." Robinson had no use for agents greedy for fees, men who told Europeans "anything necessary to induce them to emigrate." He felt that potential emigrants should be told of possibilities in trades, in forest, and on farms, since their employment at Quincy Mine depended on the mercurial prospects "for marketing copper." Farmers could live on cheap "well-timbered land with a good soil [and have] a ready market for the wood or timber." The healthy climate, abundance of work, and good pay should convince emigrants that the Keweenaw, more than any other place in the United States, was the place to come. Robinson exclaimed: "Here is room for them all: let them fish and farm or labor at the mines as they prefer. They can buy up whole townships if they choose and settle by themselves with their ministers." He described prevailing wages: $2.50–3.00 for a ten-hour day for miners, carpenters, and blacksmiths; from $1.75–2.00 for millmen and other laborers. Board was $ .66–.75 a day. The federal government owned most of the land that could be purchased for $1.25–4.00 an acre, most for $1.25.[4]

Quincy wanted men with families from central and northern Europe. Immigration agents signed up some "Swedes" who were actually Finns. At Portage Entry, by 1887, Finns already predominated, having settled at Jacobsville in 1885 and bought timberland from a Mr. Ruonavaara, described as a "good businessman" employing more than one hundred men in the woods on land he secured through the Homestead Act. A reporter described Finns as stoical and reserved, "broad-shouldered people," and often given to drink, but intelligent and frugal, with a "pertinacious adherence to their customs—properties not in harmony with the prevailing tendency toward general amalgamation as regards the other elements of the [Lake Superior] country."[5] Finns slowly accommodated to the dominant American culture with its language, law, representative government, and economic liberalism derived from England and, in so doing, helped transform that culture by maintaining singular cultural artifacts.

In contrast to the gradual process of acculturation which was almost imperceptible in 1885 (though far advanced by 1930, and so accelerated by 1940 that some feared a liquidation of ethnic cultural components), the Anglo-American gestalt prevailed. Charles Briggs was typical. Born in upstate New York in 1837 of "good old New England stock," his grandfather a Harvard graduate and clergyman, his father a prominent Massachusetts physician, Briggs came to Wisconsin to live with an uncle at Geneva and received a good business training. He located first in Ontonagon County and came to Calumet in 1868, serving in two different merchandising partnerships. By 1887, he was sole owner of a general merchandise store at Red Jacket; he was also president of E. F. Sutton Company, dealers in general merchandise at Lake Linden, president of the Merchants and Miners National Bank, member of the Calumet Township School Board, and a stalwart Republican "unwavering in support of his party and its principles." In 1879–80, Briggs represented his district at Lansing. By 1895, usually too busy to give time and attention to public office, Briggs typified many in the Keweenaw profiting from economic expansion. Described as "a man of pleasing address, genial disposition and gentlemanly deportment," he had also "a genuine interest in his fellow men."[6]

A great portion of the copper wealth flowed to New England and eastern shareholders. As early as 1875, eight hundred shareholders owned eighty thousand shares of Calumet and Hecla stock, with thirteen of the eight hundred controlling thirty-four thousand shares. The Shaw, Agassiz, Higginson, and Cabot families of Boston alone held 27,701 shares, or about 35 percent of the stock. There was an occasional caustic newspaper editorial about absentee ownership and socialist complaints from 1905 to 1915 about this outflow of wealth.

Almost from the beginning, counties had superintendents of the poor. Despite their acceptance of liberalism's central idea of progress with its hope of a possible elimination of poverty, most people accepted the Christian scripture's "For ye have the poor always with you," and the Hebrew scripture's "Oppress not the widow, nor the fatherless, the stranger, nor the poor." Bourgeois respectability demanded standards that working people accepted for the most part, although few wished to imitate the Hancock woman who on New Year's Day, 1872, gloated over surpassing a Houghton rival when she received over 372 holiday callers. The Copper Country bourgeoisie, firmly in control by then, did not set all mores.[7]

Middle-class people condemned the sale of liquor to Native Americans. Why did the authorities not do something, they asked in 1872, when Charlotte Ka-wa-zi-na died of exposure in a barn south of L'Anse after sharing two bottles of whiskey with her husband, whose toes had to be amputated later. Racism fused with sentimentality permeated many minds by the 1880s. Andreas' history states that people in Michigan generally accepted as truth that "the only good Indian is a dead Indian," adding that beneath savage exterior, however, there beat hearts "capable of the most tender feeling." Bishop Baraga had become a legend: "He was as attentive to the spiritual wants of the poorest Indian child as he would be those of any grown person, whether white or Indian. With him color or nationality or social position counted for nothing—the soul was all."[8]

Amalgamation, having begun in the 1650s, proceeded apace among whites and Native Americans. In 1826, Lewis Cass found, in a large lodge on the banks of the Ontonagon River, a French trader married to a "fine-looking Indian woman" dressed in calico, with short gown, blue petticoat, "ornamented scarlet leggins, and handsomely ornamented moccasins." Their five children ranged in age from one to six. By 1860, in Houghton County, of 279 persons listed as "Indians," many had entered "mixed" marriages. Native American women and "halfbreeds" married white or black men of American and foreign descent.

In an 1860 sampling of 151 Native Americans, selected by names, about 25 percent had so married. Many of the women, born in Wis-

consin, Canada, or Michigan, did needlework or assisted their fishermen husbands at Keweenaw Bay. They lived in Houghton village, at
Eagle River, or at scattered sites in Portage Township. Mary Steven-
son, age twenty-two, was married to forty-five-year-old Samuel, born
in England and a lighthouse keeper with real estate valued at a
thousand dollars. Margaret Beasely, age twenty-nine, had married a
Prussian laborer, age thirty-eight. All three of their children, ages one
to four, were born in Michigan. Josette Forsier, age thirty, married
a Canadian cooper, Peter, then age forty-six, and their five children
ranged in age from two to seventeen. That meant Josette bore son
Campbell when she was thirteen. At Keweenaw Bay, Mary Sinclair,
married to Francis, a fisherman, bore the first of her six children when
she was twelve and her husband twenty-seven.

Census data (1860) show that most Native Americans residing at
Keweenaw Bay made their living by fishing or hunting. As of 1888,
some Native Americans still lived along Portage River. In the Portage
Lake district, a dozen miners, machinists, woodchoppers, and laborers
of European or American extraction had married Native American
women.[9]

By the late nineteenth century, whites romanticized early experiences of Native Americans, the most spectacular story being that of
Battle Island, where Iroquois allegedly attacked Ojibwa about 1730
near Portage Entry. Francis Jacker, an early historian, said he got
the story from Madelaine Nibinekwadokwe, widow of Chief Wabos,
who had assisted Britain's King George III in the American War of
1812. She told Jacker she had the story from her grandfather Ojinini,
a mere boy at the time, who with a playmate hid in the hemlock
forest three miles above the entry as the Ojibwa, suspecting an attack,
rushed from ambush and with arrows and tomahawks killed some
sixty Iroquois who had followed the Ojibwa from Montreal after a
trading expedition.

Fortunately, Madelaine had met her lover, who, upon leaving, noticed the approaching Iroquois eager to slaughter the Ojibwa sleeping
peacefully under "mellow moonlight [while] from the dark recesses
of the woods, the hooting of the owl reverberated, answered . . .
by the sudden splash of a diving muskrat." Thus, a lovers' tryst
led to the Ojibwa victory over their eternal foe, "the last contest
between these two tribes which is on record." The improbable story
entered the folklore of the Copper Country, as did another whose
locale was the Huron Mountains, northwest of L'Anse. Jacker also
told this story of natives who practiced cannibalism, the perpetra-
tor being the woman Wazhashkons. After one rampage devouring
men, women, and children, she disappeared in her cave, then dashed
off via canoe, probably to live with relatives near the head of Lake

Superior. Asked if he thought the story were true, Jacker replied that he believed it, as the tale exemplified the struggle for existence, and the "Indian mind works with laws of nature." As late as 1950, the kettle that Wazhashkons allegedly used for her peculiar cuisine was in Houghton's Carnegie Library.[10]

In a paper read by John Chassell before the Houghton County Historical Society in April, 1872, the Reverend Edward Jacker, a student of Native American culture, argued that the Ojibwa mind, uncomfortable with dualism, rejected that philosophical concept because it recognized the "apparent disorder and eternal feud between the conservative and destructive agencies in the moral as well as the physical world."

Thomas McKenney in 1826 noticed the grave of an "Indian child," a flat stone on earth surmounted by a small wooden cross with carving in rude letters, mixing English and French: "Alexi Cadotte, *Mort*, 13 months, August 18, 1818."[11] By 1860, offspring of Native American coupling with members of other ethnic groups bore names such as Arthur, Alexander, John, Julia, Antonin, Michael, Peter, Mary, Agatha, Moses, Nancy, and Margaret. These names proliferated also among Native American families. The days when strangers like Ben, a member of the Cass expedition, trembled in his apprehension because the absence of Native Americans seemed more dangerous than their presence, seemed remote. In 1888, Native Americans identified relics unearthed at the Redstone Quarry Company at Portage Entry: The well-preserved skull and femora of a Native American buried some seventy years, a stone pipe, iron kettle, wooden ladle and bowl, a silver cross, and a small, covered, copper bowl filled with moose tallow.[12]

According to some antiquarians, Torch Lake received its name from French Canadians who observed gleams of light in the darkness on the opposite shore caused by Ojibwa moving about peaceably, carrying torches. French Canadians monopolized surface work in mining, building shaft houses, and cutting white pine timber used underground to buttress drifts. Proverbial woodsmen, they also produced numerous merchants. Fearing much would be lost, Eugene S. Vacher announced in June 1874 an evening class in French at the Calumet schoolhouse for "those desirous of learning to speak and write it in its native purity." French Canadians were prolific people: Mr. and Mrs. Peter Beaudoin of Allouez had their twenty-eighth child baptized at Red Jacket's "French" church in June 1896. The mother, age forty-four, had married at age sixteen and bore twins six times. Only eleven of the twenty-eight children survived, but the parents rejoiced that all had been baptized.[13]

Migration from Quebec continued. Madame E. Montaigne arrived in 1897, with daughters ages nine and twenty and sons ages twelve, sixteen, and thirty-one, to join three sons who had arrived eight years earlier. A widow, Madame Montaigne operated a boardinghouse in Calumet Township in 1900, for seven French Canadian laborers, ages twenty-one to thirty-five. None of the Montaigne children were married as of 1900, and the daughters worked as servants. The eldest son, age thirty-four, worked on the railroad; of his brothers, one was an engineer, others teamsters, blacksmiths, and laborers.

The French Canadian Saint Louis parish, set off from that of Sacred Heart in August 1884, consisted in 1896 of 260 families with 900 communicants and 582 noncommunicants under twelve years of age. A small school housed seventy-five pupils. The larger French Saint Anne's Catholic Church, later dominating the south end of Red Jacket's main street, was in close proximity to Swedish Lutheran, Presbyterian, and Episcopal churches. Years later, some referred to the area as God's Little Acre, though one of the churches had become a warehouse and Saint Anne's, an empty shell.

Oliver Torganeau came to the Portage Lake wilderness from Canada in 1839, when he was sixteen, and worked as pattern maker for Calumet and Hecla from 1875 until his death in 1895. He was a trustee at the Sacred Heart Church. Thomas Beauchaine worked for the company for more than thirty years, an old and respected employee who died at age eighty-two in 1907. Dolphus Tourville came from Canada in 1886 and worked as day laborer at Hancock. Their compatriots lived throughout the Copper Country with large concentrations at Lake Linden and Calumet by the early twentieth century.[14]

Francis E. Monette was *marchand de vins, liquers, cigares et glaces* on Rue Shelden, Houghton; Pierre Primeau, protonotary there; Joseph Gregoire, supervisor; and L. A. Gillet, P. Robert, and J. B. Toupin, *conseillers,* at Lake Linden, in 1891. Treffele Homier, proprietor of the Quebec House and Restaurant, competed with three other French restaurants in Hancock and with two each in Houghton and Lake Linden. J. R. Jacques's Pension et Restaurant stood near Saint Patrick's Hall and advertised "Repas a toutes heures." Francois O. Mayotte, chief of police at Lake Linden at age thirty-five and born in the province of Quebec in 1856, came to the Lake Superior district in 1881, ten years before assuming his duties.[15]

L'Union Franco-Américaine, with headquarters at Lake Linden, was only one of many organizations that worked at preserving French culture. Each year, Saint Jean Baptiste Day (June 24) found French societies out in force accompanied by cornet bands. Morning mass, picnics, and village streets "festooned with flags of different nations" and arches of evergreens marked the day, surpassing even the usually festive Fourth of July decorations.

Dolphus Tourville family, Hancock, 1909. (Michigan Technological University Archives and Copper Country Historical Collections, Michigan Technological University.)

Hancock and Houghton hosted the 1914 Saint Jean Baptiste Day celebration at Electric Park; the Reverend Father Arthur Deschenes of Montreal preached the sermon at Hancock's Saint Joseph's Church. Dinner, concerts, a speech by the Honorable Hector Laferte of Quebec, a parade of chapters of the Saint Jean de Baptiste Society from various villages, songs, and more speeches filled the day, which ended with dancing at the park's pavilion. The society leased Tamarack Park, west of Calumet, and in 1908 changed its name to Saint Jean de Baptiste Park. In June, 1919, women of Saint Anne's parish served *un banquet superbe* free to all men in uniform. Earlier, a parade featured people in costume representing Joan of Arc, Cartier, Lafayette, and Saint John the Baptist. Young men in uniform carried flags of Franco-American parishes. The 1928 midnight mass at Lake Linden's Saint Joseph's Church featured Vito Cornavali's "Rosa Mystica," with the choir assisted by the Calumet Theatre Orchestra and Edna Briere, organist.[16]

French Canadians had been among the first nonnatives to join the Native Americans in the Keweenaw Peninsula as they trod the paths of fur trader and French missionary. Groups of Cornish miners clustered in the northern part of the Keweenaw Peninsula in the 1840s as mining began. A "colony" of Germans—three hundred of them—was established around the Minesota Mine in 1859. The Civil War, a time of a major labor shortage at the copper mines, opened the doors of the peninsula to an avalanche of European immigrants.

A look at the origins of the Keweenaw Peninsula population shows the great diversity of inhabitants. Joining Anglo-Americans and African Americans from many sections of this country and Native Americans came people from the British Isles—from Cornwall and parts of England, Scotland, and Wales. Others were Germans, Austrians, Belgians, Bohemians, Bulgarians, Croatians, Danes, Dutch, Finns, French, Greeks, Hungarians, Irish, Italians, Lithuanians, Norwegians, Poles, Rumanians, Russians, Slovaks, Slovenians, Swedes, and Swiss. Still other emigrants were Armenians, Turks, Syrians, Chinese, Japanese, and Australians. This hemisphere was represented not only by French Canadians but also by English-speaking Canadians, Mexicans, and West Indians. Censuses do not list precise origins of a few Asian-born. Such was the ethnic tide between 1650 and 1930. The Calumet public schools in 1908 enrolled children of forty different nationalities.

In 1870, of the 7,869 foreign-born (57 percent) in Houghton County's total population, Irish constituted 31 percent; English, 22 percent; Germans, 18 percent; and Swedes and Norwegians, 5 percent. Forty years later, the foreign-born totaled 33,333 (38 percent) of the county's total population; Irish made up 2 percent; English, 13 percent; Germans, 5 percent; Swedes and Norwegians, 8 percent. By 1910, Finns, Italians, and Slavs had made impressive changes in the county's ethnic configuration. In 1870, 51 percent of Keweenaw County's population and 40 percent of Ontonagon's was foreign-born. Baraga County (not organized until 1875) had a foreign-born population of 31 percent in 1880.[17]

The Irish, driven from their island by famine and oppression in the 1840s, came in considerable numbers. The Cornish found them volatile. Many Irish who began as miners became successful merchants or proprietors of livery stables. Edward Ryan with his Hancock and Red Jacket stores achieved outstanding merchandising success. Many found their way eventually into local politics. Finns and Italians who arrived later often chose the Republican party as their vehicle partly because of their envy of, and hatred for, the Irish.

C. H. O'Rourke, born at the Norwich Mine in Ontonagon County in 1859, was the fifth of twelve children whose parents settled nine years earlier. O'Rourke began as a teamster, worked as a blacksmith in the iron country, built bridges and roads in Gogebic County,

and published the *Knights of Labor* newspaper in 1886, when he
also became sheriff of Ontonagon County for four years. Later, he
served as county treasurer. In 1890, he went to Ewen, engaged in
the livery business, and opened a stage line from Ewen to Choate.
M. A. Powers, Ontonagon County Clerk in 1895, born in New
York in 1845 of Irish parents who arrived in Michigan that year,
began work as a carpenter, and lived in Vermont, Ohio, Minnesota,
and Wisconsin, before arriving in Hancock in 1858. He worked
in the mines there, then in the Franklin stamp mill, where he lost
his left arm, went to school in Canada, and returned to Houghton
when he was twenty, in 1865. The ambitious Powers moved soon to
Ontonagon and worked as hotel clerk, then a mining company clerk
until 1868, when he was elected county clerk and recorder of deeds.
In his leisure, he studied law and was admitted to the bar at age fifty.
He was married to an American of German descent; the couple raised
four daughters and three sons. Powers was a staunch Republican.

Patrick H. O'Brien was not. He began work at age fourteen in the
Osceola Mine, taught school, studied law, became the workingman's
advocate, and eventually circuit judge. His prominent role in the
1913–14 strike was the culmination of years in which he sought
justice and financial remuneration for injured copper workers and
widows of men who perished in mines. After the strike, O'Brien
became an attorney in Detroit; and eventually, Michigan's attorney
general. John O'Connor, born in 1841 in Ireland's County Cork,
came to the United States in 1852, fought in the Civil War, settled in
Houghton afterward, and held office in both Houghton and Baraga
counties. An aggressive realtor, he lived in L'Anse. Dennis Coughlin,
born in County Cork in 1832, was working at age fourteen in Irish
mines before coming to Eagle Harbor at age twenty. He worked
in numerous mines; lived in the first house built in Hancock; and,
after eight years in a mine there, embarked in the express business, in
which eventually he utilized thirty teams of horses. His son Thomas
took over the livery business when Coughlin decided to retire before
he was sixty years old.[18]

The Irish for decades celebrated Saint Patrick's Day with a great
parade, religious services, and much drinking. Hancock for many
years witnessed assemblages of Irish and Irish Americans from all
parts of the Keweenaw. Many Irish moved to Butte, Montana, or
cities "below" when economic conditions deteriorated after 1920.
But many Irish couples, such as Honora and Peter Murphy, raised
their families in the Keweenaw. Their children were Mary, Michael,
William, Jeremiah, Peter, James, and John.[19]

When the Frimodig family emigrated to Quincy Mine in 1871, in
search of better pay than that earned at the Altens copper mines at

Kaafjord, Norway, they joined miners they had known there. They brought a seventy-eight-year-old grandmother. Isaac Frimodig, who had begun work at age eleven in Norway attended school briefly, then worked at the Quincy, Calumet and Hecla, Centennial, and Osceola Mines before entering the mercantile business at Red Jacket. By 1894, he was elected by Republicans to serve as Houghton County treasurer. A member of several lodges, including the Finnish Kaleva Benevolent Society, he also championed prohibition. He returned to Norway when he was twenty-one, worked for two years, married, and came back to the Copper Country.

Some Norwegians left for California in 1896 to work in orchards; a group of them purchased land, dividing it evenly as they began new livelihoods after eight to fifteen years of labor at Calumet and Hecla. As long as they lived in the Keweenaw, Norwegians celebrated their independence day each May, established a thriving Norwegian Lutheran Church, created the Viking Glee Club, and sometimes imported well-known Scandinavian American contraltos and tenors to perform at local theaters.[20]

Norwegians were often confused with the Swedes, who were among the area's pioneers. The Swedish Benevolent Society was foremost in assisting Swedes in times of sickness and death. Most Swedes had Lutheran affiliations, although some belonged to the Swedish Methodist Episcopal Church. When the Finns began arriving soon after the Civil War, Swedes shared their churches with them. All celebrated holidays they had known in the old country. The Juleotta (Christmas) service, most sacred to the Swedish Methodists, began at six on Christmas morning. Swedish women, among the most progressive socially, formed the Swedish Woman's Club in 1902. They cooperated with activists among Finnish women, insisting on social legislation to benefit their families and worked to procure the vote for women. Many of the Scandinavians excelled in carpentry and found jobs at mining companies and in small manufactories, turning out doors, sashes, and other wood products.[21]

Judge O'Brien remembered Germans as mechanics, adept with machinery, distinguished-looking men who would enter mine shafts "with beautiful drilling clothes." Mining was a stepping-stone for them. John H. Forster summed up the situation as early as 1887:

> The German makes a capable miner but he does not stick to the business long after coming to this [Lake Superior] country. He prefers to keep store, run a hotel or saloon, and manage a brewery. He is convivial but looks out for the main chance, accumulates property and becomes an alderman.

German emigration slowed, and World War I halted the flow; but a new wave of Germans brought several hundred in 1923–24. Germania Hall at Hancock in the 300-block of West Quincy Street saw numerous festive gatherings for decades. At Lake Linden, the Maennerchor Liederkranz sponsored a grand ball at the Opera House just before Lent began in 1898. Scott's popular orchestra of Calumet played, a special feature being a number of old-style German cotillions. Next day, the faithful wended their way to churches for ashes or long sermons at German Lutheran evening services held on each Wednesday of Lent.[22]

About twenty-five years after the Lutheran Church–Missouri Synod organized in 1847 in that state, Germans at Hancock organized. Their Saints Peter and Paul Lutheran Church was the mother church of Saint Paul of Laurium–Calumet. Pastors named Wuebben and Wambsganss lived in Hancock but carried on mission work north of there and in the southern part of Keweenaw County. Once known as the German church, Saint Paul's became the English Lutheran (the adjective was used in the 1920s and 1930s) about the time of World War I, when Germania Hall became Lincoln Hall and Copper Country high schools dropped the teaching of the German language. In a Calumet bakery, as late as the 1930s, the jelly-filled doughnuts known as Bismarcks became Pershings (after America's general).

Saint Paul's pastors preached some sermons in German, alternating with English, until about 1930, when the pastor announced at a funeral service that this would be the last time preaching in German would be heard. In the beginning, nothing but the native language was used, typical of the "ethnic" churches in the Keweenaw. Young Henry Fedderson, a Detroit German who became a coachman for a Calumet and Hecla official, walked the twelve miles from Calumet to Hancock each Sunday simply to worship in a church in 1872. He persuaded Hancock clergy to hold services in homes of Lutherans at Calumet until the growing congregation built its own church on Scott Street, Red Jacket, in 1881, on land leased from Calumet and Hecla. To preserve Germanic culture, the pioneers organized a parochial school. By 1887, they built a church addition used solely as a school. When the company requested them to vacate the Red Jacket lot, the German Lutherans built an imposing, larger structure in Laurium. By the early twentieth century, an altar with elaborate wood carving, three steeple bells, and an organ enhanced this church. The Reverend Andrew S. Lucas attracted non-German communicants; in the 1930s, his Holy Week preaching at the Calumet Theatre proved a novel experiment in evangelism. W. E. Maas, its pastor in 1954, recalled then that Saint Paul's had, at one time, communicants of fourteen different nationalities.

Like Finns, Scandinavians, and French Canadians, Germans created aesthetic practical things in wood, carving and painting chairs, tables, cabinets, and numerous novelties to adorn homes and halls. Otto Dietze, who came to work in the mines in 1923 spent a year-and-a-half building a model carousel with miniature horses, chariots, hand-painted scenes, mirrors, crystal, and electric lights. The Keckonen Hardware Store at Calumet featured this merry-go-round in its windows one Christmas. A Painesdale artificer molded lead soldiers and painted them in the early 1930s, much to the delight of some Calumet boys until they showed them to English-American playmates, who gasped, "Those are *German* soldiers!"[23]

Leslie Chapman's grandmother operated a candy shop in Red Jacket and had brought her "secret recipe" for candy when she migrated from England in 1852. Chapman recalled his mother's herbal remedies, made from her garden: "You got more out of that," he explained, "than going to doctors and paying $10.00 for an examination and some pills that won't do you any good."[24]

Catholics found strange the English-Cornish observance of Good Friday, which had "always been looked upon as the Englishman's day in Calumet and vicinity," according to the *Mining Gazette* in 1908. Lodges of the Sons of Saint George paraded and ate a big supper that day, followed by entertainment. South Range hosted the Copper Country lodges in 1914. The grand climax came with a concert at the Painesdale Methodist Episcopal Church. Participating lodges were W. E. Gladstone (Mohawk), General Butler (Houghton), Mistletoe (Hancock and Quincy), George Washington (Lake Linden), and One and All (Calumet). South Range's lodge was Duke of Wellington, Sons of Saint George. Members of the Duchess of Wellington Lodge, Daughters of Saint George, served the meal. For decades, Saint George's Day, April 23, was celebrated with parades, banquets, and concerts. Saffron cake (baked in a loaf pan so that it looked like bread), its yellow texture rich with raisins or currants, remained a favorite among those of English descent. Mrs. Claire Moyer, recalling some forty years later that non-English people in the Copper Country sometimes called it saffron *bread*, exclaimed, "I nearly die when I hear such sacrilege!"[25]

Scots excelled as merchants and entrepreneurs. In a sampling of prominent citizens of Houghton County in 1882, seventy were born in Great Britain, 26 percent of them in Scotland. Forster described them in 1887: the Scots "are canny bodies, and succeed in the mines as elsewhere, but most of them, like the Yankees, prefer to work above the ground." The Saint Andrew's Society of the Scots sponsored picnics with highland dances and games, including always a tug-of-war. Annually on January 27, they commemorated, with poetry and

feasts, the birthday of Robert Burns. Bannockburn Camp, Sons of
Scotland, offered such "a grand entertainment" in 1896 that the
merrymaking was moved to the Red Jacket Opera House so that
even more Scots could toast Bobby Burns with song and verse.
Their Presbyterian religion's emphasis on striving for moral perfection
assisted local Puritanism in all the range towns.[26]

The Cornish—the most prominent group at the inauguration of
mining in the northern tip of the Keweenaw Peninsula—also played
important roles in developing Upper Peninsula iron mines. Mining
seemed almost intuitive for men from Cornwall in southwestern England. How they learned their profession, or when, is as nebulous as
the fogs that so frequently visited both Cornwall and the Keweenaw.
They had a voluminous vocabulary of mining terms: *adit, shaft, kibble,
collar, burrow, pass, gob, jig.* To "taper-off" meant to "rest from
work." They had little schooling. Most, by the time they reached
age ten, worked nine or more hours in Cornish copper or tin mines.
Yet, it was said of them that they possessed "the mathematics of the
mole," with an unusual sense of direction underground. Asked by a
supervisor how he had arrived at results to solve a problem obviously
requiring trigonometry, a Cornish miner answered, "Why, Sir . . . I
tell 'ee I mizured 'im up brave and careful, and I found the length of
un was two showl [shovel] hilts, three picks, a mallet, four lil' stones
and so far as I cud spit, jus' zachly." He nudged his coworker as he
spoke. Perhaps a practical joke, for the Cornish played them often,
with subtle sardonicism.[27]

The Keweenaw, with its copper riches, seemed almost heaven-sent
for the Cornish, whose tin and copper mines in Cornwall reached
a peak of production, with some mines nearing exhaustion, in the
1840s. The first of the Cornish in the Keweenaw loved strong drink
and a good fight. One of their historians described them as "tall,
muscular, upright, with sort of a swaggering gait about them," with
never a complaint about hard work, their spirits low only when a lag
in the copper industry brought temporary unemployment. Professor
James Fisher said, "Of fighting, feasting, and fasting there was much,
but of murders and robberies almost none." Schoolmaster Henry
Hobart at Cliff Mine, in July, 1863, recorded his view of Cornish
women in his diary:[28]

An old English [Cornish] woman is as tight as the bark to a tree
& the perfection of tyranny in her management always boasting
about how smart she is & how her hired help & everyone else
are good for nothing . . . .The children of such a woman are
self-conceited, tyrannical, foolish, silly things who are superior
to everyone in their own minds.

He was not the first to resent what he considered a superior air assumed by the Cornish. Finns and other peoples at times bristled in mentioning the Cornish and used the term Cousin Jack derisively. The Cornish coined the term simply to describe the Cornish miner. The Cornish went their way, nonplussed by what anyone thought. Their confidence is shown in such proverbs as "A miner has nothing to lose" and the miner is "never broke till his neck's broke." Several generations later, about 1937, a Calumet High School youth wrote to a Slovenian classmate, saying initially, "Let a good Cornishman set you, an Austrian, straight."

Many of the Cornish invested small earnings in the mines that employed them. They resented patronage. A visitor once tipped a Cornish miner a dollar for explaining work procedures. The miner spat on the money and stuck the bill to the end of lumber loaded on a skip so that the demeaning gift would be lost in the earth. Some described the Cornish as "gruff in speech, forceful and rough in manner, with fear . . . for no man." Yet they were among the most mellifluous of Christmas carolers, sometimes to a flute accompaniment, on Copper Country village streets.[29]

In the Keweenaw, newcomers from Cornish villages found warm welcomes. If in financial want, Copper Country Cornish assisted them; and once established, they helped other Cornish immigrants. The Cornish, envied by some, displayed courtesy, hospitality, and civility to strangers. Witty, sometimes sarcastic, they expressed thoughts creatively. In the 1850s, Jinny Penhale, at the Northwest Mine, south of Cat Harbor, between Eagle River and Eagle Harbor, told relatives in Cornwall of life in the Keweenaw, using rhyme in her letters:

> We're livven at the North West-Mine
> And eer we found old Stephen Vine
> And Joey Blewett and lots more
> We war acquainted with before;
> And they were glad to see us too,
> And gov us hall a tastie stew;
> And cooked a oggon and a caake
> And put a pasty in to bake
> And gov us coffee and good tay
> And made us appy right away

She and her family eventually returned to Cornwall, where they amused relatives and friends with tales of their American experiences in Keweenaw's wilderness. Many of the Michigan Cornish drifted to western mines in the late nineteenth and early twentieth centuries, but a core and their descendants left an indelible imprint. A Copper Country newspaper in the 1880s printed a weekly column of news from Cornwall, including prices of mine shares there, "carefully collated from [Cornish newspapers] giving the items of interest from the different towns for the benefit of our Cornish readers."[30]

Finns published several newspapers in their own language and sometimes referred to well-known English-language newspapers like the *Daily Mining Gazette* as "the Cousin Jack papers." To many people in Michigan today, the Copper Country is known as the land of Finns and the Cornish. Of the seven members who made up the first class to graduate from the Michigan Mining School, five were sons of Cornish mining captains.

As Americanization proceeded, the descendants of the Cornish became even more self-conscious of their culture. Their pasty—the meat pie filled with potatoes, white turnip, onions, and diced beef— became a hallmark of Copper Country cuisine. An advertisement for the Cornish picnic in 1934 at Electric Park read, "Whether you are from St. Anstell, Camborne, Mevagissey, or [are] a 'Devonshire dumplin' makes no difference, for we are all together on this big Cornish picnic." Competition in Cornish wrestling (popular for decades in the Keweenaw), boxing, cricket, softball, horseshoes, and baseball comprised the sports activities open to "men only who are Cornish or of English descent." Some two thousand people attended. But the times were changing, and by the 1950s, community residents debated whether Cornish or Finns had invented the pasty![31]

Deeply religious, the Cornish exuded enthusiasm and produced fluent and original speakers, lay preachers, men who mined all week and then delivered "eloquent, earnest sermons." Extemporaneous prayer at Methodist meetings, with members calling out "Glory to God!" or "Amen!" or "Thanks be to God!" resounded at the Cliff and Central Mine located about seven miles east of the Cliff. Central Mine opened in 1854 and operated until 1898; ten years later, the company went out of existence. The mining company had helped build a Methodist Church in 1868, seating about 200, and the Sunday School reported 338 members in 1890. At Christmas there was a huge tree with small presents affixed for the girls and boys. John R. Bennetts once received a pocket knife, his friend Billie Hall, a pair of suspenders. In summer, while fishing, Billie fell into the creek; his mother scolded him when she saw the soaking wet suspenders, telling him the suspenders were "intended to hold your pants up in going to Sunday school."

Bennetts recalled his father's renting a four-seater canopy-top wagon in which the family, joined by others, drove to Fort Wilkins, where they slept on the floor of deserted barracks after playing all day. "Father seemed as young as we Boys and Girls," Bennetts wrote years later. The temperance lodge formed at Central in 1882 provided the main social affair weekly at Philanthropy Hall. Here, also, the young delighted in dances, though frowned upon by Methodists generally. Some Central folks turned an old building into an indoor ice rink and held masquerades, with music supplied by Bung Ivey playing the mouth organ.[32]

After 1907, families who once lived at Central began annual reunions. They attract hundreds to this day. The Central Church in its heyday (1868–98) served as a vibrant community center, planning Fourth of July picnics, maintaining a circulating library, and sponsoring programs at the public school. People who lived at Central formed lasting associations and considered those days of hardship and happiness incomparable. Those who moved downstate or elsewhere enjoyed reliving the past with the Cornish and others who remained in the Copper Country. They remembered people like Mrs. Jane Bryant, milliner and candy store proprietor, who boiled water in wash kettles for tea to accompany pasties, saffron cake, and seedy buns at early reunions. Grace Lee Nute wrote: "The buildings still stand around the deserted shaft, unpainted like most of the simple frame dwellings in the Copper Country. When I saw them [at Central] in the dusk of a late October day in 1943, only one weak, solitary light gleamed from a window in this otherwise deserted village."[33]

Methodist conferences in Michigan divided the Upper Peninsula into districts in the 1880s and appointed men to further the Gospel in eleven different areas from Central to Ontonagon. Many of the Copper Country young rebelled against Methodist opposition to dancing, drinking, and card playing. Some Methodists spoke disparagingly of one Methodist church as catering excessively to "bosses" or "the upper crust" at Calumet. Laurium's Methodist Church by 1912 was extremely active in relieving some of the wants of the needy in the community.[34]

African Americans worked and lived in all the towns from Eagle Harbor to Mass City. Sixty-two appeared in the 1860 census for Houghton County (when the county included what is now Keweenaw County and parts of Baraga County). By 1870, their number dropped to twenty-eight, then rose to thirty-four in 1880 and to sixty-one by 1910. Thirteen blacks lived in Ontonagon County in 1870; twenty-four had lived there a decade earlier.[35]

In 1860, five years before a constitutional amendment ended slavery officially in the United States, Rebecca Gleeves, age twenty-five, an African American born in Virginia, operated a hotel at Eagle River. Five English miners stayed there. Other inhabitants were Jane Jeffry, age thirty, her black cook; and Josiah Champlin, her white barkeep. A total of eleven blacks at Eagle River are listed in the 1860 census: barbers, homemakers, servants, children, and a musician. At

nearby Clifton, Lenisa Custer, age thirty-four, served in the home
of Dr. and Mrs. Mortimer Senter. Born in Washington, D.C., she
had an eleven-year-old son born in Michigan. The John Slawson
household included Harriet Butler, age twenty, born in Tennessee, a
black servant who worked alongside two fellow servants from Saxony,
Germany, ages thirteen and nineteen.

Twenty African Americans lived in Houghton Village in 1860,
fourteen in Portage Township, and one in Hancock Village. The men
worked as cooks in boardinghouses or hotels, as barbers, laborers,
and servants; the women were generally servants in hotels or private
homes. In Houghton, Charles Baker, age fifty, a barber, had married
Margaret, age thirty-six, a Native American. Their daughter, age six,
and sons, ages eight and nine, were born in Wisconsin. The African
Americans hailed from Alabama, Canada, Connecticut, the District of
Columbia, Kentucky, Louisiana, Maryland, Massachusetts, Michigan,
New York, New Jersey, Ohio, Pennsylvania, Tennessee, Wisconsin,
and Virginia. Asa Jeffry moved his barber business from Houghton
to Calumet by 1870. Like the Cornish from Clifton and Central who
inundated Calumet, the African Americans moved with the economic
tides. In Ontonagon County, their numbers dwindled to eleven in
1900 and two in 1910.[36]

The African American experience resembled that of other ethnic groups, in that strangers from everywhere came to the Copper
Country, worked, settled, and then moved on to other parts of the
Keweenaw or out of the peninsula entirely. It differed in that some
members of other groups sank roots and established themselves, so
that today one can find members of the fifth to seventh generations.
Blacks did not, but some African Americans married whites or Native
Americans and added to the gene pool in the Keweenaw. Since part
of the pre–Civil War Underground Railroad passed through Michigan's Lower Peninsula, with Sault Saint Marie as a crossing point to
Canada, one can understand how some escaped slaves decided to try
their luck in the Keweenaw, rather than Canada. The movement of
free blacks from the East to the Keweenaw was part of a general move
west by Americans in the northeast states.

The early settlers felt challenged as the nineteenth century matured, for a flood of immigrants from Finland and from Italian and
Slavic polities within old empires changed much of the Keweenaw
Peninsula. Historian James Jamison said of Finns in Ontonagon
County, "They came and they came to stay." The statement needs
qualification. Like all other strangers migrating to the Keweenaw,
Finns moved about in the Copper Country. Underground mining
and tramming proved, for many, Finns, a phase, as they became agricultural pioneers. Several Finnish businessmen distinguished them-

selves locally long before the heaviest immigration of Finns began; and others followed them into businesses and service industries, some after working in mines.[37]

Oscar John Larson, born in Finland in 1871, attended public schools until age sixteen, then pursued a business and literary course at a Valparaiso, Indiana, normal school and studied literature and then law at the University of Michigan. He returned to the Copper Country to practice law after admission to the bar in 1894. Tailors who learned to sew in their youth in the Finnish colony at Saint Petersburg, Russia, gave a particular flair to the city of Hancock. J. H. Jasberg, who once worked as railroad agent for the Duluth, South Shore, and Atlantic Railroad, seeking Finnish settlers to inhabit towns along the line, operated a bookstore before developing a line of enterprises that made his name famous in the Upper Peninsula. Henry Sakari, who arrived in 1887, conducted a slaughtering business and other enterprises, including a grocery store. Many Finns gained business experience working for Sakari.

Edward Waara, born in Alkkula, Oulu, Finland, in 1855, arrived in Calumet at age twenty-six, followed his father's trade as watchmaker and goldsmith, then moved his business to Hancock in 1885. His son Charles carried on until 1950. Finns competed with other peoples in various enterprises. By 1900, Henry Haapapuro operated a butcher shop, Sam Junttila and John Wäyrynen, a general store and bakery. Isaac Tolonen entered the lumber business. William Anttila and John Kermus, with two others, opened saloons. At Calumet, by the turn of the century, Oscar Keckonen's hardware store was already one of the largest there. Mrs. M. E. Mikkola's candy store near the Bijou Theater, Edward Keisu's bakery, and the meat markets of William Frederickson and Akseli Keskitalo served many. Finns worked as cobblers, and Charles Ojala sold shoes. Abram Väänänen not only sold jewelry at his Pine Street store but also served as broker and steamship agent. He had come to Red Jacket in 1879 and moved to Detroit in 1920. His children called themselves Warren. At the shore of Lake Superior, not far from Calumet and known as the Waterworks, Finns worked as fishermen and found good markets in neighboring mining towns. One of the oldest and best known of the fisherfolk at Calumet Waterworks was Pekka Remali.[38]

Fifty percent of total Finnish emigration to the United States in the late nineteenth and early twentieth centuries originated in the *laani* (counties) of Vassa; the majority of the immigrants came from South Ostro-bothnia, "an amazing localization of emigration." In 1900, 73 percent of the 18,910 Michigan Finns lived in the Upper Peninsula, 38 percent (7,241) in Houghton County.[39] Finns introduced churches, the sauna, cooperatives, and their cuisine to the developing

Copper Country culture. A particular intonation that many in the Lower Peninsula associate with the Upper Peninsula springs—in large part though not completely—from Finnish speech patterns.

Miners from the Norwegian Alten mines included some Finns. In 1865, for example, thirty Finns departed from Trondheim, Norway, bound for the Quincy Mine. Some brought families to Quebec, whence they traveled to Hancock by ship; among them were Olli Danielson, Matti Maikko, Olli Sutinen, and Peter Lampa. Happy to arrive on Saint John's Day (June 24), they began by living in Norwegian boardinghouses and commenced work next day. More than five hundred Finns arrived in the 1870s, about twenty-seven hundred, in the 1880s; and when iron mines shut down in Ishpeming in 1879, Finns poured into the Copper Country, creating such a labor surplus that companies lowered wages. Hundreds left Hancock then for Duluth, half of them Finns.[40]

Agricultural settlements, almost exclusively Finnish, grew like mushrooms after the rain, in the late 1880s and early 1890s, among them Toivola, Tapiola (from Tapio, a Finnish forest-god), Nisula (from August Nisula, who served as first postmaster), all in Houghton County. French Canadian woodsmen settled at a place in Baraga County in 1885 known as King's Land; but when farmers arrived to till the cutover land, the place became Pelkie, named after an early settler. Wainola, a village in Greenland Township (Ontonagon County), remained home to Finns who settled it, using the legendary name for the Finnish family, Waino. A community of Finns turned from mining to farming in Ontonagon after brief stints as woodsmen in Ontonagon County; they named their village Wasas after a province in Finland.[41]

Finns who arrived at Otter Lake to settle in September 1890 began an illustrious history of cooperative house building, farming, hunting, fishing, and conducting a school where children learned the rudiments. Trapped otters provided caps, mittens, and bedcovers. Land ownership served as a source of pride, and a farm served as a link to the European past. This Finnish "dream" was identical with that of hundreds of thousands of European emigrants from the 1790s on, but the new culture Finns developed in an American setting proved singularly rich.[42]

Copper Country Finns succeeded better than most groups in settling cutover timber land for five reasons: (1) their love of the agricultural life allowed an autonomy not possible working for Cornish and other shift bosses; (2) their communal organization—helping one another—formed social associations to enrich their lives; (3) they had a deep-rooted fear of debt; (4) they had a passion for dairy cows' production of milk, cream, and cheese to banish ancestral

Some Finns moved from mining to farming. (Michigan Technological University Archives and Copper Country Historical Collections, Michigan Technological University.)

fears of privation and starvation; and (5) they skillfully handled the dynamite (a task learned in mines) needed to rid land of stumps. A county agricultural agent said in 1918 that Finns worked hard and did not fear challenges and that where others eventually gave up and pulled out, Finns stayed and were Houghton County's "only hope" in agriculture. Their children "taught to work on the farm" served as valuable assets.[43]

Oskar, a region of dense forests in 1875—where Finns applied the axe for logs, railroad ties, and cordwood demanded by copper companies and others—became a farming settlement named Ojanperä. When its Finnish founders applied in Houghton for a postmastership, Oskar Eliasson could not spell his surname in English, so the impatient official asked his first name and recorded that in the official papers as the settlement's name. Eliasson became one of the most important lumbermen in the area. By 1882, a school and a place for church services appeared. Later, a general store selling products from "salt fish to pocket watches" joined a small tannery, shoemakers, a brickyard, and public sauna. By 1896, fire destroyed everything. Most of the original settlers left; but others came, cleared the land to the Portage Lake shoreline, and planted oats, wheat, and potatoes.

Thus began additional communities: Liminga, Heinola, North Superior, and North Canal, where Finnish dairy and strawberry farms still flourish.[44]

Finns lived at Ripley, adjoining Hancock, by the late 1860s and at nearby Dollar Bay by 1887, working in sawmills and smelters. Their presence in quarries and later at strawberry farms at Jacobsville was pronounced beginning in the late 1870s and reached a peak by 1910. A party of ten Finnish families moved to Fitchburg, Massachusetts, in 1904, after earlier compatriots sent them glowing accounts. A reporter commented, "These people are well adapted for the work of tilling the soil and stock raising, so there is not the least doubt that they will make things boom." A post-1914 move from Houghton and Keweenaw counties to Pointe Abbaye in Baraga County, to land and log houses there, was only one instance of Finnish migration. Some left for Butte, Montana, after the disastrous 1913–14 copper strike.[45]

In Houghton County, by 1920, Finns owned 66,896 acres assessed at about $1.5 million and real property assessed at $876,290. Seventy-nine percent of the acreage lay in the townships of Stanton, Portage, Laird, Chassell, and Torch Lake. By 1918, Finns who first began to clear lands and farm in Carp Lake Township in Ontonagon County formed a cooperative, each buying a share at ten dollars to pay for a thresher, portable sawmill, and later a hay baler. By the 1920s and 1930s, Finns belonged to various cooperative stores and organizations. Some of that seemed "socialistic" to Yankee and other ethnic groups, many of whom failed to comprehend the Finns. Some of the Finns averred that they lived on "Kuparisaari [Copper Island], outside the American mainland." Considering themselves "Copper Islanders" lent a unique cast to their cultural lives as they attempted to perpetuate much of the traditional civilization as they accommodated to the new.[46]

Historian Armas K. E. Holmio visited Nisula in 1925, admiring broad, tilled fields, crops, apple trees, farmyards with silo, machinery, and automobiles; but his farmer–guide "spoke the whole time about *Suomussalmi* . . . with tears in his eyes and sorrow in his voice." Like all immigrants who worked so hard in the Copper Country, nostalgia for the "old country" often led in the beginning to homesickness. This pain generally disappeared. Descendants of Nisula pioneers eventually "scattered all over America."[47]

Some Finns tended their farms in summer and worked in the copper mines in winter. Others remained entirely faithful to mining. At the 1916 semicentennial celebration at Calumet and Hecla, five received gold medals connoting over forty years of work for the company, sixteen received silver medals for thirty-to-forty years' work, and forty-two had bronze medals for twenty-to-thirty years' service.

By 1883, Finns arrived to work in Baraga sawmills and instituted a church temperance society and social activities in private homes by 1892; but as "the older generation gradually passed away, Finnish-language cultural activities also died out," wrote a Finnish archivist and historian. Never numerically great at L'Anse, Finns worked in nearby lumber camps and, after 1958, for the Celotex Corporation. Many Finnish girls and women worked as maids in homes of the well-to-do at Calumet but lived in Tamarack, where they enjoyed the Thursday "maid's day off." In Copper Country towns, the larger stores, "regardless of the owner's nationality," employed, by 1910, at least one Finnish employee to serve Finnish customers as the Finnish population grew. Of 2,529 births in 1917 in Houghton County, 879, or 34.7 percent, were to Finns. Finnish children accounted for 34.4 percent of pupils in Hancock public schools in 1911 and 53.9 percent in 1916. By 1910, about 13,894 persons born in Finland lived in Houghton, Keweenaw, and Ontonagon counties.

By the 1960s, affluent descendants of the original Finns enjoyed summer cottages at Dreamland, which extended many miles along the tree-lined channel from Torch Lake to Portage Lake. Atlantic Mine, where the Keiski, Keranen, Hiltunen, and Kallio families pioneered, had an opera house, hospital, churches, and the Aura Temperance Society (*aura* being Finnish for "plow") by 1899–1900. Painesdale, Trimountain, Redridge, Mohawk, and Fulton all felt the Finnish cultural imprint. At South Range, Finns built a brick building to house their Knights of Kaleva, a hardware store, the Royal Theater, and a confectionary and restaurant, as well as offices, kitchen, and smoking room. Simple, austere wooden churches appeared everywhere.[48]

Religious congregations formed as early as the mid-1870s. As towns rose, so did dissenting groups. Copper Country Finns divided themselves due to intense individualism, narrow-minded doctrinal interpretations, partisanship, and zealous pastoral leadership, so that by 1917, twenty-two churches had been established by Finns in Houghton County alone: eleven Evangelical Lutheran with fourteen congregations, three ministers, and 5,702 members; one National Lutheran with two congregations and 748 members served by one minister; nine Apostolic Lutheran, with ten congregations and 1,675 members led by two ministers; and one Methodist congregation with 187 members and one minister. In these churches, 8,312 Finns sponsored thirty-six Sunday schools where 2,735 girls and boys received initial instructions in the faiths.[49]

Temperance halls served as valuable social centers. Painesdale's Kyntäjä Hall, of wood, had many windows, gables, and an open cupola. There were sixteen halls in 1917 in Houghton County, including Pohjan Tähti (North Star), Koitto (Morning Twilight), Onni

145

(Luck), Soitu (Torch), Hyvä Toivo (Good Hope), and Säde (Ray). Here the immigrants sang folk songs; played games native to their culture; recited stories and poetry; presented dramatic skits; organized athletic clubs, glee clubs, and bands; held concerts; and collected books for loan to members. Here many became acquainted with the epic *Kalevala* and learned of Ilmatar, the Water-Mother—Creatrix, for "she then began Creation, and she brought the world to order"— and some could sympathize with lines such as "Here my life is cold and dreary, every moment now is painful."[50]

Socialism attracted a minority of Finns; socialist halls existed, the most famous being Kansankoti at Hancock. But the notion that Copper Country Finns divided themselves between "red Finns" and "church Finns" is an oversimplification. Many of the "socialists" used Marxist rhetoric to achieve ends such as collective bargaining, which even the most conservative Americans today accept. Copper Country Finns could at the same time be fiscally and socially conservative and call for liberal—even radical—institutions (sounder public education, shorter working hours, cooperatives, government aid to communities). Most maintained a fierce independence, differing with one another in religious practices. Some dabbled in agnosticism, atheism, and free-thinking. Others championed "the strong-minded woman," as feminists were known toward the end of the nineteenth century. Unfortunately, the stereotype of complacent Finnish reactionaries critical of progressive-minded radicals persists. Overall, a strong social consciousness prevailed, a reaching out to the unfortunate among the group. Among the temperance halls' most ardent endeavors were rescuing addicts to alcohol and mitigating sufferings of relatives who endured Russian rule in far-off Finland.[51]

Croatians and Slovenians—each group proud of its particular language, customs, and culture—found themselves labeled "Austrians" in the Copper Country, since the provinces from which these Slavic peoples migrated formed part of the empire known then as Austria-Hungary. They began arriving in the late 1870s and continued to come throughout the 1880s, with a huge migration after 1890 as economic difficulties in the empire forced them out. So many Croatians left one province to work and live at Calumet that they referred to Calumet by the name of their province, prefixed by "New."

Slovenians and Croatians endowed with entrepreneurial skills contributed much to the building of communities after 1900. Workingmen saved from meager wages in order to buy copper-mining shares; more often, a family saved to open a business or saloon. By 1910, Croatians at Calumet started a cooperative store with a capital of thirty thousand dollars. The hundred members—mainly trammers in mines—also included construction workers and other laborers. In 1900, Stephen Kasun, age thirty-three, a naturalized Slav, worked as a miner; but he and his wife Margarita, age twenty-two, conducted a boardinghouse with thirteen miners and the seventy-eight-year-old father of one of them—all aliens and all Slavs, ranging in age from nineteen to fifty-one, with most in their twenties. Three Popovitch brothers (Gabriel, Nick, and Peter) had arrived that year; but Mark Belabolavitch came to America at age thirty-two in 1893. Mish Badevinitch came in 1898, the same year as Joseph Verbanitz. Of the fourteen boarders, nine could read, write, and speak English. The Kasuns had a six-month-old son, Stephen, and a three-year-old daughter, Barbara. This assemblage was typical of households ranging from South Range north to Mohawk.[52]

In the process of living in the Copper Country, names changed. The Sälz family became Shaltz simply because their name sounded that way when enunciated to immigration and other authorities.[53] Slavs were second only to Finns as the largest foreign-born group by 1910 in the Keweenaw. In Houghton, Keweenaw, and Ontonagon counties, 4,006 lived along with 2,996 native-born Americans whose parents were born in Slavic provinces, a grand total of 7,002.[54] Slovenians came as early as 1858 to Hancock, some peddling watches, trinkets, clothing, and kitchen utensils. Peter Ruppe engaged in door-to-door selling before establishing his large department store in Red Jacket. This was surpassed later by Vertin Brothers store, which became a Calumet institution, in business for over a hundred years. Ruppe, who died in 1923, had invested in mining stocks and was "the first Slovenian millionaire in America." Saint Joseph's lodge, with its Slovenian Fraternal Benefit Society, established in 1882, paid death and sick benefits. Its bylaws had to be sent to Slovenian print shops, as no shops with the needed diacritics existed in the United States. When membership reached five hundred, a band was organized to escort funerals of members to the cemetery and it also played at picnics and dances.

Slovenians built Saint Joseph's Church in 1889 and, after it burned three years later, constructed the imposing, twin-towered neo-Gothic edifice (now Saint Paul the Apostle) still in use at Eighth and Oak Streets in Calumet. Poles and Croatians also worshiped with the Slovenians in their church until they built their own church buildings, Saint Anthony's and Saint John's, both on Seventh Street.[55] Poles celebrated Polish Constitution Day each May, organized clubs for dancing and convivial gatherings, and John and Albert chapters of the Saint Stanislaus Society, providing concerts, parades, and suppers. The Slovenian-Croatian Union was the grand lodge encompassing the Saint Nicholas Croatian, Saint Jacob, Saint Barbara, Saint Florian, Saints Cyril and Methodius, Saint Roch, Saint Peter,

Old St. Joseph's Church, Red Jacket, c. 1890, ministered to Slavic peoples. (Michigan Technological University Archives and Copper Country Historical Collections, Michigan Technological University.)

and Saint John societies, plus some others. All joined in 1907 to celebrate the twenty-fifth anniversary of the grand lodge "in the good old way," with parades, dramatic entertainments, beer, and roast lamb.[56]

Saint Joseph's Church in 1907 had 2,950 members, Saint Anthony's 1,259. Of the 27,238 persons living in Houghton County in 1907, Roman Catholics in Calumet Township's six Catholic churches accounted for 13,141. Local Italians built their own church, Saint Mary's, by 1897. In 1907, its membership was 2,800 (350 families). The opening ceremonies in 1897 included blessing the bell dedicated to Saint Barbara, patron of miners, and an outpouring of ethnic participation in the parade through Red Jacket: Cornish musicians, Irish from the Hibernian Rifles and Ancient Order of Hibernians, French Canadians from the Saint Jean Baptiste Society, Poles belonging to Saint Stanislaus Kostka Society, and others, including Italians from three different lodges. Despite their many differences, in 1889, the Finnish Coronet Band and Finnish Temperance Society members,

Polish Hussars, French Canadians, and other ethnic lodge members, marched with Italians in celebrating the American Fourth of July.[57]

The Italian Mutual Benefit Society, formed in 1875, began "for the purpose of assisting the members and their countrymen in every way, possible" and incorporated under Michigan law in 1889. The opening of its Italian Hall in Red Jacket was festive with well-wishers from all of the county. The general manager of Calumet and Hecla delivered a speech. He praised the society for uniting Italian residents in fraternal bonds and extending assistance to needy members yet never allowing an opportunity pass "to strengthen the principles of Americanism which already strongly exist among those affiliated, . . . for every man connected with the society is in America to stay and is desirous of becoming everything that a citizen should be." He thus summed up not only for Italians but for all ethnic groups the singular role of mutual benefit societies as both protectors of a precious ethnic heritage and a help to immigrants and their children in becoming acculturated.[58]

The first Italians settled on Quincy Hill in 1859, when the Coppo family arrived to usher in thousands who came to work in mines or open businesses. James Lisa, appointed first vice consul in 1895 to assist the immigrants, helped with advice, loans, and mediation. Made a knight by King Victor Emmanuel III of Italy by 1910, Lisa was also a successful businessman whose "Lisa block" at Sixth and Oak Streets, Red Jacket, housed his store, where Italian and American products pleased compatriots, who made the place a virtual social center. Lisa sold dry goods, shoes, miners' boots, nails, tools, plates and cups, kitchenware, and steamship tickets. About 80 percent of the Italians in Houghton and Keweenaw counties came from Piedmont; others arrived from Tuscany (10 percent), Lombardy, and Liguria.[59]

Several Italians kept boardinghouses. In Hancock, an Italian "factory" turned out pasta for wholesale and retail sale. Doctor Joseph Vercellini advertised himself as the "Italian Doctor" with an office in the "Lisa block" and consultations in English, French, and Italian. A 1910 guide to Copper Country Italians listed them in every town and village from Mohawk south to Painesdale and Greenland except for Lake Linden and Ontonagon. Antonio Giuglio, proprietor of the Torino Hotel, Houghton, advertised "Pasti all'italiana." At South Range, Luigi Basso was village marshal; and the village had five Italian lodges, including Toscano di Mutuo Soccorso. Hancock had one lodge; Franklin Mine, three; Trimountain, three. At Calumet, six lodges flourished, including Garibaldi Celibi, restricted to bachelors of Italian descent. Battista Bigando, born near Turin, worked two years at mining and delivered milk before going to the mine. Then he worked fifty-seven years in the Calumet and Hecla paint shop and also distinguished himself as musician in the company band. In 1973, he recalled those hard but heady days with all the lodges and reflected that now there was only one lodge "and there's hardly [anybody] in it."

Bernard Bracco, baker, and the Barsotti Brothers, ice cream makers, with other small businessmen, formed a nexus with bankers Tinetti and Castiligano, liveryman Michael Richetta, contractor Vincent Vairo, dealer in wholesale liquor and epicurean foods G. Martini, and thousands of Italian-born miners and trammers. Italian women of the Copper Country defied tradition and spouses to form organizations like Daughters of Italy in the southern section of the mineral range and Daughters of the Eternal City in the north. There was nothing parochial about the Italians.[60]

Italians added a convivial flair to Copper Country cosmopolitanism, as did the Jews. On January 7, 1915, Rabbi Koplewitz of Hancock's Temple Jacob read the funeral service for Jacob Baer, who with brothers William and Kaufman, had in 1862 begun a retail meat market called Baer Brothers. By the time of his death, Baer had entered into a partnership with a Scot named Dymock in a store in Red Jacket, opened a store at Dollar Bay, and owned Houghton Pure Food Company, besides maintaining the original Hancock store. Baer, like the Leopold brothers, ranked among the earliest merchants in the peninsula. David Haas came from Ohio to L'Anse in 1853, moved to Houghton where he first sold whiskey, then became a haberdasher, hauling underwear and boots in wagons or sleighs to mining locations and eventually operating excellent men's clothing stores at Houghton and Calumet. His sons Ed and Ike, along with Martin and Herman Haas, carried on, with Ike's grandson Bob operating the Houghton store until 1980.

Jacob and Isidore Gartner came to the United States in 1880 and eventually to Hancock, where they learned English and Finnish. Gartner's Department Store continues to this day, a century after its founding. A recent historian wrote that Gartner's was "a business that began with a cardboard suitcase and a sturdy pair of shoes (the founders began as peddlers), and has moved into its second century of operation."

At Red Jacket, Benjamin Blum, who left Lithuania in 1881, operated a saloon for thirty-one years at Pine and Fifth Streets before prohibition turned him to selling groceries and clothes. By 1913, Jews who had celebrated high holidays in third-floor rented halls or similar locations, opened Temple Jacob at Hancock, near the bridge. More than a hundred Jewish families lived in the Copper Country then, among them those of I. Abel, Hugo Field, Isidor Gartner, Mandel Glass, Herman Joffee, A. L. Levy, and H. Pimstein.

Jacob Hevesh served as first rabbi. After 1914, visiting rabbis assisted their compatriots in observing Rosh Hashanah and Yom Kippur. Local newspapers carried syndicated material on these and the spring holidays, even minor ones. In 1898, kosher meat was prepared at a market on Tamarack Street, Laurium, when local Jews formed a corporation for that purpose.

Like the Gentiles, second-generation Jewish women entered teaching as a means "up." Lillian Neimark demanded much of her violin students. C. Harry Benedict, prominent engineer at Calumet and Hecla, who later wrote its history, was of the Jewish tradition and lived at Lake Linden. The Glass, Hoffenberg, Blum, Tecotzky, Rosenbaum, Mawrence, and other Jewish families resided at Calumet–Laurium in the 1930s and 1940s. One discovers no recorded untoward incidents involving Gentiles and Jews, although Jewish youngsters sometimes resented singing Christian hymns in public schools at Christmas. One lad who voiced his displeasure with having to sing such songs at a Calumet elementary school in the mid-1930s played Saint Joseph five years later in a holiday tableaux at Calumet High School with nary a murmur. About that time, a first-year woman student at the high school found reading *The Merchant of Venice* most unpleasant. She said nothing, but expressed her displeasure by ignoring the text, quite the contrary of her usual dedicated work.[61]

Solomon Kirkish, an entrepreneur of Lebanese origin, opened a drygoods store in Houghton in 1913 and later with members of his family operated three grocery stores simultaneously. Still later, their furniture store attracted many customers. The Kirkish family served Portage Lake and other communities for more than eighty years and presently continue to maintain the business. They added much to community life as did those families in Houghton County, some of whom called themselves Syrians, who operated small businesses. Like the European immigrants, those from the Middle East urged their children to assimilate to the middle-class American way of life; one family at Calumet used the name Kelly. In the 1930s, Irene and Hameda Nicholas held important secretarial posts in the state government at Lansing.

About six hundred Hungarians lived in the Copper Country in 1907. They had a Magyar church at Wolverine and celebrated the anniversary of Hungarian independence, but the great strike of 1913–14 led to their almost complete abandonment of the Keweenaw. Mike Miczkynys, Lithuanian, applied for citizenship in 1915. He was already known to others as McGinnis, another sign of powerful acculturation forces at work. Despite hard work, accidents, deaths in mines, drudgery, and complaints about hours and wages, many mine workers believed something similar to T. J. Rickard's 1904 assessment: The miner "in this region is better off than the higher paid men who live amid the desolations of Arizona, . . . Nevada, or among the even more brutalizing environments of . . . Butte City and Broken Hill." Scores of ethnic groups, themselves singularly diverse, lived richer lives by associations with other groups at school and work.[62]

Diverse peoples with a common experience of living near forests, lakes, and streams with the "freedom . . . from the thousand cares of the busy world" easily available by absorption in nature or participation in their own social organizations, the humble hospitality that folk offered one another, and the social democracy often unconsciously fostered over many decades—these fashioned the Keweenaw "experience" immediately recognized by those who lived it and usually incomprehensible to tourists and others who passed through. Nostalgia often ignores the hardships of those times. Many people from various groups agreed with Progressive representative William MacDonald in the early twentieth century that "human rights are greater than property rights" and fulminated against big copper companies and their dictation to smaller ones. Despite all civilizing forces, men retained "the somewhat common custom" of firing guns and revolvers at midnight on New Year's Eve at Houghton, 1914.[63]

Life was often painful. John R. Bennetts recalled his Cornish grandmother, who, in the 1850s left father, mother, and six sisters and never saw them again. He added, "But [in] that way [the] U.S. was settled by such partings from every Foreign country." At evening concerts, where Finns offered instrumental numbers and choirs sang Finnish songs, such events "often became the climax of long repressed memories, sentiments and emotions about the old country." A Finnish woman who found the Copper Country ugly, English and other speech abhorrent, and the United States "strange" often burst into tears but twenty years later felt "perfectly at home [in the Copper Country, with] plenty of wholesome food and everything we need."[64]

The singular social democracy prevailing was shot through with class distinctions, snobbery, and cruelty. Phillipa Aldrich, an English mining captain's wife, found herself shunned by Atlantic mine women for "putting on airs" when she hung lace curtains in her living room. Grievously homesick, she left on a long visit to England and, upon her return to the Michigan mining community, found such curtains in many homes. For the pioneer woman, life in the forest was at first a romantic novelty; but soon monotony set in. Said one who lived that life: "Her domestic cares are onerous and trying . . . .She is expected to be nurse, cook, housekeeper, seamstress and governess, while a man thinks he does well if he is a specialist in one line." At the

Adventure Mine in 1859, Thomas W. Buzzo reassured his superior in the East that he did not allow miners to board with him; for it was "a wrong policy to mingle too freely with laborers, . . . as it destroys in a great measure the respect they should bear to their employer and the command the employer should have over them."

Annie Aldrich recalled Irish and English fighting every Saturday night at Calumet in the early twentieth century; but at school, all children—Finns, Swedes, Germans—were equal, though they might shout "Dirty German!" or "Dirty Finn!" on playgrounds.[65] In the 1930s, Ngan Lee's shop, filled with packages of laundered shirts, seemed a house of horror to some small boys whose parents had threatened to sell them to the Chinese proprietor to be butchered for chop suey. One lad remembered being sent there for his father's shirt collars and discovering Ngan Lee to be a jolly, friendly, enthusiastic man. Anna Isola recalled youngsters of different ethnic groups playing together. In the alley between Fifth and Sixth streets in Calumet in the early 1930s, children played at hide-and-seek; they came from families descended from Croatian, French, German, English, and Scandinavian families who lived as neighbors. Frances Rozich remembered the difficulty some Slavic children had learning English in school while speaking Slovenian, Croatian, or Polish at home. So many Finns lived on Red Jacket's Pine Street that scoffers called it Shoepack Avenue or Shoepack Alley. Finns were often called "herring chokers," too; but their numbers, strength, solidarity, and industry allowed them to emerge unscathed from the "petty nationalistic battles of a mining town."[66]

The discrimination at work whereby Finns, Slavs, and Italians were often relegated to the most menial jobs in mines and mills by Cornish, Irish, Scandinavians, Germans, and Anglo Americans was paralleled in most American mines, mills, and factories between 1890 and 1930. At Tamarack Mine, emotions ran high between Cornish and Finns in 1898, and one petty shoving match had Eric Rytilahti bringing charges against John Reynolds. Irish miners hoping to become machinists in the early days found those ambitions thwarted by Cornish in control of the machinery, who "never would hire an Irishman for a machinist." A prominent, Progressive magazine said in 1914 that the Finns, though hardy, were inclined toward socialism and "often ignorant and racially sullen." Some people at Red Jacket in 1896 protested against the flying of Italian or British flags on holiday occasions.[67]

In the late nineteenth century, the *Copper Country Evening News,* in reporting mine accidents, often garbled names or gave no names at all, saying two Swedes were injured in a premature blast, an Italian trammer suffered a broken leg when a rock fell, or a Frenchman had his leg broken in North Tamarack Mine. In 1898, when "Cuba libre fever" ran rampant, a "Citizen" wrote the newspaper about "chronic growlers," who should hold their tongues or go back to where they came from—and "good riddance." But the mix of peoples was so great that the American liberal ideas of tolerance and accepting *individuals* for their accomplishments prevailed. In the early twentieth century, at Ontonagon, the funeral of Jewish veterinarian Dr. Bernhard was held in the Presbyterian church and conducted by a Methodist minister, with an Episcopal choir singing and devout Catholic "Bud" Corgan serving as chief mourner.[68]

Although not the industrial Arcadia touted by journalists, neither was the Keweenaw Peninsula's Copper Country an industrial hellhole where tyrannical companies crushed proletarian lives. Many immigrants (and especially their children) took advantage of opportunities for social mobility, usually through business. Ralph Paoli migrated from Italy in 1896, worked in mines, then left to form at Houghton a great wholesale produce business with Harry C. Cohodas. John Gasparovich emigrated from Croatia at age twenty-four, worked in the mines, and after twelve years opened a Sixth Street saloon in Red Jacket. He served on the village council, became a prominent businessman and was highly regarded. He and his wife raised four daughters and four sons. They, with their grandchildren, distinguished themselves, spreading to various parts of the United States. Paoli and Gasparovich typify hundreds of individuals who moved from mines to business enterprises, men who, with their families, loved their ethnic heritage but blended it with a new American heritage.[69]

Acculturation developed slowly, as some ethnic groups, more than others, shed cultural elements in order to succeed as Americans. Groups divided over language. Knowledge of English proved a decided advantage for Cornish, Scots, and Irish in a Keweenaw society culturally dominated by Anglo-American leaders joined by American descendants of Germans, Irish, Jews, Finns, and Scandinavians in commercial, educational, and political activities. Champions of Americanization, they maintained superior positions in an evolving society. By 1910, due largely to fewer chances for economic advancement in mining, more recent arrivals from Finland, Italy, and Slavic countries challenged these elites.[70]

Former ethnic hostilities between Cornish and Irish or among Swedes and English gave way to bitter polarization between Finns, Italians, and Slavs on one side and English on the other. Between 1904 and 1914, Marxian socialism, with its emphasis on class conflict, pitted some ethnic groups against others and created divisions within ethnic groups. Despite the violent suppression, by economic and social elites, of the socialist movement between 1913 and 1918, hostilities generated by this "purge" lingered for decades as Finns were unjustly blamed for violent labor disturbances during the 1913–14 copper strike.[71]

Copper Country Finns, like Irish in the eastern United States in the 1840s and Poles in urban centers in the 1920s, found themselves targets because other ethnic peoples found their speech, appearance, and demeanor "foreign" and complained about their clannishness. Children of all ethnic groups, whether German, Italian, Norwegian, or Croatian, felt the sting of ridicule on school playgrounds, as "Americans" and the previously acculturated laughed at accents.

Religion also worked as a divisive factor. American Protestantism's pervasive, centuries-old distrust of Roman Catholicism caused personal anguish at times. As late as the 1940s, irate Lutheran fathers denounced daughters marrying outside the fold and severed familial ties. Many young Methodist and Congregational males refused to date Catholic women. At times, they related stories of errant priests and nuns. Although generally discreet at school and work, where they encountered many Catholics, Keweenaw Protestants derided them for "superstition" and "foolish rituals." Torch Lake Protestants howled at the story of a Lake Linden priest's announcement at Sunday mass that the congregation was invited to visit the parish's Little Gem movie theatre that afternoon to see *Million Dollar Legs,* a 1932 comedy (actually about Olympic track competition). Catholic and Protestant clergy, especially in the 1930s, debated, via radio and church sermons, their respective beliefs. Antagonisms prevailed among English Protestants between "high church" and "chapel" adherents.[72]

The Cornish "hold" in mining militated against hopes of Finns, Slavs, and Italians to rise in the ranks. That was constant from the 1860s on. By 1910, the situation festered and threatened to erupt with dire consequences. "The Cousin Jacks have everything sewed up" was a common expression into the 1930s. The newer arrivals (1890–1910) from Europe lacked skills enjoyed by the Cornish and Scots who predominated as foremen, smiths, carpenters, pattern makers, clerks, and managers. In the 1920s, Finnish lumber workers lived in camps, where filthy blankets, lice, and bedbugs prevailed.[73] In 1882, John Callihan several times impersonated an officer and, according to a newspaper account, "arrested ignorant Finns and others," releasing them on payment of five dollars—a fortune in those days.[74] Italians from Piedmont, in 1904, treated other Italians as "outsiders;" and Italians often feuded according to the states or provinces they hailed from in Italy.[75]

Education proved potent in the process of Americanization. The combined demands of Anglo-American elites and desires of Europeans for education for their children wrought wonders. Keweenaw people were highly literate. By 1910, school attendance was high for youngsters in elementary schools, ages six to fourteen, and ranged from 88 to 95 percent (see Table 5.1).[76]

Table 5.1. Percentages for School Attendance,
Ages 6–14, 1910

County	Native White, Native Parentage	Native White Foreign/Mixed Parentage	Foreign-born White
Baraga	95	90.6	91.4
Houghton	92.3	93.2	90.4
Keweenaw	88.3	92.2	94.1
Ontonagon	91.1	91.6	91.6

The public school system continued for decades as a remarkable engine promoting literacy. By 1910, only .4 percent of Hancock's foreign-born remained illiterate. Many emigrants attained literacy in Europe and quickly adapted to English in the Copper Country. Of Hancock's total 1910 population of 8,891, only 152, or 1.5 percent, were illiterate.[77]

At the same time, Houghton's illiteracy amounted to only 1 percent. At Laurium in 1910, .1 percent of native whites ten years and older were illiterate; but among foreign-born whites there, 7.2 percent could not read or write. Red Jacket's illiterate native whites also numbered .1 percent; but among foreign-born whites ten years and older, the illiterate percentage was high—13.6.[78] Clearly, a major difference lay in the advantage natives enjoyed vis-á-vis literacy; but the schools continued to enforce reading, writing, arithmetic, tolerance, democratic liberalism, and the ideal of unlimited human development. Their success in eliminating illiteracy is shown in the 1910 percentages for illiterates ages ten to twenty in the four counties of the Copper Country (see Table 5.2):[79]

Libraries at Painesdale, Houghton, Hancock, and Calumet, either in schools or housed in handsome public buildings subsidized or owned by mining companies, rank high in the acculturation process. Here immigrants first read books in their own languages, while their children read in English. Americanization meant participation "in all respects of American life"—the opportunity to become productive members of society, with rewards, political rights, and some

Table 5.2. Percentages for Illiterates, Ages 10–20, 1910

County	Percent Illiterate
Baraga	1.3
Houghton	1.1
Keweenaw	4.3
Ontonagon	3.2

understanding of the evolving mix of peoples that was America. Acculturation combined, in a singular manner, "long cherished American principles" with the "best ideals and contributions brought from other countries." Much of that was manifested as individuals of different ethnic groups continued to intermarry. Individuals retained some ethnic customs while accepting the ways of the larger American culture. As the mother of one pupil expressed it in a note to school authorities who questioned the child's "nationality" in 1897, she was German, her husband, a Swede, and "therefore [our] little Willie is American."[80]

6

The "Golden Age" of Copper

1890 – 1920

FROM 1890 THROUGH 1920, OVER 5 BILLION
pounds of copper were produced in the Keweenaw Peninsula as
population in the area mushroomed.[1] Despite economic depression
in the 1890s, work was available; and Americans and Europeans
poured in to do it. New mines along the south range, lumbering
in Ontonagon County, and new industry in Baraga County helped
provide jobs.

A burgeoning population increased pressure on the existing in-
frastructure. The Copper Country responded with new settlements,
improved transportation, more schools and other institutions, business expansion, and improved recreational facilities. Census figures
show the magnitude of population growth (see Table 6.1).[2]

Table 6.1. Keweenaw Peninsula, Population 1890–1910		
County	1890	1910
Baraga	3,036	6,127
Houghton	35,389	88,098
Keweenaw	2,894	7,156
Ontonagon	3,756	8,650

As always, the future was bright, golden with promise—certain to reward if only one seized opportunities. So argued a visitor, who praised the "great district" with its industrious people and "opportunities for the young man that cannot be excelled. . . . Dig, and your fortune awaits you, [said another]. These rocky hills, studded with copper must yield up vast riches to him who will delve." Hyperbole, yes, and certainly most unrealistic, because almost all the land had already been acquired; but such expressions satisfied many; for as long as mines remained productive, persons who offered services to feed, clothe, educate, amuse, and comfort the living and bury the dead could succeed. Patrick H. O'Brien, who had good reason to feel bitter about the Copper Country, recalled late in life that it "was the most prosperous area of any activity in the whole world at the time [1899, early 1900s]." Quincy stock reached a peak of $189 a share in 1899 while Calumet and Hecla's soared to one thousand dollars a share in 1907. Due to the worldwide expansion of the electrical industry, consumption of copper continued to increase.[3]

Visitors to Chicago's 1893 world's fair saw evidence of the Keweenaw's copper wealth—a large mass—as well as ingots, bars, and cakes—of the red metal. Models depicted mining at Tamarack and Calumet and Hecla. A twenty-five-foot-high arch of light red and brown sandstone from Portage Entry quarries and Marquette testified further to the north country's bounty.[4]

In Ontonagon County, the famed Minesota Mine's output had declined after the 1860s; in 1882, the mine shipped just slightly more than ten thousand pounds of copper. Seven Ontonagon County companies produced in 1896 only 117,520 pounds. By then, lumbering was more important. The Ontonagon Lumber Company had organized in September, 1881, with thirteen thousand acres of pine and a mill capable of cutting two hundred thousand feet of lumber and three hundred thousand shingles daily, marking a turn in the county's economy. The next year, Sisson and Lelley from Michigan's Ottawa County bought a mill site west of the river and by 1883 cut five hundred thousand shingles daily and employed 250 men.[5]

The Diamond Match Company gained control of Ontonagon Lumber and purchased even more pine land. Lumbering helped spur rail service. Soon, Diamond worked round the clock with up to four hundred men in mills, depending on the season. In less than a decade, Diamond was capable of producing up to seventy million feet of lumber annually in its mill and became the "single biggest timber cutter in the Upper Peninsula." One of the first great monopolies of its time, Diamond cornered between 85 and 95 percent of the market.[6]

A new culture accompanied the new economy. The lumberjack was "a man handy at most all wood work,"[7] and gangs of men recruited in Wisconsin and Michigan lived in camps and applied axe and saw to thousands of acres of pine forest. Most were "sober, industrious . . . loyal to their employers," men with values, energetic, great tellers of tales, often profane but men with a grand sense of humor. An old-timer recalled Jack Arvey kicking open the door of a camp bunkhouse and shouting, "Turn out you fellers; today is Monday, tomorrow will be Tuesday, the next day Wednesday—half the week gone and nothing done yet." Disciplines at some dining tables forbade talk; and each "jack" had his particular place, priority given to seniority, with foreman at the head, straw boss at the end of the table. New men applying for work often asked who would cook, for a bad chef could mean a winter of agony in the forest. Men created a veritable dictionary of slang: *punk* for bread, *red horse* for corned beef, and *sowbelly* for pork.[8]

Settlements rose, named for the lumber companies creating them: Calderwood, Paulding, Barclay, Choate. O'Brien was a Thomas Nester lumber camp with a brief existence (1888–93) on the Duluth, South Shore, and Atlantic Railroad route. Ewen, a famous logging camp, began as Ewen Station in 1889, its name altered from the original Ewing, the name of a lumberman. On Highway 28, Ewen

Lumber camp crew, October 1894. (State Archives of Michigan.)

today calls tourists' attention to its being the home of the "1893 World's Fair Load of Logs Replica, consisting of 50 White Pine logs, masterfully assembled on a magnificently handcrafted sleigh." Craigsmere developed as a sawmill town named after the Craig Lumber Company, which began operations about 1885. By 1892, it was a station on a branch of the Chicago and Northwestern Railroad. Near Ewen was Matchwood, founded by Diamond in 1888 to supply its logging camps. Wiped out by forest fire in 1893, Matchwood rebuilt only to be destroyed by another fire in 1906. With access to supplies such as Matchwood provided, camps could be maintained less expensively deep in the woods.[9]

The high-water mark of pine logging in northern Michigan occurred in 1894–95. When fires swept vast acreage, scorching, but not consuming, pine forests, Diamond hired jobbers to assist in cutting; and six thousand lumberjacks worked through the winter. Some thirteen million feet of pine fell in one week. Twelve hundred horses hauled logs to the Ontonagon River; and great log jams occurred, some lasting until 1897. The port was invigorated. Boosters reveled in the giant cut of 1894–95 as proof of Ontonagon's prominence as the locus of the industry. Then on August 28, 1896, disaster struck. After weeks of acrid stench from nearby burning forests, the central business district of Ontonagon disappeared as fire hit, with seventy-five-mile-per-hour winds tossing brands through the air. Hundreds of people escaped from what an eyewitness called a "monster tidal wave of flame." An estimated 340 buildings lay in ashes and charred lumber. More than two thousand men, women, and children roamed homeless, without possessions. The curious came on excursions from Hancock and Houghton to "visit the ruins."[10]

H. M. Powers, editor of the *Ontonagon Herald*, visiting Houghton, spoke optimistically of Diamond Match's expectations to resume activity and of a hundred buildings under construction by September 24. But the company decided not to rebuild mills and plants. In bad straits financially, Diamond applied the insurance money to its corporate debt, cut the remaining timber, floated it to Ontonagon, then sent the lumber by rail to its Green Bay, Wisconsin, mill. The county's leaders groused, threatening tax increases; but Ontonagon's lumber boom had ended. A recent historian concluded, "Ontonagon's unhappy fate presaged the future of other northern boom communities built on pine."[11]

Undaunted, the Copper Country moved forward with other timber ventures and the opening of even more copper mines. In Keweenaw County, the organization of the Wolverine Mining Company (1882) and the Mohawk Mining Company (1898) provided employment to many, as did their mills at Gay, where today tons of stamp sand cover the Traverse Bay shores. Kearsarge, Wolverine, Gay, Copper City, Ahmeek, Allouez, and Mohawk were new towns and villages, as were Freda, Redridge, Beacon Hill, South Range, Baltic, Trimountain, and Painesdale—the latter group spawned either west or south of Houghton by the Atlantic Mining Company or the Copper Range Consolidated (1901), a holding company merging several smaller enterprises. Everywhere, excitement ran high. In the company store at Beacon Hill, J. R. Bennetts, the aggressive young manager, raised monthly sales very quickly from five hundred to five thousand dollars.[12]

The Atlantic Mining Company, organized in December 1872, became famous for management's successful processing of low-grade rock, the average yield of copper being twelve-and-a-quarter to fourteen-and-a-half pounds per ton. Joseph Gay, president of Atlantic, was ably assisted by John Stanton, a mining entrepreneur of almost legendary repute. Stanton involved himself in the Winona, Phoenix, Michigan, Mohawk, Wolverine, and Copper Range companies. Along with William A. Paine and a few associates, he controlled, by 1904, nine mines producing about sixty-two million pounds of copper. During tense times in 1893, with miners' wages low and depression settling over the entire United States, many Finns homesteaded thirty miles west of Houghton along the way to Ontonagon. Families left Atlantic Mine to form, by 1901, Toivola (Place of Hope). Many would combine subsistence farming with part-time mining or lumbering.

Calumet and Hecla, the giant among Keweenaw mines, produced 59.5 percent of Michigan copper in 1890; but the percentage gradually sank, reaching 35.7 by 1920. Dividend payments reached seven million dollars in 1900 after hitting a high in 1899 of ten million.[13]

Foster and Whitney had said in 1850 that there was "a limit to the productiveness of all mines; for, when once fairly opened, their exploitation becomes more expensive the farther it is prosecuted." Managers, especially at Quincy and Calumet and Hecla, did everything possible to cut costs and ensure greater efficiency. Some critics complained of the extravagances of Agassiz in duplicating machinery; but he argued that this had been done "to guard stockholders against disasters incident to a mining company's work [and] nothing else could have insured . . . employees the steady work which they have enjoyed since the opening of the mine, [for] a more parsimonious policy would have entailed many delays."

Calumet and Hecla faced not only declining copper content of rock at greater depths but also competition from western mines in the nineteenth century. Since 1872, Calumet and Hecla had entered into agreements guaranteeing copper sales to eastern middlemen. In

October 1883, the company entered into a pooling agreement with Quincy, Central, Atlantic, Franklin, and other companies whereby Calumet and Hecla regulated sales, restricting them when the market price was low and pooling its output with that of other companies to protect all. But by 1888, Montana produced twelve million *more* pounds of copper than did the Lake Superior mines. The Western mines continued to lead. By the 1890s, Calumet and Hecla was no more the important cog in regulating the world copper market; but it continued, for years, to stabilize conditions in "various movements organized for mutual protection."[14] A later historian summed up the situation well: "The handwriting was on the wall, but it was hard to read in the blinding light of the pure masses of copper gleaming in the walls of the mass mine drifts and stopes."[15]

Calumet and Hecla refused to join the Amalgamated Copper Company created by Standard Oil interests at the turn of the century in an attempt to form a monopoly and corner the copper market. The Calumet company's output in 1896 was 19.6 percent of the total United States production of copper. The company had, as of October 1, 1897, capital stock of $1.2 million and up to then had paid stockholders dividends amounting to $50,850,000, "in addition to perfecting an expensive mining plant and making numerous surface improvements of a modern and superior character." The company owned more than 2,600 acres of mineral land in Houghton County and more than 20,352 acres of timber land in Keweenaw, Houghton, and Ontonagon counties. By 1907, it possessed 125,000 acres of the best pine lands in the Upper Peninsula. The stamp mills occupied about another thousand acres.[16]

The Calumet and Hecla Mine had seventeen shafts; and the new, very expensive Red Jacket Shaft, begun in late 1889, connected with No. 4 Calumet at the thirty-sixth, thirty-ninth, and forty-second levels. The new shaft was sunk to a depth of forty-nine hundred feet; and accoutrements like the boiler houses, hoisting engines, and brick smokestack 250 feet high seemed the apex of the company's development. Boston financial circles believed the Calumet conglomerate would last another twenty-five years, that is, until 1932—an accurate appraisal. The Calumet and Hecla mines employed about 16,500 men in 1904; in 1907, employment reached a peak of 21,014 and subsequently fell, slowly at first.[17] Many workers labored underground in hives of feverish activity with shafts and drifts corresponding to the streets and avenues on surface.

An early historian described life underground:

> Hundreds and thousands of feet below the surface of the ground there are railroads, cars, telegraph and telephone lines,

and great chambers bright with glittering spars and copper, illuminated by artificial light and filled with miners, trammers, and timbermen. The solid rock is pierced with rapidly revolving power drills, moved by compressed air sent down in tubes from reservoirs on the surface. The dynamite cartridge explodes with terrific force, tears asunder the hardest rock held together by tough native copper. Great blocks come crashing down and are seized upon by the trammers, thrown into cars which are pushed to the shafts.

There the rock was dumped into skips, hoisted to the surface, and dumped into cars of an automatic tram road to be carried to the rock house, where a large gang of men began their treatment of the ore before sending it off to mill and smelter.[18]

About forty-five thousand people lived in a radius of three miles of Calumet; housing remained at a premium, and ground "upon the Calumet location proper could not be had for any price." Rumor had it that Calumet and Hecla opposed a streetcar system; but by 1899, the high price of rental housing drove many from places near

Quincy miners about to descend into mine, c. 1902. (Michigan Technological University Archives and Copper Country Historical Collections, Michigan Technological University.)

their work. Men who lived at Florida location (adjoining Laurium) and worked at Red Jacket Shaft walked two-and-a-quarter to two-and-a-half miles each way. Agassiz said he favored a street railway when the masses of workers demanded one, and now the time had come. The Houghton County Traction Company was incorporated in 1900 and by 1902 had completed a trolley system running cars from Houghton's Hubbell Street through Hancock, Calumet, and terminating at Mohawk. Double tracks ran through the towns, and the fare was five cents. The new iron bridge over Portage Lake (1895) added to modernity, but businessmen and editors complained of late trains, which meant late mail.[19]

By the early twentieth century, the Mineral Range; Chicago and Northwestern; Chicago, Milwaukee, and Saint Paul; and Duluth, South Shore, and Atlantic Railroads operated in and out of the Copper Country, with the Copper Range railroad operating within the Keweenaw Peninsula. Some railroad officials, inspecting the area for the first time in 1896, were "favorably impressed [with] the evidence of prosperity . . . encountered" at Calumet. At Hancock, they admired the "new business blocks and handsome residences." Houghton had, they observed, a "metropolitan aspect," what with recent additions of the Shelden–Calverley and Shelden–Dee blocks and the magisterial Douglass House. Twenty-seven guests at the Douglass House on August 6, 1891, came from Duluth, New York, Chicago, Cleveland, Muskegon, Toledo, Milwaukee, and Saint Paul and Wisconsin towns and cities. The fifty-eight guests of July 26 that year included a couple from the Transvaal, South Africa, ten men from Chicago, three from Detroit, and others from the Upper Peninsula towns. Salesmen arrived daily to service the lucrative market that was the Copper Country at the turn of the century.[20]

Despite the denuding occasioned by mining and timbering and growth of "cities in the wilderness" around the mines, most of the Copper County in 1890 remained a land of forest. Most settlements were attached to mines. Seemingly parasitical but independent and vigorous, they helped to create a melting-pot culture. Copper Country population centers, such as Hancock (which alone enjoyed the status of "city"), Houghton, Red Jacket, Laurium, Lake Linden, and Ontonagon increasingly impressed visitors with establishments and institutions as fine as those in many urban neighborhoods.

Despite occasional business slumps, towns could hardly supply the demands of customers. Although Ontonagon's population grew only from 1,267 in 1900 to 1,964 in 1910, with major growth taking place outside the town, the story elsewhere was remarkable (see Table 6.2).[21]

**Table 6.2. Growth in Copper Country
Population Centers, 1890–1910**

County	1890	1900	1910
Houghton	2,062	3,359	5,113
Hancock	1,772	4,050	8,981
Red Jacket (Calumet)	3,073	4,668	4,211
Laurium	1,159	5,643	8,537
Lake Linden	1,862	2,597	2,325
Baraga	1,090	1,185	1,071
L'Anse	1,468	620	708

Red Jacket, often known as Calumet and officially renamed in 1929, was already overcrowded by 1900. Between then and 1910, part of Red Jacket's population gravitated to nearby Laurium. As for Baraga and L'Anse, township figures are better indicators of growth in their areas (see Table 6.3).

Table 6.3. Township Figures, Baraga and L'Anse, 1890–1910

Township	1890	1900	1910
Baraga	1,090	2,097	2,548
L'Anse	1,468	1,360	2,083

By 1909, a small group of taxpayers who owned automobiles saw Houghton County's road building and maintenance as inadequate. The board of supervisors submitted the issue to the electors in 1910, when a thousand automobiles and light trucks travailed over poor roads; and 7,100 citizens voted for a good road system, with 989 opposed. Thus was born the Houghton County Road Commission, composed of three members who estimated finances for 1910–11 at twenty-nine thousand dollars.[22]

When, in 1913, progressive-minded politicians attempted to secure legislation at Lansing to prevent pollution of streams and lakes and to protect fish and fisheries, Allen F. Rees, of Houghton, attorney for Calumet and Hecla, argued that the bill was so broad it would prohibit the deposit of tailings from stamp mills and not only injure the operation of mills worth more than eight million dollars but also end the entire copper-mining industry. A bill to license and regulate hunting and killing of wild animals and birds found opposition from Representative Albert E. Petermann, also associated with Calumet and Hecla. Petermann explained that he would vote *no* because he did not believe "in discrimination against resident aliens"; that is, such legislation would hurt Copper Country hunters who with their families enjoyed the small game and pheasants so abundant there. Senator Frank James at Lansing, on April 10, 1913, introduced Petition No. 1279 of "Matt Kangas and 25 other citizens of Houghton county, in favor of the passage of the bills removing state protection of skunk and black bear."

The bill on pollution was introduced February 24, 1913; debated; read a third time by April 19; and then referred to committee— and that was the last of it for this legislative session. The incident is one of many that, seventy years later, returned in larger forms as environmentalists battled those who wished industrial development to help the Upper Peninsula. The case for the environmentalists was put neatly in the Michigan Senate on March 20, 1913, by Peter Jensen, representative of Delta County:[23] "Nature will take care of itself, it is true, when all goes naturally; but just as soon as the white man gets into a country and what you call civilization comes in, the wild fowl and fish and game cannot get along with it."

Such arguments fell on deaf ears of men and their families who needed work. Except for Progressives advocating conservation in the early twentieth century, few challenged the inexorable exploitation of timber. When Mass City was platted to accommodate those who worked for the Mass Consolidated Mine, a mile-long boardwalk, along which lay thirty-eight saloons, connected the new town with Maple Grove (Greenland).[24]

The district population grew to 110,031 by 1910; and new facilities gradually arose to meet needs. Keweenaw Peninsula residents who originally relied solely on company hospitals were provided with additional facilities at the turn of the century. The Sisters of Saint Joseph of Carondelet, of Saint Louis, Missouri, operated a hospital from 1899 to 1904 at Hancock, after which the institution moved into its new, five-story brick-and-sandstone building with pillared entrance. Here a nursing school was organized in 1920. The venerable "Saint Joe's" hospital by 1951 became the Portage View Hospital— the present medical center—and in 1960, a long-term care unit was added. Between 1953 and 1963, the center cared for 32,124 patients; and 4,512 babies were born there. Outbreaks of near epidemic proportions of measles and scarlet fever were common in the early twentieth century. At Calumet, besides the company hospital, a public

hospital was organized at the turn of the century; and after World
War I, this institution, the Calumet Public Hospital, built its red
brick building and continues to serve the community. Despite the
existence of medical institutions, folk remedies persisted. Having read
in an almanac that arthritis was "only a phase of indigestion," Lucena
Brockway fasted "*four whole days*"; and though feeling "a goneness"
at her stomach, she slept better.[25]

Within slightly more than ten years, three new libraries were
erected to serve various parts of the Keweenaw Peninsula. The Calumet and Hecla Library was built in 1898. As early as 1874, a
worker argued that many would enjoy a reading room. When it
was established, it deteriorated into a facility where snobs frowned
upon the "lesser breeds." Company officials then opened a room
in the school at Calumet Avenue and School Street in 1896; and
in one month that summer, 969 persons drew 2,737 books from
a collection of 3,792. Agassiz then decided to establish a library in
an architectural gem for all inhabitants of School District No. 1 of
Calumet Township, not just for company employees.

The development of the magnificent library on Red Jacket Road
was a classic example of the curious amalgam of Calumet and Hecla
wealth, Boston intellectual activity, the peculiar attributes of Agassiz
(who had once taught in a school in his parents' Cambridge home),
and the creativity and independence of Calumet people. This mix
of New England, Copper Country, and European influences produced admirable results. Calumet and Hecla purchased 3,000 books
in Boston, adding them to the original 3,792. Original plans called

Calumet and Hecla Public Library.

for basement rooms, where games such as darts could be played and for bathing facilities for men and women. Fifteen years later, the company constructed nearby a huge red-brick bathhouse. In one month in 1913, 11,536 men, women, and children bathed there, a number that would have strained the twelve library baths which had been removed and replaced with stacks.

Constructed of mine (poor or discarded) rock, the Calumet Library became a community center; by 1935, it housed 50,000 volumes. In 1914, the diverse peoples of Calumet had access to 142 different English-language, and 28 foreign-language, newspapers and magazines. Languages included German, French, Italian, Swedish, Norwegian, Finnish, Polish, Slovenian, Croatian, and Hungarian. There one could find the *American Journal of Sociology, American Historical Review, Scientific American, Annals of the American Academy of Political and Social Science,* and *American Labor Legislation Review* but also the *Étude, Good Housekeeping, Collier's, London Illustrated News, McClure's, Little Folks, Mining World,* and the *Manual Training Magazine,* among others. In 1912–13, the circulation of books was 131,291. That year, 27,430 adults and 29,849 juveniles used the reading rooms. About 7,000 foreign-language books circulated. Finnish accounted for the largest number—1,694—with Italian at 977, and German at 870. Fiction withdrawals totaled 51,282, ranging from Dickens, Jane Austen, and Conan Doyle to Carolyn Wells, Frank Stockton, and Jack London. The plays of George Bernard Shaw with their militant and provocative socialist prefaces circulated along with works of Ibsen, Goethe, and Victor Hugo.[26]

William A. Paine, one of the founders of the Copper Range Consolidated Company and a Boston financier, established the Sarah Sargent Paine Memorial Library in Painesdale to honor his mother. Originally intended for Painesdale residents only, the library quickly offered its services to Baltic and Trimountain and eventually to all in Adams Township. The red sandstone building was dedicated in 1903.

The third of these new libraries in this era was built at Houghton, after John A. Doelle—first a teacher and then, beginning in 1906, superintendent of schools at Portage Lake—contacted Andrew Carnegie to obtain funds. It was completed by 1909. Doelle solicited money from businessmen to defray cost of the lot for the library. This library housed 13,344 books plus another 315 volumes of public documents.[27]

The tremendous surge in population, with its increased ethnic variety, challenged educators. School attendance jumped in Ontonagon County from 1,185 in 1895 to 3,266 in 1915; Houghton County's, in the same period, rose from 9,000 to 20,000; Keweenaw County's grew simultaneously, in part due to opening of new mines there, from 536 to 1,672, while Baraga's school population rose 58 percent, to 1,850 pupils in 1915. Attendance records were broken at Calumet in 1907, when 6,012 pupils enrolled. More and larger schools were required; but they existed alongside small rural schools, one composed of only sixteen pupils. School attendance rose sharply, from 88 to 96 percent in Ontonagon County in 1915, a trend evident in other counties, too, as truant officers clamped down on absentee pupils.[28]

Dedicated and talented teachers and school supervisors emerged to meet the educational challenge. John Doelle, at Portage Lake, became a veritable legend in his time, spurring the building of more schools and working endlessly to have students receive an outstanding education. He hired the best teachers available and introduced courses in music, home economics, and physical and manual training. James K. Jamison came from Isabella County to Ontonagon County, becoming superintendent of schools from 1913 to 1917. He left briefly but returned in 1920 and made a solid imprint, insisting on quality education.

Teachers usually boarded with families. One Mine Street boardinghouse at Calumet contained so many teachers that wags labeled it The Hennery, a slight that failed to acknowledge the truly noble work carried on for decades by devoted women. Ida Blum recalled working at Swedetown's Eugene Field School on a hill west of Calumet, where the principal installed a bathtub used by pupils who had none at home. Miss Blum taught children of Finns and Poles for forty-five dollars a month with a promise of seventy dollars after five years. She and others enjoyed transportation to and from their homes but ate their lunches in furnace rooms at times. Later, this beloved teacher, who truly understood children, taught elementary school for forty-six years at Calumet.[29]

A most singular instance of dedication to their charges was manifested for more than half a century in Adams Township in Houghton County by Frederick (Fred) and Cora Jeffers. Born downstate, Fred Jeffers was orphaned early and was ill treated by the father of a family that took him in. But one of the daughters of the family taught him to read, so that by the time he entered school at age six in Jackson County, he read fluently. He ran away soon after graduating from high school, worked as a farmhand, and, later, in a Kalamazoo grocery store. He left the store when he discovered scales set to give short weight and the proprietor adding water to oysters. His goal was to work as a lumberjack in the Upper Peninsula, but an Ypsilanti family persuaded him to attend college at Ypsilanti. He developed into an outstanding leader in student affairs and graduated with honors in 1891. There he met Cora Doolittle; and their friendship ripened, during a three-day lake trip from Detroit to Houghton, into an engagement to marry. After graduation, Jeffers was hired by the superintendent of the Atlantic Mine to go to the Copper Country to teach. The knowledge that the Atlantic schoolboys "had thrown out the last three men" did not daunt him.

The Atlantic school was "redolent of garlic, unwashed children and the odors of stable and latrine," said one observer. Scabies and lice existed. Some children had been sewn into their underwear for the winter. Challenged by a bully, Jeffers gave him "a severe drubbing"; and when the bully returned with his father, the new schoolmaster invited the father to an encounter. He declined and later became one of Jeffers's admirers.[30]

Cora and Fred married in 1894 and set about their great work together. She served fifty-five years as principal at Painesdale High School. He served as Adams Township superintendent from 1891 and for eighteen years on the state board of education, taught summers at Marquette's normal school, and retired only in 1948.

The couple lived through waves of ethnic groups: Cornish, Welsh, Scandinavians, Germans, Italians, and finally, Finns. At first meeting resistance, the Jeffers gradually convinced working people that an education—a sound one—was the key to success in life. Parents first said their daughters needed no high school: they should marry and become housewives. High school would only "spoil" their sons and daughters and make them dissatisfied with the "class" into which they were born. A German father, hearing his daughter *speak* well after some time spent at school and win praise from neighbors, withdrew her, asserting, "She is smart enough." But persistence, excellent books, and novel techniques worked. In 1907, Painesdale's first high school graduation occurred with no formal commencement address; for the pupils spoke. Cornishmen who once said of education for daughters, "What good is it to she?" now boasted, "My maid has graduated." Cora Jeffers recalled that "they had something new to talk about over their teacups."[31]

Mrs. Jeffers taught Shakespeare and German and substituted for teachers of every other high school subject. She emphasized personality growth, introduced class discussions, and had students reenact great moments in history. She and Fred did all possible to satisfy "the need of every child to be understood and recognized as an individual." They developed child-centered schools, sent groceries to the destitute, visited the ill, paid for the correction of crossed eyes, persuaded wayward pupils to mend their ways, cajoled parents into seeing the value of education, had graduates assist teachers, and financed college educations for many of their promising but indigent students. They had shower facilities installed and required all students to bathe as the first order of activity on Monday mornings. They pressed democracy by refusing to allow a girl to wear an expensive dress at the junior prom and encouraging students of all backgrounds to participate in creative projects in classrooms. All boys took shop; girls, four years of homemaking. Young women graduates had to sew their own graduation gowns. Each morning, the pupils enjoyed a half-hour of music. During the school year, Cora and Fred Jeffers prescribed much homework. At the prom, Fred danced with every girl. Seniors stood in line at the junior prom to welcome the juniors.[32]

Cora, described once as "the tireless woman of the range," also gardened, canned produce, and developed into a militant public speaker when she took up the cause of woman suffrage. A lifelong student, she studied aeronautics and taught a class in that during World War II. Education seemed elitist to many Copper Country workers imbued with cultural values learned in Europe. Cora Jeffers believed the couple's real achievement as educators lay not in their long service but in that in a mining community, "where European ideas prevailed that . . . children of working people were not to be educated beyond the grades, . . . it was possible *to establish a high school.*" That only the wealthy and privileged should be educated was the aristocratic notion that the parents knew.

Mr. and Mrs. Jeffers insisted on the decorum and discipline that aristocrats believed children of the proletariat needed. At dismissal, children lined up silently and marched out. In time, the two educators became "more gentle, understanding, sympathetic yet decidedly firm." Under their tutelage and in the Copper Country schools generally, where American democracy's values juxtaposed with aristocratic principles, schools were places for work. Here one acquired academic knowledge and "the qualities of character, habits of courtesy, proper conduct and intelligent service that would develop intelligent and worthwhile citizenship [and] deep respect for constituted authority, . . . for the rights of others, and . . . habits of observation of regulations, punctuality, orderliness."[33]

A former student who achieved much success said, in 1946, of the couple, "They are part of the cement which holds society together." By then a Christian minister, the former student had spoken in synagogues and invited rabbis to speak in his church, actions inspired by the tolerance taught him by Cora and Fred Jeffers with their high regard for individuals of all ethnic groups and religions.[34]

So successful was Fred Jeffers in Adams Township that he was offered the superintendency of the Detroit schools in the early twentieth century. He said *no* to Detroit. Asked in the 1930s why they did not leave (because before long, only ghost towns would remain in the Copper Country), the couple said they had long ago cast their lot

Cora and Fred Jeffers, c. 1931. (Houghton County Historical Society.)

with the community. Fred quoted Saint Luke 9:62: "No man, having put his hand to the plough, and looking back, is fit for the kingdom of God." They had to remain faithful to whatever new generation of young strangers entered their classrooms.[35]

At Calumet High School, Superintendent W. E. Trebilcock summarized well in 1942: "The qualities which made the mine a well-managed, profitable business and the town a thriving community made of the schools an institution whose reputation deservedly spread afar and, what is more important, was a matter of general pride and proud concern on the part of the residents of Calumet." At Calumet, Portage Lake, and Painesdale High Schools, by 1915, students read American history texts written by Andrew C. McLaughlin and John Bach McMaster—books that today many college students would find formidable. Some schools offered classical curricula, including Latin, alongside a growing practical emphasis on commerce, manual training, and home economics.

In all the schools, censuses took place before the school year opened. School inspectors who were local citizens donated much time to visiting schools and writing annual reports. A one-mill tax and other direct taxes provided for improved school financing. Quincy Township spent about $12,000 in 1894–95 on its schools. In 1914–15, Adams Township spent $140,000, and Portage Township, $179,751. In Calumet Township, District No. 1 spent $62,559 in 1894 and $282,117 twenty years later. Hancock city spent $80,182

173

on schools in 1914–15 when there were 1,664 pupils with an average daily attendance of 96 percent. Such was progress in Houghton County.

Ella Chamberlain, superintendent at Ontonagon in 1901, strove, like the Jeffers couple, to democratize society in the forests. She announced, with her June commencement committee, that "no flowers or other gifts will be received at the opera house on the night of graduation for any members of the class."[36]

As early as 1891, a Miss Nye reorganized the primary school system at Houghton; and it was another instance of the variety of approaches used to meet children's needs. She brought parents and teachers together. Teachers visited homes and parents held meetings twice a year in various schools, with fathers in attendance. By 1917, mothers met eight times a year. Miss Nye promoted pageants to instill civic pride and encourage children's creativity.

Catholic schools did their share of educating the young at Baraga, Hancock, and Calumet. About eight hundred enrolled in 1905 at Calumet's Sacred Heart schools, which provided a library for each of its classrooms in two buildings housing elementary and high school. The Sisters of Notre Dame taught reading, writing, and arithmetic, as well as music (vocal and instrumental). Girls learned needlework and in the 1930s, boys and girls were taught to dance. Botany and zoology manifested themselves in a large museum collection of animal and plant life from the community and from the Atlantic and Pacific coasts. By 1915, these schools and the German Lutheran parochial school at Laurium (Saint Paul) enrolled 1,056 pupils. For years, adults recalled stern male taskmasters at the Saint Paul school, where American curricula combined with elements of German Lutheran culture.[37]

Graduates of public and parochial high schools sometimes went on to the University of Michigan or South Bend's Notre Dame or to study in Europe. Many teachers in the Copper Country received their basic training at what was, in earlier times, the Marquette Teachers College; and a few received part at the Michigan School of Mines. At the latter, the autumn term opened on October 2, 1899, with seventy-nine students, thirty of them new, most studying mining engineering. Few came from Houghton or Calumet: that was a later development. In 1896, the new entrants included young men from Detroit, Chicago, Ann Arbor, Toronto, Cincinnati, and Durango, Mexico, as well as from Pennsylvania, Iowa, Colorado, and California. J. J. Murray arrived from Castle Milk Mill, Lockerbie, Scotland. "These mining school students are a queer lot of boys, although of a very industrious nature," said the *Portage Lake Mining Gazette* in 1896, voicing the tension that at times existed between town and gown at Houghton.

After three years of study, one received the degree of bachelor of science; and an additional year's study could become the nucleus of a master's degree. Students attended classes from six to seven hours each day or worked in laboratories, mills, or mines. By 1900, enrollment reached 121. By 1908–9, 292 students were enrolled, 119 of them new students. The crowded campus (it had only Hubbell Hall and the Engineering Building) expanded with new mining and chemistry buildings and—pushed by students, faculty, staff, and Houghton citizens—a gymnasium. By 1908, landscape artists developed an appealing campus. In 1911, the college celebrated a quarter-century of development, with an illuminated boat parade on Portage Lake, music, and visits from Michigan's Governor Chase S. Osborn and President William H. Taft's personal representative. By 1922, enrollment reached more than 300.[38]

In 1899, Suomi College and Theological Seminary opened its doors at Hancock with twenty students enrolled from Michigan, Minnesota, New York, Ohio, Montana, Pennsylvania, and some young men from Finland. Board and room, including laundry, fuel, and light, cost twenty-six dollars for three months. Merchants donated flour and supplies, while farmers sent potatoes, tubs of butter, and other produce to help feed the scholars. Its interior finished in Norway pine, the Old English Gothic building with elliptical Gothic arches also contained a dining room in the basement and a gymnasium on the top floor. Student chambers were described as commodious, with ten-foot-high ceilings. President J. K. Nikander, scholar and clergyman, taught from 8:00 A.M. to 5:00 P.M., edited two newspapers, and involved himself with numerous social duties.[39]

Employers did not always find it easy to obtain workers from the expanding local population. First-class mechanics remained in demand; and a Hancock contractor who had to produce forty thousand railway ties in 1907 had difficulty finding workers, for they frowned on short-term employment. He paid three dollars per day "clear," complaining that the men found steady work—and did not have to work as hard—at other Copper Country locations.

Various ways of community development unfolded in this "golden" era. The Lake Superior Produce and Cold Storage Company completed, in December 1899, a huge five-story building of Portage Entry sandstone. The seventy-five-by-seventy-nine-foot edifice faced the Copper Range Railroad tracks at Houghton. It contained general offices; huge storage rooms for apples, oranges, and lemons; a poultry dressing room; and storage rooms for hay, grain, oats, potatoes, turnips, onions, beets, parsnips, and carrots. Some

rooms had a capacity of five carloads. The pioneer days of scraping
through the winter had ended.

By 1907, building expansion at Portage Lake provided three hun-
dred thousand dollars worth of work: a new schoolhouse at Franklin
Mine, repairs at Hancock High School, a new Episcopal church at
Houghton, a three-story addition to Gartner's Department Store in
Hancock, new bottling works for Park Brewery, a two-story build-
ing for Ed Haas and Company, haberdashers, and new store fronts
on Quincy Street (Hancock), along with palatial residences in East
Hancock and in Houghton.

Some businesses had begun with owners peddling goods door to
door, as Jacob Gartner and son Isidor had done before opening their
first store in Hancock in 1886. By 1895, established on Quincy Street,
Gartner's Store was on its way to becoming a Hancock institution.
Sakari's was another store that evolved from peddling to the selling of
clothing, shoes, furniture, carpets, tinware, woodenware, dry goods,
crockery, meats, and groceries. Richard Vollwerth, sausage maker,
founded his one-room business in 1915 at Hancock. Thirty years
later, it was a most successful enterprise operating throughout the
Upper Peninsula.[40]

Hancock needed street signs, argued the *Mining Gazette* early in
the twentieth century. A soap salesman offered them free if he could
list the name of his company below the street name. The city council
refused, but signs appeared; and by 1910, cement walks replaced the
many wooden walks. Thrifty miners' families utilized the Northern
Michigan Building and Loan Association (organized in 1889), which,
by 1914, became Detroit and Northern Michigan Building and Loan
Association. Mining companies, workers, financial institutions, and
merchants formed a grid at Hancock; and the pattern was repeated
elsewhere. The opening in Hancock of the elegant Hotel Scott in
1906, the Kerredge Theatre in 1902 on Quincy Street, and Calumet's
Opera House in 1900 marked a coming of age for urbanity in the
Copper Country.

The Kerredge had parquet, a balcony, and a gallery reached from
a side door; the theater accommodated 1,250 persons. It had a big
orchestra pit, which was augmented when Broadway musicals came
to town. Next door to the Kerredge, the Scott Hotel hosted visiting
theatrical troupes. The Kerredge was the city's answer to Calumet's
Opera House, which opened March 20, 1900, and seated 1,200 (419
in parquet, 400 in the first balcony, and 380 in the gallery). Its
chairs were upholstered (except in the gallery, where rude benches
prevailed) in Waldorf tapestry of greenish tint to blend with the
crimson, gold, and ivory of the interior and faced a stage sixty-six-

feet wide, twenty-eight deep, and sixty high. The grand proscenium arch measured twenty-six by thirty-two feet. In anticipation of the opening, the *Gazette* related, "In appointment and furnishings on the inside it will be the peer of any theater in the West." Lake Linden also built an opera house, hoping to attract shows ordinarily headed for Hancock or Calumet. Its manager in 1908, Thomas O'Rourke, provided a connecting buffet.[41]

The Houghton Club building, constructed by Herman Gundlach, Sr., in 1906, found many admirers for its classic simplicity, with neo-Renaissance facade and projecting balcony and columns. Businessmen in 1900 lunched in the Board of Trade Garden and Cafe, where potted palms hung from an elaborate inset ceiling, and arches and small tables allowed for confidential talk. At the best stores, blue serge suits sold for nine dollars to twenty dollars, and a woman's fine tailored suit for $22.50—high prices, considering wages. All manner of industries related to mining continued to produce. Charles Ojala, Jr., of the Northland Shoe Manufacturing Company, announced in 1915 that 80 percent of mining footgear was manufactured locally. His plant could turn out 250 pair per day.

Baraga and L'Anse developed new industries. A huge brickyard just outside L'Anse could store enough clay to make seven hundred thousand bricks in 1895. Several Baraga newspapers, following each other in succession, attested to civil growth and boosterism. The old rivalry continued. An item in a Baraga newspaper in 1897 mentioned a Houghton newsman who put up at L'Anse's Thomas House, "the only hotel in that pretty but desolate village." The desolation resulted from the 1896 fire; and Baraga, despite its rivalry, had been among the first to call for assistance for its sister city then.

As the nineteenth century matured, the Ojibwa lived in and about Baraga and L'Anse and wore "citizens' dress." About 50 percent of them belonged to Christian churches, most knew enough English for everyday conversation, and about 60 percent could read. The Bureau of Indian Affairs records indicated that "civilized pursuits" provided the sole support of the Keweenaw Bay Native Americans. They, like their white counterparts, continued to hunt and fish but surpassed them in the cultivation of wild rice. Newspaper stories of Native Americans perishing in fires or snow because they fell intoxicated, tales of whites illegally selling hard liquor, and pitiful accounts of demoralized people indicated that social problems remained, despite the federal government's rosy accounts of acculturation.[42]

At Lake Linden, ethnic changes occurring there by the early 1890s were evident in the names of local enterprises. J. B. Tibor, Epiceries et Vivres, advertised *bonbons et cigares*; Quai Robert served customers who arrived by water; and the newspaper was titled L'Union Franco–Américaine. The newspaper's editor, Telesphore Saint-Pierre, published, in 1895, a history of French Canadians in Michigan.[43]

Between 1895 and 1907, Red Jacket abounded in sturdy sandstone-and-brick business blocks. The four-story Ernest Bolman block, with shops below and three floors of apartments—a massive hunk of Romanesque architecture made of Portage Entry sandstone—dominated the corner of Eighth and Oak streets. A block away, the Nelson–Schroeder block, built circa 1903 by Gundlach of Houghton, remained for years an architectural prize, with arches, pilasters, roundels, and wrought-iron balconies. In the same year, Saint Anne's neo-Gothic church, pride of local French Canadians, joined such imposing structures along Fifth Street as the Peter Ruppe and Son store, selling general merchandise. The Richardsonian Romanesque style appeared in many variations, as did the Victorian Eclectic and the Neoclassical Revival styles. Sandstone and mine rock —materials peculiar to the Copper Country—joined brick, glass, and wood in creating a beauty particular to Red Jacket, Laurium, Hancock, Houghton, and Lake Linden. By 1907, the imposing Glass Block Department Store advertised millinery copied from the smart shops of Paris's Rue de la Paix. The village macadamized some streets in 1899–1900 but kept many of its raised wooden sidewalks for another fifteen years. By 1906, some of the first cement walks appeared. The majestic Town Hall and Opera House of 1900 marked a maturity for Red Jacket, where only twenty-five years earlier, tree stumps and log houses were beginning to give way to frame structures.[44]

At Laurium, all agreed in 1907 that Hecla, the main business street, should be paved. But who should pay? The village council said businessmen and property owners ought to pay part of the cost but were told that the village should shoulder the expense, as paving would benefit the entire community. By 1895, Laurium, having changed its name from Calumet, had also increased its size six times; and three further additions followed. The village boasted of being the home of the first indoor ice rink, the Superior Ice Palace, built shortly after 1900. Gas mains laid about 1906 brought a new fuel to residents of Calumet, Red Jacket, Laurium, and the Portage Lake towns. Laurium's First National Bank at Hecla and Third Streets had architectural rivals in the State Savings Bank across the street and the sandstone Town Hall nearby, which housed the fire engines. The vast Palestra, used for winter skating and other sports, as well as meetings in other seasons, served the community until 1921, when it was sold and moved to Marquette.

Rural and urban lived in uneasy tension. In 1907, Laurium authorities, after a roundup, impounded fifty cows found wandering, fined irate owners two dollars per stray, and announced they would keep up this "warfare against stray cows." Wandering bovines also plagued South Range, West Hancock, and Houghton's College Avenue. Seven years later, the practice having persisted, village fathers warned owners of strays that they would be arrested next. Angry owners released their beasts from the pound, where unpopular pound masters tended to resign after short tenures.[45]

Population pressure on housing brought expansion into new areas. By 1910, East Hancock's reputation as a most desirable residential location was fixed. But the city was crowded, and the move of some to Dollar Bay on the northeast shore of Portage Lake had begun. Known also as Dollarville, Dollar's Mill, and Clark, Dollar Bay began when Ransom Shelden set up his sawmill in 1861; it witnessed several logjams before its transformation into an ideal residential area.

The success of the Tamarack Mining Company, organized in 1885 west of Calumet and Hecla, with an output of over sixteen million pounds of refined copper by 1896, allowed a virtual new town to develop. Accompanying that was the Tamarack Co-operative Association, founded about 1890. The famous Tamarack Store, one hundred by seventy feet in area, had four giant departments. It sold goods at "virtually the middleman's price." By early 1913, the Tamarack Co-op had annual sales of $845,000 and, since organizing, had paid members over a million dollars in dividends. Stores in nearby Red Jacket governed their prices by those fixed by the Co-op, which also delivered in villages for a distance of fifteen miles. The par value of a share of Co-op stock was ten dollars. Customers received 12 to 13 percent returns on the amounts of their annual purchases.[46]

As population and communities expanded, social institutions ranging from ethnic lodges, societies, and religious organizations to musical groups, literary associations, and libraries remained one Copper Country defense against ever-present vice and crime. Legal authorities in Ontonagon County carried out raids on houses of prostitution and insisted on proper licenses for selling liquor in 1906, provoked, in large part, by public-spirited men and women. A variation on an old theme, such action was hardly novel. The Red Jacket newspaper fulminated against "dance halls" in 1897, declaring that they hardly differed from brothels and blaming certain Italians whom the "better part of the Italian colony" found shameful. Two years later, Lake Linden and Grover parents, outraged at liquor dealers selling spirits to their fourteen- and fifteen-year-old sons, took their case to the *Mining Gazette*. The lads, having just begun working and "exhausting every effort in endeavoring to imitate men," hired rigs, drove round to dives, even spent Sundays in them, and created nuisances as they drove home "under the influence." Some Hancock residents worried about "dangers that surround[ed] boys and girls of tender years . . . permitted to rove about the streets at night till they chose to go home." Citizens petitioned the council for a curfew bell but were ignored. Much crime was petty: Ontonagon boys stole pies or cakes from Edward Bergeron's bakery wagon, and adolescents formed informal gangs with, for example, Hecla boys hostile to Red Jacket youths.

At Red Jacket, mine workers assaulted and battered one another in saloon fights. Sometimes knifes were brandished. Patrons often purchased drinks after legal closing hours, with Sunday morning rows common. Editors wondered why the constables did not do their duty. The "rock building saloon" on Red Jacket's Sixth Street in 1896 was especially notorious. A foolish quarrel near a Baraga lumber camp in 1893 resulted from the overconsumption of whiskey, after which a homesteader fired a gun loaded with fine shot, wounding a lumberjack whose wife and four children lived at Houghton.

By 1908, saloons at Red Jacket closed at 11:00 P.M. daily and completely on Sunday. Police hauled violators to court as the county sheriff periodically attempted to stem vice. The court blotter contained numerous cases of drunk and disorderly men on the streets of Copper Country towns. Laurium in 1908 witnessed a rash of robberies, holdups, and burglaries. A young woman charged with killing her baby and placing the body in a ten-quart pail in a timber car in the Calumet and Hecla yards was said not to "realize the enormity of her crime." In 1914, "highwaymen" operated near Osceola, relieving streetcar passengers of cash. A 1918 raid in Red Jacket resulted in an African American pimp and his four white prostitutes being fined up to twenty-one dollars each plus costs, after which the "quintet also were ordered to leave [Houghton] county."[47]

Probably the most exciting crime occurred in 1893, when masked robbers, after placing logs on the Mineral Range Railroad tracks between Hancock and Calumet, took seventy thousand dollars from the Adams Express Company safe. It was part of the Calumet and Hecla payroll. Pinkerton detectives fanned out into the countryside, for experience taught them that in the "loneliness and vastness of rural areas" the unusual was quickly noticed. A farmer's wife who told of seeing a strange red buggy and a blanketed horse led sleuths to study hoofprints; and within seventy-two hours, assisted by information from a "madam" with knowledge of two men meeting with an express messenger, the detectives knew all they needed to solve the case. All but sixty-five dollars of the loot was recovered even though the thieves had managed to hide the money at Marquette.

Zoning laws to keep saloons out of neighborhoods, ministers' crusades to stop Sunday games of baseball and football and horse racing, periodic crackdown on houses of ill fame (with occupants given a choice between county jail or state reformatory), children sent to reform school, males who drank excessively to bolster egos and forget the sheer drudgery of tramming in mines—all seemed commonplace between 1890 and 1920, when journalists penned stories of the Copper Country as an industrial arcadia, the best place for a workman.[48]

By 1917, the Hancock Civic League materialized as an all-female club intent on "improved living conditions, attractive surroundings and the care and welfare of children." Beginning with garbage pickups and "paint-up-clean-up" campaigns, the women achieved enormous success; the group branched out to beautify the city, sell war bonds, and collect used clothing for overseas victims of war.

The Copper Country in the early twentieth century was part of a circuit graced by entertainment stars of the time. Artists who appeared in Hancock also performed in Red Jacket. Among those who appeared locally were Otis Skinner, Fiske O'Hara, John McCormack, Fritz Kreisler, and Sarah Bernhardt, who was said to have taken a trip down into the depths of the Quincy Mine. Richard Mansfield starred in Booth Tarkington's *Monsieur Beaucaire* (1902), and Joseph Jefferson, Jr., and William Jefferson came with Sheridan's *Rivals* in 1903 and 1908. Lillian Russell (1909), James O'Neill in the *Count of Monte Cristo*, Sarah Bernhardt in *Camille* (1911), Maude Adams in *Peter Pan* (1913), Ibsen's *Doll's House* (1904), and John Philip Sousa and

Red Jacket (Calumet) town hall and opera house. (Michigan Technological University Archives and Copper Country Historical Collections, Michigan Technological University.)

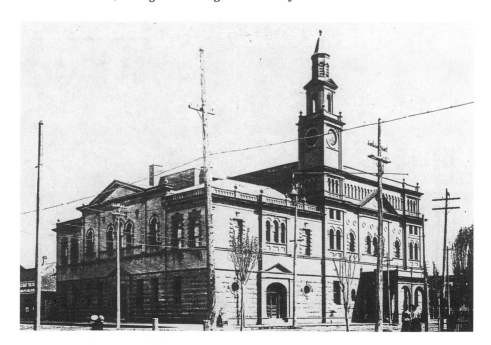

his band (1902, 1906, 1912) delighted thousands. Between 1900 and 1916, artists offered sixteen plays of Shakespeare, including *Hamlet* (twice in 1900) and Helena Modjeska in *Macbeth* and Schiller's *Mary Stuart* on December 6, 1900. Red Jacket's Opera House offered repertoire that included *Faust* and a short version of *Parsifal*.

Victor Herbert musicals, Wagnerian opera, *The Wizard of Oz*, and George M. Cohan's *Forty-Five Minutes from Broadway* alternated with slight comedies that some found vulgar, such as *The Maid and the Mummy* (1906), with its hit song, "Gee, but It's Great to Be Crazy." The new Red Jacket Opera House was a far cry from the former opera house on south Fifth Street (1887), where old chestnuts like *Uncle Tom's Cabin* still played in 1896. One entertainment at Lake Linden's opera house was a play, *Wedded and Parted* performed by a stock company alternating with vaudeville artists who traveled with the group.[49]

The Perils of Pauline, the exciting silent movie, spelled peril for stage productions by 1914. The Orpheum Theatre in Hancock showed movies by 1915, but stage and musical events continued at the Kerredge and at Red Jacket off and on until the Great Depression of the 1930s. By that time, Red Jacket had become Calumet, and the Red Jacket Opera House, the Calumet Theatre. Among speakers at Red Jacket before World War I, sculptor Lorado Taft, social settlement leader Jane Addams, and socialist Eugene Debs drew large crowds. In April 1914, Taneli Hurri, Finnish tenor, sang at the Kerredge Theatre in English, Finnish, Italian, German, and Swedish, offering Leoncavallo's "Arioso" from *Pagliacci* and songs by Grieg, Schumann, and Sibelius, including "Ajattelen Aikojani" (Think of the Past.)[50]

Much entertainment was locally spawned. Lodges and sports served as magnets, drawing together residents in need of ideological ballast in making the transition from European to American culture. People of many nationalities turned holidays into exhausting festival commemorations. The editor of the *Portage Lake Mining Gazette* complained about Hancock's and Houghton's dividing the Fourth of July celebration between them in 1896. Only saloonkeepers, main contributors to the holiday fund, rejoiced with such an arrangement. Why did the towns have to engage in so much rivalry, he asked. The "better element" decried this. Folks flocked to Hancock for its callithumpian parade in the morning. The main attraction at Houghton, a balloon ascent scheduled to occur in the afternoon, had trouble with wind, heading skyward only in the evening. The two towns held separate celebrations in later years.

Jilbert's Palace Restaurant, Red Jacket, charged thirty-five cents for its 1899 Christmas dinner. The menu included claret, bluepoint oysters, celery, and olives, then choice of soups, whitefish, capon, turkey, or duck, with vegetables and jellies, three kinds of potatoes, mushrooms, and frogs' legs. Dessert included a choice of English plum pudding with brandy sauce, apple or lemon meringue pie, vanilla ice cream, cheese, or cake. Then came California fruit, mixed nuts, and a choice of coffee, chocolate, or green tea. Such a Dickensian display of food was common in restaurants and hotels in those golden times.

Hancock and Calumet, from their early days, presented amateur productions. At Hancock, the Home Dramatic Club offered *Two Orphans*, a seven-act melodrama, in September 1896, at Saint Patrick's Hall, which was "packed to the doors"; the group raised seventy dollars. By 1908, the city's amateurs presented *The Pirates of Penzance* with a cast of more than eighty, directed by Professor L. A. Collom, teacher of music in the city's public schools. Two performances delighted hundreds at the Kerredge Theatre. Michigan Tech's Micomi Club produced musicals there, then toured by railroad to Calumet, Ishpeming, Marquette, Iron Mountain, Crystal Falls, and sometimes the Sault.[51]

In September 1906, the Italian fraternal societies sponsored dances and picnics: Laurium's Garibaldi Society, headed by the Red Jacket City Band, first paraded the Laurium and Red Jacket streets, then ascended to Tamarack Park for a picnic with sports, refreshments, and dancing. Red Jacket's Giuseppe Garibaldi Celibi, whose membership was restricted to Italian bachelors, hired the Calumet and Hecla Orchestra to play for their dance two weeks later at the Town Hall. Before the evening's entertainment, the 250 bachelors paraded through village streets, led by the Calumet and Hecla Band.

When the Red Jacket Band in 1908 lacked funds to buy uniforms and meet other expenses, a local businessman proposed that the band play on village streets Wednesday and Saturday evenings and that fellow businessmen contribute one or two dollars per week during summer months. This would bring people out on the streets and, they hoped, into their shops. In all the range towns, men and boys with musical inclinations formed brass bands, a practice that continued for decades. Days and nights preceding the Fourth of July, as well as the Christmas season, rang with their lively music. In the 1930s, young women of Slovenian descent formed drill teams affiliated with their church.

By 1914, the Chautauqua attracted many to Electric Park, where the Portage Lake Glee Club sang and learners saw travelogues or heard lectures on such topics as "Modern Italy," "Why God Made a Woman," and "Adam and Eve, and the Baby." Many sought the high culture. As a young girl, Alma W. Swinton took the train from

Ontonagon to Calumet at the turn of the century to study piano under a German Jew named Davis, who had studied at the Royal School of Music in London. Hundreds of Copper Country girls and boys studied piano and played "pieces" by Schubert, Grieg, Beethoven, and Mozart.[52]

Forty men attended the Honorable Jay A. Hubbell's sixty-seventh birthday party at the Onigaming Yacht Club, southeast of Houghton, in September 1896. The Copper Country male elite toasted the guest at tables decorated with pink roses and smilax. Reporters noted tables "laden down with one of the most elegant spreads ever given in this section, where many are noted for good dinners." The meal lasted three hours. By the early twentieth century, Women's Clubs at Portage Lake and Calumet had existed for years. Many a musically inclined girl and boy had been invited to musicales by such clubs to play piano or violin pieces, sing, and recite. The Fortnightly Club, probably patterned after Boston clubs—composed of doctors, lawyers, teachers, and heads of Calumet and Hecla departments—met in homes of members. They usually heard a scholarly paper, then enjoyed cake, coffee, and tea.

Social hierarchies and class differences prevailed, but groups and individuals created for themselves every conceivable kind of social relaxation. Businessmen, profited by responding with satisfactory measures to the demands of working people and their families. In the heat of summer, the Copper Range Railroad ran its "3-H Special" several times on Sunday, leaving Calumet but stopping to take on passengers only at Hubbell, Hancock, and Houghton, on its way to Freda Park. There, "cool, fresh lake breezes" made people forget momentarily the heat, daily toil, and effort of raising large families.

Excursions by water were popular summer diversions. Steamers continued to arrive in season, ships such as the *Northwest* and *Juniata* carrying and picking up passengers bound for the head of the lakes in 1907; freighters included the *Easton* and *Northern Light* and the *George Williams* bringing coal. The steamer *Mariposa* docked at Houghton from Isle Royale with a large catch of lake trout. The ship covered 150 miles of Lake Superior in setting and taking up nets. On July 12, members of the Hancock and Calumet Hibernian Rifles left Houghton via special train for Saint Ignace. There they boarded a ship for "a grand excursion to Detroit." One of the largest local excursions occurred one week later, when twelve hundred Finns boarded the Croze and Hennes barge and sailed leisurely to Portage Entry. Sponsored by the Finnish Lutheran Sunday schools of Hancock and Calumet, the outing was acclaimed "a financial success."

Calumet Presbyterians, in early September 1896, chartered the whaleback steamship *Christopher Columbus* for a one-day trip to Port

Arthur, Canada, The Fifth Regiment Band furnished music. A special train left Calumet at 5:30 in the morning and the ship sailed an hour later from Houghton, arriving at Port Arthur at noon. In 1913, some people booked Cunard line steamship tickets for international voyages with a large party sailing on the SS *Olympic* on August 2. Newspapers advertised rail excursions to the shrine of Saint Anne du Beaupré in Quebec and cheap fares, at times, for trips to Great Lakes cities.[53]

Some idea of the variety of entertainment sponsored by various groups is provided by the agenda for Labor Day, 1906. The Lady Foresters of Houghton hired a special train for their annual excursion, which took them to Ontonagon. The Odd Fellows of Calumet entertained at Tamarack Park. Organized labor's craft unions began the day with a Shelden Street parade that crossed the bridge to Hancock Grove for speeches by Patrick H. O'Brien and others, including one in Finnish. Sports and picnics followed in the annual event sponsored by the Hancock Trades and Labor Council. Cigar makers, longshoremen, teamsters, and railroad workers, among others, and their families and friends enjoyed hours of fun and solidarity. Others who sought to fill leisure hours roller-skated at Laurium's Palestra. Some paid fifty cents for a round-trip Houghton-to-Eagle Harbor excursion, a nine-to-five one-day journey with music furnished by the Laurium City Band.

Most organizations invited the public to special events, charged from ten to twenty-five cents admission and thus replenished their tills. Sometimes women were invited free. The annual Pequaming Fair in Baraga County, in September 1895, attracted people from all over the Copper Country, as well as visitors from Chicago, Pittsburgh, Norway, Sweden, Finland, Canada, Ireland, and England. A reporter wrote, "A few aborigines added to the cosmopolitan character of the crowd."

The variety of gatherings is evident in an 1896 listing. Women of Hancock's German Lutheran church (Saints Peter and Paul) had held their annual picnic at Hancock Grove. The following Sunday, Kaiser Wilhelm Lodge of Houghton held its annual picnic at Haas's Park: a procession left Hartman's Hall at one in the afternoon, led by the Houghton Silver Cornet Band, as Teutons and their descendants made known their presence at Portage Lake. In mid-week, Saint Ignatius Church held its annual gathering at the Canal, a popular picnic spot. Another group ate and drank aboard a barge that left Houghton one Sunday at 9:30 and Hancock at 10:00 in the morning. Musicians played old favorites.[54]

A popular resort for summer entertainment was Electric Park, created by the streetcar company halfway between Calumet and Hancock, in the woods near Boston location. It attracted 54,355 adults

185

Norwegian Sunday school classes, Frenchtown, Quincy Mining Company, c. 1900. (Michigan Technological University Archives and Copper Country Historical Collections, Michigan Technological University.)

and 7,000 children in 1909. Here, amid birch and poplar trees, parents opened wicker baskets at picnic tables while children rushed for swings and slides or played in sandboxes. The park—usually open by early June and closed by late September—hosted band concerts and dances. Bat Bigando recalled ten- and twelve-piece orchestras playing for dances in the Copper Country, some at this park—a vivid contrast, he thought, to the two- and three-piece combos that in the 1970s made "more noise than twenty. . . . No music, just noise." Park attendance, though declining as novelty wore off, averaged 45,000 between 1910 and 1912 and dropped to 34,790 in 1913.

In the early twentieth century, White City, a popular amusement park near Houghton, drew thousands. Boat trips on the canal with four or five barrels of beer were picnics in themselves, as the boat made its way to White City. The Keweenaw Central Railroad ran special trains to Crest View, near Phoenix—an attractive spot with picnic tables and dance pavilion. One could walk from there to the beach at Eagle River and bathe. For decades, miners, merchants, and a score of ethnic groups created places long remembered by their descendants as ideal summer recreation spots. One of the oldest was known as Section Sixteen Park (Calumet Township), a short distance from the Lake View Cemetery west of Red Jacket, a natural beauty spot amid sylvan peace. Opened about 1889, the park had little in the way of accoutrements. People loved going there for the rustic quality of the sparsely wooded retreat enclosed by forest. The German Aid Society used it for years but found the distance from Calumet a drawback until the automobile (few used buggies or surreys) eliminated that objection in the twentieth century. The *Portage Lake Mining Gazette* announced, as summer began in 1896, that the road from Oskar to Lake Superior had been completed and "affords a drive [via horse and buggy] from Houghton. . . . A Pleasant Drive." Today, the drive west from Houghton, past Oskar, to Lake Superior, remains exceedingly pleasant.

Claire Moyer recalled childhood days in the family yard at Boston location, "right after dawn, listen[ing] to the birds sing as they greet[ed] the new day . . . [the] silence of the village, the sun in the celestial blue, the fragrance of the green grass still wet with dew and the aroma of good coffee brewing, floating upon the freshness of the pure air, . . . the peaceful atmosphere." She recalled salesmen with carpetbags displaying colorful shawls and trinkets, a living room with flowered carpet and pump organ, Christmas trees with candles and a pail of water nearby (just in case), and her father leading the church choir while her eldest sister played the organ and "red-headed sisters sang in the choir." Local children remembered, with affection, Louis Moilanen, known as "Big Louie," born in Finland, who once worked at Quincy Mine before traveling with a carnival. He was eight feet, five inches tall and weighed 480 pounds. He wore shoes size 32, gloves size 15, and had great strength but died at age twenty-seven on September 16, 1913.[55]

The accelerated pace of American capitalism by 1913 manifested itself also in the introduction of dances considered vulgar and "freakish": the "Turkey Trot," "Grizzly Bear," "Bunny Hug," "Texas Tommy," and similar foxtrots. Puritans reeled at the sight of the tango not because it was fast ("It looked like a funeral procession," ventured one woman) but because of its sheer sexuality. Students home from the University of Michigan danced these "freak" dances almost exclusively at private parties in the Copper Country, and the public outcry against any attempt to stop such terpsichorean delights forced village dance halls and public places to allow them. "These dances are here to stay," proclaimed a letter writer signing as "A Freak" in the *Calumet News*, reminding conservatives that they had once found the waltz and the two-step shocking. Once again, Copper Country people had their way. But the Puritan influence remained potent.[56]

Many obtained an education teaching self-discipline and collegial-
ity in sport. The evolution of sport in the Copper Country tells
much of the course from aristocracy to democracy. Racing on frozen
Portage Lake, with horse-drawn cutters especially built for racing
and horses clad in colorful blankets with names printed on both
sides, reached a peak in the years 1865–89. Accompanied by betting
pools and enough excitement to dispel winter moods, racing ended
rather abruptly by 1913, despite two-hundred-dollar purses. Cricket
led to clubs formed at Calumet and Hecla, Tamarack, Kearsarge,
Ahmeek, Quincy, Mohawk, Trimountain, and Painesdale by 1908.
Soccer was played. Curling, once extremely popular at Calumet–
Laurium, was almost a forgotten sport, as many of the most talented had left the district by 1914. An exodus of Cornish workers
and the tendency of young people to abandon English and Canadian sports (except hockey) for the more American ones ended curling's repute.[57]

   After 1865, baseball's popularity rose. Every town and village and
location had a team. So did the Methodist Mission, whose team
suffered defeat by Bay Shore 37–4 in 1893. Local teams played
against other Upper Peninsula teams. When Baraga beat the Whitings
of Champion 31–0 in September 1893, the *L'Anse Sentinel* chortled,
"The Whitings should change their name to Whitewash." George
Gipp, who made his name later in football, began as a baseball star,
hitting the ball four hundred feet at Calumet High School. Legends
arose from a Baraga–Hurontown game in which a player sent the
ball flying to the deck of a passing freighter—the longest home run
in history. The ball was discovered later, miles away at Houghton,
when the boat docked.

   Teams sought the championship of the Upper Peninsula. Special
trains carried fans between Houghton and Marquette, with stops
at intermediate points like Ishpeming and Baraga, in 1896. Labor
Day, 1906, proved memorable when Houghton and Calumet ended
their series before twenty-five hundred in grandstand and bleachers
at Calumet's Athletic Park. The Calumet Aristocrats won 3–1 in
the afternoon game, fourth in the series. Houghton forfeited the
morning game by leaving the field, having protested an umpire's
decision allowing Calumet to score two runs. Spectators rushed to
the field to join players in "an excited throng," with much arguing
but no fisticuffs.

   Both teams belonged to a league extending to Canada; and the
Houghton Giants, who had not fielded a team in years "certainly
made the others go some." The *Copper Country Evening News* hailed
the triumph: "Naturally we cannot help crowing. Calumet's magnificent victory has simply overwhelmed the fans with joy, to take four

out of five games was not an easy task, and its accomplishment is occasion for local rejoicing." Some idea of local and extraterritorial rivalry can be seen in the final standings:

	Won	Lost	Pct.
Calumet	62	38	.620
Houghton	56	38	.615
Winnipeg	56	41	.577
Duluth	54	44	.551
Lake Linden	40	57	.412
Fargo	35	59	.371

Excitement over local teams paralleled that over Chicago that year, when its White Sox opposed the Cubs in the World Series. A thousand fans, many with brooms indicating the "sweep" of the series, marched along Red Jacket's streets, the brooms becoming torches, lighting the way for local magnates and players riding in carriages as a "teeming mass of people" cheered. Many feasted that night at the Arlington Hotel. Some recalled the bitter feelings earlier, when Calumet fans believed the game schedule had been rearranged to benefit Houghton. The two towns always furnished "a first-class" rivalry in baseball and other sports. By 1908, a league in Keweenaw County, composed of teams from Mohawk, Gay, Kearsarge, Wolverine, Ahmeek, Alloucz, and Ojibway played in a season from mid-May to Labor Day, their champion playing the champion of the Houghton County league at the end.[58]

Mammoth ice rinks at Lake Linden, Calumet's Colosseum, and Houghton's Amphidrome hosted hockey. Houghton was the birthplace of organized and professional hockey in the United States. The Portage Lake team became world champions, defeating Pittsburgh on March 3, 1903. A decade later, teams vied to win the MacNaughton Cup, thirty-one inches high and insured for thirty-five hundred dollars, in the American Hockey Association. This was amateur hockey. In 1912–13, Portage Lake defeated Cleveland to win the U.S. Amateur Championship. Hordes of fans came on special trains run by the Copper Range Railroad from the south and on streetcars from all over Houghton County to watch Houghton play. After the games, many stopped for bowls of oyster stew at the Board of Trade restaurant or invaded bars and bistros. Many a child recalled first impressions of glittering ice, bright lights, echoing cheers, wool clothing, mittens, and air redolent with hamburgers and onions at hockey games in the Amphidrome or Colosseum, as well as the walk afterward as snow crackled under boots on frosty winter nights.

Sport activity dominated the lives of many boys and young men, who built their own ice rinks in backyards or at locations adjoining towns. Children cavorted with sleighs and toboggans, many home-made, on numerous hills and slopes in the Keweenaw. Almost as soon as children could stand, someone introduced ice skates. Youngsters joined parents and friends on neighborhood rinks. Warming sheds and electric lights followed in some places, so working people could enjoy skating during long evenings when "moonlight nights were sparkling clear and the snow squeaked with the coldness." In 1889, twenty-two members of a Snow Shoe Club traveled from Calumet to Phoenix, some thirteen miles, enjoyed refreshments at the Brockway home, then left at one in the morning. In spring, boys eagerly awaited the resumption of fishing in ponds and streams. In summer, when heat descended, children cavorted in inland lakes; and many plunged into Lake Superior.[59]

Quincy No. 6 in the "golden age" of copper. (Michigan Technological University Archives and Copper Country Historical Collections, Michigan Technological University.)

After 1920 and continuing to fairly recent times, many spoke of the "great days" of the golden age, when mines flourished, population grew, and communities expanded. For many, this was real. But "golden age"—a vivid perception in the minds of many—was a misnomer, often conjured up by the nostalgic yearning for a past that was forever gone and that for many people, had never existed at all. For many years, beginning in the early 1890s, all was not well in this north-country Eden. In 1913, after decades of slow gestation, an explosion in the form of a long, violent, and devastating labor struggle changed everything.[60]

7

The 1913 Strike

THE BITTER LABOR WARFARE ERUPTED ON JULY 23, 1913, with tragic long-term consequences for the Copper Country. It pitted neighbor against neighbor; brought malice, mayhem, and murder; and left a badly divided community in its wake. After more than forty years of relative industrial peace, few on July 23 could contemplate the nearly nine months of virulent industrial strife ahead.[1] Michigan's governor, Woodbridge N. Ferris, received a telegram dated October 23, 1913, from his chief military representative in the Copper Country reporting on the strike of copper workers:[2]

> Lawlessness broke loose throughout the district today. Northwestern train windows smashed with rocks. 30 men broke into workmens home at Quincy. Row with deputies at Quincy. Paraders at Calumet armed with clubs. Three fights, 2 deputies badly cut up. 13 strikers arrested. 4 arrests near Ahmeek for shooting up workmens premises. 2 arrests at Allouez. Picketing throughout entire district.

Long-simmering grievances between mine workers and management exploded into class warfare abetted by inflammatory propaganda of the Western Federation of Miners (WFM). By early December 1913, as outraged middle-class citizens, encouraged by mine managers, paraded and assembled in giant rallies; a reporter wrote, "Up in the northern peninsula of Michigan there exists a

Strikers march along Fifth Street, Red Jacket, to rally at Laurium, July 1913. (The Archives of Labor and Urban Affairs, Wayne State University.)

condition of warfare . . . and bloodshed that should not be tolerated in any civilized community."[3]

As the strike began in July, Guy Miller, WFM Executive Board member, announced the union's demands: (1) an eight-hour day, (2) a minimum wage of three dollars a day for all underground workers, (3) abolition of the one-man drill, (4) a formal system for hearing workers' grievances, and (5) recognition of the WFM as bargaining agent for mine workers. A militant socialist, Miller advised local union leaders until mid-October, when he realized that the strike had been lost. The initial goals gave way to later demands for a $3.50 minimum per shift for miners and a $.35 increase per shift for surface workers, but the main objective was to procure a three-dollar minimum for all underground workers. In 1889, the average wage per shift in Montana was $3.50, in Michigan, $2.00.[4]

The Western Federation argued that the Michigan copper companies enjoyed "an unfair advantage over the Amalgamated and other companies at Butte" and that to remedy this "discrimination against Butte" the Michigan copper workers must be unionized. A spokesperson pointed out that the Amalgamated paid "from $3.50 to $4.00 per day, according to the price of copper, and it makes no difference to the miner whether there is ore or not. If rock is drilled through without results, . . . the Amalgamated stands the loss." In Michigan, men working under the contract system made living wages only

193

"once in a while."[5] One study made by investigators for the federal
government indicated that 64.74 percent of miners, but only 16.34
percent of trammers, worked on the contract basis. Michigan mine
managers preferred the contract system as an efficient means of raising
production. Many miners approved of working via contract, for they
could "earn more than by ordinary monthly rate." They took their
chances on the inevitable months when they mined poor rock and
earnings plummeted.[6]

The Western Federation, in 1910, boasted that once it had organized the Lake Superior mines, the workers would "be benefited
financially and every other way." The federation did not mention
that Michigan underground employees had guaranteed employment
in good years, working 314 days per year, while their Montana counterparts worked only 281. Furthermore, management's "benevolent
paternalism" allowed its spokespeople to ridicule the "rank nonsense"
of the WFM's claims:[7]

> Everyone of good sense knows that the miners of Lake Superior
> are as well off, if not better, than those of Butte. Lake Superior
> is a region where many miners own their own homes. It has a
> settled population. Many of the men working in those mines
> today are the sons and grandsons of miners working in the
> same district. A comparative glance at the living conditions in
> Lake Superior and Butte is all that is necessary to show the
> relative welfare of the miners in the two districts. In 1907,
> when an advance of wages occurred at Butte and there was an
> extraordinary demand for miners, many men went there from
> Lake Superior to try their fortune. Later on they were glad to
> return to Lake Superior.

But by 1910, the Michigan copper district suffered a severe labor
shortage as many Irish and Cornish workers headed west for more
money. By 1911–12 and the first six months of 1913, the labor
shortage became acute. Managers complained frequently of their inability to hire men at wages offered by their companies.[8] Cost cutting
had become imperative everywhere in the Copper Country. Quincy
manager Charles L. Lawton prided himself on reducing costs as the
average copper content of a ton of rock fell from eighteen pounds in
1904 to fifteen by 1913.[9] The district's mines produced over one
billion pounds of copper from 1906 to 1910 at an average cost
of 10.7 cents per pound. At Calumet and Hecla, where efficiency
and cost cutting reigned supreme, the average cost was 8.95 cents.[10]
Its miners and trammers sometimes resented "college boys" from
Michigan Tech armed with pencil and pad, noting what worked

and what needed improvement, young men serving apprenticeships underground. The *Engineering and Mining Journal* editors hailed all this as good in these times of vast changes in America. The country was moving away from personal management toward an intensely impersonal corporate management. Students who would one day manage mining industries needed to understand "the man on day's pay," who liked or disliked the company because of the foremen he worked immediately under.[11] In the Michigan copper mines, where 10,900 of the 13,000 workers in 1910 were foreign-born men—many of them Finnish, Slavic, or Italian—who saw only Cornish or Americans of English extraction as foremen and managers, the situation was volatile.[12]

"Scientific management is now almost oozing out of the air in all branches of engineering" proclaimed the distinguished mining journal. Low prices for metals in 1910–11 caused companies "to study costs closely." When Michigan copper workers began leaving the district in 1906, Calumet and Hecla raised wages 10 percent, and Quincy followed with 5 percent—direct bids for labor in a market of insufficient supply.[13] Angry workers and their propagandists denounced capitalistic excesses, while apologists for corporations defended their cost-consciousness and profit making. In August 1913, Bingham (Utah) Miners Union No. 67 appealed to the Michigan strikers: "You are bound to win if you only refuse to listen to the capitalistic jawsmiths who try to buy you with the money they have stolen from you."[14] But a Harvard professor of economics argued that copper mining seemed to be "more than almost any other sort of enterprise, in the nature of a lottery" and that the profits accruing to investors were "not pertinent" to the Michigan contest. What was vital was "whether the employers have paid full current wages, and paid them regularly, without cavil, and without taking advantage of the men's weakness in bargaining; and whether they have arranged the hours of labor and the other conditions of employment on a high plane of management." For a great many observers, Michigan managers had done their "duty in full measure to [their] employees, and in full measure to the public, and yet . . . secured large profits" for stockholders.[15]

A Minnesota mining engineer in spring 1911 marveled at management's conservation of mineral deposits in the Michigan Copper Country. Here miners stoped copper rock at depths a mile deep, securing twenty pounds or less of copper from a ton of rock, while others trammed the ore to shafts where it was lifted at express-train speed to the top, then loaded into hopper-bottom cars and sent on to "vast mills filled with costly machinery," where metal was separated from rock, refined, and cast into bars or ingots—"all being done at a cost that permits the sale of the final product at 12c. per lb., or a total of $2.40 for the original ton of rock."[16]

Claude T. Rice, in one of a series of articles on Michigan copper mines, hailed, in 1912, the introduction of the one-man drill as probably the greatest economy for the future. Having tested the new drills at several local mines, management believed it was only "a question of getting the men to use them without any friction arising." At Quincy, management achieved, in a few years, vast gains in productivity, reducing costs and securing additional profits by 1914; but the introduction of the drills was the issue that pulled together various miners' and trammers' grievances and attracted many men who had given the WFM very short shrift previously. Historian Gates concluded that "many of the men considered the new machine dangerous, in that its use often required the driller to work alone in a stope [and] contended that no clear-cut system was provided in case a man needed help in setting the machine up."[17]

Forty years after the strike, popular historian Angus Murdoch commented that "in three weeks' time, the one-man air drill accomplished more for the [Western] Federation than four years of speech-making." The new drills, already used widely in Western copper mines, were the first major cost-saving innovation in rock drills since power drills had largely replaced hand drilling in the early 1880s. A new technology frightened many workers, who listened now to WFM leaders charging that the drill would throw many out of work and severely reduce opportunities for trammers ever to become miners. Progressive lawmakers in Michigan, as well as throughout the nation, curtailed work in the mines by very young boys. In the Keweenaw Peninsula by 1913, men and women, already incensed due to the declining job market for their sons in the mines, now saw further reduction in family income as companies ceased hiring drill boys and introduced the one-man drill. Calumet and Hecla management would not, in 1913, hire anyone under eighteen years of age, because the Michigan factory inspector considered mining a dangerous occupation. Earnings of boys, though small, aided considerably in large families. Parents expected their children to work once they finished school. Educators shared their concern. Why have boys idle for two years after leaving school? Resentment against a diminishing job market rose quickly and broadened resistance to the one-man drill. Workers parading in mass demonstrations during the first months of the strike carried hand-drawn posters denouncing the drill as a "widow-maker," claiming that the "one-man machine" was their "agitator"—the epithet hurled by supporters of management, who blamed a few foolish noisy persons for instigating the struggle.[18]

Mine managers had known for years that the situation was building to trouble. They had decided to break the Western Federation in the Keweenaw if and when a strike came; they would throttle the monster at birth for three reasons. First, the WFM was a threat by Western radicals and others to the long-established "paternalistic" system in numerous mines in Michigan; mine operators firmly believed in the system they had installed long ago to prevent labor struggles. Second, recognizing the WFM would increase wage costs and might eliminate the wage differential between Michigan and Western mines. Finally, to accept the WFM meant that general adoption of the one-man drill was in jeopardy. To these may be added a genuine fear of socialism; for many of the federation's leaders either believed ardently in various forms of Marxian reconstruction of society or gave lip service to them, whetting workers' appetite for social democracy badly needed in the Michigan copper fields.[19]

The 1908 constitution of the WFM recognized the existence of class struggle brought about by economic conditions in capitalistic society: workers did not receive a fair share of wealth produced; theirs was stolen by men for whom they slaved. Workers needed to emancipate themselves. The constitution's preamble stressed that only in an industrial union and through concerted political action could the momentous changes be made. This credo was merely the extreme expression of a nationwide call for reform in American institutions—economic, social, and political—by millions, including middle-class men and women in the Progressive movement by 1912.[20]

But the WFM worked pragmatically, often using socialist rhetoric when demanding higher wages, shorter hours, and amelioration of working conditions. Copper Country mine management regarded the federation's constitution as a declaration of war. General manager James MacNaughton at Calumet and Hecla had personally known Bulkeley Wells, who, in the 1903–4 Colorado labor struggle, had been the target of an assassination attempt that authorities blamed on the WFM. Wells had done much to suppress the WFM in Colorado. MacNaughton, with an almost neurotic fear of the federation, stepped forth boldly at the strike's inception and until its end waged furious campaigns against it. As in Colorado, management called upon the police power of the state. The Michigan National Guard—2,765 men (212 of them officers)—assembled in Houghton County in four days, after the Western Federation commenced the strike on July 23 and 24 as enraged strikers became a mob and hurled rocks, sticks, iron bolts, clubs, and brickbats, chasing deputized company employees out of mine buildings, kicking and knocking down men who emerged from underground. How dare they work? Anyone carrying a dinner pail on July 23 was assaulted. The crowd marched along the stretch of

Calumet and Hecla shafts. Men refusing to stop work when com
manded were attacked. Mining captains were driven from posts on the
surface. Nonstriking workers emerging from man cars were ordered
to leave, and many were roughed up.[21]

The WFM concentrated its first day's fury against Calumet and
Hecla, the heart of the district, the majority of whose workers wanted
nothing to do with the Western Federation. If Calumet and Hecla
could be subdued, then the strike would succeed; for copper workers
north and south of Calumet and Hecla's domain supported the strike
more energetically, with noticeable exceptions. At Copper Range
and Quincy, men who had worked for years felt less sympathetic
than did the mass of trammers and newly arrived contingents. For
many, the Michigan copper district was a complex of stable, productive communities inhabited by hard-working, frugal, God-fearing
people—ethnically diverse but bound by common interests stimulated by middle-class aspirations. They hoped to realize satisfying
modicums of success within the region's peculiar blend of capitalistic
paternalism and business enterprise. Many had grievances—low pay,
long hours, bad conditions, and no one to hear their complaints—but
felt satisfied with the basic structure at work.[22]

A minority numbering several thousand scorned these views. Many
only recently come from Europe—Finns, Croatians, Poles, Italians,
Hungarians—joined with Americans of English and Irish extraction
who found the copper companies' paternalism stifling. Attracted initially by talk of good wages, many of the Europeans labored in the
bowels of the earth as trammers, loading and pushing heavy cars laden
with copper-bearing rock. They sold their labor for what seemed a
dismal future and were often seen by miners and foremen as easily
replaceable, foreigners, uncouth, incomprehensible, men who did not
speak English. Some of the malcontents—men of English, Cornish,
Irish, German, and Scandinavian descent—had worked hard with
little success, drifting from location to location along the range, from
Mohawk to Ontonagon, some trying their luck in Canadian copper
camps or in Montana and Arizona only to return to proletarian
wanderings in the Michigan Copper Country. A great many were
obstreperous, footloose, angry single men stuck on the bottom rungs
of economic and social ladders.[23]

The angry minority despised those they called "company men,"
who, despite complaints, felt that the companies could do no real
wrong. This dichotomy between those who believed that the companies provided the good life and those who believed that the companies
battened on exploited workers produced the division among copper
district workers that determined the outcome of the 1913–14 strike.

Violence continued on the second day, and strikers closed down all the mines as leaders issued press releases claiming that sixteen thousand men had thrown down their tools and walked off in protest. Of Calumet and Hecla's 4,337 miners, trammers, mill employees, and other surface workers, perhaps one-third refused to work. The total number of men employed as the strike began in the Michigan copper mines was 15,157. Federation records at Denver, Colorado, listed 7,085 as union members; but many of these were honorary members: clerks, railway workers, businessmen, farmers, and nonmining socialists.[24]

The WFM scored greater organizational success at Quincy, the Copper Range mines, and among workers in the northern reaches of the peninsula at Centennial, Kearsarge, Ahmeek, Allouez, Copper City, and Mohawk. Union records showed only thirty-three hundred members in the entire Copper Country as of June 1913.[25] Many men who shunned union participation but sympathized with the strike's goals found themselves repelled by the crude, violent behavior of strikers the first two days of the strike and decided either to work or lie low until some semblance of order was restored. The recklessness with which the WFM inaugurated the strike alienated many sympathizers. Overall, the Western Federation did not have the allegiance of a majority of copper workers initially; and as the strike wore on for eight-and-a-half months, the total number of strike supporters dwindled.[26]

Residents watch Michigan National Guard encamp at Calumet, July 1913. (Michigan Historical Collections, Bentley Historical Library, The University of Michigan.)

By July 28, the Michigan National Guard brought temporary peace. Thirty-six infantry companies, two cavalry troops, two artillery batteries, one company of engineers, two ambulance companies, mounted signal corps, and three brass bands (men from Detroit, Adrian, Ann Arbor, Bay City, Big Rapids, Coldwater, Flint, Grand Haven, Port Huron, Alpena, Cheboygan, and Sault Sainte Marie) joined Calumet and Houghton companies, setting up camps on property of various companies. Federation leaders protested, claiming the governor had answered "the just demands of the workingmen with bayonets." Although WFM and socialist publicists made much of military brutality and overpowering numbers—of soldiers protecting hundreds of "scabs" returning to work—the military force quickly diminished. Half left after two weeks; 732 remained by September 3. Three months after arrival, only 22 officers and 191 enlisted men of the initial 2,765-strong force remained in the Copper Country. By December 6, the remaining 5 officers and 84 men moved out of Houghton County to be stationed in Keweenaw County. By January 12, 1914, Governor Ferris ordered out all remaining guard members—4 officers and 62 men—within a week's time.[27]

The Western Federation, unsuccessful in defaming the Michigan militia, turned on the "hired gunmen"—the notorious Waddell–Mahon guards hired by James Cruse, sheriff of Houghton County, over protests from MacNaughton and his security chief August Beck. Fifty-two Waddell employees trained local deputies, including those protecting property at Calumet and Hecla, Quincy, and other mines. Cruse claimed that the violence of the first two days of the strike caused local men to fear serving as deputies. MacNaughton admitted in March 1914 that four Waddell men trained deputies at Calumet and Hecla. The Quincy Mining Company hired 28, and the Copper Range Mining company, 32—112 in all.[28] Federation publicists spread nationwide stories of terror imposed by Waddell men. This seemed credible after mid-August, when Waddell men participated in a bloody shoot-out at Seeberville, near Painesdale. Two Croatian strikers died violently. Their funeral rites became a massive demonstration of striker solidarity, with five thousand mourners on parade. Joseph Cannon, WFM organizer, declared that the "crime" for which Steve Putrich and Alois Tijan died was trying to bargain collectively with their employers. Strikers saw themselves as victims of the violence of mine managers, aided and encouraged by the governor, sheriff, and allies using troops and thugs to destroy a strike. A Waddell–Mahon circular boasted to employers elsewhere that the firm was "maintaining the integrity of the law . . . 'policing' the 1,019 square miles of territory contained in Houghton County . . . protecting the lives and homes of . . . 80,098 men, women and children" and concluded, "We are sure of defeating the [WFM] because we have met and defeated them before."[29]

James MacNaughton wrote to Calumet and Hecla president, Quincy A. Shaw, Jr., on July 31, 1913, of his chagrin at learning that Red Jacket businessmen had signed petitions asking Ferris to remove the troops. Small businessmen sympathized with strikers and had profited from large orders of groceries and bakery products that the WFM had procured early in the strike. MacNaughton told businessmen in a conference he called that management "would never recognize the Western Federation and that grass would grow in the streets here" before Calumet and Hecla or any subsidiaries would resume operations, for law and order must first be restored, and the Western Federation, annihilated. The general manager praised local Catholic priests, a delegation of whom had visited him, writing, "They are very strongly with us." As for WFM ruffians beating men who wished to work, each act simply put another "nail in the coffin of the Western Federation of Miners."[30] The Protestant clergy, with a very few exceptions, opposed the strike. Most Finnish ministers remained faithful to issues like temperance and social conservatism. When the WFM's tactics turned to shooting at trains carrying men to replace striking copper workers and firing into houses where they lived, in late autumn 1913, the Reverend William Reid Cross of Houghton declared, "This is not a strike at all, . . . it is rather an assault on civilized society, . . . sedition pure and simple."[31]

Federation officials at Denver had attempted to persuade local leaders not to initiate a strike in the summer of 1913. Having always fostered democracy within its locals, the executive board now saw Copper Country democracy with the four locals (Calumet, Hancock, South Range, Mass City) as impetuous and premature. Denver hoped for a delay until spring 1914, when the anticipated membership would be larger and six months of good weather lay ahead. Copper workers in the Keweenaw Peninsula did not wish to wait. They forced the district board to meet on June 29 to schedule a strike vote. When the district board delayed, waiting upon Denver's executive board, expected to meet on July 14, angry workers compelled their district board to send letters to all mine operators asking for conferences and replies by July 21. If managers would not meet with workers, the men had approved a strike. When management made no response—Quincy returning its letter unopened—the strike began, on July 23.[32] Charles Mahoney, WFM vice president, in charge while President Charles H. Moyer attended a European labor conference, did everything possible to prevent a strike but was overruled by actions taken by the Copper Country's locals. He had spoken at a meeting at Calumet in 1911 to advance unionism, and hardly sixty men showed up. He was not surprised, for resistance to unionism at Calumet and Hecla had always prevailed. Mahoney, like others, could not understand why these men earning from $55 to $90 a month would leave for Butte and other Western camps, where they earned $90 to $120 a month, only to return to Michigan after a year's stay in the West.[33] Mahoney had spent much time in the Copper Country. He was well aware that by June 1, 1913, the four locals had only 3,287 members.[34] He and other officers worried about the threats to strike.

Moyer had notified organizer Thomas Strizich on March 25, 1913, that although he was pleased to hear that recruitment of workers went on apace, he hoped the Michigan workers would "realize the importance, in fact the absolute necessity, of deferring action that may precipitate a conflict with the employers until they have practically a thorough organization."[35] The Western Federation was broke.[36] The available documents fail to make clear why the WFM decided to conduct the Michigan strike against such odds. A majority of workers failed to support the federation; opposition from management and local and state police power loomed ominously; the American Federation of Labor, with whom the WFM had reaffiliated in 1911, looked unfavorably at the strike decision; and raising money would prove arduous.

Moyer arrived back in the United States on August 9 and immediately set about raising funds in September—a hundred-thousand-dollar loan from the United Mine Workers (Illinois Division) and one for twenty-five-thousand dollars from the United Brewery Workers of America. He arrived in the Copper Country about Labor Day with attorney Clarence Darrow, whom he encouraged to begin arbitration of the strike, first with company officials, then with Michigan's governor. Moyer, impressed with the enthusiasm and determination of the striking thousands at Hancock, Calumet, and Keweenaw towns, gambled now on a successful strike. Victory was possible! Mass picketing to prevent men from working, (with many women involved in daily demonstrations, publicity, and propaganda); heightened class consciousness; adherence of a small but powerful socialist group; and a solid core of bitter, angry, fighting Finns, Slavs, and Italians—all seemed harbingers of victory.[37]

The momentum would be accelerated. Success in this big strike would enhance greatly WFM power and prestige. The federation's efforts to become a truly stable, respected, and progressive organization had been damaged by complaints about its national leadership, democratization within its locals that had allowed internal wrangling to weaken its structure, difficulties encountered in organizing workers, and disastrous defeats in Colorado strikes of 1903–4. Moyer told reporters at Lansing, "I'm not willing to admit yet that James MacNaughton will not recognize organized labor before he dies."[38] Moyer and Darrow had come to confer with Governor Ferris, who was pessimistic about his chances to arbitrate the strike. He realized that MacNaughton was the key man whose decisions could resolve or prolong the struggle. As in the past, the smaller copper companies' managers followed the lead of Calumet and Hecla. MacNaughton came to the governor's home at Big Rapids. "I went at him from every angle," said the governor later; but he could not budge the stubborn general manager. The only encouraging note was Mac-Naughton's belief that sooner or later, the mine operators would have to come round to the eight-hour day. MacNaughton expressed no fear of investigation of conditions in the Copper Country; in fact, he told Ferris he welcomed them: the crux of the matter was that the Western Federation would not be recognized as agent for collective bargaining under any conditions.[39]

The federal Department of Labor sent investigators in mid-September, who took copious notes and assembled statistics. John A. Moffitt and Walter B. Palmer met with MacNaughton in mid-September and "tendered the good offices" of their department. MacNaughton said he wanted no go-between; furthermore, he knew of nothing to arbitrate. If any workers wished to return to work, they must first give up WFM membership and promise not to rejoin. He would never deal with the WFM. Should the federation waive its claim for recognition, would he meet a committee of employees on strike? MacNaughton snorted at the idea: "Oh, no. They can't work that on me—form a local organization and subsequently join the Western Federation."[40]

At another meeting, this time with Calumet and Hecla attorney, A. E. Petermann, the men from Washington, D.C., were told that the real issue was recognition of the WFM and that the company would be derelict, remiss in its duties to the majority of workers if it made any sign recognizing the WFM. He spoke for all the managers of the twenty-five mines in the district. Petermann thought the visitors would better use their time persuading union officials of the "futility of any attempt to secure recognition." The companies would never give up using the new one-man drills. They had also considered the eight-hour day for a long time past and if a majority of workers wanted that, the companies would consider the proposal. The variety of conditions and extensive use of the contract system throughout the Keweenaw Peninsula mines militated against a minimum wage for all. Petermann told Moffitt that the managers "were determined to drive the Western Federation of Miners out of the copper fields, if they had to fight all winter to do so." Would that not bring great suffering in winter for many? Petermann replied that "the price paid made no difference" to him.[41]

Strikers had not only demonstrated ably on village streets and at all mine locations, they also served as political activists. In August, strikers urged the United States Senate to act so that the nation's metal and coal mines could be nationalized. They also called for a Senate investigation. Nothing came of these efforts.[42] After the disastrous turn of events in December, the House of Representatives decided to send a subcommittee to Michigan to investigate the copper strike. Organizers began relief payments. From August 22 to September 26 alone, WFM support for the Michigan strike averaged ten thousand dollars a week. Initially, a striker and his wife received four dollars weekly, single men, three dollars. Families with two children, five dollars, with fifty-cent increases for each additional child. Families with five or more children received seven dollars. In emergencies, the maximum could be extended to nine and even eleven dollars. All WFM locals assessed members two dollars per month for the Michigan strike, but the total was never adequate to cover the enormous expense of conducting the Michigan strike over a long period. Recourse to collections from women and men at dances, theaters, and political gatherings and from socialists became an important part of life among the nation's working people.[43]

Strikers succeeded in shutting down all the mines and did all they could to prevent men from returning to work. In dawn parades each day, hundreds of stalwarts, set out from Hancock and its vicinity. They climbed Quincy hill—their ranks orderly, American flags flying—shouting "Scabs!" and assembling as close as possible to change-houses. They so infuriated military officers that General Pearley Abbey one day called in the district president and ordered a halt. But the parades resumed the next day only to be broken up by soldiers. Strikers complained about abridgement of constitutional rights and continued to march.

Hundreds in Keweenaw County rose daily at four to march in semidarkness to Calumet, where, by six o'clock, they joined hundreds of others parading along streets bordering the Calumet and Hecla shafthouses. Soldiers and deputies monitored them. Residents of Calumet, Red Jacket, and Laurium complained of the noise disrupting their sleep. A group that attempted to reach the Red Jacket Shaft Mine was forced by village marshals, deputies, and soldiers to retreat to the union hall on Sixth Street, near the Opera House. Innocent citizens were attacked. William Kissanieme, who worked for a private contractor, was assailed by Ana (Annie) Clemenc and Maggie Aggarto, who grabbed his pail and slapped and pommeled the bewildered man. Four other women clashed with deputies rushing to the rescue. At Ahmeek and Allouez, striking men blew horns and rang bells as they picketed. Men and women fought in the streets of villages almost every day in September and October.[44]

Many looked upon the daily parades as solemn undertakings. Strikers argued that trouble arose only when deputies and gunmen provoked it. William Hanninen said the strikers hoped to stir consciences. When a working miner "would see the silent, determined men walking along the road in large numbers, men with whom he had worked, and he knew their conditions were the same as his, . . . he would know that these men were trying to better his as well as their condition [and] it would have a moral effect upon him." The mass demonstrations succeeded in keeping most men from working. They also intensified fury and tension. Deputies increased, carrying riot sticks the size of baseball bats, manufactured in the Calumet and Hecla carpentry shop. They feared that the strikers, imitating the WFM's wild West violence, carried concealed weapons. By November, parades were often halted and the marchers assembled in a building and searched. Many had discarded knives, blackjacks, "knuckles," revolvers, and razors when arrests were made, hurling them into shrubbery or passing them to friendly bystanders.[45]

Women worked actively in the strike, viewing the struggle as one against privation, uncertainty, and endless hours spent caring for home and children. Many begrudged a privileged class that they felt received more than a just share of wealth produced by husbands, fathers, brothers, and lovers. They lived among complaints, trouble, crying babies, and dirty diapers, cooking and scrimping to make ends meet. They cultivated small gardens, made over clothing, and sometimes hired out as maids. Always, despite frequent prosperous times, fears haunted their minds, fears of injury to, or death of, their men in the mines.

Some fought savagely during the strike. In late August, they had come out at Quincy, South Range, Painesdale, Calumet, and in Keweenaw County, to snatch lunch pails, slap scabs, hit men with their fists, hurl rocks, spit, throw eggs and tin cans, argue, cajole, and call names. Some dipped brooms in human excrement at outhouses, then prodded their enemies who dared work in the mines. A few soldiers expressed shock at the language some women used. Captain Robert G. Hill told reporters of the *Grand Rapids Herald* early in September that many men let the women do the fighting for them, as the military found women more difficult to deal with than men— women who used "the filthiest means in their fights," like the woman at Baltic who "pounced upon a little boy carrying a dinner to his father," who had returned to work in the mine.[46]

205

Federation publicists and socialists lionized Mrs. Clemenc, a regular in Sunday parades of strikers bound for Laurium's Palestra for rallies who was active daily in the streets. She became "Big Annie" and won nationwide fame during a mid-September confrontation when soldiers and strikers fought over the Stars and Stripes, accidentally torn by a soldier's saber. In the scuffle, she draped the tattered flag across her body and dared soldiers to harm her. Refusing to move, she threw the flag to the ground and challenged the soldiers to step on it. The incident led to her interrogation before a military tribunal during the month of October.

"An exceptionally tall woman, [she] does not convey the impression of bigness that the popular name has given rise to," a reporter wrote. He described her as "not unattractive, . . . though dressed in the manner of the . . . working class." She often carried the flag in daily demonstrations; and this miner's daughter whose husband had sung so eloquently in the Slovenian Saint Joseph's church at Red Jacket became for many a heroine—a modern Joan of Arc, as a socialist journalist described her.[47]

The governor continued to withdraw troops from the Copper Country resulting in deputies' inability to control the mass demonstrations. Strikers' parades, timed to pass mine shafts and traverse village streets as men walked to work, retarded, most successfully, the resumption of meaningful operations at the mines. Attorneys for seventeen companies applied for an injunction. Judge Patrick O'Brien, of the circuit court, issued one on September 20, ordering strikers to cease interfering with persons employed by the complainants, picketing in or about the mines, interfering with free access of any employees from their homes, and gathering and parading in large numbers around the premises of complainants.

Federation lawyers protested, arguing that the men had the right to picket peacefully. O'Brien, sympathetic to the strikers, dissolved the injunction and refused the companies' request for a second one. Calumet and Hecla attorney, Albert Rees, then carried an appeal to the Michigan Supreme Court, which, on October 8, reinstated and continued in force the September 20 injunction but modified it: strikers could parade and hold peaceful meetings, but they must not interfere with men who wanted to work. This ruling was temporary—in effect only until the high court could rule definitely on the original injunction.

What appeared as a WFM victory, however, contained elements of inevitable defeat. The mass demonstrations, as reported in the nation's press, only reinforced the picture of union excesses deplored by middle-class citizens. Street violence was conducted by local men and women, many influenced by WFM organizers Ben Goggia, Mor

Oppman, Steve Oberto, John Välimäki, Thomas Strizich, and others. They harangued groups and individuals in Italian, Hungarian,
Finnish, and Croatian. Oberto once complained that the Michigan
conflict was "no damn strike at all"—that the Michigan workers were
damned fools and cowards who could never succeed unless they
employed violence, as did the WFM in the Western battlegrounds.[48]

By October 8, eleven weeks after the strike began, an investigative
group partial to the companies counted only 5,445 men at work—
2,079 of them underground. While Calumet and Hecla had about
80 percent of its employees back, Quincy had only one-third of
its prestrike labor force, Copper Range, a little less than one-third.
Smaller mines remained completely shut down underground. Operators everywhere suffered from the severe shortage of workers.
Their solution was to import workers. Quincy began this as early as
September 19, hiring men from the Austro–American Labor Agency
in New York City to work nine hours daily for $2.50. Reimbursement
to the company of $24.50 for cost of transportation from the east
would be deducted from their first six months' wages. Of thirty-three
who left New York, six left the train before it reached Hancock,
and all but fourteen "deserted and joined the union." Some told
strikers they knew nothing of the strike until soldiers boarded the
train in Houghton. Quincy hired more, but all seventy-five quit by
October 1.

MacNaughton had said late in July that his company would not
import workers; but in late September, Ocha Potter, mine superintendent, convinced him to seek laborers from Saint Paul, Minneapolis,
Duluth, Fargo, Milwaukee, and Chicago. The WFM countered this
with an educational campaign urging all to stay away: "Don't be
a scab. Wages are low, the labor required excessive, hours long.
No real man will come to the copper district until a settlement
is made." Such appeals to masculinity fell on many deaf ears. The
United States had entered economic depression. Men everywhere
sought work. By November 1, an estimated fifteen hundred imported
workers had arrived in the Keweenaw Peninsula. More than thirty
nationalities were represented among the men hired by Calumet and
Hecla, some from ethnic groups never before counted in the Keweenaw mix: Russians, Armenians, Romanians. Slovenians, Germans,
and Americans from farms and factories arrived, some of them to
remain forever. MacNaughton called many of them "rolling stones."
His company imported 1,606, all but two hundred of whom stayed,
taught by foremen and shift bosses and living in bunkhouses peculiar
to an ethnic group. In November, some of the once-resident Cornish
trickled back to work, along with numerous Lithuanians along the
south range.

To encourage recalcitrant local miners and trammers to return, operators announced, on November 28, that the eight-hour day would be inaugurated December 1. A nine-hour day was granted to surface men. The long-established practice of paying miners for a half-day shift Saturdays that they did not work would be abolished. So was pay for a sixth night shift when men had worked five nights. Employees would work at their discretion a short, Saturday-night shift. Some men had opposed the eight-hour day; for under the new rules, some would work only forty-five minutes less per week in return for giving up their previous long weekends. All workers would now be required to put in the same hours underground. Conformity had arrived, as rules and practices peculiar to early Cornish miners now gave way to modern ways.[49]

The success of the companies in building a new work force infuriated the strikers. Deputized company men replaced the military, which Governor Ferris wanted out. Their continued presence, he thought, signaled the state's taking sides in the labor struggle. Soldiers should be used only in emergencies—to curb riots and protect life and property "of the employee along with the employers." By October, about two hundred of the military remained. General Abbey told the governor that about three thousand strikers remained, keeping up the strike; but they still prevented some six thousand from working. Obviously, he related, the seventy-seven thousand people of Houghton County had wearied of the strikers' aggressiveness and sought an end to the dispute. In Keweenaw County, with sheriff and governing supervisors extremely sympathetic to strikers, things were really bad. Abbey described the northernmost county as "absolutely without officials to enforce the law, and furthermore, they do not try to." Ruffians intimidated would-be workers, threatening to dynamite their homes. Trains arriving in the county with imported workers met with showers of rocks and gunfire. In other parts of the two counties, barns were burned, dynamite bombs, exploded; and shots blasted windows of boardinghouses inhabited by imported workers.[50]

By late October, Judge O'Brien issued an order for an enforcement of the injunction—until now roundly abused by strikers and strike sympathizers. On October 24, mass arrests were made at the Allouez streetcar station for strikers' interference with arriving workers. At Mohawk, a parade was halted, and its marchers, detained in a mine shed. Over two hundred arrests were made; and the 111 who showed up in court that afternoon (as the WFM insisted on immediate hearings) heard Judge O'Brien say it was their duty to obey the law lest the republic perish. But he had good words—even encouragement— for strikers on December 5 when he suspended the sentences for 139 he had found guilty of contempt of court for violating the injunction: strikers, "through enthusiasm for their cause rather than with any intention of deliberately violating the order of the court, . . . [were] engaged in a heroic struggle for the mere right to retain their membership in a labor organization."

As he viewed the situation, a set, deliberate, and relentless purpose on the part of the mining companies to crush out the spirit of organization was being met by a self-sacrificing and determined devotion to unionism on the part of the strikers. He said also that class interests inspired different moral codes; therefore, strikers regarded as a traitor anyone who worked. The October 24 events at Allouez were hardly peaceable, but there was no actual violence. The companies had done nothing to conciliate strikers, while doing everything to "increase their bitterness and hostility." He implied that the companies acted as a law unto themselves, whereas "law is simply the concrete expression of those rules that experience has taught to be for the best interests of all the people."[51] His legal realism—the idea that human experiences called for new interpretations of law—infuriated many of the local establishment. The workers who had launched and conducted the strike had seemingly scored another victory. But two days later, an event occurred that turned everything in the direction of their total defeat.

At two o'clock in the morning on December 7, 1913, a volley of rifle shots crashed into Thomas Dally's house in Painesdale, killing, almost instantly, Arthur and Harry Jane and mortally wounding Mr. Dally, who died at five o'clock that afternoon. In an adjoining house, bullets ripped through, wounding a thirteen-year-old girl. The assailants could not be found; but Western Federation ruffians fell under suspicion immediately, as Arthur and Harry Jane had returned from Canada only the day before to resume work at the Champion Mine. The cold-blooded murders galvanized the mining communities. Houghton businessmen assembled in the village hall with the mayor presiding and made speeches having only one message: the Western Federation and its paid agitators "had sealed their own doom in Houghton County."[52]

Later, they and others boarded a special Copper Range Railroad train to meet with hundreds of citizens at Calumet and to prevent any Sunday meeting of strikers. Citizen rage silenced the strikers temporarily. At the rally at the Calumet Armory, citizens set in motion a series of offensives that over the next five days demolished the strength of the strikers. Instrumental in this drive to rid the mineral range of all "outside agitators" was an organization, the Citizens' Alliance, that had announced its existence on November 10. At its core, businessmen rallied thousands of citizens disgusted with constant strife in their communities. When the labor struggle had reached stalemate, a group of businessmen took hold of an idea that had been afloat as a potential means of combatting the WFM. The Citizens' Alliance was simply a copy of others like the Colorado Citizens' Alliance, which in 1904 had effectively curbed the WFM there.[53]

The WFM's *Miners' Magazine* claimed that once the federation had opened relief stores selling food and life's necessities at wholesale prices, indignant businessmen, some of whom had profited earlier by federation purchases in large quantities, decided to take action. Their principal object was to eliminate the WFM and end the strike. The magazine charged that businessmen had cut off credit to strikers in hopes the men would return to work.[54] Leaders of the new organization set up headquarters in Houghton's Douglass House, from which they solicited assistance from a broad stratum of editors, doctors, barbers, butchers, bankers, lawyers, clergy, teamsters, shopkeepers, and homemakers. One could sign up at any bank or clip the membership application from the *Calumet News* or *Mining Gazette* and return the completed form to their offices.

The Citizens' Alliance published *Truth*, which appeared periodically with stories ridiculing WFM claims, questioning the union's efforts, and printing stories from citizens. One who signed himself "Calumet Miner" declared, "We are Finlanders but not socialists. . . . I do not approve of the socialist soup, especially when mixed with unionism." Intraethnic rivalry inflamed by the strike came under attack: "You come from the same place in the old country, . . . were friends, now the Federation agitator, whom you believed, has made you enemies." *Truth* claimed 5,236 persons belonged to the alliance when it printed its first issue. In nine days, membership had risen to almost nine thousand. *Truth* serialized Harry Orchard's sensational autobiography detailing how Moyer and other federation officials paid him to lie, destroy property, and assassinate their enemies in Colorado, California, and Idaho. Mining company officials remained discreetly in the background but obviously supported the alliance, as shown by lavish praise accorded the companies in *Truth*. MacNaughton's assistance was evident in the paper's references to his friend Bulkeley Wells, who had been terrorized in Colorado and came close to being shot to death a decade earlier by assassins unknown.[55]

The murders of the Jane brothers and Mr. Dally—Cornishmen—as they slept was the catalyst that turned the fledgling Citizens' Alliance into a juggernaut as the outraged rose in fury. Speakers at the December 7 rally subtly criticized businessmen who had until now hesitated to join the growing desire to get rid of the Western Federation. Many citizens who did not approve of all the WFM stood for saw the federation as a collectivity attempting to resolve real grievances, such as low pay, discrimination, long hours, and the arbitrariness of mine captains. Many saw the paternalism begun by Alexander Agassiz as a passing phenomenon in the twentieth century, for its constrained system of work and welfare had outlived its time. Many businessmen had either worked underground or had kin and friends who labored there. They knew how hard life could be for miners and trammers. Now many of them fell into line, joining the swelling opposition to the Western Federation.

Final rites for the three slain miners under the auspices of Duke of Wellington Lodge, Sons of Saint George, at Painesdale's Methodist church, and consequent funeral procession in Houghton, followed by mass rallies at Calumet and Houghton, dramatized the human tragedy that had gripped the Keweenaw Peninsula. Following the funeral, 10,000 milled about in Houghton's streets, 6,000 of them attending a giant rally at the Amphidrome. Another 40,000 at Calumet marched, 4,000 of them crowding into the Armory while 8,000 pushed into the newly opened sports and exhibition arena, the Colosseum. Prominent figures from schools, the legal profession, and companies' legal staffs, joined by ordinary workingmen, sang the praises of the companies—the peace they had known prior to the advent of the Western Federation—and denounced the Federation, described as "a hotbed of socialism," the enemy of the home, community, law and order, good citizenship, good morals, and the church and "the enemy of the gospel of Jesus Christ." So said the Reverend J. R. Rankin, Civil War veteran, pastor of Houghton's Grace Methodist Episcopal Church. "What had the WFM cared for laboring men?" he asked. The audience screamed, "Nothing! Nothing!"[56]

The governor, courts, mining companies, and militia received praise; and the WFM was attacked "for criminal conspiracies and plotting . . . willfully, and directly [imposing] upon this district, a reign of lawlessness and crime that is a disgrace to the community and to the state." Company lawyers cautioned against unlawful means in ridding the community of the WFM. In the five days that followed, deputized citizens stood "shoulder to shoulder" with law enforcement officers as scuffles broke out between them and strikers. The district seemed "to be on the verge of a little civil war"; and Governor Ferris was notified by his representative on the scene, with men "on both sides arming themselves." The tinderbox was about to explode. Threats had been made against WFM organizers. On the day of the funerals, strikers opened fire on Quincy workers assembling near a mine shaft for the Houghton parade.

On Quincy Hill, homes were searched; trunks, opened; and men, beaten. Innocent women and children, along with strikers, stood by in terror as deputies without warrants ransacked their dwellings.

The South Range headquarters of the WFM fell victim to an attacking party of deputized citizens from Houghton in search of hidden weapons. Thirty guns from the socialist quarters downstairs were confiscated; forty men, arrested; red flags, taken. On December 12, the WFM store on Red Jacket's Pine Street was raided, with five rifles, nine revolvers, a shotgun, and three hundred rounds of ammunition confiscated. Deputies with warrants searched homes at Franklin location near Quincy, confiscating twenty rifles, four revolvers, and six swords. Men protested that the weapons were used for hunting; but marshals and the deputized pushed on. Mor Oppman was arrested when two half-sticks of dynamite were found in a coat hanging in his closet. His claim that they had been "planted" by authorities was repulsed.[57]

When Paddy Dunnigan at Ahmeek heard of the South Range raid, he allegedly exclaimed, "We have 300 rifles right here and I will be goddamned if any of the officers of Houghton and Keweenaw County can get them without bloodshed, to give them to the Citizens Alliance to shoot the shit out of us." A few days later, Ahmeek was raided; but the dragnet picked up only nine riot sticks, a couple of rifles, three shotguns, one revolver, and a hundred feet of fuse. A number of private homes were searched as the number of sworn deputies increased to twenty-one hundred by December 18. Only five Waddell men remained, along with some seventy men from the Ascher Detective Agency. At Houghton and Calumet, arrangements were made to use fire whistles to summon aid in case of trouble. This gradually mounting counterattack, with men wearing Citizens' Alliance badges or buttons and bragging of having the Western Federation on the run led directly to the confusion of Christmas Eve, 1913. Then came the monumental tragedy that engulfed the Copper Country.

The Houghton Trades and Labor Council had wired Governor Ferris on December 11, saying it feared bloodshed because of alliance aggression and asked for an immediate investigation of district affairs.[58]

Charles Moyer returned to the Copper Country shortly after the Dally–Jane murders, his fifth visit in the course of the strike and his first since the end of October. The Houghton County Board of Supervisors summoned a grand jury, which indicted Moyer and thirty-seven other WFM men on January 15, charging them with conspiracy to restrain laborers from going to work, interfering with imported workers, and depriving workingmen of property and their rights. From mid-December until the twenty-sixth, Moyer worked to have both state and federal governments arbitrate the strike, as colleagues like C. E. Mahoney, John C. Lowney, Ben Goggia, Mor Oppman, and many others fled the wrath of the Citizens' Alliance and the evolving legal prosecution. For some reason, Moyer still believed that the cause of the workers could be salvaged.[59]

On December 24, he had reason to believe that state and federal governments could be utilized to secure a victory for the strikers from the ashes of defeat. The women's auxiliary of the Western Federation entertained hundreds of children and their parents at an afternoon party at Red Jacket's Italian Hall. More than 500 children and about 175 adults had gathered to hear carols, recitations, and receive gifts. In the noise and confusion, as children moved toward the stage where auxiliary members tried to quiet them, an ominous cry of "Fire!" rang out. In the panic that followed, seventy-three lost their lives, trampled in the stairway leading out as an avalanche of terrified men, women, and children cascaded down. Those who fell first could not regain their footing and were trampled to death. Boots came down on a child's head or smashed a breast. On they came, hurtling down, grasping, clawing in efforts to get out while others behind them fell (some descending head-first) upon them. The more agile leaped down upon others wedged in the mass of bodies below. Arms and legs meshed as body piled upon body. Within minutes, the stairway was tightly blocked. At the bottom, children were "jammed into one solid mass from which no one could emerge."[60]

There was no fire, but soon whistles pierced the December darkness of late afternoon. Firemen, as well as others (some wearing Citizens' Alliance buttons), arrived to help take bodies to the Red Jacket Town Hall, where a temporary morgue had been arranged. Hysterical adults inside the hall believed the Citizens' Alliance had come to attack them. Several later spoke of an intruder wearing a Citizens' Alliance badge, who entered and uttered the fatal cry. Ana Clemenc, in charge of the party, told reporters such a story, although at the inquest five days later, she denied she had seen a person wearing such a badge. The Finnish-language newspaper *Työmies* issued an extra charging that a man wearing an alliance button was responsible. Next day, the seventy-fourth person died in hospital, as a stunned Copper Country attempted to fathom the tragedy. In a statement to the press printed widely on Christmas morning, Moyer stated: "My information is to the effect that no striker or any one in sympathy with the strike brought about this catastrophe. There are many who testify that a man from the outside came up the stairs and yelled 'Fire!' " Even before all the bodies had been removed from Italian Hall on Christmas Eve, Moyer had wired President Woodrow Wilson, Governor Ferris, Secretary of Labor William B. Wilson, and Frank Morrison of the American Federation of Labor, asking for immediate state and federal investigations of "the cause of the disaster." His precipitous action initiated what Clarence Darrow criticized as an

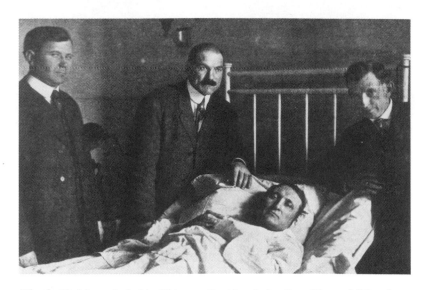

Charles H. Moyer, in bed in Chicago after his eviction from Hancock/Houghton December 26, 1913. With him are, from left, John Walker of the Illinois Federation of Labor, Yanco Terzich of the WFM Executive Board, and M.J. Riley, WFM representative. (Archives, University of Colorado at Boulder Libraries [General 2056].)

attempt by attorneys and officers of the union "to capitalize on the terrible tragedy of Christmas eve."[61]

Moyer's refusal in the days that followed to accept thousands of dollars contributed by local men and women to assist survivors and bury the dead infuriated the people of Calumet, Hancock, Houghton, and other communities. A small group of "vigilantes" accosted him in his room at Hancock's Hotel Scott; beat him; discharged a revolver, wounding him; and dragged him over the bridge to Houghton, where he was put onto the Milwaukee-bound train at 9:35, the evening of December 26. He claimed that James MacNaughton appeared on the station platform, telling him that if he ever returned he would be hanged. Later, Moyer retreated from this positive identification. He spent much of the night on the train composing telegrams to Denver and other places notifying all that the cause of the Michigan miners was not lost. The stories of his deportation made front pages across the country, convincing many that the Copper Country was indeed a "feudal fiefdom" ruled by King James and his corrupt court. Later, Moyer admitted there had not been a deliberate attempt to shoot him but that the gun had discharged as it was used as a club.

Governor Ferris's legal representative in the Copper Country, Ernest J. Nichols, collected affidavits from some who had witnessed the deportation. The accused included MacNaughton's brother, a Calumet businessman, a Laurium police officer, a Houghton haberdasher, a Calumet druggist, a coal dealer, an impetuous young

Calumet and Hecla security officer, and ten others. The grand jury investigated, but no one was ever convicted of the assault. Moyer served briefly as martyr. A lawyer said of the deportation: "If it was illegal, we are willing to stand it. Few men were engaged in it, and exercised great restraint." But the Italian Hall tragedy and the deportation simply gave the strike a new lease on life. A striker told a reporter: "They half killed Moyer and run him out because he is the best friend we miners have. He was bringing the mine agents [managers] to time. He knows how to fight them; we don't. They had to get rid of him, so they mobbed him. But he'll come back and this thing is going to keep on until we win."[62] Moyer returned briefly in January, then disappeared forever from the Copper Country; but the most immediate result of the events of December 24–26 was the decision by the U.S. House of Representatives to investigate the Michigan copper strike thoroughly.

The congressional subcommittee worked four long weeks and heard eloquent spokespersons from both sides to the dispute, in February and March 1914. Its final 2,357-page transcript covered all aspects of life for working people in the Michigan Copper Country. Some members held additional hearings in Chicago, where Moyer participated and in Washington, D.C., where they heard from the Copper Country's Representative William J. MacDonald. Chairman Edward T. Taylor (Democrat) of Colorado told reporters in the nation's capitol after all was ended that the Copper Country was a little kingdom with James MacNaughton reigning over men who were practically serfs but not oppressively treated and that little could be done to end the strike. Not allowing men to join unions was un-American, and he accused the Citizens' Alliance of working to wipe the union "off the map."[63]

But one member of the committee, identified only as "a strong union man" said, as the hearings neared an end:

> There isn't any case here. Undoubtedly the operators could have done more for the men but at that, if a miner from Pennsylvania, West Virginia or Ohio were transported up here he would think he was in paradise. I came here, firm in the belief that the men were being oppressed by greedy corporations, and that we could accomplish a great thing for the workingman generally, by showing the nation what was and [what] had taken place. But I find that I had an entirely wrong idea of the situation, and our report must, in all fairness, be entirely different from what I thought it was going to be when we started in. We have found things to criticize of course but, on the whole, the men are far better off than two-thirds of the workingmen of the country.

The committee never issued an official final report.[64]

The congressional investigation—the most important of a dozen investigations conducted by federal, state, and local groups—was followed by an announcement from Denver three weeks later. The WFM Executive Board cut strike relief by $25,000 a month. Single men received $2.25, families with six or more children, five dollars. Moyer advised the district union at Hancock that the United Mine Workers of America had ended assistance, that the WFM had only $5,303 in its treasury, and that unpaid bills totaled $48,450. "While we still believe your *cause* is just," he told them, "we cannot be expected to do the impossible. We have done our full duty. . . . We now leave it up to you. We can make no promises as to length of time we can furnish relief."

On Easter Sunday, April 12, 1914, strikers voted to end the strike with only Calumet voting to fight on (see Table 7.1).

Table 7.1. Vote to Terminate Strike, April 12, 1914

Local	End Strike	Continue Strike
Ahmeek	600	17
Calumet	291	382
Hancock	491	18
South Range	485	90

Next day, the executive board at Denver decided "that in view of the unsatisfactory conditions under which the strike was terminated, and on the advice of counsel, the Board take the responsibility of changing the [1914 WFM national] convention from Hancock, Michigan to Denver, Colorado." So ended the Western Federation of Miners' hopes of substantial expansion east of the Mississippi. Their strategy had been organization of the fifteen hundred copper workers, and then an effort to win the iron workers in Michigan.[65]

Already, two rival legends had been created that persist to the present day: (1) that thousands of workers, ill paid, oppressed by awful working conditions, and unable to participate fully in crucial decision making had been starved out, betrayed, in their attempts to reorder their lives, by mining executives, who used police and military power and were assisted by courts and businessmen and (2) that thousands of copper workers had been misled by outside agitators, socialists, and gullible local foreigners bent on destroying peaceful patterns of community life, where miners and managers had worked for seventy years in basically wholesome cooperation. The bitterness and emotional frenzy of the long strike influenced all future life in the Keweenaw Peninsula.

In addition to nine men who died from gunshot wounds, twenty-six other persons were shot. At least 168 persons were beaten or injured by missiles. Intimidation terrorized hundreds. The idea of home as sanctuary ended with the outbreak of the strike, in part because of the peculiar residential pattern wherein company houses nestled together, so that many families were vulnerable to pressures from neighbors. Six homes were set afire. Three were dynamited, and threats made to destroy others kept many worried. Private residences and numerous bunkhouses were shot into. Windows shattered in scores of homes as culprits hurled large stones that lay in abundance everywhere in the Keweenaw. Three families fled their homes, traumatized by cursing strikers. Deputies searched homes ruthlessly, at times without warrants. Occupants accused them of personal abuse, destruction, and theft. Men and women lashed out at one another physically in street demonstrations.

Intimidation ran rampant. Hundreds of shots fired to frighten those who struck and those who worked shattered the crystalline sky of the north country. At least thirty gatherings turned into riots. Women fell victims to, and also perpetrated, violence. Opposing views on the strike resulted in meanness and such petty aggressions as despoiling gardens. For all, the grimmest and saddest memory was the Christmas Eve tragedy, where so many innocent children perished in Italian Hall.[66]

The cost was enormous. The Western Federation weakened itself enormously with its tremendous expenditures in Michigan. Its failure to win in Michigan prompted its most powerful local in Butte, Montana, to rebel two months after the Michigan strike ended. Workers there, furious with Moyer's mishandling of the strike and the large assessments they had expended, shouted him down, refused to let him speak, and drove him from the city. Although Moyer remained in charge until 1926, the WFM barely clung to life. Stalwarts like Mahoney, Lowney, and Terzich—all of whom played important roles in Michigan—left the WFM by 1915. The Copper Country strike saddled the WFM with enormous debts. For the year ending June 30, 1914, the WFM spent $783,454 on the strike; half of the amount was paid by Western mine workers via assessments. Enormous unpaid legal bills, money owed for commissary supplies, and $168,000 in loans—such was the state of affairs confronting the WFM in April 1914.

Services of the militia in the copper district cost Michigan almost $400,000. As of December 1, 1913, Houghton County expended

$150,000 on strike costs; and the congressional investigation exacted another $40,000. Public services deteriorated; all road work was suspended in Keweenaw County in 1913, the money being used, instead, for relief costs and police protection. The loss in mining company income ran into the millions, and the loss in wages was enormous. (In 1909, in Michigan, seven operators and twenty-one mines had paid copper workers wages of $14,047,665.) The total cost of federal, state, and local governments was reckoned conservatively at $700,000.[67]

Although any man wishing to return to work had to turn in his union card and thousands who refused left the Copper Country forever, the strikers had achieved the eight-hour day and its resulting increase in wages. Management at all mines instituted better methods of hearing grievances. But the one-man drill remained. Worst of all, collective bargaining via union auspices had been defeated resoundingly. Almost thirty years after the strike began, the major goal of the Michigan rebels of 1913–14 was achieved. Between 1939 and 1943, Michigan copper workers chose the *same union* to represent them, under the name adopted by the WFM in 1916: the International Union of Mine, Mill, and Smelter Workers (IUMMSW). Affiliated now with the Congress of Industrial Organizations (CIO), the IUMMSW became sole bargaining agent for the Michigan copper workers.

In attempting to account for the strike's failure in 1913–14, the following are crucial: (1) the premature beginning of the strike by Copper Country locals; (2) the inept tactics of the Western Federation of Miners once Denver officialdom decided to support the strike; (3) the peculiar personalities of Charles H. Moyer, Alexander Agassiz, and James MacNaughton; and (4) the unique Copper Country communities, which benefited from mining companies' treatment of employees.

COPPER COUNTRY LOCALS

Victory by the strikers was virtually foreclosed from the outset because a *minority* of workers challenged united managers, who vowed to close the mines, rather than recognize the federation. Due, in large part, to "the kind of paternalism that kills unionism," Michigan copper workers in the prosperous years 1904–7 had little time for Western Federation organizers. Local unions had been set up in 1904 but had disappeared by 1907, for all practical purposes. When the WFM split with the Industrial Workers of the World and moved toward more conservative positions, affiliating with the American Federation of Labor (AFL) in 1911, organizers returned. As companies cut costs to maintain efficiency, especially from 1910 to 1913, a resurgence of interest in unions occurred. But recruiting was slow. In part due to company "blackballing" of those who dared join unions, recruiting moved at a snail's pace, because a great many workers looked upon the Western Federation as an intrusion that might seriously disturb the "welfare capitalism" that the workers themselves had helped develop over many years. They worked for lesser wages in Michigan but enjoyed various forms of social insurance provided by workers' fees and company largesse. A fine hospital, excellent physicians, superb schools supported in part by companies' beneficence, admirable libraries, disability and death benefits, relief funds, pensions, extremely cheap rents for housing, public baths, and company encouragement of workers owning their own homes—all this, which benefited a majority, militated against change.[68]

However, by 1913, a large minority did *not* benefit from most of this. Thousands had become convinced that they were forever doomed to remain at the dirtiest, most exhausting, lowest-paying work in the mines. Most of them foreigners, many bore bitter resentments toward English-speaking miners, trammers, foremen, mining captains, and managers. The 1910 census indicated that only 31 percent of foreign-born males were naturalized. Thus, they had no political power and correspondingly, no "say" in affairs at their work. The appeal of the WFM for the men to assert themselves in order to control their lives was enormous; but too many of the foreign-born truly believed they could improve their lives and those of their children by remaining faithful to the companies.[69]

By 1910, class consciousness, envy, and feelings of inferiority permeated many workers' minds. Graham Romeyn Taylor, social worker, in his 1913 article on the strike, wrote of a Finnish servant at Calumet who allegedly told her mistress: "Some day you be in kitchen and I be in parlor."[70] The anecdote is illustrative of the reality many faced. On the second day of the strike, two to three hundred men marched from South Range, "carrying clubs, rocks in bags or cloths," and some, revolvers. They demanded that the Baltic Mine and office be shut down. "We are the bosses now," they told mining captains as they searched men believed to be deputies and ripped their clothes. The long hours, low wages, and bad conditions underground forced such men to rebellion. *They* demanded that the district union stop hesitating and listening to Denver and begin the strike.

Western Federation officials torn between socialist and conservative approaches in guiding the strike failed, too; for they failed to understand the unique conditions prevailing in the Michigan Copper Country. The violence used there (as in the past, in Colorado and Idaho) backfired among many Michigan people who initially sympathized with the striking miners' desire for change. The frequent injection of socialist calls for nationalization of the copper mines frightened many middle-class people. They saw the WFM as a divided body, using, first, all the approved methods of arbitration and then violence while blaming imported gunmen and avaricious mine managers. Evidence indicates that the WFM leaders from Denver realized that the strike was essentially lost by October when the companies began importation of workers. Still, they persisted, with Moyer callously using the tragedy of Christmas Eve, 1913, as a last-ditch attempt to secure state or federal assistance in achieving a victory of the WFM.[71]

MOYER, AGASSIZ, AND MACNAUGHTON

Although the "great man" theory of history is invalid, one must not discount the *human factor* in what happened in history. Charles H. Moyer was a man torn between middle-class respectability, the rational approach to problem solving, and a recklessness that resulted in incredible behavior damaging the cause of labor. He courageously worked for improvement in the lives of workers but thought nothing of exaggeration, lies, and foolhardy acts to achieve victory.[72] Alexander Agassiz stifled a revolt of copper miners in 1872; and when Finnish trammers initiated a strike in 1874, he asserted: "We cannot be dictated to by anyone. The mine must stop if it stays closed forever, . . . we have always treated our men fairly, . . . they have received higher wages than [from] any other corporation. . . . They spit in my face as it were. . . . Wages will be raised whenever we see fit and at no other time." If the workers did not like that, they must seek work elsewhere.[73] In May 1893, he signed a notice printed in English, Polish, Italian, and Slovenian: "As the trammers of the Calumet and Hecla Mining Company have of their own accord abandoned their places, they are requested to call at the different mining Captains' offices and obtain their settlement."[74]

Agassiz used profits from the successful mines to further his life's work as oceanographer; therefore, no interruptions in mining would

Calumet and Hecla's Red Jacket Shaft Mine surrounded by company houses. (Michigan Technological University Archives and Copper Country Historical Collections, Michigan Technological University.)

be tolerated. His obsession with control can also be understood as compensation for the chaos in his own life when, at a most important stage of life, between ages twelve and fifteen, his father deserted him for America.[75] Agassiz' attitudes toward unions, strikes, and providing for workers were carried on by his successor James MacNaughton, who told the congressional subcommittee: "I do not consider this a war of extermination. If they [WFM members] do not want to subscribe to the conditions that we impose, they are perfectly free to go to other places." His talk was laced with expressions of Calvinistic perdition and union proposals "conceived in iniquity," mixed with Christian charity: "I pride myself on being something of a Socialist," he told the inquiring congressmen, not a red militant; for his was an enlightened concern manifested in the long-established principles of capitalistic paternalism.[76]

The Protestant ethic ruled supreme for MacNaughton. The 1913 strike was really an attack on the capitalist system, which could not be tolerated: "I personally will not agree to let any power on earth, [state or federal,] arbitrate a question between 4,700 [Calumet and Hecla] employees who are faithful and loyal to the company and two hundred forty-odd employees who are on strike, the conditions of which arbitration shall be imposed upon the men now [February 1914] at work. I think it would be outrageous and uncalled for and unjustifiable." The evidence clearly shows that his decisions during the strike's duration found willing adherents in all of the smaller companies in the Copper Country.[77]

COPPER COUNTRY COMMUNITIES

Although all did not benefit equally, the workers in copper mines and mills accepted what has come to be called "welfare capitalism" or "benevolent paternalism."[78] They did not live behind fences, shop at company stores, or experience deliberate discrimination. Indeed, the companies, for the most part (and especially at Calumet and Hecla), recognized that they owed much to their employees. Good workers made for continued production. As one investigator wrote in 1911, "The men that operate the mines are those who have worked as miners themselves during a part of their life and they appreciate the fact that the good will of the workmen helps largely in cutting down costs."

The companies through their support of schools and libraries encouraged foreigners to become citizens of vital communities without destroying their precious ethnic heritages. They might have erred in their advocacy of an Anglo–American civilization; but the truth is that in those times acculturation to the American ideal of freedom (especially free enterprise, as in the contract system, for underground mining) found many takers. It has become fashionable now to deride all this, to accuse Copper Country management of the early twentieth century as intent only on profit making at the expense of employees. But when the editors of the *Mining Gazette* wrote in October 1899 that Calumet and Hecla was a corporation with a soul and that workingmen "are nowhere better cared for than in this district," the language was not hyperbole.[79]

Where the companies erred, however, was in their failure to admit that in 1913–14, "a new principle of industrialism" (collective bargaining) was "struggling for expression and acceptance." This was, as an astute reporter noted, *"the issue between yesterday and today,"* with the companies looking backward to yesterday. Paternalism, noble and beneficial, was not in keeping with a dynamic economic order, peculiarly American, in which labor demanded justice. "The mistake of the [copper] companies," said the *Engineering and Mining Journal,* "was in not recognizing the basic economic condition in the first place. . . . Benevolence is not an asset in labor disputes. No matter how altruistically an employer may seek to improve living conditions, no matter how extensive may be his endowments of schools, hospitals and public improvements, the employee will reject them all and prefer to live amid conditions of discomfort . . . for the sake of a few cents more in the daily wage." Another twenty years would pass before an American social democracy emerged, encouraging collective bargaining and recognized working people's rights to shorter hours, higher wages, and better conditions at work.[80]

In July 1913, militant strikers who launched the action had many sympathizers among nonunion workers desirous of major changes. An astounded MacNaughton, told of what his assembled workers listed as desired changes, exclaimed that they asked for even more than the federation had asked for! They wanted more money and shorter hours without recognition of the WFM, but the general manager told them that the federation would be encouraged should he concede. After that, workers realized the futility of opposing inflexible mine managers backed now by the military power of the State of Michigan.[81] Although the strikers destroyed no property during the first two days, their beatings of men who wished to work and closing down of the mines triggered management's decision to have the sheriff send for the troops.

One can also understand the strikers' pent-up fury releasing itself on such a scale. One hundred and fifty years earlier, Thomas Jefferson wrote, "It is unfortunate, that the efforts of mankind to recover the freedom of which they have been so long deprived, will be accompanied with violence, with errors, & even with crimes."[82] But the tumult, intimidation, beatings, and arrogance of the rebels alienated increasing numbers of copper workers. Many of them, along with the local bourgeoisie, deplored Moyer's slurs upon their human decency when he refused money they raised for victims of the Christmas Eve panic. Determined by decisions made by thousands of men and women at all levels of society, the 1913–14 copper strike remains the most traumatic event of the history of the Keweenaw Peninsula.

In late summer 1914, World War I began; and by November, copper prices dropped 7 to 11.3 cents per pound. A steady rise followed. By autumn 1917, after the United States entered the war, copper sold for 36 cents. War revived the industry. The "golden age" seemed reinvigorated. Producers arranged to sell the federal government forty-five million pounds at 16 3/8 cents when Congress declared war on Germany in April. Government price fixing bolstered Michigan output; but labor shortages continued, and most companies halted development of new properties.[83]

Copper Country producers made their money before price fixing had its effect, paying $12,200,000 in dividends in 1915, almost $19,000,000 in 1916, and $23,900,000 in 1917—"the highest and most sustained profits in the industry's history." War's end in 1918 and glutted markets transformed "gold" to "ashes." Managerial efficiency reduced work forces. At Quincy, miners' wages increased 43 percent from 1912 to 1916 as the one-man drills "brought large gains in productivity, reducing costs and raising profits."[84]

Some saw the "golden age" as truly ended with the imposition of prohibition, adopted by Michigan, effective May 1, 1918. Quincy women allegedly sat at doors of saloons, where husbands drank all through the night even though liquor sales should have halted legally at midnight. Some tried to revive "the best of times" they had known before 1913, with Christmas tree parties on Quincy Hill and at Mason symbolizing the nexus of company and employees. At Quincy Mine, in 1919, some 1,150 children of workers enjoyed ice cream, candy, Santa Claus, gifts, and carols sung by a twenty-six-member Cornish choir.[85]

Calumet and Hecla celebrated its fiftieth birthday in 1916 with a gala holiday and gold medals for 140 men who had worked for the company forty or more years, silver medals for 480 who had served thirty to forty years, and bronze medals for 824 with twenty to thirty years' service. The sons of Agassiz and Shaw arrived from Boston, along with Higginsons, Hunnewells, McKeans, Fennos, Livermores, and others, including Scott Robinson, the janitor of Calumet and Hecla headquarters at Ashburton Place. Some twenty thousand men, women, and children—"the extensive Calumet and Hecla 'family',"as a Boston newspaper described them—gathered in the old Calumet Common separating Red Jacket from the line of shafthouses. The area made pleasant with recently sown grass, banners, and bunting for the event, became beautifully landscaped Agassiz Park in 1923. A bronze statue of Agassiz was dedicated that year in the park.[86]

Seventy years after the Keweenaw was "discovered," the copper companies reached maturity. They paid $146 million in dividends from 1905 through 1918. Less impressive was the refrain sounded in Quincy Mining Company annual reports after 1920: "Due to the light demand and continued low prices at which copper sold during the past year, it has been impossible to operate the mine at a profit notwithstanding every effort to reduce prices."

The massive funeral service for Calumet's football celebrity George Gipp in December 1920 evoked tales of the strength and talent possessed by Copper Country people. Elderly men and women recalled pioneer days, while a new population emerged. The births in Calumet Township dropped from 738 in 1910 to 475 in 1914. In births, Finns now led, with Americans and Slavs running second and third. With 191 deaths, the township's 1914 increase in population amounted to 284; in 1910, the increase had been 473. Economic facts plus the 1913 strike had taken their toll; many had left the Keweenaw Peninsula forever.[87]

War brought changes. Some five thousand men left during World War I. As they had since the Civil War, men in 1917–18 responded to their country's call. Later, many created romantic versions of experiences, as had those who went off to war before. For instance, the Houghton Light Infantry in 1898 became part of the Thirty-Fourth Michigan Volunteers; and in the "splendid little war" of that year, eight died, victims of fever, malaria, and other afflictions. Some lads wrote home that powerful Cuban rum gave one the "jaggiest kind of a jag . . . made one feel as if he had fallen into Quincy mine; been dragged through the murky waters of Portage Lake and mopped over the Mining College campus." Survivors welcomed the Copper Country's cool air, for they had been "worn down and debilitated by the long service in a climate for which the boys were not fit to serve in." The Calumet Light Guard, Company D of the Thirty-Fourth, fought at San Juan Hill (Cuba), on July 2, 1898, using antiquated Springfield rifles. Suffering in broiling sun as they helped construct a road, many fell ill. Sixteen died of malarial fever, typhoid, consumption, gastritis, and fatigue, a few, from injuries received in a railroad accident.

Later, veterans marched proudly in parades. In 1916, local companies of the National Guard patroled at the Texas border when war with Mexico loomed. With draftees, they served when war came in 1917 with Germany. Some wrote home of the "old country" from which parents had emigrated.

The Peter Gatzen family had five sons in service (four in France) by 1918. One wrote of a seven-day raid amid machine-gun bullets and shellfire. American Legion posts in the Keweenaw were named for men who died in war. In World War I, eighty-seven from Houghton County died, thirty-nine from Ontonagon, eight from Baraga, and four from Keweenaw.[88]

Once home, many veterans left for places with more promise of employment. An observer in 1906 had described the entire Upper Peninsula when some $45 million[89] worth of copper was produced: "Mountains of iron and millions of tons of copper ore have been removed, and like the pine forests . . . have gone to enrich other localities in the east, leaving Michigan the 'stump land' and the worked out mines"[90]—a harbinger of economic distress that came in the 1920s.

8

The Truly Great Depression

1920 – 1940

L'ANSE, IN 1923, WAS "BOOMING FROM A LUMBER deal." At Keweenaw Bay, everybody "seemed busy and new houses were going up all around, making everything look prosperous." Native Americans, "a mere handful of descendants from proud tribes which once roamed the entire peninsula . . . living contentedly, [were] eking out a living fishing and small farming." Like tourists before her, Mrs. Turrell, the author of these observations, marveled—when she reached Houghton, Hancock, and Calumet—at the mines that had made the district famous.[1]

After the 1913–14 strike, Michigan's copper mines had rallied quickly. They produced a record 266,839,000 pounds of copper in 1916; but production tumbled to 178,366,000 pounds in 1919 and 92,262,000 pounds in 1921, when the United States copper-mining industry underwent the sharpest production curtailment in its history. Employment in Keweenaw copper mines fell from about fourteen thousand in 1918 to about eight thousand in 1922. What Mrs. Turrell witnessed was a Keweenaw Peninsula struggling out of a postwar depression.[2]

The depression (1921–22) hit the district severely due to world-wide overinvestment in copper mining. As copper markets became glutted, the price fell. The Quincy Mining Company cut wages almost in half between December 1920 and August 1921 and operated its mines and mills only four days a week, expecting to close

226

momentarily. Calumet and Hecla curtailed production in 1919 and shut down completely for one year beginning in April 1921. Everywhere, cost-cutting ruled. At its subsidiary, Isle Royale, the company reduced the total cost (mining, transporting, and stamping a ton of rock) to $2.73 in 1920, $2.62 in 1921, and $2.36 in 1922. In Houghton County in 1923–24, only 4,267 men worked in the mines, and twelve mines were idle. Men worked an average of 258 days a year at Calumet and Hecla, 296 at Quincy, and 302 at Copper Range. In 1924, beginning in March, Calumet and Hecla operated only five days a week. Even the "prosperity" that returned that year and lasted through 1930 in the Copper Country was illusory, relative to former years.

Attorney Edward Le Gendre, employed by the WFM during the 1913–14 strike, penned a letter on Christmas Eve, 1925, asking the union's president, Charles H. Moyer, when he might expect the $14,500 still due him for his services. He noted that more than twenty-five thousand people had left the Copper Country since 1921.[3] Henry Ford's offer of five dollars a day in pay had drawn many Keweenaw workers to Highland Park after the strike. In 1917, Copper Country workers began to move in large numbers to Detroit and Flint as mine wages lagged behind those in the automotive plants. Scores of people were still boarding trains, in 1924, at the Mineral Range depots, for Detroit, Milwaukee, and Chicago. The movement to downstate cities became a genuine exodus as auto building succeeded the lure of copper as an economic incentive. Some who departed had long chafed under Quincy's or Calumet and Hecla's domination; others left sorrowfully out of economic necessity and fashioned, in downstate cities, continuing links with the Keweenaw through clubs, sport teams, and periodic reunions.

Agents from automobile factories scoured the Keweenaw to recruit employees. The downstate auto centers received vital transfusions from the large investments made in the Copper Country in excellent education and on-the-job training. Energies, talents, diligence, and aspirations of transplanted Keweenaw copper workers contributed to the productivity of the Lower Peninsula. As a result of this exodus, once Michigan copper mines began to resume normal production after the recession, they faced a labor shortage.

By the 1920s, despite one historian's talk of "the seven fat years of the roaring twenties, 1924 to 1930" at Calumet and Hecla, the copper-mining industry faced poor long-term prospects. Its future decline was foretokened by (1) the increasing depths of mines, (2) exhaustion of the major deposits, (3) declining copper content in the rock, and (4) the high cost of mining.[4]

Costwise, the Michigan industry operated at a disadvantage to other United States copper mines despite the generally lower wages it paid. For 1928–30, the total costs for producing a pound of refined copper were 10.24 cents in Michigan, 9.73 in Arizona, and 8.62 for all other United States companies. The Quincy Mining Company operated with a labor force less experienced and more transient and inefficient than in earlier years; and it also faced big expenses to repair damage done by fires and 1924 air blasts, which alone caused forty thousand dollars' damage. Its production dropped to about 1,220,000 pounds of copper by 1928 before recovering to 11,000,000 pounds in 1930. An underground fire at the Red Jacket Shaft and No. 4 Calumet caused considerable damage in 1924.

Much of what Copper Country people thought was the acme of the "golden age of copper" was in reality a period of deterioration. The relative position of the Michigan copper industry to other United States and world producers had actually worsened substantially during its period of maturity between 1905 and 1918. In 1929, the Lake Superior copper companies accounted for only 9.3 percent of this nation's copper output. From 1924 to 1925, increased output of the red metal in Chile and central Africa kept the price of copper down. In October 1926, a cartel, Copper Exporters, Incorporated—formed by firms that controlled 90 percent of world copper output—worked to stabilize the European market. In 1927, the Copper Institute, a cartel fabricated by American companies ostensibly for "sharing information," functioned to fix the price; but the voice of Michigan companies proved "a minor, if strident, one" in such councils. Alex Skelton, industry analyst, commented in the mid-1920s: "The querulous voice of the white-haired Grand Uncle from Michigan, Calumet and Hecla, jealously guarding the last of his treasure, was insistently heard protesting at the growing influence of foreigners about the court."

In 1923, the Copper Range Company called for a tariff; and in 1924, the entire Copper Country demanded one. But the bill died in Congress. The call for a tariff became a shout by 1932; but by then, American capitalism had collapsed in one of its fiercest downturns, never to regain the commanding position held between 1890 and 1929, creating a situation beyond the capacity of a tariff to remedy.[5]

The *Calumet News* hailed improving business conditions in 1924 with an editorial, "Give Prosperity a Chance." The Rosenbaum stores in Red Jacket advertised, "We will slash, sacrifice and price cut" to move a stock of men's and women's cloth coats. The Hancock Rotary Club, organized March 17, 1921, argued, "He profits most who serves best" and raised funds for various charities while extolling President Calvin Coolidge's maxim, "The business of America is business." In 1927, Houghton and Keeweenaw county banks had twenty-three million dollars on deposit, "close to the highest point in the Copper Country's history." J. H. Jasberg of Hancock said, "Not a man in the district need be without a job, and incomers are being put to work as fast as they arrive." Pay, he continued, was lower than in downstate cities; but so was the cost of living.[6]

Calumet and Hecla, operating in the red in 1924, enjoyed a net profit of $5,326,933 in 1929 and paid $9,024,759 in dividends. Some found signs of optimism in scattered instances of population growth. L'Anse had 1,013 inhabitants in 1912 and 2,240 in 1930; Ontonagon had a 1920 population of 1,406 and 2,403 by 1930. But the population of Houghton County fell by more than 25,000 people between 1920 and 1930, most having left in the early 1920s. Hardwood logging enjoyed a burst of activity, although the peak period for lumber production in the Upper Peninsula was over by 1920. Tourists, told that the "Ahmeek Mine never shuts down," believed that that made for prosperity.[7]

By 1923, the consolidation of Calumet and Hecla with other smaller companies led to extensive explorations as geologists sought new mineral deposits. Beginning in spring 1920, a corps of men supervised by L. C. Graton of Harvard University surveyed Calumet and Hecla properties. The company had acquired the property of the Lake Superior Smelting Company and the Superior Copper Company. In 1927, Calumet and Hecla began unwatering the old Phoenix Mine, abandoned in 1888, and announced in 1928 that for the past two years, explorations at both the Phoenix and Cliff mines "indicated the wisdom of conducting these explorations." That sounded good to stockholders, but attempts to find new life in these mines came a cropper. By February 3, 1931, expenditures caused all work there except pumping to be suspended. Meanwhile, scientists and engineers scrutinized Hecla, Calumet, and Tamarack Junior properties only to find mostly "poor" grades of copper. By 1926, exploratory work along the crosscut from the Osceola Lode to the Allouez conglomerate drove a distance of 2,437 feet, exposing twenty-four amygdaloid and conglomerate lodes; but none "offered any encouragement for further work, and the exploration was therefore abandoned."

Optimists, such as President W. E. Hotchkiss at the Michigan College of Mines, argued for viewing the future with "sane optimism"; for estimates indicated that less than 10 percent of the copper had been "systematically and thoroughly prospected." The reality was that the 8,000-foot-deep (on the incline) Quincy shaft, the No. 4 Calumet at 9,070 feet, and the almost-mile–deep No. 3 Tamarack proved too expensive to operate, the ratio of copper to rock almost negligible. Explorations in the three copper-producing counties revealed no new rich deposits to tap. Baraga County's involvement in mining had been limited to a Mass Mining Company stamp mill, which closed at the end of 1919. Quincy paid no dividends after 1921. The company did invest in new technologies, always hoping for a rise in the market price of copper.

One harbinger of success was reclamation of copper, at Lake Linden and Tamarack plants, from tailings that had been flushed into Torch Lake. This operation, by 1929, produced 250,799,000 pounds of refined copper.[8]

J. N. Wright, once superintendent of the Calumet Mine, had said as early as 1899 that while every speculator hoped to find "another Calumet," the mining of copper remained hazardous in that millions had to be spent to determine whether or not a mine would pay. Patience was required of shareholders. He recalled that men had predicted that the Calumet would not pay and that it took a good five years to prove them wrong. Wright's was an interesting story. He had first gone to the Copper Country because a relative mentioned possibilities of getting rich there. In 1899, he was the largest individual owner of Calumet and Hecla stock (900 shares) and trustee of an additional 3,850 shares. He left to live in Detroit in 1896. Then a millionaire, he had once worn rough miner's clothes and commanded Cornish workers. He had spent thirty years in what the *Detroit News–Tribune* described as "that bleak and desolate Lake Superior country, with its deep snows, its long winters, and . . . insufficient modes of communication with the outside world." In later life, Wright took a house in France from which he moved about that country to savor its culture. His interviewer in 1899 found him refined, cultured, and "bookish" and seemed surprised that the Lake Superior district was capable of producing such a person.[9]

For those who remained in the copper district, hopes of finding new mineral deposits sprang eternal. A veritable legend grew of great days coming if only explorations uncovered vast new riches in copper, silver, or other metals. Such faith flamed anew at every new utterance of the old capitalist ethos, including the 1923 consolidation of Calumet and Hecla properties with those of Ahmeek, Allouez, Centennial, and Osceola.

William Alfred Paine, Boston financier who almost single-handedly founded the Copper Range Company, admitted in 1928 that for mining entrepreneurs, the 1920s disappointed all. Paine Webber had experienced several depressions but had gathered a surplus "in the big years" to help through the lean years and thus remained "comfortable until the next big copper period" began. He learned this lesson early, he pontificated, one "every young man *must* learn" if he wished to succeed in America's capitalist society. He had built Copper Range "from a hope into a fortune" and said, in effect, "Go, and do thou likewise." Like many other capitalists, he failed to see, or refused to admit, that the times had changed—forever. Most Americans, including those in the Keweenaw, accepted this philosophy of working, saving, and waiting for the rain to stop falling. They erred, later, in failing to see that the 1930s Depression was unlike any other.[10]

As the copper-mining industry moved toward recovery from its 1921–22 depression, the value of Michigan copper mined rose from the $12,620,000 of 1921 to $33,540,000 in 1929, the year of the great Wall Street financial crash, while dividends paid had risen from nothing in 1921 to $11,170,000 in 1929.[11]

Development of both agriculture and tourism were promoted during the 1920s as potentially beneficial for the Keweenaw Peninsula, where nonmining ventures had met little welcome in the past: Red Jacket Village had been diffident to a 1914 proposal from a Milwaukee firm to open an overall factory in the North Country. Agriculture could never become a sustaining component of Copper Country life, however, because of the relatively short growing season, the scarcity of high-quality soils, and the distance to potential markets.[12]

But agriculture did blossom in the Upper Peninsula between 1900 and 1920. The number of farms rose from sixty-one hundred to more than twelve thousand. World War I's worldwide stimulation of food prices made farming "lucrative even in marginal areas like the northern Michigan [cutover land]." The 1860 census had listed but nineteen farmers in Houghton County. Now men with families left settlements like Boston, Coburntown, Concord City—all north of Hancock—and once-thriving mining locations in search of new livelihoods. By 1940, many Finnish miners had "exchanged their pneumatic drills for plows and . . . cleared extensive farms."

Michigan's Department of Agriculture exclaimed in 1921 that the Upper Peninsula was "boundless in its agricultural opportunities" with thousands of acres awaiting brains and hands of farm families "to yield [a] flow of 'milk and honey'."[13] This was five years after Roger Andrews, publisher of the *Menominee Herald–Leader*, had called for transforming seven million acres of cutover timberland into farms. He helped establish the Upper Peninsula Development Bureau by 1911, and its monthly newsletter in the 1920s and early 1930s promoted not only farming but the economic possibilities of tourism.

Andrews coined the name Cloverland for the region "he hoped would become an agricultural cornucopia of the Upper Great Lakes." At the annual banquet of the Calumet Business Men's Association on January 5, 1916, he began with the proposition that the Upper Peninsula should become a separate state named Superior—not entirely a new proposal, for legislators from the Upper Peninsula had argued that in Lansing as early as the late 1860s. The *Detroit News* found statistics accompanying the proposal "impressive, [presenting] the Upper Peninsula in a prouder light than many of us have been accustomed to view it." The *Detroit Journal*, thinking of copper, quipped sarcastically, "We suggest Boston as the capital of the new state." The *Grand Rapids Press* sniffed, "Let the wise men of the north country think more of the state and less of their peninsula." The *Calumet News* argued that the proposal "will at least open the eyes of the country to . . . the great opportunities [the area] presents agriculturally, industrially and economically." The separate-state idea gestated for another half century before squirming for attention once again.[14]

Tourists in Ontonagon County in the early 1920s noticed "thriving farms," dairy herds grazing on cutover lands at Ewen, and much agricultural progress. Statistics confirmed such observations (see Table 8.1).[15]

Table 8.1. Keweenaw Peninsula Agriculture, Early 1920s

	Farms		
County	1919	1922	Acreage, 1922
Baraga	653	698	51,710
Houghton	1,741	1,952	149,517
Keweenaw	72	152	8,932
Ontonagon	917	1,119	82,700

George Bishop, secretary–manager of the Upper Peninsula Development Bureau in 1926, lauded Finns as "the outstanding and most progressive tillers of the soil." Leo M. Geismar praised William Soumis, Finnish farmer, for conserving seedlings and young native trees while removing fallen timber to guard against forest fires. Soumis worked his father's eighty-acre farm but found time to put up a tiny bungalow in a secluded grove on his own forty acres, where he spent "a little time now and then, watching the progress of my little forest, seeing the bushes and wild flowers blossom, the birds build their nests, . . . rabbits and squirrels rear their young in the safe retreat which I have provided for them." Thus, Mr. Soumis busied himself with his private "Walden" on the county road between Chassell and Painesdale.

John Doelle's agricultural school and demonstration farm at nearby Otter Lake [Houghton County], grew from 87 students in 1914 to 250 in 1927. Forty acres large, with twenty-five cultivated, the Doelle school served also as community center for rapidly expanding agricultural activity. The school won sixty first prizes and fifty-one second prizes at the autumn 1927 Copper County Fair. Paul P. Banker, a University of Wisconsin graduate with work, also, in rural sociology, and Florence Limmata, assistant principal, worked with six other faculty, women of Finnish and Scandinavian descent. Young people installed a moving-picture booth in the school's auditorium and invited the entire community for movies each week.

At Ontonagon, women organized clubs where girls learned canning and gardening. In summer 1928, nine girls put up more than two thousand quarts of fruit, jelly, and vegetables. They learned how to raise poultry, sew, till the soil, and also attended discussion sessions with adults, learning new ways of husbandry.[16]

By 1931, farmland sold better than ever as prices hit rock bottom and closing mines in the Keweenaw Peninsula sent more to the land. Potato yields tripled due to fertilizers, rotation, and sprays. By 1933, Houghton County had about two thousand acres in potatoes, in 1940, four thousand. In 1934, the Houghton County Emergency Relief Commission furnished labor for constructing a potato warehouse capable of storing sixteen thousand bushels.[17]

Michigan State College pushed sheep raising, in a five-year program toward the end of the 1920s. Daniel Brockway had anticipated that, as early as 1884. He wrote a friend from this "poor country . . . except for miners and tradesmen" about the fourteen-thousand-acre

Potato farmers, Houghton County, 1940. (State Archives of Michigan.)

estate under his supervision—five thousand being pastureland, which Brockway thought the owner could covert to a sheep ranch. Some four to five thousand head a year could, he opined, be sold in a ready market within twenty-five miles. The estate already had barns and buildings that could accommodate one thousand sheep, the "very best water and healthy high country for stock." In the early 1930s, one did see sheep in Keweenaw County but not on the scale Brockway or others envisioned.[18]

The Upper Peninsula Development Bureau increasingly advertised the region as a summer playground and tourist haven. By 1954, it reported that the automobile, road building by state and federal governments during the 1930s Depression, and the desire of city dwellers to seek recreation, beauty, and peace had caused the local tourist industry to become one of the largest in the Upper Peninsula. With this development came better hotels, resorts, souvenir shops, and cafés, although occasional downstate people as late as the 1990s cultivated the story that one "could not find a good meal in the U.P." For decades, not much in the way of dining places was to be found "along the road" in the four counties of the Copper Country, where natives found tourists "quaint" and did little until the 1940s to really serve them.

Bishop estimated conservatively that four-hundred thousand tourists visited the Upper Peninsula in 1925. The next year, one-hundred thousand pieces of literature were distributed at Chicago's Outdoor Life Exposition at a booth where signs proclaimed, "All Trails lead to the Upper Peninsula: The Tourist's Paradise." That year Michigan governor Alex J. Groesbeck advocated more financial aid for both peninsulas. By 1929, James C. Bowman of Marquette hailed the Upper Peninsula as "the Cape Cod of the Middle West," where, in June and July, "there is almost a midnight sun [and] at two-thirty in the morning the birds begin to twitter, and the long twilight advances against a pageantry of slowly brightening colors," where towns and small cities bordered forests of hemlocks and maples, a country as varied and picturesque as the proverbial Joseph's coat of many colors. Those in cities who could vacation chose shorter trips during the Great Depression, and the Upper Peninsula benefited as thousands of new strangers discovered the Copper Country.[19]

Visitors praised the pollen-free Copper Country where Leo M. Geismar had come at age thirty-five, ill "and with a limited expectation of life," then lived until age seventy-six, his most productive years spent as county agricultural agent. Public relations people slowly abandoned the name Cloverland for Hiawatha Land; and tourists bought postcards in the 1930s bearing the legend, "In the Land of Hiawatha." Had not Longfellow written of the Taquamenaw

(Tahquamenon) and "the fatal bowl Onagon" (Ontonagon)? If you came to the Upper Peninsula, you were in what the poet called "the land of the Ojibways, in the pleasant land and peaceful." Warren Manning, celebrated landscape architect and city planner from Cambridge, Massachusetts, said he always found new vigor in "this fair northland, [which] might fittingly be called 'The Ozone Land'." He seconded a suggestion to conserve the enormous forests. Others argued that "Hiawatha Land is [en]visioning the day, not far off, when all its counties will be traversed by ribbons of concrete laid once and for all and permanently."

Tourism prospered as part of the affluence that changed America so drastically in the last half of the 1920s. Arthur W. Stace of Ann Arbor, an official for the Michigan Public Utilities Commission, said in August 1929: "There is a new era here for the upper peninsula. Once [it was] down and going but now it is up and coming. Mines are working. Docks are busy. Copper country stacks are pouring smoke. Agriculture is looking more prosperous. Hotels are filled to capacity. Things are entirely different up here than they were a few years ago." Electricity helped transform rural areas. Manning pointed out that in 1918 state ferries carried 700 cars with visitors over the Straits of Mackinac; in 1928, 107,560 automobiles crossed into the Upper Peninsula. He foresaw hiking trails, shelters, and camps—comparable to Vermont's Sky Line trail along the Green Mountain summit—for the Upper Peninsula "wilderness" and other projects to turn the peninsula into a vast recreation area.[20]

Dining on whitefish and trout at Ontonagon, A. W. Burr, of Beloit, Wisconsin, thought the food made up for the clambakes he once enjoyed on the Maine coast. "The tonic Lake Superior air" was identical with that of the seaside, and glimpses of deer and other wildlife and miles of sand beaches delighted the tourists. "The Ontonagon river valley has all the natural charm of the most picturesque New England country," Burr acclaimed.[21]

With the completion of the Brockway Mountain Drive in the early 1930s and installation of wayside tables for picnics on the way to Brockway's majestic views of Lakes Upson, Bailey, and Medora, with thousands of evergreens—of various shades, depending on the position of the sun—tourists found unforgettable pleasure in such escapes from the Depression's difficulties. In the period June 16–30, 1939, the Keweenaw County Information Booth at Ahmeek, staffed by National Youth Administration (NYA) clerical help, reported 9,802 automobiles entering the wilderness wonderland and 5,991 in the first week of July. Tourists came from thirty-five states and Canada, and one, from Panama. By 1934, Austin C. Raley reported that his Lake Breeze Hotel had had its best year since 1929. Tourists feasted on the hotel's turkey dinner with all the trimmings for seventy-five cents in 1933. Leon Lundmark, marine painter, visiting the Copper Country, was so impressed by the Keweenaw's unique beauty that he decided to move his base of operations from Marquette. Tourists found in the Cliff Mine's ruins, the deserted Central, the Phoenix's Church of the Assumption, vivid reminders of the once great days; and they noted how Nature encroached upon these remnants. At nearby Eagle River, a general store, summer homes, and huge reels for drying fishnets gave no impression of the once-busy center.[22]

A visiting botanist at the Lake Breeze Hotel arrived to collect seven hundred varieties of the Keweenaw's wild flowers, many of which were then found only west of the Rocky Mountains, some of them "survivals of the pre-glacial age." Ontonagon advertised itself as a hay-fever haven. Students arrived each summer at Eagle River for six weeks of conferences and fun at the Gitche Gumee encampment maintained by the Northern Baptist Convention. Louis Bockert of Detroit said he met about a hundred people from all over the country on Isle Royale but that only two were from Michigan. That was 1934; but by 1939, Charles Kauppi's *Isle Royale Queen* made day trips each Tuesday and Thursday from Copper Harbor to Rock Harbor. From the Lake Breeze Hotel dock, Holger Johnson's *Awahnesha* made two trips per week to the island. These craft held twenty-five to thirty passengers each. Paul Pawler, automobile dealer from Calumet, operated a fast motorboat carrying five on chartered trips around the isle. Devotees of Isle Royale, which was about to become a national park, spun legends of prehistoric miners and Viking visits to a "copper island." Between 1920 and 1940, shops selling newspapers and magazines carried souvenirs of copper or copper-plated materials, as did the "five-and-ten-cent" stores. Dolls in Native American dress, postcards of Fort Wilkins, lamps, ashtrays, medallions, candlesticks, bowls, and plaques of hammered copper now entered the local market.[23]

Prohibition hit the Keweenaw area hard from 1920 to 1933. In 1913, 152 saloons flourished from Calumet to South Range, with another 11 scattered nearby; there were nine wholesale liquor establishments. In the early twentieth century, there were 121 persons for each of the 59 saloons in Ontonagon County. Mrs. Aurora Toivanen, Mass City, sued four dealers there to recover $3,000 she claimed was a small part of what her husband had squandered at their saloons. A South Range woman had been awarded $850 in a similar 1910 case. A Louisville salesman considered Calumet one of the biggest beer-drinking towns in the Copper Country. Exaggerations persisted. James MacNaughton of Calumet and Hecla testified in 1914 that as a class, "our local people . . . are very sober and steady," not hard-drinking people.

Prohibition divided people along class and ethnic lines. The Protestant middle classes—many of them descendants of pioneers—favored the ban generally, with Catholics and Jews opposed on grounds that they drank temperately, for the most part. Homemade beer and wine complemented many a meal, especially on feast days, in working-class homes. Many continued to brew during the 1920s. Some manufactured potent beverages that blinded some men and caused others to fall asleep in snowbanks and suffer consequent amputation of limbs.

Raymbaultown, a residential section near the Hecla shafthouses, became notorious for bootlegging. Al Capone was rumored to visit there. "Raymbaultown Rye," a volatile moonshine, led to fights. Leslie Chapman, security officer for Calumet and Hecla, once sent a bottle's residue to a friend at Michigan College of Mines. After he had analyzed the brew, the friend asked, "Is the guy who drank this stuff still living?" But some said the wine and other liquors from Raymbaultown were good, not like those of amateurs. Raids by county sheriffs proliferated—twenty-five in a few weeks in 1927. The officers found "moonshine" in a Houghton saloon selling soft drinks, "booze" galore and slot machines at Red Jacket, Laurium, and North Tamarack.[24]

The Great Depression knocked out prosperity with terrifying swiftness in the Copper Country. There was no demand for copper. Its price fell to seven or eight—sometimes five—cents a pound. At Calumet and Hecla, the cost of pumping and maintaining the deep conglomerate mine—its mainstay—caused the company to announce in 1936 that this principal producing unit "will be exhausted in the course of the next twelve or fourteen months." The inventory of refined copper on hand in 1932 consisted of 78,595,192 pounds. Many operations were suspended and wages cut 10–15 percent by 1931; the company dismissed all single men, and the rest worked only two to three shifts a week. Copper had become more expensive to produce and unable to justify the price received in the market. Slowly, the giant company retreated in the 1930s, closing mines, abandoning most of its expensive exploratory work, and dismantling some buildings and hundred-foot-high smokestacks. Only part of the Calumet conglomerate and the Champion Mine of the Copper Range Company operated in the depths of the Depression.[25]

Senator Arthur H. Vandenberg, speaking at the Calumet Armory on October 26, 1932, told his large audience that only "a fully effective copper tariff would be [the] cornerstone of a new Copper Country prosperity." One word all Keweenaw children knew at spelling bees was *tariff*, as everyone called for protection. A half-page political advertisement reasoning that Democratic tampering with the tariff was "vague and meaningless" appeared in the *Calumet News* three days before the presidential election. This referred to a tariff measure that had been enacted the previous May. Much was at stake for the Copper Country, readers were advised; for the Democrats would bring disaster, and "a Republican victory is our only hope of restoring happy, prosperous times." The writers cried out, "Must we compete with African copper, produced by jungle labor living under jungle conditions?" Ocha Potter, a Calumet and Hecla official who had made "a First-Hand Study of the Subject, in the African Field" was to speak at Ahmeek on that subject.[26]

Before the Depression, local governments, the copper companies, and local charitable organizations assisted the needy. Probate Judge Herman A. Wieder announced that for the year ending September 30, 1924, 268 mothers in Houghton County received "pensions" totaling $46,012 for the support and maintenance of 965 children of widows, three deserted women, and three whose spouses had been committed to the state hospital for the mentally ill at Newberry. The Depression left so many in need that people began to look to the federal government for some of the social welfare once supplied locally. Until 1933, Calumet and Hecla assisted sixteen hundred laid-off employees.[27]

In 1934–35, 34.7 percent of Baraga County's population, 36.3 percent of Ontonagon County's, 40.1 percent of Houghton County's, and 74.6 percent of Keweenaw County's received relief.[28] The capitalistic welfare state that emerged from twelve years of the New Deal reshaped local attitudes, as well as lives. Politically, that meant a tempering of Republican ascendancy. Generations who came of age in the 1930s and 1940s formed attitudes startlingly different from those who once benefited from capitalism's hectic heyday.

Calumet and Hecla announced in 1932 that it operated at a loss of $1,377,884; and its dollar-a-share dividends of late 1928 through 1930 (with a high of $1.50 in 1929) disappeared entirely from 1931 through 1935, then remained at about $.25 a share until World War II. The company's conglomerate mine produced copper at $6.75 a pound and sold it for $6.82 in 1933. The corporation surrendered all options on Keweenaw lands, which meant that the Cliff and Phoenix areas became attractive studies for antiquarians in what once was. Pessimists predicted that Quincy and Calumet would suffer the same fate.[29]

For many, Calumet and Hecla had seemed like the Rock of Gibraltar. Now, ruin faced almost all. An exception was James F. Wiggins, local furniture retailer, who operated more than a hundred stores scattered throughout the United States. Striking an optimistic note, he recalled past business downturns and concluded, "After the storms things always were better and brighter and I feel that we shall come out of this troublesome period in the same way.' But population loss and the Depression transformed Hancock and Calumet as stores closed and businesses folded. By the early 1930s, Calumet's Fifth Street was the site of bankruptcy and "going out of business" sales. No longer did the street have its early-twentieth-century commotion when, Bertha Jacka recalled, on Saturday evenings, one "could scarcely move or get a baby carriage through the crowds of people." Now stores closed, cafés waited for customers, idle men gossiped on street corners, and everyone complained of "hard times." The immense cavity half filled with bricks, which was the Glass Block Store until it fell victim to fire, now peered blankly at phenomena that had arrived later: F. W. Woolworth, J. C. Penney, and Rexall Drug, none crowded with customers. Hancock stores sold goods at ridiculously low prices. On Quincy Street, grim-faced men and women walked slowly. Young people with nothing to do wondered about their future.[30]

The Depression had other consequences. In 1933, at Calumet, only 134 sets of license plates for passenger autos and 40 commercial plates had been sold by mid-February. Governor Frank Fitzgerald announced that 1932 plates would be legal until March 1. So many people had sold their cars that midtwenties' worries about traffic jams evaporated. Progressive ideas highly critical of capitalism, dormant during much of the twelve-year-long Republican bacchanal, revived. After describing an area west of Ontonagon devastated by forest fire in 1933, F. G. Westphal wished former lumber magnates could see the havoc they had perpetrated: They cut trees they never planted and left "detritus of their greedy march to litter the land and become a menace to fire [for] the generation that followed." These strangers who had fled were representative of "the army of enthusiastic Americans who went after the great natural riches of the country with just one idea: [get] as much of the cream as possible for themselves; and let the devil take the hindmost." Now, argued Westphal, others must seed the charred earth to prevent weed and brush from feeding future fires.[31]

In the face of the grave economic situation, Houghton and Keweenaw counties in the 1932 presidential contest voted Republican, as they had faithfully since 1896 except for the 1912 deviation in support of Theodore Roosevelt's Progressive party. Baraga and Ontonagon counties, however, swung into the Democratic column in 1932, after years of voting Republican. Ninety percent of registered voters in Calumet Township (about one-third of the vote cast in Houghton County) voted in 1932.

Republican dominance in Copper Country politics ebbed considerably between 1932 and 1940, as New Deal money poured in to provide work relief. The district's electorate had proved erratic in the past, with much progressive, even radical, sentiment expressed early in the twentieth century. Many of the most vocal then did not vote, however. Socialists and union advocates in 1914 urged them to vote and participate. In 1896, miners convinced by arguments favoring high tariffs ignored class differences and voted Republican; but at the Portage Lake Smelting Works and similar places, workingmen leaned toward the Democratic party's William Jennings Bryan and free coinage of silver. Silver Clubs held debates and challenged the establishment. One speaker in 1896, William J. MacDonald, became the Progressive party representative in the United States Congress in 1912 and eloquently supported striking workingmen in 1913–14. His congressional district included the entire Upper Peninsula at that time. He had interrupted a line of Republican representatives that began with Jay Hubbell in 1873.[32]

MacDonald carried Houghton and Baraga counties in 1912. Even rock-ribbed Republican Calumet Township cast many votes for Theodore Roosevelt for president, rather than for William H. Taft. When Roosevelt spoke at Laurium's Palestra in 1912 on short notice, thousands turned out to hear part of his husky-voiced twenty-minute talk, many leaving after catching a glimpse of him. The desire for change was deep. Roosevelt carried Baraga, Houghton, and Keweenaw counties. Democrat Woodbridge Ferris, amiable reform candidate in the gubernatorial contest in 1912, fared well in townships where Democratic votes usually did not materialize. Although copper companies practically shut down on major election days, so that the men could vote, and although Calumet and Hecla attorney Albert E. Petermann represented Houghton County's First District at Lansing in 1912–13, many voters sought through political action, change from establishment ideas and policies. General Coxey had drawn thousands when he toured in 1896, preaching the populist doctrines of more government responsibility for the people's welfare. Senator Benjamin F. Tillman of South Carolina—"Pitchfork," to admirers, for his thrusts at the smug—stopped at Houghton in 1907 but did not leave his ship. "The copper country probably has no more enthusiastic friend than Ben Tillman," wrote a *Gazette* reporter, appalled at the senator's rabid racism but recognizing Tillman's advocacy of change and challenges to Republican elitism. A basic problem was that voting among non-English-speaking people was low. Leslie Chapman's immigrant father told him that by voting, he had "as much power as the queen of England," for nobody knew how he would vote.[33]

In the spring 1933 elections for state offices, all four counties voted Democratic. Murray D. Van Wagoner, who had done much to provide work building roads, defeated Highway Commissioner Grover C. Dillman, 385,768 to 298,994, another indication of how voters pursued their economic and social interests via the ballot box. In 1936, socialist and communist candidates received less than 1 percent of the votes in the presidential race, while Houghton County— foremost recipient of federal money for public works—voted heavily for Franklin D. Roosevelt and Frank Murphy, who became governor (see Table 8.2).

Table 8.2. 1936 Presidential Election Results, Keweenaw Peninsula

County	Alfred Landon, Rep.	Franklin Roosevelt, Dem.	Norman Thomas, Soc.	Earl Browder, Comm.	William Lemke, Union
Baraga	2,035	2,218	0	34	48
Houghton	9,345	11,642	23	66	129
Keweenaw	1,070	1,060	9	12	2
Ontonagon	2,162	3,233	15	114	37

(William Lemke was a North Dakota radical farm leader whose Union Party attracted Dr. Francis E. Townsend, who advocated paying all unemployed over age sixty $200 a month, as well as neofascists like Gerald L. K. Smith and Father Charles Coughlin.)

In 1940, Baraga, Houghton, and Keweenaw counties supported Republican Wendell L. Willkie; Ontonagon stood fast with Roosevelt and gave 114 votes to Communist Browder. From the 1930s on, the Copper Country wavered among Democratic and Republican candidates for various offices, depending on issues, interests, and localities.[34]

In politics, 1934 had been a watershed; for Frank E. Hook, Democrat, defeated Republican W. Frank James, who had represented the Twelfth Congressional District since 1915. That was truly the "top news story for the region," concluded David Halkola. The Twelfth Congressional District composed of Baraga, Houghton, Keweenaw, Ontonagon, Marquette, Dickinson, Iron, and Gogebic counties found in Hook an ardent champion of New Deal progressivism until the latter fell into some disfavor about 1948. Hook, born at L'Anse, lived in Ironwood and became the champion not only of labor but also of a new generation that approved of the Washington, D.C.— Upper Peninsula nexus. An older order of reactionaries had met their superiors in the New Deal.[35]

Hook was reelected three times before the 1942 reaction against Democrats (they lost forty-five seats); then Republican John B.

Bennett of Ontonagon served two years in the Seventy-Ninth Congress, 1945–47. Bennett returned in 1947 for eighteen years. Raymond F. Clevenger (Democrat) of Sault Sainte Marie (but originally from Chicago) served in the Eighty-Ninth Congress, 1965–67, before the Republicans returned under the aegis of Philip Ruppe and, later, Robert W. Davis, following a major redistricting. Frank Hook ran for the Senate but was defeated in 1948. He contested the election, claiming that Homor Ferguson and confederates had engaged in gross irregularities in several counties. Ferguson enjoyed a twenty-five-thousand-vote plurality over Hook; and the Senate Rules Committee upheld the results, admitting evidence of some irregularities in Michigan but not including participation by Ferguson. Hook returned to the fray in 1954, hoping to regain his House seat; but Bennett defeated him by 8,344 votes. In 1948, labor leader Gene Saari opposed Bennett but lost, 32,485 to 75,192. Many middle-class voters feared what they perceived as Saari's radicalism; nevertheless, Saari's receiving 30 percent of the total votes cast indicated new political forces at work.

The 1940 election for governor found Houghton, Keweenaw, and Ontonagon counties voting heavily for Van Wagoner. Their champion failed to gain a majority only in Baraga County—and that by only 178 votes out of more than 4,600 cast. Houghton County Democrats, in a 1941 caucus, asked Governor Van Wagoner, Representative Hook, and Senator Prentiss Brown to initiate defense industries to employ local surplus labor and to plan a long-term program of rehabilitation for the industrial–commercial development of the entire Upper Peninsula.

The change from stalwart Republicanism to a politics often in support of Democrats from 1934 on resulted from the following, according to an astute analysis: (1) The Depression decade's "searing effect upon traditional party preferences"; (2) the unemployed's turning for assistance to the Civilian Conservation Corps (CCC) and Federal Emergency Relief Administration (FERA) in Washington, instead of Calumet and Hecla and other copper companies; (3) the special concerns of the entire Upper Peninsula and Republican callousness to those needs at Lansing; and (4) more independent voters, who, from the 1930s to the 1990s, often saw Democrats as more amenable to the peculiar conditions prevailing in the Upper Peninsula. Voters in the four Copper Country counties gave Dwight D. Eisenhower big majorities in 1952 and, two years later, granted Democratic candidate for governor G. Mennen Williams huge margins of victory.[36]

The Hoover administration's Reconstruction Finance Corporation had helped furnish funds for Michigan highway construction; and by

March 1933, state highway commissioner Grover C. Dillman had authorized ten million dollars for improving the Ontonagon–Greenland road, in preparation for its later transformation into a trunk line highway.[37] Soon, the New Deal, with its expansion of the Reconstruction Finance Corporation and an array of assistance programs enacted in the first hundred days after Franklin D. Roosevelt's March 4, 1933, inauguration put to work Copper Country people who, for so long, had depended on private mining enterprises. Quickly, leaders in the Keweenaw became conversant with the alphabet of New Deal programs that funneled assistance into the area. The Copper Country towns held parades to celebrate the National Industrial Recovery Act of June 16, 1933, setting up the National Recovery Administration (NRA). The shops, stores, and industries displayed the NRA Blue Eagle posters until 1935, when the U.S. Supreme Court declared the act unconstitutional. By that time, the act had helped increase wages and assist workers insisting on collective bargaining.

In early April 1933, impatient farmers and workers demonstrated at Hancock's City Hall and demanded $20.00 a month relief for a married couple and $4.00 for each dependent, $10.00 each for single men and women over age eighteen, whether they lived alone or with others. They also asked for $3.20 a day for eight hour's relief work and free milk—a quart for every child and a pint for each adult—regardless of other relief. The implementation of relief, recovery, and reform measures galvanized people as Roosevelt began his presidency. An Ontonagon editorial in August 1933 said, in part, "The man who isn't 100% with President Roosevelt in his effort to bring back industry and trade to a normal basis is either a fool or a knave."[38]

A FERA supervisor suggested to the Houghton County Welfare Relief Commission that federal funds should be used to operate Quincy Mine. Miners would receive sixty-eight dollars a month, double their relief payments. The plan died aborning but indicated some desire to involve the federal government in creating social and economic democracy, as had long been advocated by some residents of the Copper Country. Workers at Toivola in 1936 formed an alliance with 117 members to combat unemployment and help those in need, sending representatives to Upper Peninsula meetings, as well as downstate. The group lost momentum eventually, due to internal dissensions and the economic recovery that accompanied the national defense buildup after 1940. Patrick H. O'Brien, working at a new career as a lawyer, advising autoworkers in the 1920s at Detroit, hoped, by 1933, to introduce a bill at Lansing calling for government confiscation of factories, mines, and other private property. Socialism, he said, was the only alternative to chaos. His bill was only the "entering wedge," he told the press; for "before long the nation will adopt pure Socialism, with government controlling all industry and wealth."[39]

Local organizations continued to work to help meet needs. The Portage Township Welfare Association joined Calumet and Hecla in supplying plots for community gardens. The association also supplied food and clothing to the neediest. The mining company allowed some people to cut wood for fuel in its forests and stored flour in company warehouses until needed. In April 1933, Houghton County's expenses for assisting the poor with food, clothing, fuel, rent, and medical attention amounted to $7,157, the fourth highest of counties in the Upper Peninsula. From May 1932 to July 1933, the Red Cross distributed flour, clothing, and bedding valued at $57,100 to about 6,200 people in Keweenaw and Houghton counties, while local relief agencies helped 4,600 in the Calumet district and 1,600 in Keweenaw County. Some people bartered garden produce or berries for bread at family bakeries. Some small businessmen simply exchanged products.[40]

Far too many people in distress exhausted local supplies and funds. The Roosevelt administration's relief brought "relief" in the form of work for many and outright gifts to the needy. The Washington "revolution" funneled hundreds of thousands of dollars into the Copper Country, one of Michigan's hardest hit areas, between 1933 and 1940. Keweenaw County relief expenditures for July 1934 totaled $26,306, with $18,750 of that coming from Washington and $5,570 from Lansing. By August 1934, 836 persons worked at cutting wood and building a new dock at Eagle Harbor, while 124 worked on the golf course and clubhouse for what eventually became the Keweenaw Park Resort. The golf course (eighteen holes), one-and-a-half miles south of Copper Harbor on U.S. 41, begun by the Civil Works Administration (CWA) and completed by the Works Progress Administration (WPA), involved clearing the land of 187,000 trees—some, tiny saplings, others, huge conifers cut for the market. This formed only one part of what was known as the Keweenaw Park Development. By 1938, Michigan legislators announced a closed season on hunting black bear there because the animals invaded garbage pits created by the invasion of tourists.

Employment by the CWA and then by its successor, the WPA, helped business revive. The *Mining Gazette* reported, "With thousands of dollars in CWA pay checks in the hands of workers, merchants have found [Christmas, 1933] business unusually brisk this year." The twenty-five hundred CWA employees in Houghton County also enjoyed Boxing Day, forced idle on December 26 by temperatures eight to ten degrees below zero.[41]

By the hot summer of 1934, Hancock residents could enjoy improved facilities at the public bathing beach, thanks to the CWA. The WPA, by 1939, paid thirty-four cents an hour for unskilled and forty-nine cents for skilled labor for an eight-hour day, five days a week. The total federal share for that year was $3,406,916 for the four counties, the money used mainly for roads, roadside improvements, public buildings, recreation facilities, and services attendant on these. Public schools benefited also. Surplus commodities were distributed to those in need. For the first time in their lives, some Copper Country people tasted grapefruit. Laborers received the bulk of the funds in the form of wages. Shares paid by local sponsors and figures for the years 1936–39 inclusive for Baraga, Houghton, Keweenaw, and Ontonagon counties are shown in Table 8.3.

The colorful WPA mural by Joe Lasker depicting miners at their underground work can still be admired at the Calumet post office, also built by the WPA and completed in the early 1940s. People in their late sixties today can still "hear" the music of the WPA Band, which presented 157 concerts from July 1, 1938, to July 1, 1939, and continued to play into the 1940s. Known formally as the Houghton County Federal Band, its director, John Bigando, and musicians—recruited from those who loved music and had played in local bands—entertained thousands with public concerts and many at public schools.[42]

Houghton County, with a population of about fifty-three thousand, provided relief to 8.9 percent of its population in June 1936 and spent $7,822 on care for residents in mental institutions, as compared with $2,606 spent by Ottawa County with a slightly larger population but with only 1.2 percent on relief. Social workers theorized that the "hopelessness of the economic situation in such counties as . . . Houghton is undoubtedly a contributing factor in the incidence of mental disease." They blamed the closing of mines, which had been occurring since the early 1920s.[43] When the Quincy Mining Company sought to collect rents of three to five dollars a month in the mid-1930s from WPA workers who had lived rent-free for several years in company houses, one tenant wrote on behalf of others there: "You know we are all on relief or New Deal which pays us $44 a month which we can't make reach all over. . . . There are 7 in my family and at present prices of things we have to skimp and scratch to make ends meet."[44]

Some high school students helped by the NYA worked part-time. Of enormous assistance was the CCC, created by Congress "to provide for the restoration of the country's natural resources" and other work. Men between ages seventeen and twenty-three, under the direction of the Departments of Agriculture and Interior, organized

Table 8.3. Work Projects Administration Expenditures, 1936–39, Baraga, Houghton, Keweenaw, and Ontonagon Counties ($)

Year and County	Local[a] Share	Federal Share	Uses (Besides Labor and Roads)
1936			
Baraga[b]	10,532	130,889	school services, recreation facilities, sidewalks
Houghton	146,866	1,163,205	public buildings, surplus commodities
Keweenaw	14,051	162,872	recreation facilities and services
Ontonagon	54,422	149,231	sidewalks, school services, public welfare
1937			
Baraga[c]	25,456	150,109	sidewalks, school services, public buildings, publicly owned utilities
Houghton	241,018	2,108,908	roadside improvements, school buildings, recreation facilities, public buildings, utilities
Keweenaw	24,289	283,897	roadside improvements, recreation facilities, publicly owned utilities
Ontonagon	84,265	244,528	education, public buildings
1938			
Baraga[c]	41,409	234,167	school services, public buildings, utilities
Houghton[d]	192,585	1,681,332	streets, sidewalks, school buildings and grounds, recreation facilities, public buildings
Keweenaw	25,953	296,779	publicly owned utilities, recreation facilities, public welfare buildings
Ontonagon	56,674	264,971	professional services in education, school buildings, recreation facilities, publicly owned utilities
1939			
Baraga[c]	66,757	452,861	school buildings and grounds, publicly owned utilities, recreation facilities
Houghton	347,685	2,063,339[c]	sidewalks, roadside improvements, school buildings, public buildings in towns and at the college, public welfare

Year and County	Local[a] Share	Federal Share	Uses (Besides Labor and Roads)
Keweenaw	41,623	298,266	streets in Ahmeek Village, recreation facilities, publicly owned utilities, surplus commodities, school buildings
Ontonagon	157,465	592,450	roadside improvements, sidewalks, public buildings, school buildings and grounds, recreation facilities
Totals	1,531,050	10,277,804	

Source: Work Projects Administration, Tabulation of Sponsor and Federal Participation in All Michigan Projects for Fiscal Years Ending June 30, 1936–39 inclusive, State Archives, Lansing, pp. 7, 31, 42, 66, 90, 114, 125, 149, 173, 197, 208, 232, 256, 280, 291, 315.

[a] Sponsors were county, townships, villages, cities, school districts.

[b] Does not include expenditures by townships and school districts.

[c] Does not include expenditures by townships.

[d] The Village of Calumet participated for first time with funds spent on street repair.

[e] Of $1,837,928 contributed by the federal government for the county alone, $1,581,484 was expended on labor; federal participation usually amounted to 82–85 percent in all categories of expenditures, at times, 89 percent.

camps like No. 635 (Ontonagon County) and No. 1617 (Baraga County). They received monthly thirty-dollar stipends and were required to send twenty-two dollars to their parents. Thousands of hours spent in forest culture and protection, learning of tree diseases and cures, fighting forest fires, and observing nature resulted in healthier youth with skills they would not have learned elsewhere.[45] In Ontonagon County, the CCC was vital as early as the summer of 1933. During one fire in the county that year, the camp at the Sawyer Goodman location furnished thirty-eight hundred man-days' labor. Residents praised the camps for reporting and fighting forest fires that year—ten in Keweenaw, sixty-one in Houghton, eighty-two in Baraga, and eighty-six in Ontonagon County.[46]

Men served relatively brief terms, their places taken by others from the ranks of the unemployed. H. Beadle reported from Reforestation Camp No. 662 (near Kenton, Baraga County), in August 1933, that the young men, besides working hard, enjoyed baseball, swimming, volleyball, the radio, and mail from home. Most here hailed from Detroit; and they got along well with the local population, attending dances and singing in church choirs. "All in all we are a happy camp; one big family of about 200 men of different nationalities, creeds and views, but united firmly together by one cause: [the] need of clean honest work." Quite a change, he recalled, from the first days when the urban strangers did not speak to one another! A youth from Hubbell told his family of a story current in his camp where a disgruntled, taciturn fellow each day in the chow line looked at the food and said only, "Hebrews 13:8." Checking their Bibles, colleagues found the verse, "Jesus Christ the same yesterday, and to day, and for ever."[47]

The Hancock Public School Library broke an attendance record in its reading room for the year ending July 1, 1934, when eighty-six thousand people used the facility. On some days, lack of chairs forced children into study halls to make room for their elders. Under the NRA, wage rates increased about 20 percent by 1934 at Calumet and Hecla. The codes of fair competition set hours of labor and rates of pay with the expectation that industry would stabilize and operations be restored to a sounder economic basis.[48]

By 1936, Calumet and Hecla produced over fifty-nine million pounds of copper and the Lake Linden Reclamation plant, more than nineteen million pounds. The average 1936 selling price was nearly ten cents a pound, almost double that of the worst years of the Depression. The company both cut and raised wages between 1937 and 1939 as New Deal experimentation ushered in a recession when President Roosevelt succumbed to advice from Democratic conservatives eager to balance the budget. Most of the company's mines lay idle; but gradually, the Ahmeek Mine assumed the dominant role among the company's lodes. In the mid-1930s, the company resumed bonus payment to employees equivalent to the dividend paid on fifty shares of stock. In 1936, with two dividend payments, that amounted to twenty-five dollars an employee.[49]

Calumet and Hecla explored for gold in the old Ropes ore body in the Ishpeming area in 1936 and at Goldfield, Nevada, where work continued via two subsidiaries. Some $512,000 in gold was produced from small ore bodies, but the future seemed uncertain for this venture. There was no uncertainty remaining about the great Calumet conglomerate. The company announced in October 1939 that No. 12 Calumet had been permanently closed. After seventy-three years, during which 3.275 billion pounds of copper had been mined, the end had finally come. The company diversified beginning in the early 1940s and operated mines mainly in Keweenaw County. Often pronounced "dead," Calumet and Hecla, by 1939, had another thirty years of life remaining. In the 1930s, the Copper Range Company also moved to diversify its holdings by purchasing the C. G. Hussey Company of Pittsburgh, a sheet copper fabricator.[50]

Businessmen, industrialists, scholars, and politicians met at trade recovery conferences in May and August 1933, in Houghton and

Hancock. In May, A. T. Sweet sounded the refrain of conservatives already alarmed by the New Deal "revolution": "We cannot continue to build public works, dole out direct relief, shovel snow and the like and expect the taxpayers to return this money into government coffers." The consensus, however, was one of accepting all government funds available to complete highway construction halted by the Depression. Governor William A. Comstock attended the August conference and toured part of the area, after listening to men explain the possibilities of using public funds to keep men working as they enhanced Keweenaw County's attractiveness to tourists with roads, lodges, picnic tables, and recreation facilities. Patrick O'Brien accompanied him and spoke on the NRA. A sales tax initiated in 1933 by Democrat Comstock astonished the Copper Country. Merchants told customers, "That will be a dollar, and 3 cents for the governor." At Calumet's F. W. Woolworth emporium in summer 1933, a clerk told a customer purchasing a kit to repair shoe soles that the cost would be forty-five cents and one cent for the tax, only to have the customer respond "I don't want the tacks; I use glue." Copper Country individuals maintained a sense of humor in these worst of times, which under the New Deal became almost the best of times. By November 1936, a Republican who lost his bet that Roosevelt would be defeated fulfilled his promise and trundled north on Fifth Street a wheelbarrow containing his Democratic betting partner.[51]

The New Deal also helped change the lives of the descendants of the Ojibwa. For decades, the federal government had emphasized their assimilation "into the white world" in order to end their financial and psychological burden on taxpayers. Militating against this were reservations like that at L'Anse (where climate and soil proved not the best for agriculture), loss of allotment lands by sale or lease, and effects of the Great Depression. Here few allottees raised crops or livestock. By the early 1930s, only six hundred out of fifteen-hundred acres had been cleared and cultivated. Work in nearby towns and lumber camps attracted some. By about 1925, more than half the eligible children attended state-maintained special schools but were encouraged to attend public schools.[52]

In 1930, an official of the Bureau of Indian Affairs reported that at L'Anse, the Ojibwa were "so far advanced in the way of industry, self-help, modern living . . . that they do not engage to any extent in the old tribal customs and pastimes." About 40 percent had left the reservation in search of work. Those who remained voted and paid taxes. In World War I, 705 went to fight in France, while others bought war bonds and donated to the Red Cross. The Catholic Sisters, Order of Saint Agnes, in 1922, taught thirty-six children in

249

their day school; a Catholic boarding school for Native Americans enrolled forty-six, all on the west shore of Keweenaw Bay, two-and-a-half miles from Baraga. During the 1930s, a rehabilitation division served as CWA, providing cash for repair of houses and public buildings and the manufacture of furniture. Native Americans did not go to CCC camps but benefited from the program, receiving, for their labor, $43,350 by March 31, 1937, as they worked seeding wild-rice paddies, planting trees, and in fish hatcheries.[53]

In 1930, Baraga County, with 493 individuals, had the third largest Native American population in Michigan. The Wheeler–Howard Act of June 1934 reversed the Americanization, assimilation, and allotment practices and recognized Native Americans not as rugged individualists but as human beings functioning best as "integrated member[s] of a group." This "Indian New Deal" provided cash to help tribes organize and create their own community responsibility "and new incentives for collective action." On June 14, 1935, the local Native Americans voted 13–8 to organize in this way out of an eligible voting population of 558. Thus began the Keweenaw Bay Tribal Council, with six representatives each from Baraga and L'Anse. By 1941, the factions clashed; but a new practice began of fostering Ojibwa culture and empowering members to negotiate with governments at all levels and most important, legislate for the good of all. In Washington, D.C., Indian Commissioner John Collier suggested that Ojibwa and other Native American values—individual and tribal—could also have value "for modern, industrialized, urban America."[54]

Despite the hard times of the early 1920s and the economic and social despair of the 1930s Depression, the Copper Country was not about to die, although some early mining locations did gradually take on the character of ghost towns. Feisty Houghton in 1926 boasted of its advantages, calling itself "the biggest little town" in the world as it sought a factory to offer steady employment and to lure back many of the residents who had migrated. From 1920 to 1940, Houghton County's population fell about one-third to 47,631 persons. Baraga County alone, among the four northern counties, gained population in that period. Keweenaw County's population dropped to 4,004 from 6,322, while Ontonagon County suffered a lesser loss, from 12,428 to 11,359. Houghton County boasted of its agricultural industry, its mining college, sound banks, schools, and churches in 1920s promotional literature. Despite the Depression, with diminution of commerce, Houghton's position as a lake port remained secure. In July 1934, the Keweenaw Waterway carried a heavy tonnage of freight, including 4,724,000 pounds of copper. Fifty-one vessels carried twenty-one tons of eggs and eighty of wool

"down" and automobiles, butter, and 32,275 tons of coal "up."
About a thousand passengers also traveled on the ships.[55]

Streetcars gave way to motor buses by 1932; and beer gardens
and saloons returned with such impact that the Houghton County
sheriff, in late summer 1934, ordered them to halt music at midnight.
(Michigan law allowed places selling liquor to remain open until two
in the morning.) Harold J. Skelly, who managed Hancock's Scott
Hotel, flew his own airplane from Saint Louis to the Isle Royale Sands
Airport, made by leveling stamp sand dumped by the Isle Royale Mill,
near Houghton. By 1930, Laurium had been selected as a site for
the joint Keweenaw–Houghton County Airport; but the project was
stymied by the Great Depression and never materialized.[56]

Economic hard times stimulated pursuit of the many amusements
to be had out-of-doors, summer and winter. Fishing, hunting, and
berry picking provided food to stretch some meager budgets. Winter
was made enjoyable with sleighing parties, coasting, skiing, tobo-
ganing, and snowshoeing. Some entertainment centers continued to
attract residents. The Houghton Amphidrome, an enormous combination skating and dance hall, used also for fairs and exhibits, drew
people from throughout the Keweenaw Peninsula and elsewhere.
Community dances held weekly in towns along the mineral range
throughout the year entertained thousands.[57]

Entertainment groups from afar still came to Red Jacket and
Houghton–Hancock in the 1920s. On October 11, 1924, the Boston
English Opera Company presented the popular musical play *The
Bohemian Girl* at the Calumet Theatre. Two nights later, the John
D. Winninger Company entertained audiences with vaudeville. Paul
Vernon and his Cleveland Symphonic Orchestra played at the Calu-
met High School. The Cornish Club hosted the Rhonnda Welsh Male
Chorus at the Calumet Methodist Episcopal Church on October 16,
and the group sang the following evening at the Hancock Methodist
Church. Admission to Red Jacket's Royal Theater cost five or fifteen
cents for viewing the movie version of David Belasco's *Girl of the
Golden West*.[58]

As always in the Copper Country, the humble remained along
with the elegant, the sordid along with community uplift. In the
1920s, some women peeled bark from large hemlock logs piled along
Mine Street in Calumet, the chips to be used for kindling fires—a
practice allowed by Calumet and Hecla. Bootleg liquor, prostitution,
rebellious youth, and narrow-minded Puritans cast ugly lights. The
elite mingled at the Onigaming Yacht Club. Three African American
women pleaded guilty and paid ten dollars each and costs for working
as prostitutes after the sheriff raided their house in an alley west of
Eighth Street, Calumet, in late winter 1930. Flappers outraged their

elders, as did youthful use of slang. Until well into the 1930s most people thought smoking for women was scandalous. Devotees of crime news, reading of the sensational kidnapping–murder of Bobby Franks in the early 1920s in Chicago, recalled that one of the two accused was Nathan Leopold, Jr., related to the Leopolds who once were prominent Copper Country merchants. Mrs. James Wilcox, who knew young Nathan, remarked: "That nice little boy. I just can't believe it."[59]

A highlight of the Great Depression occurred on Saturday, August 3, 1935, when the George Gipp Monument was dedicated at Tamarack Street and Lake Linden Avenue at Laurium. The triangular plot had a fifteen-foot-high fountain made by WPA laborers using rocks and pebbles taken from local mines and the shores of Lake Superior. A floral centerpiece in the shape of a football in front of the fountain reminded the eight thousand who crowded into the village of the great days at Notre Dame when their "local boy" made headlines. Mrs. Matthew Gipp, the hero's mother, unveiled the plaque that read simply "George Gipp—All-American, 1895–1920." Members of the 1918 and 1920 Calumet Aristocrats baseball team attended from Detroit and other cities, because Gipp had begun his sport career playing that game at Calumet. Lyman Frimodig, assistant athletic director at Michigan State, said the memorial would inspire boys "to make the most of their abilities." Some adults remembered Gipp playing left halfback on October 2, 1920, with three other local men on the Notre Dame team: Heartley ("Hunk") Anderson, E. J. Larson, and Percy Wilcox. Dominic M. Vairo, a first-year student at Notre Dame in 1931, was a more recent hero of football enthusiasts. Grantland Rice described him as "long, lean and lanky, rough and raw-boned and tough, with the tenacity of a tiger, asking no quarter and giving none." When his team played Army, "Dom" caught a thirty-yard pass from William Shakespeare and ran twenty-five yards to score. Movie star Mae West chose Vairo for left end on her idea of an all-star team to face the Chicago Bears. Frank J. Sembello chose him for his all-American team of men of Italian descent.[60]

Depression or no, sport remained a continuing source of enthusiasm, rivalry, and excitement in the Copper Country. Never at a loss where creativity and fun were involved, local youth produced about a hundred hockey teams in the winter of 1930–31. These included the Albion Rough Riders, Tamarack Falcons, Laurium Bull Dogs, Wolverine Pla-mors, Swedetown Cardinals, and Pine Street Trojans, who chased the puck at outdoor rinks. Calumet had twenty-five rinks. Some four hundred skaters took over the rinks on nights when no games were played. That season, amateur hockey produced excitement with such teams as the Calumet Blackhawks, Hancock Eagles, Houghton Wolves, and Marquette Owls playing eighteen scheduled games. The Calumet–Hancock series drew thirty-five hundred spectators to two games. Victorious Hancock walked off with the MacNaughton Cup at season's end and went off to New York's Madison Square Garden to compete in national play-offs.

Sandlot baseball provided entertainment in all the towns and locations. Fulton's team, like others, had uniforms, batboy, and loyal followers who cheered on the men. Nearly four hundred people attended the second annual Cornish wrestling tournament at Ahmeek Village park in September 1934. Boxing featuring Russell Adams of Painesdale and Walter Wilmers of Calumet drew many to the Amphidrome that month. Houghton had its Hubbell Field, where the Copper Sox played in the 1920s, and the Houghton Camels, in the 1930s. In 1932, the Sibilisky Nine consisted of nine Sibilisky brothers coached by their father. Joe Mishica, who coached high school football at Hancock and Calumet, was already on his way to becoming a beloved legend—a dedicated man who inspired hundreds and provided winning teams. At White Pine, in Ontonagon County, Frank Zugel's basketball team combated those of Ontonagon, Mass City, Woodspur, Bergland, and other towns.[61]

Improved sport facilities and a place of beauty were provided when the Agassiz Memorial Park was dedicated in September 1923, to honor Alexander Agassiz. School children and other people of the community, Calumet and Hecla officials, and Boston stockholders gathered for the unveiling of a bronze statue of Agassiz in the park created by Red Jacket Village, Calumet and Hecla, and scores of boys and girls who had gathered wild flowers and seedlings and helped plant them under the direction of Warren Manning. The park lay between the mine area of Calumet and Red Jacket Village, an area once known as Calumet Common, where, in years past, cows grazed and the company piled its excess lumber but allowed space for an athletic field. From the statue, walks radiated to village streets. Maple, birch, and elm trees lined the paths; and Lombardy poplars surrounded three sides of the park. Paul Bartlett, a New York sculptor, known for including whimsy in his work, sculpted a seated Agassiz in academic robes with thick scholarly volumes thrust under his chair at the rear, indicating that Agassiz was an intellectual who proved eminently practical as the inscription at the base proclaimed: "A man of science, who developed a great mine and wrought the welfare of its people." The park provided playing space for baseball, football, and track and, in time, tennis courts.[62]

While cultural ethnicity at Keweenaw Bay experienced its renaissance, Americanization proceeded with strides elsewhere in the Keweenaw Peninsula. Over many decades, miners, despite some clustering in ethnic entities, found that their work forcing them to think, act, and speak like the Americans proved to be an agent for acculturation. Discrimination against Germans during World War I coerced them to assert their loyalty to the United States—some in Ontonagon County declaring, in 1918, that they could not help being born German but that they now displayed the American flag at home and in their businesses: "[for] we are . . . American to the backbone." Calumet Village had changed its name from Red Jacket in 1929; and the March election resulted in officers of French, Slovenian, English, German, Italian, and Irish descent.[63]

The aftermath of World War I acted as a solvent of ethnic attachments, interacting with ideas and sentiments expounded in schools and by veterans' organizations. On Armistice Day, November 11, 1920, patriotic businessmen closed their stores at noon in Red Jacket: "As a fitting tribute to the heroic dead who gave their lives overseas, . . . all bells [were] tolled and whistles [of mines] blown" from 10:59 to 11:01 A.M. The following year, Patrick H. O'Brien dedicated sixteen memorial elms planted at Houghton by Judson Ingram Post, American Legion. Each tree bore the name of a fallen warrior. O'Brien said, "We do this that future generations shall know of their heroism, their valor and their love for the flag." In 1920, the Hancock Civil League honored, with a monument in Montezuma Park, the 926 men from the Hancock district who participated in World War I. A bronze tablet bore the names of soldiers and sailors who had given their lives. In 1912, at Emerald Street and College Avenue in Houghton, a monument with a life-size figure of a soldier had been dedicated in memory of Houghton Company 1, Twenty-Third Michigan Infantry, and the five hundred sailors and soldiers from Houghton County who had served in the Civil War. A granite monument with a life-size figure of a soldier had been erected in May 1900 in Lake View Cemetery, a mile west of Red Jacket, to commemorate Spanish–American and Civil War soldiers who had given their lives. Their names engraved on the monument reminded visitors that the Copper Country military heritage remained strong in many minds.[64]

Private Joseph Ozanich, a tailor, often wrote to fellow tailor and friend Paul Fromholz in 1919. He took Paul's advice to see as much as he could, now that peace had come. Ozanich found Paris "the best place I could find to visit, . . . one great big museum," where he saw things from Roman times to the French Revolution. He wished he could visit his "native country Croatia," where Italy and newly formed Yugoslavia now quarreled over Fiume and Trieste. Fromholz, like many another who did not go to war, subscribed fifty dollars to the Fourth Liberty Loan and contributed twenty-five cents a month to the Copper Country War Relief League.[65]

In 1924, the Copper Country chapter of the Daughters of the American Revolution (DAR) distributed manuals to five hundred recently arrived German immigrants, so that they could learn of the U.S. Constitution and citizenship. Some seven thousand leaflets explaining the history and reverence due the Stars and Stripes inundated the public schools, a gift of Mrs. Gordon Campbell, DAR member and wife of a banker. By 1933, schools accepted the American Legion's requests for programs analyzing the pledge of allegiance, studying flag etiquette, and concentrating filiopietistically on Washington and Lincoln. Songs to be sung included "America" and "Columbia, the Gem of the Ocean."

As the 1920s began, hundreds of people signed up for night school classes in Calumet Township, which prepared alien residents for citizenship. At Portage Lake, Hilda Ruohoniemi remembered how she pulled herself up by her own bootstraps, studying shorthand under a gifted teacher after school and bookkeeping via a home-study course. Hancock's Suomi College prepared many newcomers for American citizenship by teaching English and United States history. The college had in 1918–19 announced its goal of providing American education while cherishing "the heritage of the Old Fatherland."[66]

Children from Finnish households were eager to speak English once they entered public schools. Their parents sent them also to Sunday schools where teachers conducted all instruction in Finnish, but the youngsters spoke English "whenever they [could] evade the teacher's eye." A teacher at Toivola angered some children in the 1920s, when she refused to use their Finnish first names and, according to one child, "renamed us by distorting them." While not abandoning their European cultural roots, some Finns and Slavs anglicized their surnames.

Many one-room schools closed. The neighborhood school gave way to busing long before urban dwellers made busing a social issue. In the pioneer days, said a descendant, "you did not have to be a college graduate. . . . If you could add divide subtract and multiply, you could . . . teach." By the 1930s, some sons and daughters of immigrants—college graduates from such institutions as the University of Michigan—were among those who taught in Copper Country schools admired for their excellence. Schools of the Keweenaw Peninsula were considered "far in advance of the ordinary class." Students from Chicago, whose families in the 1930s returned to weather the economic storm, declared that Calumet High

School was intellectually more demanding—"much tougher"—than their city schools. Women now dominated the teaching field: In District No. 1, Calumet, in 1928, 108 women and 22 men taught. Truant officers and dismal Depression homes resulted in remarkably high attendance (92 percent and higher of all enrolled).[67]

Ontonagon's total school enrollment in 1933 hit a new high of 756. The 1933 class of 205 graduates at Calumet High broke all records. Hancock, that year, graduated 100 in its fifty-fifth commencement. In the 1920s, migration and dropouts were reflected in enrollment. Houghton High School's 1928 first-year class numbered 125, the senior class of 1932, only 85. At Calumet, 297 enrolled in 1928, but only 170 stayed to finish four years later. The schools had become, by the 1930s, havens of security, where hundreds found an evolving American civilization attractive.[68]

Popular culture also had its impact in the sometimes happy, often grim, years between 1920 and 1940. Exposed to the latest fashions, automobiles, and movies in Keweenaw Peninsula towns, bright young women and brash young men challenged the social conservatism so long pronounced. Second-generation males of all ethnicities, uninterested in learning their immigrant parents' languages, sought to become Babbitts; their sisters spurned Mary Pickford and imitated Clara Bow. A blurb from Cecil B. DeMille's movie *Adam's Rib* summed it up: "The modern girl is all right. It's her parents who need watching." Young descendants of the immigrants in the Copper Country felt the impact of schools, libraries, Fourth of July parades, baseball, jazz, music of brass bands blaring Sousa marches, ice-cream cones, soda pop, Tom Mix, and New York movie wisecracks—all creating desires to be "like Americans." The Depression accentuated the need to help reshape *their* country, the United States.[69]

Ecumenism and toleration, longtime currents, expanded. Rudolph Svetozar Banovec, visiting tenor from the Jugoslav Royal Opera, sang Italian, English, Croatian, and Slovenian songs at the Calumet Theatre in 1930; and the Congregational Church's Anglo–American congregation invited him to sing "Ave Maria" at their church the previous Sunday, reinforcing an ecumenism long underway. Residents who performed a historical play in 1939, celebrating Laurium's fiftieth birthday, included an African American song to commemorate the blacks who had come to dig ditches for village sewer lines in the 1890s. With much intermarriage among members of various ethnic groups, romance played the role it had had since the early days of mergers of French Canadians and Native Americans, when the country was sparsely settled.[70]

Ethnicity took on new forms in confraternities and societies no longer desiring to maintain the mother tongue and customs but continuing to express pride in the heritage. Slovenians in 1935 held their annual picnic "at the maple grove west of No. 5 Tamarack," with lamb barbecue "in the old-country style." Croatians began "annual" picnics in 1933 at Electric Park with the crowning of a queen after morning mass, with picnics, dancing until midnight, a talk by their Chicago consul, and visitors from downstate Michigan, Illinois, and Minnesota.[71] People of Cornish descent planted flowers dear to their grandparents or attended homecomings at Central, a practice initiated in 1906.[72] Much of this was an assertion that blended lingering values of importance for a group with the dominant American culture. Much also represented an assertion against the inevitable shaping of an entirely new culture based on Anglo–American law, economics, and language as the old language and culture were abandoned. Ethnic groups found themselves in transition.

The Tapiola Drama Club in the 1930s produced Aleksis Kivi's *Seven Brothers*. Martii Nisonen conducted the Copper Country Symphony Orchestra in 1930 in his own Symphony in E Minor. The programmatic work told the story of a Native American who, from a lookout, watches the invasion of his kingdom by white men, then falls asleep to find himself in the modern era—truly a metaphor of what was occurring in the Copper Country in the lives of thousands assimilating, often with difficulty, to modernity. The *Opas* and *Walwoja* continued publishing for another thirty years, but "the old country" receded for most readers. The cruelest epithet schoolchildren hurled at one another was "you immigrant."[73]

The gradual diminution of copper mining from 1920 to 1940 had brought severe hardship. In 1940, 37 percent of Houghton County's residents still needed public assistance—this in the county that in 1882 had been called "the wealthiest county in the State of Michigan."[74] An era had truly ended, but some still accepted the verdict of sixty years before: "No one . . . can doubt for a moment that a great, profitable future lies open, and that centuries hence, the copper mines will be worked by a populous, intelligent and prosperous community, educated in our common schools . . . and made happy by the perpetuated blessings of civil and religious liberty."[75]

9

A New Breed

1940 – 1960

AN *EVENING NEWS–JOURNAL* EDITORIAL, JULY 11, 1939, labeled as "undesirables" communists, fascists, Nazis, spies, picketers, drunken drivers, opinionated youth, and others but concluded: "Keep your shirt on. . . . Our population is all right. . . . The American system is now on the march."[1] This blend of optimistic, liberal, patriotic, and reactionary opinion expressed the confidence of many in a Copper Country rescued by the progressive collaboration of federal, state, and local governments. Six years of the New Deal brought a new lease on life for the Keweenaw Peninsula. Unionization and an approaching war brought more change.

Cooperating with local sponsors and supplying the bulk of the funds, the federal WPA spent $10,914,532 in 1940 on public works and community service in the Upper Peninsula. This included the cost of new structures at the mining college, handsome post offices at Hancock and Calumet, and building a two-story, fireproof addition to the Houghton County Sanitorium. Conservatives decried this "socialism," but the 529 young men and women employed in Houghton County by the NYA in 1940 formed part of a new breed, along with thousands of their elders that accepted government as an active partner in the economy.[2]

An aggressive labor movement began organizing in the late 1930s and, by 1943, captured the most resistant stronghold—Calumet and Hecla. Labor's triumph proved pivotal in the development of the

258

Copper Country for the next thirty years. A new generation wounded by economic depression opened the way to unusual collaborations.

Business and labor united in seeking solutions to economic problems. Chambers of commerce at Hancock and Houghton appointed a committee in February 1941 to attract new industry. Members wired their representatives in Washington, D.C., saying, in effect, that there was no remedy for unemployment in the Copper Country unless the federal government built defense plants or involved itself with local private industry: Atlas Powder Company, manufacturers of dynamite at Ripley, "could be extended to provide manufacture of powder and explosives"; or the United States could make shells at Dollar Bay's Foley Copper Products. A local labor leader instituted joint meetings of representatives of the Isle Royale Mining Company, chambers of commerce, Elks, Eagles, and Lions Clubs, and other interested parties. A major issue discussed was whether to raise the price of copper to at least fifteen cents, so that companies could afford to haul low-grade rock to the surface, instead of throwing it aside underground.[3]

Within one generation, the state of Michigan had changed from agriculture as the "backbone of industry" to manufacturing (1906–26). Production of automobiles and associated products (engines, machine shop tools, bearings, gears, chemicals, paints, and oil) transformed the Lower Peninsula in those twenty years, while the industrial giant that was the western Upper Peninsula faltered, then fell on hard times. By 1926, more than 65 percent of Michigan's population lived in manufacturing centers.[4] Detroit became the hub, symbolizing American progress. The bitter but eventually successful labor battles fought there in the mid-1930s had their repercussions in the faraway Copper Country.

In the Keweenaw Peninsula, private enterprise and federal, state, and local governments worked in tandem, literally paving the way for the emerging tourist industry that, a half-century later, became a major component of survival. In five years, from August 1935, the Ontonagon Road Commission sponsored seven projects, supplying $484,000 of the $1,930,587 spent on them. Employing a hydraulic air compressor once used at the Victoria Mine, the Copper District Power Company, in the 1930s, constructed a dam on the south and west branches of the Ontonagon River, about five miles from the abandoned village of Victoria. Private and public and past and present merged as residents sought a better future.[5]

At Houghton, federal funds helped expand the college's administration building, built an annex to the library and new locker room facilities, and repaired the athletic field. Federal grants providing work relief financed a college dormitory, which opened its doors to 200 students in 1939. By then, total enrollment reached 874. Forestry became an important part of the curriculum. Enrollment continued to grow.[6]

Once-touted agriculture expanded in the peninsula except for Houghton County. Farms there numbered 1,840 in 1930 and 2,000 in 1935; but the total fell to 1,644 by 1940. Baraga County enjoyed the largest increases, including Native American farms (three in 1930 to thirty-four in 1940). The total value of farms and their buildings in the four Copper Country counties reached $8,826,828 in 1940; about one-third of all farms had mortgages. The Baraga County Dairy Herd Improvement Association portended a changing emphasis for its twenty-one members reported that their 216 cows produced an average of 311 pounds of butterfat in 1940. Farmers like Matt Turunen of Pelkie, who owned thirty-three cows, and Isaac Holso of Aura, with a herd that produced 8,478 pounds of milk, represented a new breed of experimenters in Copper Country agriculture.[7]

The Great Depression gave new life to social conservatism despite the radically new views circulating about the role of government. A preacher complained of young people who could name the top ten movie stars but did not know the names of the twelve apostles. The pious deplored swing music, cards, the return of saloons, and books: Scarlett O'Hara was declared a wicked woman by several readers who nevertheless stayed up all night reading about her. In 1941, the Kerredge Theatre restricted Bette Davis's *The Letter* to adults only, due to "The Daringly Modern Theme of This Picture," wherein the wife of a Malaysian rubber planter shot her lover of many years, then persuaded her meek husband to spend a large sum in order to retrieve an incriminating letter in the possession of her lover's Eurasian wife. Not once did a couple embrace or kiss in *The Letter*. The two actresses whose movies brought long lines of people waiting to buy tickets were Shirley Temple and Mae West.[8]

The traditional clashed with the modern. At the Calumet Theatre, the 1930s brought Art Deco elegance created by Alfred Messner, a Copper Country native who had studied at Chicago's Art Institute. With CWA funds, he and other artists transformed the interior. The theater, still called the "opera house" by old-timers, closed for six months and reopened in the winter of 1934. Audiences arrived to admire or scoff. Victorian gilt, pastel colors, and Watteau-like paintings had been replaced by simple, stark-painted walls of dark orange decorated with stylized figures in blue and white, nude figures of humans depicting individuals from Norse and Greek mythology. Indirect lighting illuminated sheet copper backdrops in box seats. The huge chandelier had given way to light beaming out from behind a massive disc. On balcony walls, characters from Shakespeare frolicked among others from literature in a black-, white-, and copper-colored decor. If one liked Picasso—the austere and elemental—then one liked this. Many found it *moderne*.

Messner, whose family had long lived in the Copper Country, had painted murals for the Sheltering Arms Home for Children in New York City and a nursery mural in the Ralph Pulitzers' town house. His mural for the social service exhibit at Chicago's Century of Progress World's Fair (1933–34) depicted a depressed youth surrounded by crashing, disintegrating forces of greed, crowds, jazz, whiskey, and sex lure, while above this appeared a scene of an ordered society and words from Proverbs 29: 18: "Where there is no vision, the people perish."9

By October 1939, the IUMMSW–CIO, often referred to locally as "Mine–Mill," had successfully organized Copper Range Company workers, who voted two to one for the union. By early 1941, Isle Royale and Quincy Mines operated under union contracts. But Calumet and Hecla workers were not unionized until July 13, 1943, almost thirty years after the commencement of the great 1913 strike. Two National Labor Relations Board elections were necessary to achieve this. The union victory at Calumet and Hecla also represented, in part, changes that came with a new attitude of mine managers under the impact of the New Deal upheaval; but this came slowly.

For three decades, no unions had existed at the mines; but a new contingent of workers determined to change that. At the Michigan CIO convention in 1940, McLean Smith of Local 212, United Automobile Workers, suggested meeting in 1941 at Ironwood: "Let's go up where God's country begins. I know we are going to be welcomed by the [Upper Peninsula] people who know what unionism means." Although the convention chose Jackson, the minutes noted with pleasure the assertion of copper workers' strength in an area long known for fierce opposition to collective bargaining.10

Union stalwarts faced a considerable challenge in the Copper Country's economic situation. As economic historian William B. Gates, Jr., has written, "The industry never really recovered from the impact of the depression." Even World War II saw continued decline "in spite of substantial government subsidies." An average of 3,181 men worked at mining, milling, and smelting during the war years. Mine workers in 1939 earned one-third less than iron workers in Michigan and Minnesota. Wages dropped until government subsidies, late in 1941, helped change the situation.11

Gene Saari, born in Minnesota, Great Lakes seaman, Detroit autoworker, lumberjack, and organizer of lumberjacks and other woods workers in the Upper Peninsula in the early 1930s, came to the

Copper Country in the late 1930s to help organize copper workers, beginning in South Range. He believed it imperative to gain community support, including that of chambers of commerce. He spoke to seminary students at Suomi College in the 1940s, so that these future clergy "could better understand the big influx into unions of their congregation[s]." This time, no reckless agitators arrived; only sober, determined, pragmatic men came to mastermind. Copper Range workers in late 1939, after observing what had been done to organize auto, steel, and other workers in the CIO, appealed for union help. Members of the steel workers' and woodworkers' unions came to assist. Local mine employees entered CIO Industrial Union, Local 1007; but as it had no jurisdiction for copper workers, the local organization was transferred to IUMMSW–CIO and chartered as Local 494 at South Range. The IUMMSW still remained aloof, as workers in 1940 "decided that their union security and future" were at stake and hired Saari, then fifth vice-president of the Michigan State CIO and a woodworkers' union organizer. Under his aegis, Local 494 was consolidated. Membership built up quickly.[12]

This inspired the unorganized at Isle Royale and Quincy, who formed Locals 515 and 523, respectively. The three locals then worked to win a dollar-a-day wage increase, the union shop, checkoff of dues, and other gains. When Calumet and Hecla workers organized, they took pride in accomplishing what their fathers could not in 1913–14: "The Copper Country workers have built their own unions, won their own gains under the leadership of their own Copper Country man, Gene Saari. We know unions are built on unity of members but we know too that only honest leadership can create unity." A union leader wrote that some members were veterans of the famous 1913–14 strike: "One thrills to hear the voices, now not so young, ring out again in union gatherings to defend some issue dear and vital to their hearts." But members tried to build much firmer foundations than their predecessors had thirty years earlier.[13]

Organization of mine workers led, also, to the organization of men and women in the dairy, printing, explosives, railroad, wood, and other industries in the Copper Country. Saari and others pointed out that the entire community benefited (grocers, butchers, small business, and professional people): "[for] increased wages add directly to the purchasing power of the employees. . . . And increased purchasing power means more and better food, clothing and shelter improving the general health of the community. . . . We place as foremost the welfare of the people of Michigan Copper Country communities." This was a classic rationale of the impact of New Deal advocacy of collective bargaining.[14]

When the campaign to organize Calumet and Hecla workers began, Saari, in a radio speech delivered in Finnish, said, "The representatives of the Calumet & Hecla Company have not interfered with the
rights of the employees to belong to an organization of their choos-
ing." He was happy to acknowledge this, "for it indicates that the
Company recognizes and is mindful of the National Labor Relations
Act" (the Wagner Act of 1935). But the company, in 1942, mounted
a campaign of its own, granting wage increases and vacations with
pay for some at the same time that a group—calling itself, first, Employee Representation Group, and then, Satisfied Employees—argued
that the IUMMSW–CIO could bring only unwelcome changes. Saari
wrote Nathan Witt, associated with the National Labor Relations
Board (NLRB) in the late 1930s, that the group that finally called
itself the Independent Copper Workers Union (ICWU) was "clearly
a Company dominated outfit."

On the eve of the spring 1942 election, a Mr. Langdon spoke via
radio, telling workers that should they vote to accept the CIO, their
rents would rise, along with water and fuel costs, and bonuses would
be endangered. Calumet and Hecla earlier had sold its company
houses to occupants for one dollar a room; an annual modest rent
was paid for lease of the land. One flyer, signed "Satisfied Employees" likened the tactics of CIO "agitators and radicals amongst the
C.&H. employees" as similar to those that "brought the downfall
of France [June 1940] and degradation of the workingman." These
opponents believed that union chiefs battened on thousands of dollars
of dues paid by workers, who were then at their new masters' call,
striking when commanded. As in 1913–14, these opponents foresaw
an end to the workers' "freedom to live in a peaceful and law-abiding
community."[15]

The spring election ended in a defeat for the union, 736–656. It
was contested on the grounds that foremen interfered. Union leaders
led a new attack, emphasizing long-smoldering grievances of men
from 1913–14: "C&H employees for a number of decades have been
under extreme terror of the Company. . . . Business interests are at
the mercy of the whims of the Company." Even the recent wage
increases "could be construed as discriminatory";[16] for reactionary
Calumet and Hecla managements, like the French Bourbon monar-
chs, forgot nothing and would do anything to retard democracy
among their workers. However, new leadership at Calumet and Hecla
did not stand in the way of an accomplished fact: collective bargaining
had become part of the law of the land in 1935.

In 1941, ill health caused James MacNaughton to resign from the
company. His dominance marked forty years in the wilderness for
workers desiring unionization. His close associates, however, linked

his name with those of Agassiz and Shaw, three "powerful forces which made Calumet and Hecla one of the historic copper producers of the world." He was succeeded by his son-in-law Endicott Lovell, first as general manager, then, by 1944, as president, when the last of the "old breed" from 1913–14 had passed on. MacNaughton was an enigma in many ways. Remarkably efficient, seemingly cold, removed from the public, his presence was always evident. Few knew of his generosity and concern for workers and their families provided they remained faithful to the company. Even fewer knew of his independent thinking. Patrick H. O'Brien, often at odds with Mac-Naughton during the 1913–14 strike, won his unsolicited political support in 1914. O'Brien concluded, late in life, as he reflected on those days, "He was like a god around the copper country, a very handsome man."[17]

Although probably happier had they not been confronted with unionization, management realized that momentous changes had come with the recognition, by the federal government, of workers' right to organize and bargain collectively. When men voted to accept the CIO Union in November 1942, the days of Calumet and Hecla paternalism, if they ever existed, were done with. The company closed the library, selling most of the books to the public at nominal prices and turning the core collection over to Public School District No. 1, where it was housed in the Calumet High School. Another Copper Country cycle was complete. Forty-five years before, the small library had been housed in a school building. It evolved into the grand building on Red Jacket Road and now returned to smaller, humbler quarters in another school building.[18]

Earlier, when 551 men of Quincy Local 523 went out on a three-day strike that ended February 14, 1941, Saari reported to the *CIO News* (Michigan) that the local had now completed the work left undone by the Western Federation of Miners in 1913. They had struck and erected twenty-four-hour picket lines, and Quincy had conceded a ten-cent-a-shift raise. Governor Van Wagoner promised to appoint a special commission to confer in Washington with respect to the price of copper. By October 1943, the Quincy local, made up of men of American, English, Finnish, French Canadian, Slavic, Italian, German, and Scandinavian ancestry (along with a few of Irish) was the most vigorous of the district's locals. The lively debates summarized in the Quincy local's minutes indicate an intelligent, interested group eager to ameliorate conditions.[19]

In 1943, the once-rich Calumet conglomerate was only a memory: "All that remains [are] a few surface structures from which all the machinery and equipment has been scrapped and turned into war weapons, but eventually the buildings that housed them, along with

the 250-foot smokestacks that stood as silent sentinels over what for
many years was the world's richest copper mine, will be razed." Only
Ahmeek Mine, a few miles north of Calumet, remained productive.
World War II, with its demand for copper, spurred reopening of
several mines, plus two new ones: North Kearsarge, Centennial, No. 1
Iroquois, Houghton conglomerate and certain areas of the Peninsula
and Douglass properties, both adjoining Ahmeek mine. Mining had
shifted north, close to where it had all begun exactly one hundred
years earlier.[20]

Calumet and Hecla unwatered the Centennial (closed since 1931)
under contract with the Metals Reserve Company, a federal agency.
As early as October 1940, copper's price had been stabilized when
Washington and major producers agreed informally to peg the price at
11.8 cents a pound. By autumn 1941, Metals Reserve began buying
copper produced at Copper Range, Isle Royale, and Quincy at 15
cents a pound. Throughout the war, the federal government, in
tandem with Copper Country mines, maintained production. New
leadership throughout the Copper Country helped shape war-time
events.[21]

While World War II began when Germany invaded Poland on
September 1, 1939, for thousands in the Copper Country it began
on November 30 that year, when the Soviet Union, secure in having
signed a nonaggression pact with Germany, attacked Finland after the
Finns refused to sanction ceding territory in the Karelian Isthmus
and two other areas, the USSR claimed necessary for its defense.
By December 29, the Finnish Relief Committee of Hancock and
Calumet had sent more than three thousand dollars to help Finland.
Other drives organized at Tapiola, Baraga, and Laurium. Women
formed Lotta Svard auxiliaries, knitting mittens and socks and hosting
coffees where money was collected to buy underwear and defray
expenses of volunteers who left to fight in Finland.

The Calumet–Laurium Lotta Svard announced a community supper for February 16, 1940; and the five hundred tickets sold immediately. Pasty sales netted funds as did drives by local bankers in all the
communities. Several committees worked diligently—among them,
the Herbert Hoover Finnish Relief Fund, whose flyers asked, "Shall
Communism dominate the western world?. . . . Finns have been saying *NO* . . . for the past nine weeks against odds of 40 to 1. They
need your help now." Non-Finns often served, some as chairmen.
By February 1, four thousand dollars more had been collected in
Hancock and vicinity; and two weeks later, an additional two thousand dollars was sent to the Finnish consul general at New York to
help the cause. Finnish and American national anthems played by a
band on the railroad platform at Hancock on January 30 saluted nine

young men—three from Hancock, two from the Crystal Falls area, and one each from Calumet, South Range, Elo, and Chassell—due to sail from New York on February 3 to fight for Finland.

Besides the knitted materials, Copper Country people sent bandages, soap, tobacco, sugar, shoes, galoshes, overcoats, and other old and new clothing. By February's end, the Central Committee for Finnish Relief had sent $11,890, not including funds raised by the Hoover Committee and others. By mid-March, the Finns, after a sensational defense and initial rout of the Soviet troops, succumbed to overwhelming strength, which forced them to yield the Karelian Isthmus, Viipuri, and land near Lake Ladoga. Their war had ended.[22]

In an unfathomable action, some Finnish Americans in Quincy Local 523, with other members, voted, in June, 1942, to send a telegram of congratulations to the Soviet Embassy in Washington, D.C., apparently for having withstood the German onslaught; for on June 22, 1941, the Germans, Finns, and others had invaded the USSR![23]

One hundred local men from the Fifteenth Division, United States Naval Reserve, were called to active duty March 17, 1941, almost nine months before the United States was officially at war with Japan, Germany, and Italy. Stores closed early at Hancock to enable citizens to bid them farewell. Flags fluttered, and the WPA band led the men in a procession from the Armory to the railroad depot. Some well-wishers in automobiles followed the men to Houghton and Chassell. The naval reserve men, assigned to the USS *Mount Vernon* (former luxury liner SS *Washington*), helped carry troops to strategic areas and returned casualties to the States. Some of the men were later assigned to other ships. After traveling over three hundred thousand miles, the *Mount Vernon* ended its service on January 18, 1946.

At the Houghton college campus, Elsie Honkala of Houghton announced activities of the women's rifle team she captained. The campus was changed considerably, with some 400 students in 1944 enrolled in the Army Air Corps and 469 in the army's specialized programs for officer training. The college dispensed with commencements in 1944 and 1945. More than 2,600 trainees during the war brought a military air to the campus. Margaret Marie Waters, Calumet High School graduate of 1942, served as first woman editor of the college's *Lode* yearbook.[24]

Many of the forty-five male graduates among Calumet High School's class of 1942 rode a chartered Greyhound bus to Marquette the following March 9, 1943, as draftees. In December 1944, some of these young men fought in the Ardennes Forest against counterattacking Germans in the famous Battle of the Bulge. Of the Calumet High School class of 1942, Alfred Dianda gave his life, as did 176 others from Houghton County, 30 from Baraga, 13 from Keweenaw, and 58 from Ontonagon counties. Those who stayed at home bought war bonds, served as air-raid wardens, wrote letters, sent food packages, entertained at local organizations for servicemen, or migrated downstate to work in war plants. Copper Country women served in the Women's Auxiliary Corps (WAC), especially after four members recruited at the Douglass House in summer 1943. Of hundreds who left for Detroit to earn high wages, one, owner of a small grocery store, was recruited on a city streetcar. Another, a young woman, returned at Christmas in 1941, praising the good life in the Motor City and bemoaning her inability to cash a twenty-dollar bill in her native Calumet.[25] Tony Stefanic, who had mined at Painesdale, wanted to transfer his union membership to Detroit, writing: "[I] like it Better here, more money and less dangerous."

Private Tauno Kostamo, in a letter of September 20, 1942, to his union local, asked: "Did you all celebrate Labor Day just like we did last year? Or did you work that day by digging that old copper ore out because its [sic] the product for defeating the enemy." Many wrote thanking union locals for sending cigarettes. Tobacco companies shipped—tax-free—cigarettes that union donations purchased. Members contributed at frequent collections at Hancock and South Range. In a V-mail letter, Private Matt Kusisto said his brother and brother-in-law had "written of the good work the union has done back there. I know that the unbending and persistent efforts of the union will live in the hearts of the people for centuries." Copper Workers Ladies Auxiliary, Local 111, affiliated with South Range Local 494, sent Christmas cards, the message reading:[26]

> MERRY CHRISTMAS & A HAPPY NEW YEAR,
> FIGHTER FOR DEMOCRACY
> We find it hard to express feelings deep inside,
> But our hope and prayers are for your safety,
> For victory over fascism in the coming year
> To bring you and your buddies back home again.

On Saturday morning, August 21, 1943, Gene Saari and a crew of volunteers helped level off the Hancock Driving Park parade ground and erect a fence to keep spectators from danger during a Sunday afternoon show of military power, part of a gigantic industrial rally celebrating the centenary of copper mining and increased efforts for production. Albert J. Gazvoda headed a committee composed of heads of Calumet and Hecla, Copper Range, Isle Royale, and Quincy and representatives from union locals at those companies—John Sitar, Gene Saari, Jim Miller, and Ed Spiegel, respectively. The two-day rally at Calumet, Hancock, and Houghton—expected to be "one of the biggest events ever held in the Copper Country"—surpassed all expectations. The weather was perfect, and seven thousand turned out at Calumet for the Saturday night rally in the former Colosseum (now Armory). Fifth Army contingents camped nearby, some having visited, earlier, seven mines in Houghton County. Lieutenant Colonel Alexander Browner cut short his speech so that movie actress Carole Landis could speak. Crowned next day "Miss Copper," Miss Landis, for the big parade at Houghton–Hancock, wore a gold lamé dress and perched high in an open car with a "vast horde" of small children running alongside.[27]

Sunday's parade began in Houghton, where Browner took the salute and thousands saw "soldiers march . . . with snap and precision," tanks, mounted artillery, and army equipment, then miners "many thousands strong" marching "soberly and quietly" in contingents, each behind a float made by management and labor. On the Quincy float, miners hacked at a four-ton chunk of mass copper. Banners read "Smash the Axis." In an evening rally at the Amphidrome, Miss Landis spoke of her four-and-a-half-month tour of American camps in North Africa, where she found morale high, telling the crowd, as she had on arrival in New York in March, "Our boys over there who are not in the front lines want nothing more than to get there as soon as possible to get a whack at the enemy."

President Reid Robinson of the IUMMSW offered a "ringing denunciation of Fascism" as the enemy of labor, while A. E. Petermann of Calumet and Hecla said production would be increased if the men could be found. There was a serious labor shortage. Miss Landis introduced Lieutenant Pearl Cowling of Painesdale, now an Air Corps nurse home on furlough. Corporal Edmond LaBlanc, seriously wounded on Guadalcanal in January, received the Purple Heart. The highlight was the Sunday afternoon show and sham battle staged at the Hancock Driving Park before a crowd estimated at forty thousand-to-forty-five thousand. The sounds of battle, smoke drifting across the hillside, men falling or charging, tanks churning, and guns firing all created impressive scenes. Truly remarkable was that a new generation of company managers and unionized workers that evening shared the same platform and worked together for victory. The times had changed from thirty years before, when WFM president Charles Moyer and Calumet and Hecla manager James MacNaughton did not even communicate with each other, let alone share a public platform.[28]

By 1944, the Copper Country pushed the fourth war-bond drive. The committee of ten included Gene Saari, Albert B. Lieblein, Wilho Mackey, and Mrs. Lorimer A. Eaton and represented labor, business, and women. The Houghton–Keweenaw quota was $2.6 million of the $14-billion drive, which, like all others, proved highly successful. For the first time in years, Copper Country people had money either from work at reopened mines, sales generated in local stores, or cash sent by men and women in service and relatives in war plants in Detroit, Milwaukee, Chicago, and California. The U. S. Coast Guard kept a contingent at Five Mile Point and nearby places; some appeared in full dress parade at local theaters. Most spent time off at movies, dance halls, or bars. Men and women returning on furlough or leave found admirers as the war spirit waxed strong.[29]

Keweenaw County's Board of Supervisors passed a resolution in February 1944 declaring opposition to German or other war prisoners who would compete with local labor. No plans had been made actually to introduce prisoners. From the beginning, some clergy hailed the war as a "people's war" and a fight "to preserve the American idea of democracy." Grover C. Dillman, in a 1942 commencement address at the Michigan College of Mining and Technology, called World War II an engineers' war, made possible by them more than by any other social group—a war that would usher in a peacetime era that would be "highly technical and mechanical."[30]

Corporal Anton ("Pops") Crnkovich had breakfast one spring day in 1942 at the Grand Central Hotel in Belfast, Northern Ireland, where he met "Doc" Curdy of Hancock. They decided "that someone should come show these folks how to make a good [Copper Country] cup of coffee." Corporal Frank Cekada, Calumet, served as orderly to General Omar Bradley in Sicily. Age twenty-four, Cekada's duties in summer 1943 consisted of cleaning quarters, supervising baggage during travel and (as Ernie Pyle reported in a dispatch) doing the general's laundry whenever Sicilian women could not be found for that. Kenneth Cox participated in the Normandy invasion, June 1944, later writing his brother Frederick that after being hit by shrapnel, he was flown to an English hospital; and traveling through clouds reminded him "of sleigh-riding in the Copper Country, and the memories chased away all fears." The mystique of the Keweenaw continued to haunt the souls of many.[31]

Superficially, wartime prosperity brought a healthy sheen to the range towns; but reality suggested continued decline. By 1943, Houghton County had lost 13,500 of its 47,600 residents (1940 census) to the armed forces or war plants. The mining industry continued with bursts of production but was plagued by problems. About February 1, 1942, federal government controls, limited to freezing the price of copper at twelve cents a pound, expanded as the war effort demanded copper, now in critically short supply. Undersecretary of War Robert Patterson said in August 1943 "An army without copper . . . would not last a single day in battle." Every fighter plane contained two-and-a-half miles of copper wire; each tank had eight hundred pounds of copper and brass. Washington instituted the premium price plan to stimulate the production of copper, lead, and zinc. The War Production Board (WPB) and Office of Price Administration (OPA) set quotas for all mines, so that copper sold at twelve cents but rose, at times, to seventeen and even twenty cents when companies exceeded their quotas.[32]

The labor shortage proved so severe that the army released men, who returned to Copper Country mines in 1944. The premium price plan plus subsidies by the Metals Reserve Company stabilized mines and reclamation production in 1942–43. Late in 1942, Calumet and Hecla entered the scrap copper field, recovering fifty-four million pounds of copper in 1943–45. But the government's intention to increase production basically failed, due to the low price combined with increased costs, the industry's "advanced stage of decline," and the "sharply rising labor costs." In 1943, smelter production stood at about the same level as in 1939 even though the mining company work force had increased by one-third. At Calumet and Hecla, output per underground worker declined about 45 percent from 1939 to 1943. At a July 1943 Quincy union local meeting, an officer told the men that anyone who wanted a serviceman "back in the mine" should write his commanding officer. In December 1944, at an NLRB conference, Lynn Hersey, general manager of Copper Range, said that if all the increases demanded by the union were allowed, the company would have an additional annual expense of $961,400. At the same meeting, Albert Petermann stated that Calumet and Hecla lost about $30,000 annually in connection with its complete medical and surgical care for entire families. (Employees paid two dollars monthly for care, which included house calls, night calls, and most medicine.)[33]

United States government order M-9-A, effective August 6, 1941, prohibited refiners from delivering copper except upon specific authorization from month to month by a federal director of priorities. Companies delivered copper only to those presenting Office of Production Management certificates. Calumet and Hecla reported a net profit of $1,166,207, after payment of $684,000 in taxes, for nine months beginning January 1943. In 1942, profit for the entire year, after taxes, was $618,000. Companies cooperated with the war effort but chafed at their "partnerships" with Washington bureaucrats. Eventually, something would have to give, hinted Calumet and Hecla in 1944: "The ever increasing wage burden cannot be supported by high-cost producers in peacetime unless the price of copper is allowed to rise considerably above pre-war levels." When the Office of

Production Management requested, in 1941, a survey, Calumet and Hecla obliged and reopened No. 4 North Kearsarge but complained that government control had imposed a heavy burden on the conduct of business.[34]

Still, officials explained early in 1942 that the company had "co-operated whole-heartedly with the Government in war and defense efforts, and will continue to do so." The continuing decline in the average grade of ore from the Ahmeek Mine decreased production—the basic problem the corporation had struggled with for almost fifty years. Calumet Division employment rose from 1,538 in 1941 to 2,261 in 1943 and dropped to 2,018 in 1944. The division received the Army–Navy "E" pennant for high achievement in production of materials needed for war; but company officials, realizing the mines were "played out" turned to diversification.[35]

Under Lovell's direction, Calumet and Hecla moved to broaden its scope, knowing that unless something was done, the company was "headed for liquidation, . . . a fate that [had] overtaken most of the other copper mining companies in Michigan." The program of ex-pansion, diversification, and rehabilitation involved risk and expense. Effective June 1, 1942, Calumet and Hecla acquired, by purchase, all physical assets of Detroit's Wolverine Tube Company, one of the country's largest single units devoted exclusively to the production of seamless nonferrous tube serving refrigeration and plumbing in-dustries. Wolverine Tube employed slightly more than one thousand workers, about half the number its owner employed in the Copper Country. Calumet and Hecla, like many of its former employees, had gone to Detroit! The company also constructed, by 1949, a modern tubing mill in Decatur, Alabama.[36]

To meet the demand for iron-and-steel scrap, the company began a salvaging campaign, recovering materials from unused buildings and its obsolete and unusable machinery and equipment at Calumet, selling tons to steel plants. At the end of the war, the company revealed that management and directors had, for years, built up and conserved the company's cash portion for two reasons: (1) to provide a cushion for expected postwar dislocations in the industry and (2) to take advantage of opportunities for exploration and expansion.[37]

Calumet and Hecla explored from north to south, covering all bases along the mineral range that had once flourished when copper was "king." From 1937 to 1939, it had sought new lodes at the old Mass–Michigan and Flint Steel properties in Ontonagon County, under options to purchase. The results were not encouraging, and the options were dropped. In 1944, when some indications of low-grade ore appeared, the company purchased the properties for $40,000, "affording a possible reserve for the future." In 1942, it explored, by diamond drilling, the formation between the Allouez and Calumet conglomerates. The company also purchased, for $35,000 in 1942, the Estivant property, south of Copper Harbor, some twenty-five hundred acres for future exploration. The property's timber alone was estimated to be worth $17,500. Lands of the old Torch Lake Mining Company just south of Calumet were purchased for $10,000 in 1944, and diamond drilling continued as far north as Copper Harbor. In October, the company purchased all assets of the Keweenaw Copper Company—some 35,544 acres in Keweenaw County adjacent to lands it already owned.[38]

Michigan's copper mines now existed largely upon subsidies authorized by the federal government's OPA, War Labor Board (WLB), and the non-Ferrous Metals Commission. In 1946, after the war, the Office of Economic Stabilization raised the ceiling price of copper to twenty-two cents a pound, so that wages could be increased. Workers hoped for the successful passage of Senate Bill No. 2105, which would provide subsidies so that copper could be stockpiled and conserved. Should the bill fail, argued Saari, that would spell the end of an era and present new problems for the Copper Country. Saari wrote Sidney Hillman, CIO chieftain and presidential advisor, that political action was "a serious and immediate question" with labor in the Copper Country. With mines heavily subsidized by the federal government, their future depended "on a liberal and progressive Congress."[39]

On April 17, 1946, in a statement printed in the *Mining Gazette*, Calumet and Hecla president Lovell stated, "The Management of this Company is opposed to subsidies and believe they should be discontinued as soon as possible." Five years later, he criticized copper's ceiling price (reinstated during the Korean War), arguing that his company had been "forced" to take subsidies once again and warning of a trend toward the nation's "taxing and spending [itself] into bankruptcy and thus wrecking our system of free enterprise."[40]

After 1945, Quincy, Copper Range, and Isle Royale suspended operations because subsidies were terminated or insufficient to warrant staying open. Quincy closed September 1, 1945, Copper Range, only days later, "after a futile attempt to come to an agreement with the union concerning postwar operations." Quincy's reclamation plant, built during the war with funds from the government—the loan repaid by 1947—reprocessed Torch Lake sands until 1967. The company paid a dividend of twenty-five cents a share on its hundredth anniversary, in 1948. In a sense, Quincy refused to "die"; for its history, inextricably linked with the lives of thousands of individuals, left a lasting imprint. Hundreds of visitors, one-time residents of Quincy hill locations and Hancock, returned on visits, recalling the enterprise

and rich community life that shaped them and their forebears. Like
poet Ruth Malgren, they missed[41]

> . . . the sounds of Quincy Mine;
> The sounds of the hoist wheel singing;
> The bellow's blow and the blasts below
> And the locomotive ringing.

When Congress removed price controls in November 1946, the
price of copper fell from 23.5 cents a pound to 17.625 cents. In
1947, union officials reduced, by half, their demand for a 25-cent-
an-hour increase and withdrew all demands, except one for six paid
holidays and a company-financed hospitalization plan. E. R. Lovell
said, "We did not dispute the appropriateness of a wage increase
at this time." The company offered 10 cents an hour. Calumet and
Hecla refused to honor a request for portal-to-portal pay in 1947, and
580 employees filed a suit, claiming seven million dollars. In August
1949, the company called for a wage reduction of 15 cents an hour.
Workers at the Calumet Division already worked for three dollars a
day less than in western mines. The union fumed, for workers had
made "sacrifices for years at much too high a cost for themselves and
their families."[42]

A worker wrote: "We may take the Company's offer—and the
future holds dim prospects for all of us and our families. . . . We can
also reject the Company's offer. Then the younger folks can take the
'Peterman Highway' [Albert Petermann, Jr., was a vice-president]
to a fuller life in some other part of the country. Yes, there will be
some . . . who will just have to stay here and for those folks the future
will be very dim indeed, but didn't they have the same dim future
for the past 50 years?" The company closed down from May 1 to
September 7, 1949. Officers of the CIO ridiculed the IUMMSW's
timidity in not opposing Calumet and Hecla vigorously. Workers, in
deplorable straits, accepted the wage cut.

The company, incensed at the union's push for the union shop,
continued its diversification, most of which did not benefit the Copper Country. "The Michigan copper industry is dying hard but successfully—while the fate of the community still hangs in the balance,"
observed one scholar in 1950. But once again, war arrived to cushion
the decline.[43]

The Korean War (1950–53) and consequent demand for nonferrous metals saw Calumet and Hecla production rise from 30,588,701
pounds in 1949 to 36,844,108 in 1950. A government subsidy in
1952 allowed high-cost No. 4 Kearsarge, No. 4 Peninsula, and No. 1
Iroquois to operate. Calumet and Hecla contracted to sell the federal

government a substantial part of its refined copper for three years, ending December 31, 1955. Production could not meet needs. By the end of 1950, the price of copper hit 24.5 cents a pound. Officials, aware of the temporary prosperity, told stockholders, "During 1950 we began to realize the benefits of the program of expansion and diversification in terms of profits."[44]

Calumet and Hecla mined lead in Illinois and zinc in Wisconsin, searched for uranium in Colorado and New Mexico, established a Forest Industries Division, and acquired 69,000 acres of forest when it took over Wisconsin's Goodman Lumber Company, adding to the 104,000 acres of commercial forest lands it already owned in the Upper Peninsula. Tubing manufactured at Detroit proved profitable. The company now manufactured agricultural chemicals, mixed copper oxides for industrial commercial use, iron foundry products, and drill bits. New executive offices established in Chicago (the Boston connection was long past) announced a name change to "Calumet and Hecla, Incorporated"—indicating that mining was a minor component. The hospital had long since been closed and eventually razed. The "old days" had truly ended. Slick advertising in *Fortune*, the *Wall Street Journal*, and *U.S. News and World Report* illustrated how the company now actively served the automotive, refrigerator, air-conditioning, petrochemical, construction, and atomic energy industries. By 1952, President Lovell reported to stockholders that in ten years, the company had transformed itself "from a strictly mining enterprise to a broad organization producing a diversity of products." Sales had increased fourfold.[45]

After the Korean War ended in 1953, controls and restrictions ended also; and Calumet and Hecla reported that with "free markets functioning once again, we were able to achieve record sales." The general decline of business in the country in 1954 did not affect production adversely at the Calumet Division. It had held five contracts with the Defense Materials Procurement Agency, receiving subsidies—the government paying premium prices and guaranteeing the purchase of a minimum tonnage of metal. The company was dewatering the Osceola mine, closed since 1931, and was promised government subsidies "through a guaranteed floor price to cover a minimum of 53,000 tons of copper." The government also continued to pay a minimum of 27.5 cents a pound for copper produced by two other mines, but the company could apply for "relief" from the contract and sell in the market if higher prices could be obtained. The federal government was hardly the restraining brake that company officials steadfastly claimed, except for the lengthy delay occasioned when they attempted extrication to sell in the market. In the early 1950s, Calumet and Hecla also had a contract with the Defense

Materials Exploration Administration whereby the government paid half the cost of a $568,192 exploration.[46]

As time passed, the unions became integrated in Copper Country life, their members creating and constructing, as had their forebears. Union meetings served as social events. Women formed auxiliaries. Martha Saari wrote for union journals. Men and women provided Christmas parties and tree-lighting ceremonies for children, decorated floats for parades, and brought new meaning to Labor Day picnics and new life to Fourth of July parades. In later years union members promoted youth hockey and Little League baseball and raised money to buy the boys uniforms. They donated to charities and sponsored theater parties for children and adults, hosted parties at convalescent homes and the Goodwill Farm, and prided themselves on union halls.

Union locals pushed voter registration, donated to the Salvation Army, bought war bonds, and mimeographed a nine-page "Songs of the Copper Country," with working-class lyrics fitted to familiar melodies—for instance, "Put on Your Old Union Button," sung to the tune of "Put on Your Old Gray Bonnet." They read poems or lyrics of worker–bard William Perkins, one of whose verses ran,[47]

> We are the boys of the C.I.O.
> We work at the Copper Range.
> We've had a long, hard row to hoe,
> But, boy, we've made some gains.

The more political picked up the fierce antifascism espoused by the IUMMSW. The first issue of the mimeographed *Quincy News Bulletin*—June 1942—reported that Toivo Suhonen was the first of Local 523 to die on the battlefield: "Toivo was a good union man and for those principals [sic] he has given his life to defend our freedom and that we can have labor unions and not be a slave of Fascism." The syntax at times ran askew, but the ideas were ardent. The writer asked how much the workers had done to win this war in which their colleague died and asked for renewed efforts in civilian defense and copper production to counteract propaganda of the "Dies, Wheelers, Lindbergs [sic], Coughlins and [Gerald L. K.] Smith." The writer demanded a second front be opened immediately.[48]

Local unionists condemned racism, supporting Vito Marcantonio, congressman from New York, who mounted a 1943 campaign against a national fifth column promoting the insidious doctrine. They sent money to Alabama in support of a Scottsboro boy in prison. They negotiated contracts and secured benefits like that in the Copper Range contract stating that should the wage rate fall below three dollars for an eight-hour shift because of a drop in the price of copper, a minimum of the three dollars a shift would be paid. In meetings, they discussed a multitude of issues and problems. In 1944, in regard to the problem of clerical help at South Range leaving early, they adopted a motion that "the office girl be notified of this and that she be granted vacation with pay and [notified] that if she isn't more careful, she will be asked to leave."[49]

The greatest accomplishment, however, was the material betterment and spiritual sense of dignity enjoyed by working people of the Copper Country. After 1940—and especially after 1945—many homes impressed visitors with fresh coats of paint without and new furniture within. The sons and daughters of working-class men and women acquired, along with their parents, all of the middle-class aspirations for good food, clothes, and amusements. After the United Automobile Workers achieved cost-of-living clauses in contracts in the late 1940s, the Copper Country unions pressed for such benefits as group insurance policies, paid vacations, and additional holidays. In short, a "withering away" of working-class subserviency occurred, along with the idea that they, the workers, were excluded from advancing their interests. The working class became part of the expanding middle class. An observer of workers' daughters and sons in the 1950s and 1960s would have had difficulty distinguishing them from their counterparts living at East Hancock and along College and Calumet avenues.

In a March 1943 report, Financial Secretary Edward Charles, at South Range, concluded with a plea for parsimony within the local in order to establish a sound financial basis and then confront social, political, and economic problems, because then,[50]

> each and everyone of us may look at our sons and daughters and at the Copper Country and with pride say, I was one who helped put the people of [the] Copper Country on the form of social standing where they belong. So let's all work together to help establish better Social Security laws, better medical plan[s], and a better education system for [the] Copper Country and the nation as a whole.

Much remained to be done. Some miners still wrestled with the decades-old problem of petty and arbitrary supervisors. When one inexperienced miner reported for work at No. 4 Kearsarge in 1943, he was soon removed. When he asked why, the mining captain told him, "You haven't worked underground before, I don't want to take a chance with you." The miner knew that several inexperienced men had been taken on. He tried in vain to find surface work. He was not wanted, he was not liked. He claimed that a company superintendent told him, "I am through with you, because you are against the company."

The miner believed the source of the animosity was a 1932 incident when he was part of the layoff as the entire Ahmeek Mine shut down. When all prospective recipients of relief had to turn in their automobile license plates to the company office, he protested vigorously, only to suffer the wrath of the man who, in 1943, was supervisor and chief instigator of the license plate affair. The incident—typical of hundreds that dated back fifty and more years—recalled bitterness that loomed large in the 1913 decision to strike.[51]

In 1950, "war" broke out within the Copper Country union locals as Gene Saari, dismissed by the IUMMSW, joined United Steel Workers–CIO. He claimed that "Mine–Mill" had ignored the Copper Country and that communism dominated its inner circle of officials, producing internal chaos. The CIO had expelled the IUMMSW that year for "communism," and President Reid Robinson was fired. Negotiations with Calumet and Hecla for a new contract, set to begin April 1 juxtaposed with a bitter campaign waged by workers among themselves.[52]

John Sitar, who had worked twenty-five years as a miner, succeeded Saari as leader of those faithful to the IUMMSW. He and associates took to broadcasting over local radio station WHDF that the Steel Workers had allied themselves with the Democratic party and thereby stifled criticism of Michigan's governor, G. Mennen Williams. Furthermore, Sitar and others argued, Philip Murray, head of CIO Steel Workers, ordered strikes at the worst possible times; and they claimed that Saari was fired by "Mine–Mill" for "violating and sabotaging" its program. They accused Saari of accepting the 1949 wage decrease and conducting an "incompetent one man type of unionism," for which he had become notorious. Sarcasm, invective, bullying, and anger filled meetings and air waves. Supporters of "Mine–Mill" appealed to the historic link to the Western Federation of Miners, urging workers not to desert the organization built and defended "since the days of our great-grandfathers" in the Copper Country. As for Saari, his enemies claimed he "never had a muck stick or an axe in his hand." If you vote for the Steel Workers, they announced, "you'll vote for a union dominated completely by men who go along on the idea of letting the Copper Country die a slow death."[53]

Saari and confederates lashed back, accusing "Mine–Mill" of having become so internationally political that it lost sight of workers' needs. Only with the Steel Workers could their interests truly advance. Workers, confused, voted on April 20 and gave no one a majority. The steel union received 867 votes (shy of the necessary

Signing a contract: Gene Saari, seated, center; Calumet and Hecla general manager Rockwell, standing second from left; John Sitar, union president, seated, right. (The Archives of Labor and Urban Affairs, Wayne State University.)

873 majority), and "Mine–Mill," 809, while 65 declared for "no union." The newspaper and radio "war" resumed; but on April 27, United Steel Workers–CIO won by a vote of 908–869. "Mine–Mill" threatened not to abide by the decision, but that warning evaporated. Saari and the victors looked forward to a new day for copper workers, one of their chief political aims being lobbying Congress to approve nonferrous metals' conservation and subsidies. They still labored to promote government's link to industry in providing work as the Eisenhower age dawned, with its basic idea of ending such policies and returning to the pre–New Deal notion that business, industry, and finance must be free of government interference.[54]

Negotiations for a new contract opened in June 1950, the union asking for a fifteen-cent raise and fringe benefits. The men received eleven cents, three weeks' vacation with pay for employees with twenty years' service, safety inspection by a union representative on company time, and agreement for renegotiating on ten days' notice. The total "package value" amounted to thirteen cents an hour. The new breed proceeded, believing that 1933–40 had brought a new age from which there would be no turning back of the clock.[55]

Class conflict bristled despite amelioration of workers' conditions. All companies remained "reluctant in recognizing a new era that has descended upon the Copper Country, [so] accustomed are they in this period of industrial democracy to their former habits of minutely controlling, dominating, and interfering in the economic, political and even domestic life of the workers," declared one critic. The popular 1950s ballad "Sixteen Tons" was referred to by some as "the C.&H. song." Businessmen, always suspicious of unions, blamed them for excessive demands but sometimes invited members of bargaining committees to meetings in order to explain their side of the story in strike situations. Labor researchers in Pittsburgh ferreted out statistics indicating that Calumet and Hecla did not "hesitate to dig into its piled-up [capital] Surplus to pay dividends to its stockholders . . . at the expense of the employees." The statisticians advised that one should not accept "the Company's argument that it would have done more for its employees except that its funds must always be utilized for development, exploration, etc."[56]

By 1952, Calumet and Hecla's major project in the Copper Country was unwatering and rehabilitating the Osceola Lode mines at an eventual cost of eight million dollars. Over ten years, under an agreement with the Defense Materials Procurement Agency, the company expected to produce 106 million pounds of copper to be sold at a minimum of 25.25 cents a pound. The tremendous project— involving cave-ins and blasting and transporting to the surface 5,000 tons of rock in order to construct a modern substation and pump room—fell four months behind schedule by 1953 due to a sixty-three-day strike in 1952.[57]

An eight-cent-an-hour increase offered was rejected by the union, which, in 1952, asked for twenty-five cents. A strike, hailed as the first for the Calumet area since the historic 1913–14 struggle, began on September 8, 1952, amid raucous contention. Letters notified all United Steel Workers of America (USWA) locals that after thirty-nine years, an attempt was under way "to eliminate a half century of injustice" and that Calumet and Hecla, known for its strikebreaking, would "attempt to smash the Union." Smylie Chatek, a Yugoslav native, told a Labor Day rally at the Calumet Armory, "As long as the working people stick together, we'll get pork chops, not peanuts." International Steel Workers' vice-president, James G. Thimmes, said that success in this strike meant "bread and butter on the table, a rug on the floor, music in the living room." A letter in the *Mining Gazette* discussed both sides and concluded, "Unionism is a must in any democratic society."[58]

The strike affected 2,060 workers. Houghton County's Department of Social Welfare spent $25,000 extending assistance to 390 families by October 14. Representatives of the disputants met abortively in the Copper Country, then, nudged by Governor Mennen Williams, gathered in Lansing, Detroit, and (finally) the Pittsburgh office of Philip Murray. Calumet and Hecla defended its wage scale

of $1.19–1.85 an hour, arguing that 93.1 percent of the men earned
"substantially more" than the $47.50 that the union claimed many
received for a forty-hour week. Congressman John Bennett advocated
raising the ceiling price of copper to 36.5 cents a pound. Earl T.
Bester, CIO international representative, recalled that "every inch
of the strike was bitterly fought both on the picket lines and in
bargaining conferences." Locals in Michigan and Minnesota sent
strike relief donations of $3,398; and money came from the Cheese
and Dairy Workers–CIO, at Trimountain and International Brewery
and Soft Drink Workers–CIO, at Hancock.[59]

By a vote of 638–556, the strike ended with workers accepting the
company's ten-cent-an-hour increase. Calumet Local 4312 asked for
a four-month dues' exoneration, as its treasury was exhausted. In May
1953, USWA–CIO raised dues from two to three dollars per month.
All went well at Calumet and Hecla until 1955, when discussion of
terms for a new agreement deadlocked. Conferences failed two weeks
before the contract expired. In the free market, copper hit thirty-six
cents a pound; and the company sought to extricate itself from the
government contract, which was paying twenty-nine cents. Calumet
and Hecla insisted that sizable wage increases could come only with
rising prices in the copper market. The union proposed that increases
become part of the base rate, with an option to negotiate a decrease
"if the market drops." The company favored an escalation clause to
eliminate tensions and inefficiencies. Again, deadlock ensued; a new
strike began.[60]

The company's board of directors met in Boston on May 26, 1955,
and authorized complete closing down of the Calumet Division,
declaring that the strike of seventeen hundred production and mechanical workers was illegal. They voted, also, to invest $1.7 million
"in the first phase of a program to modernize the Detroit plant of
the . . . Wolverine Tube Division." Lovell wrote Governor Williams
that the final offer was "contingent on complete relief from the [Gen-
eral Services Administration] contract," adding that the company's
offer of twenty-four cents an hour was "the most liberal offer ever
made by Calumet and Hecla." Unless the government supplied "relief
from our stockpile contract *and* unless the Union drastically modi-
fies its position, liquidation of our Calumet Division is inevitable."
Gene Saari, answering a high school student's query about the strike,
said the men "wanted 30 cents an hour and pensions." The company's offer of twenty-four cents was "mythical as it was based on
complete relief from the contract they had with the government,
which they knew was impossible to obtain. Truthfully the Company
offered nothing."[61]

Former representative Frank Hook, congratulating Saari and the union in May 1955 for going out on strike, said he knew "how the companies pull stuff and color the facts." He urged the workers to keep up the good fight: "[for] when we placed the Wagner Act on the books, we had in mind the best interest of the rank and file and not the benefit of cliques or personal aggrandizement of any particular individuals."[62]

The strike lasted sixteen weeks. On August 22, the men voted 1,120–189 to accept the company offer. Its total package, estimated at about fifteen cents an hour, included an 8 percent increase on current wages, increased life insurance benefits paid totally by the company, increases in vacation–holiday pay, and a modified union shop. Thirty days after being hired, a worker had to join the union. Two weeks before the end, the company again threatened to close down. Many strikers believed that to be crying wolf.[63]

The International Office, CIO, had loaned the local union $2,500; the Strike Relief Fund of CIO, District 33 (headquarters at Duluth), assisted with $8,700 and food vouchers totaling almost $150,000. Contributions from the iron workers in Michigan and Minnesota amounted to $161,000. The Dollar Bay local sent a sizable gift of cash. Despite the 112-day strike, the company fared well, reporting good sales as a worldwide demand for copper—combined with strikes in Chile and Africa—created shortages. The domestic producers' price hit forty-three cents in August and by February 1956 had advanced an additional three cents.

Calumet and Hecla attempted, without much success, to punish or discipline some strikers, alleging "unprotected activities"—a euphemism for minor destruction of property. The threat of the company's closing down loomed so large in 1957—with rumors flying—that A. S. Kromer, general manager of the Calumet Division, stated in letters to all employees that despite the fall of the price of copper to 29.25 cents, the lowest in years, a shutdown had not been considered.[64]

By January 1958, the copper price fell to twenty-five cents. Mine production remained at about 32,350,000 pounds for the year. The union, "recognizing the seriousness of low copper prices," agreed to extend the wage schedule without change for another year. By July 1959, the Kearsarge Lode reserves mined via No. 3 Ahmeek lay exhausted; and all work stopped there. The company mined some uranium in New Mexico, explored in Ontonagon County, and actually began production again in a new area of the famous Calumet conglomerate via No. 13 Osceola. Stockholders heard rosy reports. The union concluded a new contract to expire in August 1961, providing for wage increases and improvement in fringe benefits.

Union and company existed in fitful tension. Many people refused to acknowledge that mining had become a minor part of the company's activity.

In 1910, Houghton County ranked as the second most populous county in Michigan. By the early 1960s, employment in service industries increased annually, due, in part, to the promotion of tourism in the Western Upper Peninsula. The region consisted of Baraga, Houghton, Keweenaw, Ontonagon, Marquette, Iron, Dickinson, Gogebic, and Alger counties. Of all arbitrarily-arrived-at regions, the Western Upper Peninsula was the largest in area (9,619 square miles) among Michigan's twelve regions and the smallest in population, with 186,861 persons (19.3 per square mile).[65]

Momentous changes had occurred in fifty years. Population continued to fall, as it had since 1910. Thousands who had once worked in copper mines, mills, and smelters now worked in automobile and other factories downstate or in cities throughout the United States. In one way, the Copper Country, like much of the Upper Peninsula, had served as incubator for the young, who then found success in distant realms. After World War II, thousands of young men worked in Great Lakes towns and cities as factory foremen or junior executives in gray flannel suits or else operated small businesses. Young women worked in insurance offices, taught school, or served as business partners with husbands.

Copper Country youth made new lives for themselves and their children in far away states like Texas, Florida, West Virginia, Alaska, Maryland, Louisiana, Connecticut, California, and Pennsylvania, with some going to Panama. Women and men entered college and distinguished themselves with teaching careers in high schools and universities. Houghton young men, with degrees from Michigan Tech, worked for some of the nation's largest corporations. A young man from Calumet served long in the U.S. Department of State.[66]

Statistics told a story of continued population decline (see Table 9.1).[67]

Former residents, returning on vacations, saw evidences of a strange mix of progress and physical deterioration in towns as new protagonists carried on: the giant new lift bridge spanning Portage Lake, the expanding campus at Houghton, weather-beaten houses on windy hills, abandoned mine buildings, locations where black stamp sand lay not far from hollyhocks, shady backyards where daisies and roses bloomed. Elsewhere, houses painted in pastel colors adjoined Victorian stone mansions, whose yards in spring burgeoned with lilacs. Tidy motels beckoned tourists along Highway 41, approaching Houghton.[68]

Table 9.1. Keweenaw Peninsula, Population, 1940–1960

County	1940	1950	1960
Baraga	9,356	8,037	7,151
Houghton	47,631	39,711	35,654
Keweenaw	4,004	2,918	2,417
Ontonagon	11,359	10,282	10,584

Everyone "at home" had strong opinions on the subject of what was wrong. The most bourgeois residents had little patience with those they denounced as "union troublemakers." Working people grumbled about "the company," but unionized workers serving as church deacons and ushers seemed indistinguishable from middle-class counterparts.[69] A trickle of former residents retiring and returning after decades of work in Detroit, Flint, Milwaukee, West Allis, and Chicago became a steady flow, with pensions and social security, to form by the 1970s, another component of a society different from any that had ever lived in the Copper Country. The Keweenaw Peninsula seemed permanently in flux, but its never-changing beauty remained as quietly spectacular as ever. An incredible sunset at Lake Medora, the serene expanse of Keweenaw Bay, the scent of pines in the Porcupine Mountains, or the sight of scarlet sumac along the road near Mandan evoked the words *Plus ça change, plus ça la meme chose*. There seemed to be something everlasting about the Michigan Copper Country.[70]

10

Omega and Alpha

1960 – 1980

BELLS OF HUBBELL'S SAINT CECILIA CHURCH tolled mournfully on April 3, 1969, marking the passing of the one-time giant, the Calumet and Hecla Company. Father Michael Hale set the bells in motion "after word was out that Calumet and Hecla died here today." T. S. Eliot, in 1922, wrote,

> April is the cruellest month, breeding
> Lilacs out of the dead land, mixing
> Memory and desire, stirring
> Dull roots with spring rain.

The words seemed apt in the Michigan Copper Country, where a seven-and-a-half-month strike ended with the announcement that the Calumet Division of Calumet and Hecla would shut down forever.[1]

Reaction was mixed. The *Mining Gazette* reported that "it was a time of weeping on the streets," while some shouted: "Shut 'er down!" A trammer defended the union and groused: "The company was going to shut down in '55. We went back with a 15 cent cut and what did we get for it?" A few argued that closing was perhaps the "best thing that ever happened." Others blamed a stubborn, arrogant union. The company had been the major employer for 104 years. Someone asked "Without Calumet and Hecla would the Copper Country be a copper country?"[2]

The next day, Good Friday, community leaders met at Calumet and Hubbell in public meetings to ask what could possibly be done. A professor declared that to attract new industry, natural resources and a labor supply were necessary; these were available, but the forecast was "somewhat depressing" for an area like the Keweenaw Peninsula at "the north end of the US-41 trail." Citizens from all walks of life begged labor and management to be reasonable and settle their differences. The Reverend Robert V. Langseth conducted a twenty-four-hour vigil service at Faith Lutheran Church, Calumet, calling for a reconciliation. As Easter dawned, many realized that a historic end had come.[3]

By the end of April, the dismantling of the Ahmeek Mill was announced. Pickets refused men entry into the mill. "A Group of Very Concerned Citizens" (unnamed) ran a full-page announcement in the *Mining Gazette* for May 3, concluding, "This will be your very last chance to stop the permanent closing of this Mining Industry here in the Copper Country." The next day, Sunday, union members by a voice vote vowed to continue their strike after hearing the bargaining committee's report that all previous attempts to put management–labor relations on a solid foundation were "smashed by the Company." We, the strikers, with our families, they declared, "make up the largest single segment of this community. We are concerned Citizens too! We have deep roots in the Copper Country. Our fathers and forefathers settled this area." But the end had come; and the owner, Universal Oil Products (UOP) began a momentous dismantling and selling of what had once been a giant but now was only a pinpoint on the UOP corporate chart—Calumet and Hecla.[4]

What had led to that fateful April 1969? Mining analysts for years had pointed to declining copper content in the rock in the mines and the growing expense entailed in extracting it. The Keweenaw community had seen one mine after another close and many an exploration seeking new copper resources end fruitlessly. Calumet and Hecla had been short of miners before the strike began in 1968. In 1966, the company had sought a hundred young men as trainees; as the 1968–69 strike began, it called for "the inclusion of a miner training clause [in its contract with the union] which would allow for the training of new people into a fast disappearing basic skill." In mid-January 1967, the Michigan Employment Security Commission had reported a continuing need for underground miners. Fewer young men wanted that kind of work. The local work force made up of older men encouraged sons to seek a better life but themselves remained faithful to the only work many of them knew. Winter halted construction work and often work in the woods. In early 1967, the average weekly earnings in manufacturing in the Upper Peninsula were $99.00, in metal mining, $138.50.[5]

After the 1955 strike at Calumet and Hecla, the work force dwindled from two thousand to about one thousand by 1968. Still, expectations of better times rose as the company continued explorations at Osceola and the newly discovered Kingston Lode (1960–62). The sight of silver-colored shafthouses symbolized another beginning: Calumet and Hecla was coming back! Investment of nine million dollars to begin in 1964 and to spread over three years at Kingston Mine, Centennial, and Osceola indicated that Calumet Division earnings should increase steadily as these new mines reached "planned production levels," officials announced in 1964.

As late as 1966, hopes ran high as diamond drilling began at the Hills Creek Project, an offshoot of the famous old Calumet conglomerate. In September, directors announced plans to develop this mine, hoping to procure fifty million pounds of copper annually, as projected in a Bechtel Corporation report. The company's announcement in the spring of the year that the ore body contained forty-five million tons with grade in excess of 1.5 percent a ton set off such extensive buying of Calumet and Hecla stock that the New York Stock Exchange held up trading in that stock for six consecutive days. Like many another venture, Hills Creek came to nothing. In 1963, Burton C. Peterson, president and general manager at Calumet and Hecla, said that management "has long been convinced that there are many good copper deposits remaining undiscovered in the vast mineral holdings of this Company in the Calumet area, and that persistence in exploration ultimately will disclose them." Marginal mines had been kept operating to maintain skills that would be required when explorations revealed new, rich deposits.[6]

The "warp" of Calumet and Hecla was no longer copper, but some Copper Country people seemed to live in a time warp. Miners, trammers, mill workers, and just about everyone else believed that untold riches lay there waiting to be worked. The myth died hard. In 1964, the company announced that in its tubing plants and production of copper chemicals, it consumed more copper than the company mined. Fifty-pound bags of Calumet C-line Copper Concentrates were sold to "help the farmer grow more and better crops and the cattleman healthier cattle [and were] widely used by industry for fungicides, preservatives and ceramic coloring." As early as 1961, officers revealed that "copper, the 'grandfather' of the [Calumet and Hecla] family, is still mined, but is not really a Company product since much more is used in manufacturing than is mined."

With the change to manufacturing, combined with aggressive marketing, an iron foundry operating at capacity grinding balls and mill liners, and determined managerial programs to control costs, Calumet and Hecla was totally unlike the company of 1943, 1913, or 1883. Yet in the minds of some, the company made money hand over fist but begrudged paying its workers decent wages. Some followed statistics: Calumet and Hecla net sales rose from $93,000,000 in 1961 to $112,000,000 in 1963 and $135,608,148 in 1965; net income went up from $187,418 to $1,267,958 to $2,230,883 in those three years. "Where is our share?," the workers argued.[7]

They felt that the company refused to deal realistically with "the workers' economic needs" and had "ignored the backlog of grievances and local issues that have accumulated." The 1913 trauma always loomed large, with miners in 1969 insisting "that they be treated as human beings, rather than just tools of production." They pointed to the Western Federation of Miners' attempt to rectify things in 1913–14; and they claimed that the company's breaking that strike established "virtual dictatorial control over its workers," whose successors now vowed that their spirit would not be broken. Gene Saari wrote a colleague in 1950 that the company's dividend-share bonus plan "was designed by the Company as an anti-union instrument to enslave the loyalties of the employees to their ruthless paternalism, [which] dates back to the origination of the Company." A year later, he told Florida miners and smeltermen, "Our life has been hard, as that of most hard rock miners' lives are; but we have found our protection and security to exist in a strong, militant and effective trade union."[8]

The "success" of the Calumet company as shown in financial reports convinced many workers that they must reassert themselves. When their contract expired in August 1965, a ten-week strike followed but did not delay the opening of the new Kingston Mine. When agreement was reached on October 31, workers won wage increases and fringe benefits worth fifty-one cents an hour. Sales rose another twenty-six million dollars in 1966 but fell by ten million dollars in 1967. A nationwide copper strike in 1967—68, in which Calumet and Hecla workers did not participate, forced the company to pay substantial premiums to obtain copper needed by Wolverine Tube.[9]

The myth of untapped riches prevailed. A deposit of native copper discovered off Eagle Harbor by a skin diver in twenty feet of water in 1967 set geologists from Michigan's Natural Resources Department investigating. Local observers opined that the copper lay on a fissure vein similar to that of the pre-1900 Central Mine, which had produced millions of dollars' worth of the red metal. The diver managed to recover eleven tons of the ore by 1969, when geologists took over. Nothing came of this. A decade earlier, W. P. Strassman, after making an economic study of the entire Upper Peninsula for Michigan State University, concluded that Keweenaw's mines were "mostly marginal producers that operate only when prices are high." For every one hundred tons of rock hauled to the surface and processed, only one ton of smelted copper resulted. Should the price of copper fall below thirty cents a pound, "all this must be achieved for less than $6 per ton of rock." The report continued, "As the mines become depleted, periods of operation will be limited to even briefer times of maximum prices, until finally no deep mine will be profitable even at the highest peaks of booms, and all must be abandoned." That sounded like Dante's "Abandon all hope all ye who enter here." The great days had long since gone. The *New York Times*, discussing copper prices in 1968, referred to Calumet and Hecla as "a relatively small producer" accounting for about 3 percent of domestic copper production—a drastic change for a company that between 1869 and 1876 produced more than half of the nation's copper.[10]

The company and Calumet Township celebrated their centennial with fanfare in 1966. The *Mining Gazette* in its Souvenir Edition proclaimed: "Even by the most conservative estimate today, one would be compelled to say the company is standing on the threshold of perhaps its most dynamic and fruitful years. . . . The next 100 years of Calumet & Hecla look bright indeed, it is said." The writer responsible for transmitting that pipe dream is unknown. Eighteen months later, the company entered into discussion with UOP, a large research and development firm, to explore a merger. By February 1968, the company's board of directors had approved joining the UOP. The *Wall Street Journal* described both companies as widely diversified. The UOP now entered mining and metal fabricating for the first time after success in licensing patents and processes and in engineering; it furnished operation maintenance and construction services to the petroleum, petrochemical, and chemical industries. Calumet and Hecla continued as an autonomous unit, known as the "C and H Group," with headquarters in Evanston, Illinois, each share of its common stock exchanged for a .6 share of UOP common. The merger was consummated at a special meeting of shareholders at Evanston, on April 25, 1968.[11]

Spring brought merger; summer brought rupture. Fully to comprehend what followed, a development at the southern end of the copper range deserves examination. Once again, mining interest had turned to Ontonagon County, where the rich Minesota Mine had brought renown more than a century earlier. The Nonesuch ore body, located two miles from the community of White Pine, had been discovered in 1865. It produced mineral wealth until 1881, and miners continued to extract some silver after that. Later, Calumet and

Hecla spent two million dollars exploring the area; and mining was resumed about 1915. Thomas Wilcox, a Houghton mining college graduate, masterminded the resumption of copper mining at this location, directing the sinking of four new shafts. By 1917–18, some three hundred men produced copper at 12.7 cents a pound and it sold for twice that.

White Pine, named in 1879 by Captain Thomas Hooper for a beautiful hillside tree, expanded quickly from its original few habitations when mining began again. It soon had "streets, houses, school, store, gambling and dance hall, theater, and uniformed baseball and basketball teams." But by the 1920s, mining ceased at the White Pine company due to falling copper prices; and White Pine became a logging area. Forest fires helped decimate the locality. Calumet and Hecla had long since abandoned plans to resume work there; the 1925 annual report listed a $32,481.51 loss, with no copper output.[12]

William Schacht, of the Copper Range Company, attending a sheriff's sale on the steps of the Ontonagon County Court House, bought the old White Pine Copper Company's land and mineral rights for $119,000 in 1929. Some scoffed at Schacht's folly. By the mid-1950s, almost twenty-five years after Schacht's purchase and due in part to the Korean War and the demand for copper, White Pine once again flourished.[13]

White Pine produced copper, some of it native, much of it laced with silver, most of it the black or dark gray mineral chalcocite "in the lower part of the Nonesuch shale . . . present in 5 different layers in amounts that average from 1 to 3 percent." The deposits were distinctly separated geographically from the famous deposits of copper in the Portage Lake lava series some forty-five-to-seventy miles north. The federal government had initiated a seventy-million-dollar project with a fifty-seven-million-dollar loan from the Reconstruction Finance Corporation. Huge construction equipment moved in along with thousands of tourists eager, in 1953, to witness another life of the Copper Country "phoenix"—consumed by its own actions, then rising from ruin, omega becoming alpha, in constant succession. The town of White Pine grew from thirty inhabitants in 1952 to more than a thousand inhabitants in two years as a new White Pine Company was created.[14]

In 1953, the new White Pine townsite had been "almost completely overgrown with brush"; but strangers from New York City, Canada, Cuba, Chicago, California, Minnesota, Wisconsin, South Dakota, and various places in the Upper Peninsula came to help plan, plot, develop, and construct mine, mill, smelter, and town. On lots 70 by 125 feet, attractive one-story houses with redwood siding (in six basic designs to avoid monotony) emerged, with "electricity, sewers, water, . . . radiant heating in the concrete floor slab, no basements, electric washers, driers, hot water heaters, graded and drained sites, . . . garages and extra storage space." The buildings gave the lie to those who viewed mining towns as ugly excrescences on the land. An arcadelike shopping center with protection from cold and snow; an elementary school; a high school with modern laboratories, cafeteria, swimming pool, and auditorium; and a twenty-bed, completely equipped, fireproof hospital—all heralded a new age of copper mining in Michigan's Copper Country.[15]

By 1955, Michigan produced considerable amounts of copper— 23,600 tons in 1954, more than 50,000 in 1955, and 61,500 by 1956. Governor G. Mennen Williams helped celebrate in 1955 as parades, dinners, and dances heralded the new age. The Michigan Tourist Council spoke of a "Ghost Town reborn: One of the world's largest-known copper deposits lies beneath the remnants of White Pine. . . . A 75-million pound annual output with productive mining for 50 years is anticipated." In a little over a decade, the White Pine smelter poured forth its billionth pound of copper (1965); plans proceeded for expansion, and newspapers claimed that ore reserves now assured continued operations for one hundred years. Governor George Romney attended ceremonies where hundreds reveled in joyous daylong festivities.[16]

Workers initiated Local 5024, organized by October 1953, after an agent of the American Federation of Labor's construction union made known their desires to CIO officials. Of the fifty-three men composing the local, about twenty-one were of Finnish descent and one, French Canadian; and the others bore Scandinavian, Slavic, or Anglo–American names. Many workers commuted from Greenland, Ewen, Ontonagon, Mass, Bergland, and Toivola. White Pine used new technologies and prided itself on an excellent safety record, receiving the National Safety Council's Award of Honor in May 1965, when disabling injuries incurred there stood at less than one-third of the national average.[17]

Al Londo recalled arriving in 1956 to teach school, his first impression that of "a sea of mud" and few houses; but the "price of copper was high and they were pouring it out of here." He found ties among people "very close, even though they were absolute strangers." Sharing in building a new community out of a copper camp drew people together. The century-old pattern had reemerged: young men and women with children, a strong economic base, prospects of steady work, constant construction and expansion, "a considerable mixing of executives and working men," and a rich but simple social life.

One major difference set White Pine apart from Cliff, Quincy, and Calumet. Ray Archambeau said that "very few people moved there because they lived within commuting distance, and several surveys indicated that most of them owned their homes mortgage-free." Why should they "move from old ties and risk it on a copper mine?"[18] The curious blend of optimism and cynicism, indigenous to the Copper Country, prevailed. Happy days were here again. Copper was king, the focus having shifted back to Ontonagon County after a century. But would it last? In 1962, the future was bright as advertising hyperbole declared:[19]

> White Pine Silver Bearing Lake Copper, . . . the copper with the *natural* silver content. And it's found in only one place— the Upper Peninsula of Michigan. Take special note of that word *natural*. It's the natural silver content of Lake Copper that makes White Pine significantly different from other coppers. . . . Available . . . in cakes, slabs, wire bars, ingots and ingot bars.

By 1968, White Pine produced 5 percent of the nation's copper. The industry had evolved as exceedingly diverse, with open-pit and vertical-shaft mines, brass mills, wire and cable plants, refineries, and smelters.[20]

Militancy ruled within Local 5024, USWA-CIO. There was a series of wildcat strikes in 1957, a 117-day strike that began in October 1959, a one-day walkout in the mid-1960s, and a forty-eight-day strike that began in September 1964. One newspaper writer commented that at White Pine, there had been "no real progress in 11 years of labor–management relations." As Calumet and Hecla mining diminished, White Pine became the larger employer of miners. It had 1,850 workers in 1968, when the Calumet company was reducing its labor force to around 1,000 men. The union activity and gains of White Pine mine workers influenced the course of events at Calumet and Hecla in the final management–labor confrontation there.[21]

During the giant, nationwide copper strike of 1967–68, managements everywhere claimed that exhorbitant demands cut seriously into their profits; labor demanded its just recompense. At the 1968 dedication at White Pine of a new union hall named for Gene Saari, a spokesperson said the edifice would "serve us as a constant reminder that only through a strong organization can the workers succeed in securing their fair . . . share of the fruits of this powerful, rich and often arrogant industry." It was claimed that management spared neither money nor force to hold copper workers in check: "Killings, beatings, oppression, low wages, and poor working conditions" prevailed before the United Steel Workers came to the Copper Country. Both labor and management exaggerated, distorting reality.[22]

The *Wall Street Journal* screamed of a power grab by arrogant and reckless union leaders, accusing the Steel Workers union of asking for increases double what companies were willing to pay. How could there be industrywide bargaining in an industry as multifaceted as was copper? In the 1967–68 strike, White Pine miners stayed out for 147 days. They gained wage increases and fringe benefits that had fatal consequences for the Calumet company. Copper Range was the second of the striking companies to reach a settlement with the Steel Workers, in January 1968. Workers elsewhere continued on strike for more than 200 days. The *Wall Street Journal* conceded that labor's strength was due, in part, to the role of the steel union in negotiating for copper workers; for management had previously played off one union against another.[23]

The White Pine strike was costly. One family's experience tells part of the story: Walter Pidgeon, age twenty-nine, grew up in Butte, Montana, but returned with his family to their native Michigan where Pidgeon worked at a machine pulverizing copper ore at White Pine. In the first three months of the strike, he used up his savings in bank and bonds. His family was assisted by Aid to Dependent Children and relief funds to the amount of $237 monthly for food, clothing, utilities, and fuel. The state took over the $53 monthly mortgage on his house and paid 98 percent of the cost of all family medicines. The union contributed $25 every two weeks in food and fuel vouchers but subtracted the amount from Michigan's payments. Pidgeon's wife, who once spent $30 a week on groceries, cut back to $12, followed sales, and entertained at home with "no going out." The Pidgeons considered themselves among the lucky families.[24]

The White Pine strike of 1967–68 and the Calumet and Hecla strike of 1968–69 typified the "war" that capital and labor continued to wage in the world of copper. In 1968, Edward M. Tittmann, chairman of the American Smelting Company, said the Steel Workers' growing power "must be resisted" lest "our" economic future become burdened. A shortage of copper that occurred in 1969 sent prices soaring. Copper Range raised its price to 60 cents a pound effective January 1, 1970; and western giants like Phelps Dodge followed. Even scrap sold at 60 cents after dealers purchased it for 56.5 cent a pound. American industry turned increasingly to aluminum as a substitute for copper used for heat and electrical transmission. Copper seemed to be pricing itself out of the market, according to capital's guardians of the flame. An eastern manufacturer, lamenting a copper shortage that had lasted almost a decade, declared, "We're going to look for an alternative material as hard as we can."[25]

The Copper Development Association conceded that "some copper users were forced to switch to substitute material" (stainless steel, aluminum, cast iron, steel, and plastics); but the copper industry expected to regain much of that business. Aluminum, however, had been substituted in markets involving production of screw machine products and air-conditioning.[26]

Bargaining sessions at Calumet and Hecla to negotiate a new contract began July 11, 1968, with the union asking for a settlement "on the wage rates and fringe benefits in effect at the White Pine Copper Co. operations." They continued for six additional days in July, discussion often centering on noneconomic issues that generated "serious dispute." The company's August 3 proposal of wage increases totaling fifty-five cents over three years and incremental increases from three-and-a-half-to-five cents plus clearly detailed information on shift differentials, pensions, hospitalization, life and accident insurance was rejected. Under the prevailing contract, due to expire August 21, the base wage was $2.12–2.57 per hour. The company offered increases that would raise this to $2.67–3.52 in the third year. In 1968, Calumet and Hecla paid $2.12 for job grades 1–3 while Kennecott, Anaconda, and Phelps Dodge paid $2.74 an hour in job grade 1. The union claimed that fringe benefits at Calumet were also below par.[27]

The old refrain of better wages in the West but better living conditions in the Copper Country sounded again, but a militant union discounted the importance of the comparison. Once the strike began, however, and some men left for downstate cities and Wisconsin, Gene Saari told a reporter: "My experience has been that the men say that they won't come back but that they do. Their families, their roots are in this community." The company, like others through the land, rang changes on the old themes of leisurely work habits. One official explaining the proposal said, "We asked that the Union include a productivity clause which, in effect, simply says that the Union and the Company agree that they will strive together toward increased productivity."

The company promised that "it would do everything within its power to reduce the wage disparity [existing] between the Calumet Division and other copper Producers." Officials told reporters that Michigan's conditions were peculiar, citing (as they had for years) low copper content and the expense involved in its extraction. General manager Cecil H. Suter explained that the offer exceeded any ever made in the Upper Peninsula and was greater than any ever offered by any company in the copper industry. He concluded his August 8 revised proposal by describing how "stunned" he and his colleagues were by the bargaining committee's rejection; for "in quite unbelievable sequence the Union's response has been to demand over and over again more and more money." Always wary, union

officials regarded the company as recalcitrant and mendacious, con-
ceding only when forced by a show of union strength. The men
voted 698–113 by secret ballot, on August 10, to strike at midnight,
August 21.[28]

Bill Kobe, a young man at the time, recalled years later, "The
older guys were leery about striking, but the younger guys were
all for it."[29] Although lacking the physical violence of 1913–14,
the 1968–69 struggle produced its share of verbal abuse. State and
federal conciliators and mediators worked from September on; but by
January 1969, they scheduled no meetings, because—a Steel Workers
newsletter reported—"of the hard-and-fast positions taken by company negotiators." The basic union demand called for "a contract providing wages and benefits similar to [those] won by workers during
the copper strike of 1967–68." Local spokespersons argued that the
company's record of labor–management relations stood as "one of the
worst in the entire history of American industry." Sylvio Guisfredi,
staff representative of the Steel Workers, said, "It is still 1913 for
copper workers in Calumet, Michigan," Repeating old propaganda,
a newsletter recalled Christmas Eve, 1913, and the panic at Italian
Hall, Red Jacket, as "the most senseless mass murder in the annals
of trade union history." Ralph Orr, reporter for the *Detroit Free
Press*, found "many old timers" still blaming Calumet and Hecla
for the panic. "Mine–Mill," for decades, had printed as truth the
false *Työmies* stories of deputies holding doors shut so that children
could not escape from Italian Hall. One man told Orr that many
strikers were victims of "inherited attitudes," a factor that did not
help negotiations.[30]

The company had not changed at all, claimed the December 1968
Steel Workers newsletter:[31] "Today the tactics are different, but the
attitudes remain the same. No less brutal are company attempts to
overturn a present State Supreme Court decision affording unemployment compensation to strikers. Efforts are also being made to
snarl procedures for payment of welfare to strikers." This analysis
concluded with the idea that Calumet and Hecla had maintained a
"stranglehold on both the economy and the industrial development
of the area," a view many accepted and one that accounted for some
opinions expressed in April 1969 that the complete shutdown of the
company at Calumet was the best thing that had happened despite
the initial shock. In November 1968, Saari told a Milwaukee reporter:

> I've been negotiating here for 25 years and the men are tired of
> promises, of an archaic labor policy. . . . We believe we should
> be finally getting 20th century treatment. . . . The underlying
> issue in this strike is the determination that the company has to

move in all kinds of ways to close the gap between White Pine and C.&H.[32]

Interestingly, at a Douglass House meeting called by the federal conciliator on September 26–27, 1968, the union submitted a counterproposal establishing wage benefits and fringe benefits "considerably below those at the White Pine operations." Calumet and Hecla claimed, to the end, that its initial offer was generous and that its offer of wage increases exceeded by 25 percent the settlement Steel had made with White Pine in 1968. Saari disputed this, charging that the company's offer failed in many respects to match the White Pine contract.[33]

As in 1913–14, strikers questioned safety in underground operations, making this a major issue by citing a new cage signaling system at Kingston Mine as unsafe. When workers refused to use the system, they were locked out from jobs. Arbitration—binding, according to the contract—failed to convince the company to change its new system. The strikers now vowed not to return to the pits before resolution of the issue. In 1913, the homologous dispute was the one-man drill.

As in 1913–14, the picket line emerged as the strikers' way to tell the community their story. As December snow fell in heavier amounts than in 1913, men in mackinaws, parkas, wool caps, and galoshes carried hand-printed signs at No. 13 Osceola: "Local 4312 on *STRIKE*," "The fine print costs us *TOO MUCH*," and (referring to the former locale of Mr. Suter's mining employment) "Local 4312 USWA *ON STRIKE*. This is not *BRAZIL*." Similarly, as in the struggle fifty-five years earlier, strikers used opportunities to publicize what they called the refusal of capital to see them as worthy human beings. The local's president, Henry Snabb, said:[34]

> Our wants are simple. We want to know that when we get on a cage to go to work in the morning that we have at least an even chance of returning in the evening. We feel we are entitled to the same wages and benefits other copper miners earn doing the same or similar work. And, above all else, we would like to be treated as humans, something that has been lacking here in Calumet since miners first mined the copper discovered here so many years ago.

Grievances and divisions sputtered within the union. Even before the strike began, the chairman of the Calumet and Hecla Trades Council wrote Saari and Guisfredi that electricians, machinists, janitors, and others felt that they had been ignored "in all contract negotiations since the Steelworkers has represented us." Since 1950,

"the increment between job classes has gone up from 2¢ to 2½¢";
and some of the members had written to other unions in hopes
that they might enter a trade union. He liked the Steel Workers
union but thought, "Our inequities are the fault of our local."[35]
One underground worker on strike said in November: "If we took a
vote tonight, we would go back to work tomorrow. We blame the
union. They didn't tell us the truth." By that time, the Houghton
County Department of Social Welfare reported that 210 strikers had
qualified for direct relief and another 150 received food stamps.[36] A
family of five received $142 per month in relief. Others received union
benefits—how many the local did not reveal. One striker, "nursing
a beer" at Shute's Bar, said he received $15 a week but had a rent
of $37.50 a month, adding that he liked "to eat, too" but that that
was difficult with such an income. Married men received $5 for each
dependent in addition to their $15 a week. Strikers waited weeks
before $20 fuel vouchers came through.[37]

A striker who had installed mine timbers when he had worked
watched television at home and hoped the strike would end; for he
felt that the company had made a good offer whose pension plan
would bring him $150 monthly in three years, when he would retire.
Still, he thought most of the men were not about to accept the
company's offer. Paul Asselin, grocer, said much of his business was
in food stamps. He expressed the belief of many businessmen: "I
think a lot of people would go back to work if they had a chance."
But in February 1969, a striker wrote Saari that most strikers he had
encountered "are more for the strike [now] than when it began."
For the first time, he said, Calumet workers were displaying some
backbone: "[We must] never say die. . . . A few would go back with a
cut in wages and then blame someone else for making up their mind."
He, his wife, and their four children had "bounced off and on relief
like a Yo-Yo and things weren't as difficult as the News Media would
have you believe." He thanked Saari and the bargaining committee
for their "fine" representation.[38]

Many of the strikers held on, unable to relocate because of their
age. They were in their forties and fifties, looking forward to retirement. One decried the fixation on the past, declaring that too
many men "keep talking about the strike of 1913. I don't care
about the sins of the past. I want to go back to work." A store
owner complained, "It's that Saari's fault"; for in the last two strikes,
workers charged him with "selling out the union" and Saari is "bound
they won't be able to charge him with selling out again." Some
townspeople at Calumet said maybe the company would close for
good, and "then we can all sing 'Who's Saari Now?'" By March 1969,
a waitress at the Red Garter Restaurant and Bar said, "It's a disaster";

for no longer did salesmen come to town and order steaks or chops. A Laurium striker fumed: "What these ribbon clerks [merchants] forget is that they don't make a buck until I chop out rock a mile under their stores. They should be on our side." Another, sipping beer at a Calumet bar, shouted, "I've had it up to here with C.&H.; we'll stay out until summer if we have to!"[39]

That was not to be. For months in 1968, union officials had warned workers that the coming strike would be long. Rumors flew, as winter settled in, that *this* strike would be decisive for both company and union. That was true. On February 26, Suter wrote Snabb: "All economic offers which have been made by this company to the United Steelworkers of America, Local 4312, are withdrawn. Your repeated refusal of terms for an amicable settlement leaves us no alternative but to take this action." Pittsburgh, Lansing, and Washington, D.C., officials now moved to settle the strike. Men from the union and the company met with mediators first at Lansing, March 10 and 11, and then at Michigan Technological University, Houghton, on March 17,[40]

Richard N. Speer, president of the Calumet and Hecla Group, wrote Local 4312 on April 1, 1969, that a study of the economics of the Calumet Division showed that it could not be "restored to economic soundness" and that "termination of some or all operations" was imminent.[41] This was no April fool. A *Mining Gazette* editorial next day called for more caring citizens and negotiators; for the strikers had "literally [chased] out of the area its young people, [drained] their own resources, [reduced] their earning power and retirements," and made themselves paupers at the expense of the taxpayers. A faithful, skilled foundry worker since 1936 wrote, "I could never quite fathom the union malcontents who bitterly preached their venomous hatred and dissatisfaction for C.&H. constantly." The strikers remained adamant: the company was bluffing. Remember 1955? They cried 'wolf' then. One man said, "They aren't going to pack up all this and leave." As fragile spring became mature summer, 1969, all had to accept the grim reality that copper mining by Calumet and Hecla was now history. Some miners migrated; others sought work in the Upper Peninsula. Some resented bitterly the most militant union leaders' scurrying to secure positions in community action posts. Some men commuted on chartered buses to White Pine to work.[42]

Thus ended, "not with a bang but a whimper," the last of four strikes of Calumet and Hecla workers under USWA–CIO.[43] They had not struck in seven years of "Mine–Mill" hegemony, although they had been without work from May 1, 1949, to September 7, 1949, when the company closed the mines after asking the men to take a fifteen-cent-an-hour pay cut that the workers finally accepted. Quincy men had struck briefly under "Mine–Mill" auspices as early as 1941. Calumet and Hecla workers struck for 63 days in 1952, for 112 in 1955, and for ten weeks in 1965 before their final protest. In 1952 and 1955, the men had accepted the company's offers. Ironically, under "Mine–Mill"—the militant, "communist-dominated" successor to the Western Federation of Miners—progress and peace had prevailed!

The *New York Times*, recounting the demise at Calumet, headlined its story in the business section with "End Comes in Michigan for Proud Copper Mine." The story announced that 300 supervisory and clerical workers found themselves unemployed in August 1969 and suggested that "the loss of Calumet may be overwhelming for the area"; for some 80 percent in Keweenaw County and 25 percent in Houghton County had been directly or indirectly dependent on Calumet and Hecla for their livelihood.

As he prepared to leave for Denver, Colorado, and a new assignment by the Steel Workers of America, Gene Saari clipped an advertisement from a Chicago newspaper: "*FOR SALE.* The Calumet & Hecla Corporate Headquarters Building. . . . 38,000 Sq. Ft. on 3 levels [at Evanston]. Agent: Gottlieb/Beale & Co., 120 S. LaSalle St., Chicago, IL 60603." Although UOP methodically shut down facilities, clearing lower levels of equipment in the mines, preparing to remove pumps so that the great shafts would fill with water, citizens rallied, hoping still, in early January 1971, to halt this tide. The Calumet–Laurium–Keweenaw Chamber of Commerce's program of declarations of support for the reopening of the copper mines attracted a huge crowd in the midst of a January blizzard. Garnet Hyslop, program chairman, said what many felt deeply: in the past, the affairs of the Calumet Division supposedly were "none of our business," but the economic survival of the area was "everyone's business."[44]

White Pine, meantime, continued as a major production success but passed through a series of owners beginning in 1977. While mining continued in Ontonagon County, Houghton and Keweenaw counties sought new sources of economic development to replace the major industry they had depended on for over a century. For a time, from 1926 to 1946, Baraga County had harbored hopes that Henry Ford would be the savior who would introduce new job-producing industry into the North Country. At Alberta, on Highway 41, about ten miles from L'Anse, Ford, in 1936, had built a settlement where thirty selected families hoped to farm on lands cleared from the forest and to work at the village sawmill. Three years later, no farmland had been cleared but the people worked in the mill. Twelve houses set in horseshoe formation opened onto the main road. An excellent example of planning, Alberta had expensive water and sewage systems, electricity, lights, a school, and a church but gave the appearance of something unreal, surrounded, as it was, by virgin hardwood forest. Ford's idea of combining industrial with agricultural work attempted to cope with a changing America; but the experiment failed, for the land simply could not sustain agriculture. The Michigan mining college acquired the village in 1954 and converted Alberta—some seventeen hundred acres of land—into the Ford Forestry Center of the Michigan College of Mining and Technology. The forestry programs helped industries like Celotex at L'Anse, established in the 1950s, and the Huss Ontonagon Pulp and Paper Company. The Ford family retained its summer home at Pequaming, where the patriarch sometimes danced to fiddler's music or entertained a hundred children when he was not planning to turn the home into a vocational school.[45]

Ford restored the Big Bay Hotel in 1944, spending more than half a million dollars; but the family rarely used their suite there, twenty-five miles north of Marquette. The inn, used as a setting for the movie *Anatomy of a Murder*, was renamed Thunder Bay Inn when Ford interests sold it in 1959. Ford had come to Calumet in 1923 to speak to businessmen who, along with a great many working people, admired his advocacy of "high-volume production, lower prices, and Universal consumption." Copper Country radicals—and many who frowned upon "radicalism"—sneered at the "Flivver King," denounced his antiunion tactics, and saw Ford as part of a rising American fascism. Ford was a hero to many at Pequaming, where he literally bought up the surrounding area and continued mill operations using timber from his lands nearby. The village of Pequaming dated to 1879 and the pioneer work of Charles Hebard and son, sawmill operators. Ford built a new school, installed handpicked teachers approved by the local board, and financed the institution with a thousand dollars a month. The population had been mainly Norwegian, and much of their heritage remained into the 1940s.[46]

As the Keweenaw Peninsula saw its major economic activity—copper mining—dwindle while White Pine through production, succeeded, a reflective resident could look back appreciatively at the foresight of those who had pressed for an adjunct to the area's greatest resource in the nineteenth century and established the Michigan Mining School in 1885. By the 1960s, the institution that had evolved —renamed, in December 1963, Michigan Technological University— had become a major employer. Known popularly as Michigan Tech, the university had expanded and given the Keweenaw important new vigor as mining ebbed. The economic well-being of the Keweenaw Peninsula from the early 1940s on seemed also to rely increasingly on tourism; but expectations that someday, somewhere, in the Copper Country new copper resources would emerge to revitalize the once vital communities persisted and hung on tenaciously.

As the Great Society of the Lyndon Johnson administration (1963–69) developed, citizens bound by "a desire and . . . need to prevent a further decline in the economy of the area and then to improve it" had formed, in 1964, the Community Action Agency of Baraga–Houghton–Keweenaw Counties with headquarters at Hancock's City Hall. Allied with the Economic Development Administration of the U.S. Department of Commerce, the group proposed a seventy-five-thousand-dollar grant to study the feasibility of reopening parts of Quincy Mine. Proponents hoped that Quincy's grinding and smelting operations at Mason and Ripley, respectively, could be continued and new jobs created by providing metal for copper-fabricating industries. Committee trustees represented industry, labor, law, and ordinary citizens. Representatives from the Salvation Army, the Ford Forestry Center at L'Anse, and Native Americans joined them in the "struggle against poverty"; for the three counties listed 3,552 low-income families among them.[47]

Quincy's president promised to refund, once profits accumulated, the amount the government paid for a feasibility study. Louis G. Koepel, longtime superintendent of Quincy, recalled that Quincy had produced from 1864 to July 1966, from its mine and reclamation operation, 981,784,108 pounds of copper. The committee argued that the Pewabic Lode still held "at least as much mineable copper" as had been extracted over one hundred years. Michigan's appraiser of mines from 1927 to 1952 wrote President W. Parson Todd in the 1960s that in all his travels underground, he was "impressed by the richness" of the Quincy at certain levels.[48]

The ninety-eight-year-old Todd agreed to a joint venture between his company and the Homestake Copper Company in February 1976, with Quincy contributing up to $425,000 to finance the mine's reopening and Homestake the men, equipment, and engineering. Homestake also explored at Centennial Mine, hoping to find the so-called "mother lode," in the 1970s. None of the schemes materialized. Much ventured, nothing gained. Younger people realized that an entire generation would eventually have to give way before new concepts of Keweenaw community would emerge. For the older generations, mining had so long been part of life in the Keweenaw that they could envision nothing else.[49]

In what might be considered the Indian summer of copper mining in the northern part of the peninsula, the Kingston ore body, discovered in 1962, had yielded 20,042,275 pounds of refined copper before Calumet and Hecla called it quits. Total production from the principal native copper lodes from the northernmost reaches to White Pine, from 1845 to 1968, had been 10,815,687,423 pounds—96 percent of that from the 28-mile section of the range stretching from Painesdale to a few miles north of Mohawk. Geologists and mineralogists defined the range as 160 miles long. By 1990, White Pine survived as the "last all-underground copper mine in the United States, [a] game survivor—now with a more assured future," announced the *Engineering and Mining Journal.*[50]

Old-timers remained amazed as copper's market price, only 5½ cents in 1932, hit $1.01 a pound in 1980—an aberration, but in the 1980s, copper sold for an average of 64–84 cents. When various corporations expected to open pulp-and-paper mills in Ontonagon and Baraga counties, they encountered a new element in the Keweenaw—environmentalists intent on preserving the area and protecting Lake Superior. Throughout the length of the Keweenaw Peninsula, many rose—militantly joined, on occasion, by advocates from Greenpeace, the Sierra Club, and National Wildlife Federation.[51]

Some saw tourism as the hope of the future. Snowmobiling had become a major sport. Why not turn the entire Keweenaw into a tourist land? The idea was now sixty years old. A core of old-timers looked with suspicion on urban dwellers invading their beloved north country. A reporter noted in the late 1980s that Copper Country people were "torn between the solitude and beauty of what is, and the infinite possibilities of what could be." That idea was 150 years old; for the Ojibwa had looked with suspicion and displeasure on entrepreneurs invading the lands where they fished, tracked deer, and enjoyed the quiet of the forests. One citizen spoke of the "overkill" of downstate environmentalists, some of whom simply wanted to make the entire Upper Peninsula "their park." Others asked simply that industrialists treat the area responsibly. Some assailed "economic terrorists"—environmentalists who threatened rights of residents to make a living. A Mohawk woman argued that all must band together and "vehemently and fiercely defend and protect this land." The Keweenaw must be "left as it is," she demanded, a "sanctuary for our great grandchildren . . . to see God's creation as He meant it to be." Many agreed with her that it was their responsibility to protect a precious heritage.[52]

In population centers like Hancock and Houghton, leaders listened to consultants who said that "cities, towns and villages cannot—and do not—stand still. . . . They [need] renewal, maintenance of usable buildings and replacement of those that are deteriorated."[53] In 1969, Houghton was characterized by critics as a "dead town" with no growth; the university was "expanding," but "the town was going downhill." In Hancock, Rob Roy, chairman for the city's planning commission, sounded like many a conscientious Copper Country citizen of decades past: it is time to do what we can, he said, to make our community the very best. A new wave of young, energetic men and women emerged after 1970 with attitudes that helped revitalize the Copper Country.

Many of the young activists came from downstate cities and towns, where the automobile industry declined. Some came from as far as California, but most, from states bordering the Great Lakes, especially Minnesota and Wisconsin. By 1989, Houghton had become a city reborn, said City Manager Roy Kestner, due to the efforts of "young, aggressive people trying to make a name for themselves"—people willing to serve on committees or in government, a new breed of "movers and shakers." Shelden Street regained much of its former robust activity, despite competition from a huge shopping mall built in West Houghton. Hancock set about, in 1969, with Operation Face Lift and renovated store fronts—sandblasting, painting, and encouraging owners to remodel shops.

Kestner worked with the university to make Houghton a "home away from home," developing housing for the elderly, preserving historic buildings, and benefiting from six Urban Development Action Grants in the two decades after 1969. Some looked forward to a future when Houghton would compete for tourists with the Wisconsin Dells and the Door County peninsula.[54] Michigan Tech's building from 1954 on resulted in "one of the largest dormitory facilities [Wadsworth Hall] in a state university in the United States." By 1962, the college's branch at Sault Sainte Marie flourished. Tech was no longer simply a mining school but offered degrees in various engineering specialties, physics, forestry, chemistry, and other fields. An enormous building program from 1964 to 1978 transformed the campus. Private and state funds totaled over $71,000,000 dollars for high-rise buildings, the rerouting of U.S. Highway 41, and demolition of some fifty private homes—all part of a plan to create a novel campus. By the early 1980s, total enrollment had increased 30 percent, women's enrollment by 70 percent. Private support increased from $86,000 in 1965–66 to $5,600,000 in 1983–84.

In 1964, besides the 384 faculty and administrators, the university employed some 475 Copper Country residents in secretarial, clerical, maintenance, and auxiliary services. Where once miners and trammers trudged or rode streetcars to work, a "steady stream of [automobile] traffic" flowed each morning from Houghton, Hancock, Calumet, Laurium, Lake Linden, Hubbell, Ahmeek, Mohawk, Dollar Bay, Ripley, Dodgeville, Hurontown, Chassell, Atlantic Mine, South Range, Trimountain, Painesdale, and Baltic. Residents of Baraga, L'Anse, and even Crystal Falls worked at the university's Ford Forestry Center at Alberta. Michigan Technological University has become "a major industry here," reported the Mining Gazette, its annual payroll amounting to eight million dollars and ten million was spent by the university for construction in 1968–69 alone.[55]

But poverty and unemployment remained for many Copper Country people. In January 1985, a local editor wrote, "Statistics show that but for a steady transfusion of state and federal funds into Houghton County, life here would cease to exist as we know it." One in every five in Houghton County received funds from a total of $15,000,000; and $60,000 of that came from the county, the remainder from state and federal treasuries. The Aid to Dependent Children case load doubled from 1972 to 1985, with an average grant of $362 a month. Food stamp recipients increased from about 1,200 in 1971 to nearly 1,750 in 1985. Medical assistance outlays grew from $364,872 in 1979 to $645,895 in October 1984, as more persons over age sixty-five required help. Social Services Director Scott Dickson said, "People may work in Detroit all their lives, but when they retire, they pack up and come north." He added: "Right now, if it wasn't for government money, I don't know what we'd do here. We've built a government economy up here and we're exporting our youth." Too many young people graduated "with no skill, or find that there is no market here for their skill." Young people continued to leave as they had since the 1920s; but others took some of their places, as shown in small shops, boutiques, and craft shops.[56]

A vast influx of retiring persons also brought with them their life savings. Their monthly pension and social security checks—money they had worked hard for in Flint, Detroit, Chicago, Milwaukee, and a host of smaller cities and towns in Michigan, Wisconsin, and far-flung regions—brought back the spirited, congenial paydays of the old-time mining days.

A May 16, 1964 conference at Marquette's Northern Michigan University—sponsored jointly by the Michigan Department of Labor, the Michigan Employment Security Commission, and the Women's Bureau of the U.S. Department of Labor—focused on "ways in which the talents and skills of women could be developed and utilized to improve the economy of the Upper Peninsula." About 50 percent of the fifty-three registrants came from the Calumet–Laurium, Hancock–Houghton, and Lake Linden–Hubbell areas, to explore the status of women, wage structures, training, minimum wages, equal-pay legislation, and ways to organize to find jobs.

Speakers urged women to become more active politically, to help develop a social climate "where a woman has the choice of going to work for a paycheck or as a volunteer, or, if she prefers, staying at home." They deplored the absence of young women at the

symposium, but all worked vigorously at stating views frankly. Copper
Country women meeting in this symposium raised the feminist standard before many of their compatriots in large urban centers began
their work five years later. In this, they simply repeated past patterns
formed by women in the Keweenaw Peninsula who saw problems and
set about solving them.[57] The Copper Country began the decade of
the 1990s with a population less than half that of its 1910 peak—
53,955 residents, where once there had been 110,031—but the spirit
insisting on high standards and maintaining human dignity amid
difficulties continued (as it had from the earliest days) wholesome
and vital.[58]

11

Strangers and Sojourners

THE HISTORY OF THE KEWEENAW PENINSULA THE HISTORY OF THE KEWEENAW PENINSULA encompasses the founding, flowering, and ebbing of a major industry —copper mining—on which a majority of inhabitants depended for a livelihood while it flourished. But more than that, this history is one of strangers and sojourners—men, women, and children who came from afar to develop communities around mines and create "a distinct character"[1] without completely obliterating the Ojibwa culture that had existed in various forms for two hundred years before the first Europeans arrived. Visiting tourists, as well as scholars from outside who later wrote of the Keweenaw, were not always aware of the mystique that prevailed. One had to have stayed long enough to experience the joy and sorrow so closely linked with the region's economy to realize what it was that made Copper Country people as distinctive as they were and are.

A recent historian has concluded that each "ethnic group . . . brought with [it] unique customs and qualities that have been incorporated into a common society, [and their descendants] still share a common concern for neighbors, . . . a brand of humor that is directed at each other without malice, and a spirit which routinely makes fun of adversity."[2] Those who too readily viewed the Copper Country as just another mining region or enjoyed the scenery while ignoring the people could never grasp the attraction the region holds for so many.

For those who stayed long enough—whether three hours or three years—the Keweenaw Peninsula also offered spiritual bounty: beauty, peace, goodness. When the Upper Peninsula was touted as "Cloverland" in 1926, visitor W. B. Fiske summed up well what still holds true: "Whether you intend to tour, camp, fish or hunt, this 'back to nature' land will make you forget your cares and worries and blot the memory of a laboring world left behind."[3] One need not be deep in forest or far afield. The visitor awakening in a Copper Country motel or resting at twilight heard the four-note song of the robin or witnessed the ever-stronger sunlight ushering in eternal spring.

By the 1940s, journalist John Bartlow Martin had discovered this haven for vacationers seeking "something new"; and Angus Murdoch, tourist turned popular historian, delighted readers with a narrative of the 1840s "boom" in copper and illustrious years that followed. Their books introduced strangers from the entire nation to the north Michigan wilderness–civilization, where rich and prosperous communities once flourished and descendants carried on.[4]

Always possessed of a deep sense of their history, local citizens, by the time of the nation's bicentennial celebration, developed a renewed interest in past achievements and continuing accomplishments. Books, booklets, and brochures told the story of those who built communities from Copper Harbor to Ontonagon. Slowly, like the rising of repressed emotions, the story of the 1913–14 labor struggle gained attention from new generations seeking identity. They took new interest in their ethnic heritage.[5]

The Porcupine Mountains (now a state park), Copper Harbor, Lake Fanny Hooe, the Brockway Mountain Drive, the agate-rich Lake Superior shores, the rugged reaches of Freda and Redridge, the magnificent Keweenaw Bay, and Baraga State Park—all drew visitors, as they had for decades. A turn to heritage marked the 1970s, as the Calumet Village centennial of 1975 resurrected myths like the story that "only a single vote in the State Legislature voided an attempt to relocate the [Michigan] Capital from Lansing to Calumet."[6] The village's theater was listed on the National Register of Historic Places, its Victorian opulence restored. Symphony orchestras, dance troupes, amateur theatricals, and a host of entertainments delight many there.

Keweenaw festivals drawing thousands to the peninsula were of long standing. The Michigan Tech Winter Carnival began officially in 1927, but its roots dated to 1922. By 1934, E. Judson Bentley built the first snow statue, a snowman in the shape of a giant hockey player. Each year, ice sculpture increased, becoming more elaborate; and by 1980, it developed into a fine art. Calumet, Hancock, and other towns offered winter carnivals in Depression years.[7]

New festivals followed: Octoberfest became established by 1980 at Copper Harbor, for two days each September. The Houghton County Fair, dormant until revived in the 1950s, celebrated a fortieth anniversary in August 1991—though a county fair had been held annually for more than forty years. As if in dread of approaching winter, Copper Country people assembled pumpkins, jams, jellies, knitted goods, cakes, pies, candy, and beverages at local jamborees, often importing trapeze artists and vocalists who, with orchestra, entertained young and old with songs like "Just a Gigolo" (1931) and "The Days of Wine and Roses" (1963). By the 1970s, Eagle Harbor gained a reputation for its annual Art in the Park, where local artists exhibited their work. German musicians came each year to help celebrate Strassenfest from Copper Harbor to Calumet, men and women housed in private homes and served bountiful breakfasts, their laundry washed by hosts who welcomed the Teutonic strangers come to help celebrate humanity.

Finns revived Laaskiainen as a Shrove Tuesday tradition in parts of Houghton County, announcing that all were welcome: "You need not be of Finnish heritage to join in." The FinnFest at Hancock attracted many and in 1992 commemorated seventy-five years of Finnish independence. At the recently opened Finnish–American Heritage Center (once a Catholic Church), the Hancock archives, museum, art gallery, and social center offered beauty, as well as information, to visitors.[8]

As mining faded into history, historical societies and museums organized or expanded to enable visitors to sample pioneer life vicariously: Coppertown at Calumet, Arcadian Copper Mine at Ripley, and No. 2 Quincy on the hill north of Hancock, where tourists saw "The World's Largest Steam Hoist" and local residents joined them in recalling great days when wires hummed, lights glowed, and thousands of men toiled in the earth's interior. At Lake Linden, one might visit the Houghton County Historical Society's museum and adjoining yards to see a one-room schoolhouse transported from the Trap Rock Valley, a log cabin built by NYA youth in the early 1940s, or brightly painted caboose and sturdy switch engines that once hauled cars filled with rock from mines. In the museum, one found school books, china, boots, badges, and photographs bringing to mind the great, glorious, sometimes grim past, when copper was king.[9]

Everywhere, Copper Country people cultivated their heritage. In 1965, a three-day presentation of Royce Willman's summer theater production, "Music International," drew capacity crowds with visitors from as far as Escanaba and Calumet to Ontonagon, where a cast of eighty performed musical numbers as Cornish and Finnish heritages received honor.[10] Historic buildings—of sandstone and rock unique to the area—at Houghton, Hancock, Lake Linden, Laurium, and Calumet became objects of scrutiny, study, and admiration of young architects, artists, and social scientists from afar, who called for their preservation. Did local citizens really know what they possessed? Perhaps not fully, but they had deep sentimental ties to the past. They joined in raising funds to repair deteriorating Italian Hall. By the early 1980s, the building was in such bad shape and the expenses necessary to repair, so great that the historic hall fell to the wrecker's ball. Where, once, local Italian–Americans presented plays they had written, sang songs, and recited their own poetry while more radically minded brothers and sisters called for a socialist America, Italian Hall gave way to a minipark honoring the seventy-four who perished when an unknown voice called "Fire!" on Christmas Eve, 1913.[11]

Reunions, family and social events, and celebrations honoring the past, continued to enliven the present, now inextricably linked with yesteryear. Hancock's Temple Jacob continued to serve on high holidays, as well as for weddings and funerals and occasions marking life's guideposts. Local churches underwent frequent renovation and published brochures detailing rich histories of people who cultivated good things of life.

At times, one remembered, with affection, outstanding persons from the past. Fanny Cash—in 1847, the only white woman living along the Ontonagon River—yearned for kin some six hundred miles distant, reachable only by overland trail or canoe. She raised children, sent a son to the Civil War, and was finally buried within a stone's throw of a hard-won wilderness home—her life typical of many. Historian Jamison remembered, writing that Fanny and others "turned ugliness to beauty, . . . gave us a heritage and a home, . . . taught us something of the nobility of self-sacrifice in which humility may become grandeur itself."[12]

Mining clerks and superintendents like John T. Reeder and William A. Childs, merchants like Norbert Kahn and Edward Lean, and untold men and women who taught in one-room schools passed into oblivion for most people. An unnamed Houghton "mining man," newly returned from the American West in 1903, reported that the "Lake Superior man" could always be recognized from others in mining camps because of "his energy and dash and vim . . . in all the work he does. . . . He is always busy." Harley Sachs of Michigan Technological University recalled a twelve-year-old boy's crisis at Red Jacket when the Jewish community there dwindled. Men whose names had been household words in mining or merchandising were forgotten.[13]

Some recalled Maggie Walz, who, at turn of century, won renown as an enterprising businesswoman. Born Maggie Tervola in Finland, she learned English rapidly and, with friend Linda Mahlbert, instructor at Suomi College, worked enthusiastically for women's rights and temperance. Maggie's death at sixty-five diminished the community's vitality, even among those who had bristled at her sonorous voice. Students recalled Ruth Lyon, who taught mathematics at Calumet High School; but few knew she was the first local woman appointed to the faculty there in 1908. She had graduated from the University of Michigan after work in other colleges and also did postgraduate work in Germany.[14] Barbara Evert of Houghton served as principal of M. M. Morrison School, Calumet, for decades. Each morning before her duties began there, she taught English (basics and literature) at Calumet High School to boys who majored in woodshop, challenging them with discussions of Eugene O'Neill's *Emperor Jones* and civil problems. She advocated "See America First"—but before that, "See the Upper Peninsula." Olive Hodges died at age ninety-eight, after years of retirement, having taught for forty-five years in the Calumet public school system. Some found it difficult to believe that Cora Jeffers had spent more than fifty years teaching—with others who knew that their pupils would succeed, after the encouragement they gave, the knowledge they imparted, and the discipline they offered.[15]

By the early 1980s, descendants of the Ojibwa turned to an enterprise long scorned by puritanical Anglo–Americans. Their casino and resort motel at Baraga attracted visitors from the Keweenaw Peninsula, as well as Wisconsin, to play games of chance and roulette, reminiscent of Las Vegas and Atlantic City. Earlier, their minimarket grocery and involvement in township affairs accompanied by activities outside the reservation spelled social involvement in a new American society. The Keweenaw Bay Tribal Council continued a decade-long discussion of where its jurisdiction lay over original boundaries of the L'Anse Reservation. A 1989 decision by U.S. District Judge Robert Holmes Bell upheld the Native Americans' rights over original boundaries, encompassing nearly sixty-thousand acres. Questions remained. Who had arrest powers in Baraga County? Only Native Americans?[16]

The history of the Keweenaw Peninsula has something to contribute to the debate over melting-pot theory versus cultural pluralism. Increasingly, throughout the United States, the so-called ethnic revival proved disconcerting, "a smokescreen for racism and other reactionary politics" obscuring realities. A chorus of social scientists agreed with historian Arthur Mann "that the common culture of Americans was much more important than the ethnic differences among them."[17] Nowhere was this more true than in the Keweenaw, where American institutions of law, education, language, and economic values attracted immigrants as the melting pot continued its slow, often laborious, constant acculturation and assimilation. In the Copper Country, descendants of various ethnic entities added

customs, folk ways, food preferences, ideals, and moral standards to
an ever-evolving social mix that made life here unique.

Methodists might still speak derisively of the Finnish "carrot
pasty"; but in time, every ethnic group made and sold pasties, introduced to the Keweenaw by the earliest Cornish miners. Churches,
lodges, and clubs raised money for charities through such sales. The
pasty's fame spread so far that Governor George Romney designated
May 24, 1968, as Michigan Pasty Day.[18] Foods such as the Slavs' *pot-
ica* (also spelled *povetica*), the Italians' *pollo alla cacciatora*, German
sauerkraut, Polish kielbasa, and Finns' *limpa* bread found adherents
among people thrown together by economic necessity who, despite
envy, hostility, and misunderstandings, mixed and merged over time.

Intermarriage and extramarital racial mixing had, from the beginning, prevailed. Whites and blacks formed liaisons, open and clandes-
tine. Europeans married Native Americans. Members of diverse ethnic
groups simply fell in love, married, and had children. As early as 1917,
sociologist Clemens Niemi noted the growing number of Finns and
Finnish–Americans marrying Americans descended from Croatian,
Italian, Norwegian, Swedish, Slavic, French, English, Canadian, or
German descent. He cited an instance of a Finnish woman who
married a Mexican, "both of them scarcely being able to express their
thoughts to one another through the English language. . . . [But]
neighbors say 'they are getting along fine'."[19]

The first generation clung to language, religion, and customs out
of sincere attachment or as needed strength in a land of hostile
strangers. Incoming ethnic groups found they had to join with others
in local congregations—as Finns did with Swedes, and Croatians
with Poles and Slovenians—before they could build their own church
buildings. Census data show that residential areas were not populated
exclusively by people of one nationality. In addition to a shared work-
place, members of diverse ethnic groups gathered at common dining
tables in boardinghouses. As population contracted and churches
closed, congregations were increasingly composed of descendants of
multiethnic groups.

Second-generation youngsters—sometimes embarrassed by what
they considered "foreign" cultural elements in speech, dress, or attitude that made them appear ridiculous in school—often broke away
in rebellion. Ashamed of their parents' accents, they also encountered
the strains of differing cultures. Corinne Olli, a second-generation
Finn, described her experiences:[20]

> The members of my generation were pulled two ways. . . . Our
> parents wanted us to retain something of our Finnishness; on
> the other hand, society, as represented by the school, wanted

us to be, as they said, un-hyphenated Americans; that is, just Americans, not Finnish–Americans. No wonder we were confused and rebellious.

By 1980, older Americans of Finnish descent worried that the young were losing much by not learning Finnish. One woman returned to Toivola about 1971 and found that for the first time in seventy years Juhannus (Saint John's Day) was no longer celebrated. With two friends at the beach, she "built a tiny fire [part of the day's ritual], decided the 'Old Days' were gone for good and sadly viewed the deserted beach"; none felt like talking. Twenty-one years later, more than eight hundred gathered, descendants of Finnish homesteaders and farmers, for a joyful Toivola reunion. Speakers recalled their teaching days at Misery Bay school in the 1930s or Toivola settlers who "suffered and died to help improve the American way of life." Typical of many reunions, this gathering blended ethnic nostalgia with American patriotism.[21]

Since the 1840s, the Keweenaw Peninsula had drawn thousands upon thousands of immigrants, many forsaking lives of misery with little economic future in Europe or Great Britain. While mining was hard and risky and fraught with accidents and death, immigrants sought opportunity, hoping eventually to own a home or farm, establish a business, and find a better life for themselves and their children. An untold number were sojourners, settling for a time in the Keweenaw, then moving to other mining fields or to towns and cities elsewhere. With later generations came education, acculturation, intermarriage, and youth cultures destructive of the old. In pursuit of their own American dreams, most of the young turned away from their ethnic heritage. They discovered that the way up the ladder of success in Detroit, Chicago, Milwaukee, and California seemed to call for the abandonment of what parents and grandparents held dear. In their eagerness to jettison old ways, later generations at times felt a loss of identity. The "ethnic revival" that began about 1968 and continued in varying strengths to the present may be understood as an attempt to supply values other than that of intense moneymaking.

But such a "revival" was more inclined to molding a new cultural milieu, in which ethnic elements juxtaposed with the dominant American middle-class culture. Purists avoided Saint Urho's Day; but hundreds of people enjoyed that winter festival combining Finnish American cultural remnants with myth, at Hancock and Calumet. Urho was concocted, some say, by Minnesota college students or businessmen weary of winter doldrums. Urho, it was claimed, "patron saint of Finnish–Americans" drove "grasshoppers out of Finland to save the grape vines." Some saw the festival's "official" date, March 16, as a not-so-subtle ridicule of Irish Americans, with whom Finns in the distant past had had their difficulties. Some intellectuals viewed part of the fascination for Saint Urho's Day to be part of the search for roots by young people who had lost much of their ancestral heritage.[22]

Much more important were scores of high school reunions in the four counties and hundreds of family reunions. In 1938, the first annual "Homecoming to Calumet" attracted hundreds of former residents. Some 150 members of the Upper Peninsula Club of Wayne County (all of them employed by the Ford Motor Company) made up the nucleus; but others came from Chicago, Milwaukee, Pontiac, Flint, and Bay City. They stayed for a week, joined local residents for a picnic at Electric Park, played ball, ran races, entertained their children, and danced from nine to one the next morning to the music of the Northern Collegians in the pavilion. At the 1950 homecoming, nine hundred danced at the Calumet Armory to the music of Steve Swedish and his Milwaukee orchestra, the leader described as "a Calumet boy who is now a leading midwestern musician." Two thousand attended a Catholic mass, where the Reverend George Laforest of Houghton "warned of the threat of communism and other ideologies . . . attempting to create disbelief in Christ and Christianity itself." Social conservatism ran deep in the Copper Country; some accused of being radical believed sincerely in established institutions.[23]

Hard-rock miners in 1968 launched a drive to raise fifty thousand dollars to assist the building of a dormitory–cafeteria at Suomi College. By this time, Suomi was an interdenominational, nonsectarian junior college offering liberal arts and business courses. A union official announced, "The union has compelling reasons for initiating this effort. . . . Our roots are deeply planted at Suomi College."[24] Many born in the Copper Country who left soon after graduating from high school retained fond memories of childhood. No matter where they might live, the Copper Country was "home." Others left and never returned, the Keweenaw communities being, for them, repressive places, their inhabitants, narrow-minded and provincial. Bitter feelings stemming from labor struggles festered for decades, but much was forgotten as time passed.

What was once resented was now accepted as amusing apocrypha, like the story of Calumet and Hecla, where general manager James MacNaughton's partiality to Scots as workers led once, in an interview, to his asking an applicant, "Are you a mechanic?" The man replied, "No, I am a MacDonald," to which MacNaughton responded, "Good! Come to work in the morning."[25] Two Cornish

miners, asked by their superintendent not to be discouraged by difficult rock underground and told by him that what they needed was
"pride and perseverance to help you," pondered the advice after the
superintendent left. One miner asked, "Say, Bill, who be they, Pride
and Perseverance?" The other replied, "I don't know, Tom—guess
they be the two Finns in the next stope."[26]

In 150 years, startling changes had come. Along with mine shafts
and locations, much had disappeared or been transformed. The commodious frame house on Red Jacket Road, where Agassiz stayed on
his annual visits, had become a hostel for abused women. The company offices now served as community medical center. The Quincy
steam hoist became a popular tourist attraction. Hancock's Hotel
Scott served, for a time, as a warehouse. Houghton's sport stadium
had undergone several transformations. No longer did a procession
of eighty "Austrian" Knights of Saint Stephen, brandishing swords,
wend its way, as in 1900 on December 26 in Red Jacket. Gone
forever was the annual harvest sale at Tecotzky's clothing store in
Calumet, where advertisements honored Halpa Jussi—mythological
Finnish figure, whose kindness and good nature served as ideals.
Gone were the energetic young women and men at Houghton who
danced the night away at the Amphidrome in the 1930s; gone was
the music of the Mandan Hayseeds at Electric Park. Local youth
continued to form musical groups. Their rock-and-roll beats thun-
dered at halls, wedding receptions, and reunions throughout the
Keweenaw. Where, once, copper workers and mine managers debated
the social structure and economic decision making, environmentalists
and advocates of new industry debated the future. A letter writer
argued: "People live here. It's not just a vacation retreat for the lower
peninsula, or an animal and fish preserve. . . . The past is the past, let's
work for a future together if we are to survive as a whole."[27]

Whatever the future would bring, one thing was certain: despite
economic hardships, community continued in the Copper Country.
Men, women, and children who continue to live there experience
the pleasures, woes, frustrations, and lustrations of community. The
annual reunion at Central Mine on a warm summer's day, where
one walked amid wild flowers and weathered miners' homes of days
past evoked the richness of community typical of the Keweenaw.
At Central, visitor Beatrice Putnam observed lilacs blooming beside
the "rubble of foundations and, mingling with the meadow grasses,
campanula, mallows and herbs [that recalled] beloved gardens of long
ago." Moving about, she found the location where, once, "Widow
Bryant's candy shop stood" and remembered that when a Bryant
daughter died of diphtheria, the physician ordered the destruction of
all the candy. The snow being so deep, the widow stacked it in the

henhouse until spring, when she discovered that her son and his friend had eaten all of it![28] All who once lived in the Keweenaw laughed over similar stories at reunions. Among drab details of everyday life, journals and diaries kept by pioneers and more recent ancestors reveal a joyous spirit, rich humor, and a sadness about life's brevity.[29]

Former residents visiting family graveplots—and those of people they never knew—at Eagle River, Clifton, and Schoolcraft cemeteries often felt a bond between the land of the living and the land of the dead. They had come together over many decades, strangers all—ambitious, restless, energetic, and hard-working. For some, the sojourn was short, for others, long—in this land where nature could be both edifying and harsh. Mines, mills, shops, dwellings, streets, and villages gave way; and others replaced them. The Keweenaw remained.

George H. Roberts, associated with the Central Mine reunion, once reflected upon the thousands of men and women who had made history simply with daily work and life in the Keweenaw Peninsula: "Places come and go, those we once knew are gone, but these hills, blue waters and the starlit heavens are everlasting."[30]

Notes

CHAPTER 1

1. John R. Halsey, "Miskwabik—Red Metal: Lake Superior Copper and the Indians of Eastern North America," *Michigan History* 67(September/October 1983): 34–35.

2. Patrick E. Martin, "Mining on Minong: Copper Mining on Isle Royale," *Michigan History* 74(May/June 1990): 19–20; George I. Quimby, *Indian Life in the Upper Great Lakes, 11,000 B.C. to A.D. 1800* (Chicago: University of Chicago Press, 1960), 49–63; idem, *Indian Culture and European Trade Goods* (Madison: University of Wisconsin Press, 1966), 18–19; George I. Quimby and Albert C. Spaulding, "The Old Copper Culture and the Keweenaw Waterway," *Anthropology*, 8 November 1957, pp. 189–201.

3. Halsey, "Miskwabik," 33–34, 37.

4. Ibid., 39, 41; Louise P. Kellogg, *The French Régime in Wisconsin and the Northwest* (Madison: State Historical Society of Wisconsin, 1925), 345.

5. Eric R. Wolf, *Europe and the People Without History* (Berkeley: University of California Press, 1982), 171; Emerson F. Greenman, *The Indians of Michigan* (Lansing: Michigan Historical Commission, 1961), 10; "Historical Notes," *Michigan History* 16(1932): 363; Henry M. Utley and Byron M. Cutcheon, *Michigan as a Province, Territory, and State, the Twenty-Sixth Member of the Federal Union* (New York: Publishing Society of Michigan, 1906), 1:86; William F. Gagnieur, "Indian Place Names in the Upper Peninsula and Their Interpretation," *Michigan History* 2(1918): 533.

6. Thomas L. McKenney, *Sketches of a Tour to the Lakes, of the Character and Customs of the Chippeway Indians and of Incidents Connected with the Treaty of Fond du Lac* (Baltimore: Fielding Lucas, Jr., 1827), 197.

7. Bela Hubbard, *Memorials of a Half-Century in Michigan and the Lake Region* (New York: G. P. Putnam's Sons, 1888), 10–11.

8. Bernard C. Peters, "The Origin and Meaning of Chippewa and French Place Names along the Shoreline of the Keweenaw Peninsula," *Michigan Academician* 17 (1984–85): 195–98, 202–10; Gagnieur, "Indian Place Names," 540.

9. Wolf, *Europe*, 167, 169; John G. Shea, *History of the Catholic Missions Among the Indian Tribes of the United States, 1529–1854* (New York: Edward Dunigan, 1855), 348.

10. George Copway (Kah-Ge-Gah-Bowh), *Indian Life and Indian History by an Indian Author* (Boston: Albert Colby, 1860), 61, 74, 77–79.

11. Copway, *Indian Life*, 29; Ronald A. Janke, *The Development and Persistence of U.S. Indian Land Problems as Shown by a Detailed Study of the Chippewa Indians* (Ann Arbor: Xerox University Microfilms, 1976), 144–46, 148–51.

12. Copway, *Indian Life*, 137–42.

13. Frances Densmore, *Chippewa Customs* (Washington: Government Printing Office, 1929), 17–18; for sampling of words, see Frederic Baraga, *A Theoretical and Practical Grammar of the Otchipwe Language*, 2d ed. (Montreal: Beauchemin & Valois, 1878), 14–16, 34, 45, 53, 71; everyday life of Ojibwa described in Ernest H. Rankin, *Indians of Gitchee Gumee* (Marquette, MI: Marquette County Historical Society, 1966), 5–17, 23.

14. W. B. Hinsdale, *Primitive Man in Michigan* (Ann Arbor: University of Michigan, 1925), 77; U.S. Congress, Senate, *Message from the President of the United States, to the Two Houses of Congress . . . December 24, 1849*, 31st Cong., 1st sess., pt. 3, 1030–31 (Alexander Ramsey Report, hereafter *Report, 1849*).

15. Copway, *Indian Life*, 104–9.

16. Frances Densmore, *How Indians Use Wild Plants for Food, Medicine, and Crafts* (New York: Dover, 1974), 344–45; Hinsdale, *Primitive Man in Michigan*, 83, 87; Copway, *Indian Life*, 130–35.

17. Copway, *Indian Life*, 129; James K. Jamison, *This Ontonagon Country* (Ontonagon, MI: Ontonagon Herald, 1939), 89–90; Charles B. Lawrence, "Ojibway Burials on Lake Superior to 1850," in *Baraga County Historical Pageant* (Baraga, MI: Baraga County Historical Society), 24–25; Warren's listings are from Densmore, *Chippewa Customs*, 10.

18. Shea, *History of the Catholic Missions*, 349–50; Walter Romig, *Michigan Place Names* (Grosse Pointe, MI: n.d.), 501.

19. Shea, *History of the Catholic Missions*, 353–54; Gagnieur, "Indian Place Names," 540, 546; Copway, *Indian Life*, 199–200; P. Chrysostomus Verwyst, *Life and Labors of Right Reverend Frederic Baraga* (Milwaukee: M. H. Wiltzius, 1900), 17–18.

20. Francis Parkman, *France and England in North America* (New York: Library of America, 1983), 1:737–38; *The Jesuit Relations and Allied Documents: Travels and Explorations of the Jesuit Missionaries in New France, 1610–1791*, ed. Reuben G. Thwaites (Cleveland: Burrows Brothers, 1899), 50:327; 121:265, 267.

21. *Jesuit Relations*, 50:267, 269.

22. Ibid., 51:259, 261.

23. Ibid., 50:267, 297–301; 51:63–65, 69.

24. Ibid., 50:241, 243, 249, 251, 257, 263, 265.

25. Edmund J. Danziger, *The Chippewas of Lake Superior* (Norman: University of Oklahoma Press, 1978), 30–31; Wolf, *Europe*, 159.

26. Danziger, *Chippewas of Lake Superior*, 4.

27. Wolf, *Europe*, 159.

28. Utley and Cutcheon, *Michigan*, 1:104–5.

29. Wayne E. Stevens, "The Michigan Fur Trade," *Michigan History* 29(1945): 489, 491; Densmore, *Chippewa Customs*, 9.

30. Danziger, *Chippewas of Lake Superior*, 29.

31. Stevens, "Michigan Fur Trade," 493.

32. Ibid., 494.

33. Danziger, *Chippewas of Lake Superior*, 32–33.

34. Ibid., 72.

35. Parkman, *France and England in North America*, 1:1319–21; the scholar quoted regarding traits is Danziger (*Chippewas of Lake Superior*, 32).

36. Grace L. Nute, *The Voyageur* (Saint Paul: Minnesota Historical Society, 1955), 3–10, 227, 260–61.

37. Joseph A. Ten Broeck, "Old Keweenaw," *Michigan Pioneer Collections* (Lansing: Wynkoop Hallenbeck Crawford, 1906), 30(1905): 140–41; McKenney stated (1826) that the *voyageurs'* songs were "for the most part not adapted to refined ears" (*Sketches of a Tour*, 254).

38. Wolf, *Europe*, 161.

39. Ibid., 163; Danziger, *Chippewas of Lake Superior*, 30; bishop quoted in Verwyst, *Life and labors*, 53; McKenney, *Sketches of a Tour*, 300.

40. Jamison, *This Ontonagon Country*, 108, 110–11; Wolf, *Europe*, 174, 194; Danziger, *Chippewas of Lake Superior*, 31, 59, 61, 67.

41. Alexander Henry, *Travels and Adventures in Canada and the Indian Territories Between the Years 1760 and 1776* (Edmonton: M. G. Hurtig, 1969), 186, 189–90.

42. Ibid., 186–87.

43. Ibid., 187–89.

44. Ibid., 195–97 and n.

45. Ibid., 220, 225–27; Helen E. Knuth, *Economic and Historical Background of Northeastern Minnesota Lands: Chippewa Indians of Lake Superior* (New York: Garland, 1974), 14.

46. Wolf, *Europe*, 176.

47. Danziger, *Chippewas of Lake Superior*, 68–69; William W. Warren, *History of the Ojibway People* (1885; reprint, Saint Paul: Minnesota Historical Society, 1984), 382.

48. James L. Carter and Ernest H. Rankin, eds., *North to Lake Superior: The Journal of Charles W. Penny, 1840* (Marquette, MI: John M. Longyear Research Library, 1970), 60; Hubbard, *Memorials*, 59–60.

49. Danziger, *Chippewas of Lake Superior*, 71.

50. Ibid., 71–72.

51. Ibid., 72.

52. Jamison, *This Ontonagon Country*, 82.

53. McKenney, *Sketches of a Tour*, 256–57.

54. Warren, *History of the Ojibway People*, 117–18.

55. Peters, "Origin and Meaning," 196; David J. Krause, *The Making of a Mining District: Keweenaw Native Copper 1500–1870* (Detroit: Wayne State University Press, 1992), 122, 134.

CHAPTER 2

1. McKenney, *Sketches of a Tour*, 242.

2. Ibid., 243, 245, 247.

3. Ibid., 245, 248, 252.

4. Andrew C. McLaughlin, *Lewis Cass* (New York: Chelsea House, 1980), 115–17; Utley and Cutcheon, *Michigan*, 3:328.

5. John H. Forster, "Early Settlement of the Copper Regions of Lake Superior," *Michigan Pioneer Collections* 7(1884): 193.

6. McLaughlin, *Lewis Cass*, 127.

7. Jamison, *This Ontonagon Country*, 91.

8. Krause, *Making of a Mining District*, 95–96.

9. Stephen D. Bingham, ed., *Early History of Michigan, with Biographies of State Officers, Members of Congress, Judges and Legislators* (Lansing: Thorp & Godfrey, 1888), 574; George N. Fuller, ed., *Geological Reports of Douglass Houghton, First State Geologist of Michigan, 1837–1845)* (Lansing: Michigan Historical Commission, 1928), 9–12, 20, 67–68; Lew Allen Chase, "Early Days of Michigan Mining: Pioneering Land Sales and Surveys," *Michigan History* 29(1945): 171, 173; for Michigan–Ohio dispute, see Claude S. Larzelere, "The Boundaries of Michigan," *Michigan Pioneer Collections* 30(1905): 23.

10. Fuller, *Geological Reports*, 370, 372, 378–80, 474, 476–77, 486–91, 558.

11. Ibid., 478, 485, 492–93.

12. Ibid., 531–33. 556.

13. Ibid., 557.

14. Ibid., 665–66, 681.

15. Ibid., 622.

16. Carter and Rankin, *North to Lake Superior*, 47–48; Bernard C. Peters, ed., *Lake Superior Journal: Bela Hubbard's Account of the 1840 Houghton Expedition* (Marquette, MI: Northern Michigan University Press, 1983), 52; Hubbard, *Memorials*, 53.

17. Fuller, *Geological Reports*, 566–67, 574.

18. Peters, *Lake Superior Journal*, 63–67; Hubbard, *Memorials*, 53.

19. Carter and Rankin, *North to Lake Superior*, 60–61, 63; Hubbard, *Memorials*, 59–60, 62.

20. Hubbard, *Memorials*, 189–90.

21. J. W. Foster and J. D. Whitney, *Report on the Geology and Topography of a Portion of the Lake Superior Land District in the State of Michigan*, pt. 1, report prepared for House of Representatives, 31st Cong., 1st sess., 1850, exec. Doc. 69 (hereafter Foster and Whitney, *Report, 1850*), pp. 14–15.

22. John Bartlow Martin, *Call It North County: The Story of Upper Michigan* (1944; reprint, Detroit: Wayne State University Press, 1986), 44–47.

23. For detailed information and reprinted government documents, see Lawrence T. Fadner, *Fort Wilkins 1844 and the U.S. Mineral Land Agency 1843* (New York: Vantage, 1966); see also notes in *Michigan History* 29(1945): 236; for visitors, see John R. Saint John, *A True Description of the Lake Superior Country* (1846; reprint, Iron Mountain, MI: Secord, 1988).

24. Robert J. Hybels, "The Lake Superior Copper Fever, 1841–47," *Michigan History* 34(1950): 309.

25. Fuller, *Geological Reports*, 12; W. H. Sherzer, "An Unpublished Episode in Early Michigan History," *Michigan History* 16(1932): 214–17; "Historical News and Notes," *Michigan History* 29(1945): 579–84.

26. Chase, "Early Days of Michigan Mining," 179; Charles T. Jackson to Secretary of the Treasury Robert J. Walker, 19 July 1848, Bentley Historical Library, Ann Arbor (original at Marquette County Historical Society); Jackson's report in *Report, 1849*, 385–86.

27. Martin, *Call It North Country*, 73.

28. Whitney field notes in *Report, 1849*, 754–58.

29. Krause, *Making of a Mining District*, 208, 211.

30. *Report, 1849*, 435–36.

31. Ibid., 464, 479.

32. Hybels. "Lake Superior Copper Fever," 226, 228, 233.

33. Forster, "Early Settlement," 187.

34. Lew Allen Chase, "Early Copper Mining in Michigan," *Michigan History* 29(1945): 26–27.

35. Forster, "Early Settlement," 188.

36. Letter reprinted in *Sunday Mining Gazette* (Houghton), 24 October 1926.

37. Forster, "Early Settlement," 186–87, 191.

38. Ibid., 186–87.

39. Chase, "Early Copper Mining in Michigan," 25.

40. John H. Forster Papers, B4-C, Michigan Historical Collections, Bentley Historical Library, Ann Arbor.

41. Quoted in Utley and Cutcheon, *Michigan*, 3:332.

42. Charles Lanman, *A Canoe Voyage up the Mississippi and Around Lake Superior in 1846*, reprint edition (1847; reprint, Grand Rapids, MI: Black Letter, 1978), 155–56; originally titled *A Summer In The Wilderness*.

43. William B. Gates, Jr., *Michigan Copper and Boston Dollars: An Economic History of the Michigan Copper Mining Industry* (New York: Russell & Russell, 1969), 12–13.

44. Chase, "Early Days of Michigan Mining," 166, 168; James Fisher, "Fort Wilkins," *Michigan History* 29(1945): 157; Hybels, "Lake Superior Copper Fever," 242, 312; Foster and Whitney, *Report, 1850*, 15.

45. Alexis de Tocqueville, *Democracy in America*, ed. J. P. Mayer, trans. George Lawrence (Garden City, NY: Doubleday, 1969), 1:347.

46. Fadner, *Fort Wilkins 1844*, 203–4; Gates, *Michigan Copper*, 3, 6; George W. Thayer, "From Vermont to Lake Superior in 1845," *Michigan Pioneer Collections* 30(1905): 549–50, 564.

47. Thayer, "From Vermont," 564–66.

48. Ibid., 562; Forster, "Early Settlement," 191–92.

49. Forster, "Early Settlement," 190–92.

50. Her diaries span the years 1866–97, with occasional omissions due, in part, to illness. See the Brockway Family Collection, Michigan Technological University Archives, Houghton.

51. Ibid.

52. Lucena Harris Brockway to her parents, 22 April 1844, printed in *Sunday Mining Gazette* (Houghton), 17 October 1926.

53. *History of the Upper Peninsula of Michigan* (Chicago: Western Historical, 1883), 177 (hereafter, *History Upper Peninsula*); see also biographical sketch of Daniel D. Brockway in this volume.

54. Daniel D. Brockway to his parents and friends, 14 October 1844, printed in *Sunday Mining Gazette* (Houghton), 17 October 1926.

55. Lucena Harris Brockway to her sister 27 April 1845, and to her parents, 10 December 1844, printed in *Sunday Mining Gazette*, 24 October 1926.

56. John H. Pitezel to his mother Mary Plane [Plain?], 9 October 1848, Pitezel Letters, Clarke Historical Library, Central Michigan University, Mount Pleasant, MI.

57. John H. Pitezel to his brother Joshua, 18 April and 24 August 1848, Pitezel Letters, Clarke Historical Library, Central Michigan University, Mount Pleasant, MI.

58. Chase, "Early Copper Mining," 29.

59. Saint John, *True Description*, 107; *Report, 1849*, 432.

60. Jackson's advice in *Report, 1849*, 473; Hybels, "Lake Superior Copper Fever," 98–99; Lanman, *Canoe Voyage*, 155.

61. Foster and Whitney, *Report, 1850*, 80.

62. Saint John, *True Description*, 78.

63. Statistics compiled by J. W. Foster and S. W. Hill, in *Report, 1849*, 760–65;

Foster and Whitney, *Report, 1850, 127,* 132, 134–43 and 146–51 (tabular statement of existing mines and numbers of men employed).

64. Forster, "Early Settlement," 192–93; Hybels, "Lake Superior Copper Fever," 326.

65. Jackson's comments on Isle Royale in *Report, 1849,* 427, 474; Carter and Rankin, *North to Lake Superior,* 37–39; Hubbard, *Memorials,* 22–23; for valuable information on Ojibwa social organization, see Peters, *Lake Superior Journal,* 48–49 and nn. 49–51, 53, 60.

66. Daniel D. Brockway to relatives, 22 April 1844, printed in *Sunday Mining Gazette* (Houghton), 17 October 1926.

67. Mrs. W. A. Childs, "Reminiscences of Old Keweenaw," *Michigan Pioneer Collections* 30(1905): 150.

68. *History Upper Peninsula,* 176–77; *Baraga County Historical Pageant, Souvenir Book,* 16, 18–19.

69. John H. Pitezel to his brother Joseph, 13 September 1844, and to his mother Mary Plane [Plain?], 14 October 1844, Pitezel Letters, Clarke Historical Library, Central Michigan University, Mount Pleasant, MI. As for L'Anse, Pitezel wrote his mother, "This is a delightful place and there is here a fine little society of intelligent white people who live all around us."

70. John H. Pitezel to his mother, 28 October, 1845, Pitezel Letters, Clarke Historical Library, Central Michigan University, Mount Pleasant, MI. In 1884, Pitezel recalled how in the mid-1840s, both sides of the coast and all of Keweenaw Bay "swarmed" with bark canoes of Native Americans and how, in 1883, he met, again, Mr. Bass, one of his 1847 Native American guides on a two-week trip from L'Anse to Grand Island, 240 miles distant. See "Fresh Breezes from Lake Superior," 1884, Pitezel Papers, folder 7:4, 6–7, Clarke Historical Library, Central Michigan University, Mount Pleasant, MI.

71. John H. Pitezel to his mother, 28 October and 19 December, 1845, Pitezel Letters, Clarke Historical Library, Central Michigan University, Mount Pleasant, MI.

72. John H. Pitezel, *Journal 1846–1848,* Clarke Historical Library, Central Michigan University, Mount Pleasant, MI, pp. 37–38, 71–72.

73. Ibid., 48, 69–71, 74–76, 80.

74. Ibid., 63–65; idem, *Journal 1848–1849,* Clarke Historical Library, Central Michigan University, Mount Pleasant, MI, pp. 15, 105–7, 110–11.

75. Idem, *Journal 1846–1848,* 39–45.

76. Ibid., 46–50, 94–95, 109–15, 118–21.

77. Ibid., 51–52, 78–80, 100–101, 121–24, 127–28; idem, *Journal 1848–1849,* 19–20. He wrote his brother Joshua from Cliff Mine, 13 June 1847, "It would astonish you to see the vast masses of copper which are tumbled out of some of the mines [but] Drunkeness, gambling and almost every species of vice stalk about with unblushing front in the day time. . . . Things must change for the better when things become more permanent." See Pitezel Letters, Clarke Historical Library, Central Michigan University, Mount Pleasant, MI.

78. Regis M. Walling and N. Daniel Rupp, eds., *The Diary of Bishop Frederic Baraga* (Detroit: Wayne State University Press, 1990), 21–31.

79. Joseph Gregorich, *The Apostle of the Chippewas* (Chicago: Bishop Baraga Association, 1932), 56–57; Romig, *Michigan Place Names,* 32; Verwyst, *Life and Labors,* 320.

80. Verwyst, *Life and Labors,* 210, 212, 214–15.

81. Ibid., 214.

82. Ibid., 209, 216–17.

83. Ibid., 209; Gregorich, *Apostle of the Chippewas,* 57–61.

84. John H. Pitezel to his brother, 11 July 1845 and 8 April 1846, Pitezel Letters, Clarke Historical Library, Central Michigan University, Mount Pleasant, MI.

85. *Baraga County Historical Pageant, Souvenir Book,* 72; Pitezel's 1883 comments on Fr. Baraga see Walling and Rupp, *Diary of Bishop Baraga,* 26.

86. Verwyst, *Life and Labors,* 224, 238–39.

87. Weather and seasons described by Foster and Whitney, *Report, 1850,* 54, 56; Saint John, *True Description,* 110.

88. Verwyst, *Life and Labors,* 234–35, 238–39.

89. Ibid., 300, 309.

90. Ibid., 232–33; for schools and agriculture at Keweenaw Bay, see *Report, 1849,* 1149, 1151; Baraga and Pitezel purchased the land on which their missions were located "and deeded the land to the Indians." See Walling and Rupp, *Diary of Bishop Baraga,* 26.

CHAPTER 3

1. John Greenleaf Whittier, "On Receiving an Eagle's Quill from Lake Superior," in *The Poetical Works of Whittier* (Boston: Houghton Mifflin, 1975), 144–45. Sarah J. Clarke [Grace Greenwood], personal friend of the Whittiers, had visited the Upper Peninsula and sent Whittier the eagle's feather. See Roland H. Woodwell, *John Greenleaf Whittier: A Biography* (Haverhill, MA: Trustees of the John Greenleaf Whittier Homestead, 1985), 218; Ralph H. Gabriel, *The Course of American Democratic Thought* (New York: Roland, 1940), 143.

2. U.S. Department of Commerce, Bureau of the Census, *Population* (hereafter, U.S. Census), 1850:882–83, 1860:264–65, 1870:630.

3. Larry D. Lankton and Charles K. Hyde, *Old Reliable: An Illustrated History of the Quincy Mining Company* (Hancock, MI: Quincy Mine Hoist Association, 1982), 11.

4. U.S. Census, 1850:882–83 and 890, 1860:264–65.

5. Danziger, *Chippewas of Lake Superior,* 86.

6. William H. Hathaway, "County Organization in Michigan," *Michigan History* 2:(1918): 586, 590–92, 598; John H. Forster, "Lake Superior Country," *Michigan Pioneer Collections* 8(1886): 136–37.

7. *Report, 1849,* 957–58 (annual report of Brown), 1032; Carter and Rankin, *North to Lake Superior,* 52–54.

8. For a description of the entire trip in the Ontonagon country, see Moritz Wagner and Carl Scherzer, *Reisen in Nordamerika in den Jahren 1852 und 1853* (Leipzig: Arnoldische Buchhandlung, 1857), 2:281–307. A typescript translation of chapter 20 is in the Keweenaw Historical Society Collection, B3, no. 147, Michigan Technological University Archives, Houghton.

9. *Report, 1849,* 1157.

10. Danziger, *Chippewas of Lake Superior,* 4–5, 86; *Michigan State Gazetteer and Business Directory for 1863–64* (Detroit: Clark, 1863), 35 (hereafter, *Michigan Gazetteer, 1863–64*); Commissioner Brown in his 30 November 1849 report argued that although Christianity helped dissipate the "ignorance and superstition" of many Native Americans, it might be necessary later to purchase all of their lands east of the Mississippi River and provide for their removal and concentration west of that river, since while many had turned successfully to agriculture, mechanical arts, and adopted written constitutions modeled on that of the United States, some simply could not

be helped, and all attempts "to civilize and christianize" them proved unavailing. See *Report, 1849*, 944, 955-57.

11. B. Frank Emery, "Fort Wilkins, 1844–46: A Frontier Stockaded Post Built To Protect Michigan's First Copper Mines" (Old Forts and Historical memorial Association, Detroit, 1932, Typescript), 7–8, 31–32, 39–40 42–43; Verwyst, *Life and Labors*, 340.

12. D. Houston, et al. *Copper Manual: Copper Mines, Copper Statistics, and a Summary of Information on Copper* (New York: Pratt, 1897), 9–10; for the 1863 observer, see Philip P. Mason, ed., *Copper Country Journal: The Diary of Schoolmaster Henry Hobart, 1863–1864* (Detroit: Wayne State University Press, 1991), 206; Forster, "Lake Superior Country," 138–39; Joseph Austrian, "Autobiographical and Historical Sketches," typescript, Michigan Technological University Archives, Houghton p. 45; Joseph W. V. Rawlings, "Reminiscences," autograph manuscript, Keweenaw Historical Society Collection, B3, no. 156, Michigan Technological University Archives, Houghton, pp. 1, 3–4.

13. Rawlings, "Reminiscences," pp. 1–3, 5; *Report, 1849*, 479; Alfred Meads, "History of Ascension Church at Ontonagon," *Michigan Pioneer Collections* 30(1905): 497, 506.

14. Mason, *Copper Country Journal*, 129–30, 143, 159, 183, 207.

15. Joseph Austrian's surname was actually Oestreicher. For biographical information, see his "Autobiographical and Historical Sketches," 1–5, 40, 48, 188; for life at Eagle River and Cliff Mine, see pp. 42–43, 48, 50–51, 67.

16. Ibid., 41, 47; Joseph W. V. Rawlings, "Recollections of a Long Life," autograph manuscript, Michigan Technological University Archives, Houghton, MI, pp. 15–16; *Michigan Gazetteer, 1863–64*: 291–92, 347, 591.

17. For Rathbone material, see various clippings, esp. *Evening Copper Journal* (Hancock), 16 May 1925, Keweenaw Historical Society Collection, B2, no. 139, Michigan Technological University Archives, Houghton, MI. For pioneer schooling, see "History of Old School" and school census, Dist. 1, Eagle Harbor Township, 1868, autograph manuscript—both in Keweenaw Historical Society Collection, B2, no. 139, Michigan Technological University Archives; School inspectors' reports, 1865, microfilm, reel 1116, State Archives, Lansing, MI; and *Michigan Gazetteer, 1863–64*:291, 567.

18. *Michigan Gazetteer, 1863–64*, 232–33, 567; R.E.R. (tourist), to editor, *Toledo Blade*, 1 September 1865, in Keweenaw Historical Society Collection, B2, no. 135, Michigan Technological University Archives, Houghton, MI.

19. Daniel D. Brockway to George S. Swartz and James Cooper, 21 March 1861; idem to S. P. Brady, 15 April and 17 June, 1861; idem to "Friend Mack," 29 April 1861; idem to Mr. McCausland, 8 June and 3 July 1861; idem to his brother, 18 October 1861—all in his Letterbook, 1857–66, Michigan Historical Collections, Bentley Historical Library, Ann Arbor.

20. Forster, "Lake Superior Country," 137; Wagner and Scherzer, *Reisen* (typescript translation) 1–2; Jamison, *This Ontonagon Country*, 152–53; *Michigan Gazetteer, 1863–64*, 78–79, 429.

21. *Michigan Gazetteer, 1863–64*, 429; Jamison, *This Ontonagon Country*, 126–27, 154–55; Wagner and Scherzer, *Reisen* (typescript translation), 6; Forster, "Lake Superior Country," 137–38.

22. Jamison, *This Ontonagon Country*, 155.

23. Ibid., 152–53; *Michigan Gazetteer, 1863–64*, 429; Verwyst, *Life and Labors*, 285, 300–301, 323–24. On his 1864 visit to Ontonagon, Baraga found the Ursuline convent growing, with fifteen sisters, novices, thirty boarding scholars, and a day school for "outside pupils" (ibid., 347).

24. Wagner and Scherzer, *Reisen* (typescript translation), 15; Meads, "Ascension Church," 495–503.

25. *Report, 1849*, 704; Schoolcraft quotation in Jamison, *This Ontonagon Country*, 114; Cornish anecdote in *Ontonagon Herald*, 31 March 1908, clipping, Keweenaw Historical Society Collection, B2, no. 132, Michigan Technological University Archives, Houghton, MI.

26. Gagnieur, "Indian Place Names," 545; for removal of boulder, see Senate, *Report To Accompany Joint Resolution S. 14, April 1, 1844*, 28th Cong., 1st sess., 1844.

27. Gates, *Michigan Copper*, 12–13; Lankton and Hyde, *Old Reliable*, 10.

28. Lankton and Hyde, *Old Reliable*, 1.

29. "In the mines as elsewhere, the American citizen possessed the happy faculty of adapting himself to circumstances to his own use" (Forster, "Lake Superior Country," 143).

30. Samuel S. Robinson, Calendar to the Letterbooks, Letterbook, pt. 2, no. 497ff., Robinson Papers, Michigan Historical Collections, Bentley Historical Library, Ann Arbor.

31. Samuel S. Robinson to J. P. Brewer, 18 December 1863; idem to wife Eliza, 13 November 1863; idem to J. N. Wright, 21 November 1863, Miscellaneous Letters; Estimate of Supplies Needed for 1866, Letterbook, pt. 3, no. 711ff.; letters to unspecified correspondents, 5–6 February 1866, nos. 690, 703—all in Robinson Papers. Michigan Historical Collections, Bentley Historical Library, Ann Arbor.

32. Samuel S. Robinson, Letterbook, pt. 3, no. 692ff.; Letterbook A, no. 28ff., no. 34, Robinson Papers, Michigan Historical Collections, Bentley Historical Library, Ann Arbor.

33. Eleanor Alexander, *East Hancock Revisited: History of a Neighborhood, Circa 1880–1920* (Hancock, MI, 1984), 3; Gordon Barkell, ed., *Hancock, Michigan Centennial* (Hancock, MI: Hancock Centennial Committee, 1963), 11; Forster, "Early Settlement," 192; *Daily Mining Gazette* (Houghton), 6 March 1901, clipping, Keweenaw Historical Society Collection, B2, no. 136, Michigan Technological University Archives, Houghton, MI; Ransom Shelden Scrapbook, Michigan Historical Collections, Bentley Historical Library, Ann Arbor; Gates, *Michigan Copper*, 12–13.

34. Barkell, *Hancock*, 11–12.

35. Ibid., 11–13; Alexander, *East Hancock*, 1; Claire B. Moyer, *Ke-Wee-Naw: The Crossing Place* (Denver: Big Mountain, 1966), 95; Austrian, "Autobiographical and Historical Sketches," 52–55, Michigan Technological University Archives, Houghton, MI; *Michigan Gazetteer, 1863–64*, 336, 572.

36. *Houghton Centennial Souvenir History and Program* (Houghton, MI 1961), 3; C. Harry Benedict, *Red Metal: The Calumet and Hecla Story* (Ann Arbor: University of Michigan Press, 1952), 40–45; Benjamin Wright to A. J. Wright, 18 May 1860, Letters 1858–60, Michigan Historical Collections, Bentley Historical Library, Ann Arbor.

37. *Houghton Centennial*, 3; Walling and Rupp, *Diary of Bishop Baraga*, 146; Verwyst, *Life and Labors*, 299–300, 310, 319–20; Alexander, *East Hancock*, 3; *Michigan Gazetteer, 1863–64*, 347.

38. Benjamin Wright to A. J. Wright, 18 May 1860, Letters 1858–60, Michigan Historical Collections, Bentley Historical Library, Ann Arbor.

39. John H. Forster, "War Times in the Copper Mines," *Michigan Pioneer Collections* 18(1892): 376; idem, "Lake Superior Country," 141. Forster recalled that sixteen years earlier, Portage Lake "reposed in sylvan solitudes; only occasionally . . . disturbed by the Indian canoe or the boat of the enterprising explorers," these waters "led to the Grand Portage on the north[west] and had been for centuries the highway

of the Indian tribes in their migrations or forages" (idem, "Early Settlement," 189; *Michigan Gazetteer, 1863–64*, 94).

40. *Michigan Gazetteer, 1863–64*, 347–48; Samuel S. Robinson to S. N. Warner, 1866, Letterbook, pt. 3, no. 722, Robinson Papers, Michigan Historical Collections, Bentley Historical Library, Ann Arbor; *Houghton Centennial*, 7, 9, 45.

41. *Houghton Centennial*, 13.

42. Forster, "Lake Superior Country," 144; idem, "War Times," 377.

43. Gabriel, *Course of American Democratic Thought*, 83, 86.

44. Ibid., 87.

45. Samuel S. Robinson to William Warner, 12 January 1864, Calendar to the Letterbooks, Robinson Papers, Michigan Historical Collections, Bentley Historical Library, Ann Arbor.

46. Samuel S. Robinson, autobiographical sketch, prob. 1865, Letterbook, pt. 2, no. 497ff., Robinson Papers, Michigan Historical Collections, Bentley Historical Library, Ann Arbor.

47. Samuel S. Robinson, Circular, 8 June 1864, Miscellaneous Letters, B 147-S, Robinson Papers, Michigan Historical Collections, Bentley Historical Library, Ann Arbor.

48. Forster, "War Times," 381; Hybels, "Lake Superior Copper Fever," 231.

49. *Evening Copper Journal* (Hancock), 9 April 1924; Austrian, "Autobiographical and Historical Sketches," 61–62, Michigan Technological University Archives, Houghton, MI; Benjamin Wright to A. J. Wright, 18 May 1860, Letters 1858–60, Michigan Historical Collections, Bentley Historical Library, Ann Arbor.

50. *Houghton Centennial*, 9; *Michigan Gazetteer, 1863–64*, 347; Forster, "Lake Superior Country," 138; Henry Hobart described an all-day journey via stage (horse and sleigh) from Cliff Mine to Houghton, 23 December 1863: "The snow was about four feet deep; still the road was very good," thirty-five miles through a dense forest and the ground "not rough—very level with the exception of a few small hills" (Mason, *Copper Country Journal*, 243–44).

51. Samuel S. Robinson to Mr. and Mrs. Franklin Norton, 1 January 1864, Miscellaneous Letters, and to unspecified correspondent, 18 December 1863, Letterbook, pt. 1, no. 59—both in Robinson Papers, Michigan Historical Collections, Bentley Historical Library, Ann Arbor.

52. Lucena Harris Brockway, Diary, 13 January and 6 May 1867, Brockway Family Collection, Michigan Technological University Archives, Houghton, MI.

53. Verwyst, *Life and Labors*, 217; on storms, see Ten Broeck, "Old Keweenaw," 144; Childs, "Reminiscences," 151–52.

54. *Report, 1849*, 706; Pitezel described in great detail a fierce Lake Superior storm 13 October 1846 as he and others aboard a sailing ship, unable to reach their Keweenaw destination, retreated to Sault Sainte Marie: "One woman . . . very much frightened . . . entreated me to pray for her which . . . I did to the best of my ability; but as I was vomiting much of the time I found it scarcely possible to offer up a vocal prayer," *Journal 1846–48*, 26–30, Clarke Historical Library, Central Michigan University, Mount Pleasant, MI.

55. A. N. Bliss, "Federal Land Grants for Internal Improvements in the State of Michigan," *Michigan Pioneer Collections* 7(1884): 63–64; Grace Lee Nute, *Lake Superior* (Indianapolis: Bobbs–Merrill, 1944), 248.

56. *Michigan Gazetteer, 1863–64*, 94; for a good description of the east end of Portage waterway circa 1859–60, see Forster, "Lake Superior Country," 139–41.

57. James Edwards, "How We Crossed Portage Lake Before and After 1875," typescript, Keweenaw Historical Society Collection, B3, no. 148, Michigan Technological University Archives, Houghton, MI; *Michigan Gazetteer, 1863–64*, 347; *History*

Upper Peninsula, 254. Ripley, near Hancock, served as oldest ferry landing on Portage Lake, service having begun in 1846. See Michigan Writers' Program of the WPA, *Michigan: A Guide to the Wolverine State* (New York: Oxford University Press, 1949), 589.

58. *Michigan Gazetteer, 1863–64*, 56, 96.

59. *Report, 1849*, 474 Rawlings, "Reminiscences," 2; Senter's shipping order, 8 September 1851, and others, B2, no. 120; Joseph A. Ten Broeck, "A Sketch of John Senter of Houghton," *Michigan Pioneer Collections* 30(1905): 157; Utley and Cutcheon, *Michigan*, 3:333.

60. Daniel D. Brockway to "Friend Mack," 29 April 1861, Letterbook 1857–66; Samuel S. Robinson to unnamed correspondent, 13 January 1864, Letterbook, pt. 1, no. 17, Robinson Papers; John H. Forster, Letterpress Book, pp. 101–2, 108, Mullet Family Papers; Correspondence, 5 June 1861, 14 November 1863, Forster Papers, B4-C—all in Michigan Historical Collections, Bentley Historical Library, Ann Arbor; Forster, "Lake Superior Country," 147; idem, "War Times," 375, 380; Lankton and Hyde, *Old Reliable*, 17–18.

61. John H. Forster to Colonel John Harris, 17 August 1862, J. H. Forster Papers, B4-C; Certificate of Exemption from Draft in Houghton County, Documents and Miscellaneous, Mullett Family Papers—both in Michigan Historical Collections, Bentley Historical Library, Ann Arbor; Verwyst, *Life and Labors*, 334, 343.

62. Samuel S. Robinson, Letterbook A, no. 103ff., Robinson Papers, Michigan Historical Collections, Bentley Historical Library, Ann Arbor.

63. William Heywood to John H. Forster, 8 October 1861, Correspondence–Business, 1852–85, Mullett Family Papers, B1, Michigan Historical Collections, Bentley Historical Library, Ann Arbor. Forster in a letter to an unspecified correspondent, 28 July 1861, described the battle of First Bull Run as "sickening," claimed he was not surprised at the Union defeat, attacked politicians "from whom come all our wars" and hoped they would leave President Lincoln and General Winfield Scott alone, and referred to the "insane cry 'Onward to Richmond'." See Correspondence–Family, 1860–62, Mullett Family Papers, B1, Michigan Historical Collections, Bentley Historical Library, Ann Arbor.

64. *History Upper Peninsula*, 111–17; Charles Willman, "Ontonagon County in the Civil War," typescript, Clarke Library, Central Michigan University, Mount Pleasant, MI, pp. 5–6, 8–10, 13; Jamison, *This Ontonagon Country*, 158–60.

65. Forster, "War Times," 379; John H. Forster to Charles Emery, 4 February 1861, Letterpress Book, Mullett Family Papers, Michigan Historical Collections, Bentley Historical Library, Ann Arbor, pp. 101–2, 108.

66. Samuel S. Robinson to unspecified correspondents, 3 October 1863 and 13 January 1864, Letterbook, pt. 1, nos. 25, 77, Robinson Papers, Michigan Historical Collections, Bentley Historical Library, Ann Arbor.

67. Samuel S. Robinson to F. G. White, 27 May 1865, Letterbook, pt. 2, no. 382ff., Robinson Papers, Michigan Historical Collections, Bentley Historical Library, Ann Arbor.

68. Samuel S. Robinson to Captain O. D. Robinson, 5 August 1865, Letterbook, pt. 2, no. 492ff., Robinson Papers, Michigan Historical Collections, Bentley Historical Library, Ann Arbor; Jane Masters' story in Martin, *Call It North Country*, 81.

69. For complaint of apathy, neglect, and migrating parents ignorant of Michigan law (Franklin Township, Houghton County)—along with contrary views, describing students as "well behaved and . . . anxious to learn . . . as a general thing, . . . very punctual" (Algonquin Township, Ontonagon County) and mentioning interested parents who came to school on examination days (Pewabic Township, Ontonagon

County)—see School inspectors' reports, 1865, Reels 1116–17, State Archives, Lansing, MI.

70. Ibid.

71. Ibid.

72. Ibid.

73. *Houghton Centennial*, 5, 23; Florence E. Paton, "History of the Schools of Portage Township in the Copper Country," *Michigan History* 2 (1918): 556–59. Jane Smith, of Algomac, MI, taught the first public school at Houghton, 1856, in a log building that belonged to a mining company (ibid., 556).

74. Benedict, *Red Metal*, 34–49.

75. Jamison, *This Ontonagon Country*, 160–61.

CHAPTER 4

1. Frederick L. Collins, "Paine's Career Is a Triumph of Early American Virtues," *American Magazine* 105(June 1928): 140.

2. *Boston Sunday Globe*, 13 September 1885.

3. Ibid., John H. Forster, "Finance of Mining—Lake Superior Mines," *Michigan Pioneer Collections* 13(1888): 348–49.

4. *Daily Mining Gazette* (Houghton), Copper Rally Supplement, 20 August 1943; letter signed "State Street," 21 January 1876, *Portage Lake Mining Gazette* (Houghton), 27 January 1876.

5. *Boston Sunday Globe*, 13 September 1885; Forster, "Finance of Mining," 344.

6. Unidentified newspaper clipping, Papers of and Relating to Alexander Agassiz, Agassiz Museum Archives, Library, Museum of Comparative Zoology, Harvard University, Cambridge.

7. Carter and Rankin, *North to Lake Superior* p. 8, no. 20; Lew Allen Chase, "Edwin James Hulbert, Copper Hunter," *Michigan History* 16(1932): 406–8.

8. Anthony S. Wax, "Calumet and Hecla Copper Mines: An Episode in the Economic Development of Michigan," *Michigan History* 16(1932): 15; *Daily Mining Gazette* (Houghton), Green Sheet, 5 April 1969; Edwin J. Hulbert, *Calumet–Conglomerate* (Ontonagon, MI: Ontonagon Miner Press, 1893), letter 2, pp. 15–17.

9. Hulbert, *Calumet–Conglomerate*, letter 2, pp. 18–20.

10. Ibid., 22–29; ibid., letter 11, pp. 137–38.

11. Benedict, *Red Metal*, 33, 40, Channing Clapp (vice-president, Calumet and Hecla) in a letter to Alexander Agassiz, 18 September 1885, reviews chronology of officers for 1865–71, in Papers of and Relating to Alexander Agassiz, B-AG-202-5, Agassiz Museum Archives, Library, Museum of Comparative Zoology, Harvard University, Cambridge.

12. George R. Agassiz, ed., *Letters and Recollections of Alexander Agassiz* (Boston: Houghton Mifflin, 1913), 4, 6, 8–9, 13–14; for estrangement, see Edward Lurie, *Louis Agassiz: A Life in Science* (Chicago: University of Chicago Press, 1960), 111–14.

13. Lurie, *Louis Agassiz*, 111, 113, 152, 162–65, 168–69; Louise Hall Tharp, "Professor of the World's Wonders," *American Heritage* 12(February 1961): 56, 58.

14. Lurie, *Louis Agassiz*, 170–71; Agassiz, *Letters and Recollections*, 124–25.

15. Agassiz, *Letters and Recollections*, v, 124–26, 446; Lucy Allen Paton, *Elizabeth Cary Agassiz: A Biography* (Boston: Houghton Mifflin, 1919), 172.

16. Agassiz, *Letters and Recollections*, 125.

17. Ibid., 61, 91–92. His son George Agassiz concluded, "Agassiz made it his personal interest to see that the men were well paid, well housed, and provided with the best of schools, libraries, bath-houses, and churches" (ibid., 89). At Alexander's death in 1910, Henry Adams wrote, "He was the best we ever produced, and the only one of our generation whom I would have liked to envy" (ibid., 447). Alexander Agassiz, like Henry Adams, can probably be understood best in psychobiographical terms; but such analysis has not yet been attempted by scholars.

18. Houston, *Copper Manual*, 49–50; Wax, "Calumet and Hecla Copper Mines," 24; Benedict, *Red Metal*, 48–49, 53–54; for Hulbert's story of Shaw cheating him, see his *Calumet–Conglomerate*, app.; for the best objective narrative of Hulbert–Shaw controversy, see Chase, "Hulbert," 409–11.

19. Houston, *Copper Manual*, 47, 49–50; Samuel S. Robinson to G. F. Bagley, 4 June 1866, Letterbook, pt. 3, no. 778, Robinson Papers, Michigan Historical Collections, Bentley Historical Library, Ann Arbor; for D'Aligny story and newspaper quotation, see *Boston Sunday Globe*, 13 September 1885.

20. Story of unnamed pioneer woman related by interviewer Mrs. Robert Grierson, *Sunday Mining Gazette* (Houghton), 27 March 1932; for Royal's Halfway House and Jones family, see Austrian, "Autobiographical and Historical Sketches," esp. 59–60 and 70 and Bessie Phillips story, *Daily Mining Gazette* (Houghton), 25 October 1952; the "pig story" is related best in Ira B. Joralemon, *Romantic Copper: Its Lure and Lore* (New York: Appleton–Century, 1936), 56–57.

21. Agassiz, *Letters and Recollections*, 15.

22. Ibid., 73; *History Upper Peninsula*, 299, 301.

23. Hubbard, *Memorials*, 358–59; Lucena Harris Brockway, Diary, 19 February 1867, Brockway Family Collection, Michigan Technological University Archives, Houghton, MI; for the road, see Samuel S. Robinson to Quincy directors, 1866: "Should you wish some explorations made in that neighborhood they can be better done after the next few months when a good road will have been made to Calumet" (Letterbook, pt. 3, no. 777, Robinson Papers, Michigan Historical Collections, Bentley Historical Library, Ann Arbor).

24. *History Upper Peninsula*, 302–3; Clarence J. Monette, *Laurium, Michigan's Early Days* (Lake Linden, MI, 1986), 5–10.

25. Edward Ryan to M. Freud and Co., 14 March 1871, and North and Briggs, to M. Freud and Co., 14 April 1871, Keweenaw Historical Society Collection, nos. 102 and 106, Michigan Technological University Archives, Houghton, MI; *Portage Lake Mining Gazette* (Houghton), 26 May 1870; *Calumet News*, 17 May 1921.

26. School inspectors' reports, 1875, Reels 1137–38, State Archives, Lansing, MI.

27. Ibid.; Union School described in *History Upper Peninsula*, 273; for poor attendance and racing through texts, see *Lake Superior Miner* (Ontonagon), 22 January 1870.

28. *Portage Lake Mining Gazette* (Houghton) 2 June 1870, 23 May 1872; Lucena Harris Brockway, Diary, 1–2 January 1876, Brockway Family Collection, Michigan Technological University Archives, Houghton, MI; *History Upper Peninsula*, 301.

29. *History Upper Peninsula*, 254, 301, 304; U.S. Census, 1870:170, 1880:215; unidentified newspaper clipping on railroad, Ransom Shelden Scrapbook, Michigan Historical Collections, Bentley Historical Library, Ann Arbor.

30. *Michigan State Gazetteer and Business Directory 1889–90* (Detroit: Polk, 1889), 110 (hereafter, *Michigan Gazetteer, 1889–90*). Edwards, "Crossed Portage Lake," typescript, Keweenaw Historical Society Collection, B3, no. 148, Michigan Technological University Archives, Houghton, MI; *History Upper Peninsula*, 254.

31. Unidentified newspaper clipping (prob. *Daily Mining Gazette*) 11 April 1919, Keweenaw Historical Society Collection, B2, no. 134, Michigan Technological University Archives, Houghton, MI; John Scott, Diary, 11 April 1869, Brockway Family Collection, B2, Michigan Technological University Archives, Houghton, MI, Alexander, *East Hancock*, 1–2.

32. Austrian "Autobiographical and Historical Sketches," 79, 92.

33. John Scott, Diary, 15 April 1869, Brockway Family Collection, B2, Michigan Technological University Archives, Houghton, MI; Fred Kausler, photocopy, Michigan Historical Collections, Bentley Historical Library, Ann Arbor, (original at Marquette Historical Society).

34. Lankton and Hyde, *Old Reliable*, 15; Alexander, *East Hancock*, 4; *History Upper Peninsula*, 286–89.

35. *History Upper Peninsula*, 253, 291, 296–97; Samuel S. Robinson to H. Hallock, 9 November, and to S. A. Godey, 29 December 1862, Robinson Papers, Michigan Historical Collections, Bentley Historical Library, Ann Arbor; Alexander, *East Hancock*, 3; *Evening Copper Journal* (Hancock), 19 March 1913, p. 4. *Portage Lake Mining Gazette* (Houghton), 26 October, 23 November 1871, 6 July 1876. A "knock-down . . . drag-out argument, [with] numerous black eyes and sore heads," occurred at Charbonneau's saloon, Frenchtown, as fists struck and chairs flew amid broken glass, on a Saturday night (ibid., 21 February 1884).

36. *History Upper Peninsula*, 290–91; *Portage Lake Mining Gazette* (Houghton), 14 February 1884; Catherine Mullett Hall to Martha Mullett Forster, n.d., Mullett Family Papers, Correspondence–Family, 1860–62, Michigan Historical Collections, Bentley Historical Library, Ann Arbor; *Michigan Gazetteer, 1889–90*, 1046, 1048.

37. *Portage Lake Mining Gazette* (Houghton), 21 December 1871. Mid-1930s rivalries and antagonisms belong to the personal recollections of the author.

38. *Portage Lake Mining Gazette* (Houghton), 26 October and 21 and 28 December 1871, 9 May 1872; *History Upper Peninsula*, 252.

39. U.S. Census, 1880:395; *History Upper Peninsula*, 252–54, 275–76; *Michigan Gazetteer, 1889–90*, 1090–96.

40. *Michigan Gazetteer, 1889–90*, 72; Michigan Writers' Program *Michigan*, 94.

41. Copper Range Historical Society newsletter, May 1992, Copper Range Historical Society, Houghton, MI, p. 2; Forster, "Lake Superior Country," 144–45.

42. "Notes," *Michigan Pioneer Collections* 13(1888): 404 (where the date is given incorrectly as 1857).

43. *Portage Lake Mining Gazette* (Houghton), 28 February 1884, 11 June and 2 July 1885; *History Upper Peninsula*, 274, 284; Douglass House Register and unidentified newspaper clipping regarding the governor's visit, Ransom Shelden Scrapbook, Michigan Historical Collections, Bentley Historical Library, Ann Arbor; Mason, *Copper Country Journal*, 244.

44. *History Upper Peninsula*, 252.

45. *Evening Copper Journal* (Hancock), 15 August 1916.

46. *Portage Lake Mining Gazette* (Houghton), 9 February 1871.

47. Utley and Cutcheon, *Michigan*, 4:304–5; *Evening Copper Journal* (Hancock), 15 August 1916.

48. *Michigan Gazetteer, 1889–90*, 1221.

49. U.S. Census, 1880:395; ibid., 1890:183; *History Upper Peninsula*, 192, 197–98, 201, 301; *L'Anse Sentinel*, 2 July 1969; *Baraga County Historical Pageant, Souvenir Book*, 31–32; *Michigan Gazetteer, 1889–90*, 263–64.

50. Mark Keller, "The Chippewa Land of Keweenaw Bay: An Allotment History," (Keweenaw Bay Tribal Council, Baraga, 1981, typescript), Central Michigan University Library, Mount Pleasant, pp. 21, 23, 31–32.

51. Ibid., 36–38, 50.

52. *Lake Superior Miner* (Ontonagon), 18 June 1870.

53. U.S. Census, 1870:38–39; ibid., 1880:395, 514; Gates, *Michigan Copper*, 56; *History Upper Peninsula*, 324–27. Michigan contributed a massive block of copper weighing 2,100 pounds, from the Cliff Mine, as a gift for the building of the Washington Monument, where, in 1903, a visitor observed the block on the nineteenth landing. See "Early Mining in the Upper Peninsula," in *Lake Superior Copper and the Indians: Miscellaneous Studies of Great Lakes Pre-History*," ed. James B. Griffin, Anthropological Papers, no. 17 (Ann Arbor: University of Michigan, Museum of Anthropology, 1961), 75.

54. Keweenaw Historical Society Collection, B2, nos. 102–3, Michigan Technological University Archives, Houghton, MI.

55. Daniel D. Brockway, Diary, 27 and 29 January, 12, 14 and 17 February, n.d. September, 1868, and list of business notations, 1868—both in Brockway Family Collection, Michigan Technological University Archives, Houghton, MI.

56. Lucena Harris Brockway, Diary, 1 and 21 January, 17 February, and 3 March 1874, and 12 January 1884, Brockway Family Collection, Michigan Technological University Archives, Houghton, MI.

57. Ibid., 16 April 1866 and 16 March, 8 July, and 21 August 1874.

58. Ibid., 4 March and 6 December 1874, 22 June 1882, and 14 January 1884. On her thirty-first wedding anniversary, she wrote, "Wish I was well[;] how I would like to celebrate it by giving a nice dinner" (21 January 1867); for record of strawberries picked, see final pages of 1878 diary; for additional information on Daniel D. Brockway as pioneer, see *History Upper Peninsula*, 344.

59. *History Upper Peninsula*, 311; *Michigan Gazetteer, 1889–90*. 1212; John Pitezel, "Fresh Breezes from Lake Superior," Clarke Historical Library, Central Michigan University, Mount Pleasant, MI, p. 12.

60. *History Upper Peninsula*, 311–13.

61. Lucena Harris Brockway, Diary, 20 May 1887, Brockway Family Collection, Michigan Technological University Archives, Houghton, MI; *Michigan Gazetteer, 1889–90*, 1212–14; *Memorial Record of the Northern Peninsula of Michigan* (Chicago: Lewis, 1895), 632–33.

62. *Michigan Gazetteer, 1889–90*, 1041–42; Donald Chaput, *Hubbell: A Copper Country Village* (1969; reprint, Lake Linden, MI: Forster, 1986), 16–19.

63. *History Upper Peninsula*, 510, 512; Wagner and Scherzer, *Reisen* (typescript translation), Keweenaw Historical Society Collection, B3, no. 147, Michigan Technological University Archives, Houghton, MI, pp. 16–17.

64. Knox Jamison, *A History of Rockland–Greenland–Mass* (Ontonagon, MI, 1969), 3–4, 8; *History Upper Peninsula*, 544; *Lake Superior Miner* (Ontonagon), 18 June 1870.

65. *History Upper Peninsula*, 546; Jamison, *A History of Rockland–Greenland–Mass*, 8–9, 31.

66. Samuel S. Robinson to unidentified correspondent, 4 July 1865, Letterbook, pt. 2, no. 444ff., Michigan Historical Collections, Bentley Historical Library, Ann Arbor; John R. Neph, *The Adventure Story* (Greenland, MI, 1976), 11–13.

67. Jamison, *Rockland–Greenland–Mass*, 16, 24–25, 31; Romig, *Michigan Place Names*, 357.

68. *History Upper Peninsula*, 515, 537; *Lake Superior Miner* (Ontonagon), 8, 22, and 29 January, 5 February, 9 July and 3 September 1870.

69. For women's clothing, see *Michigan History* 2(1918): 64; for maids, see U.S. Census, 1880, Houghton County, microfilm, T9-581, National Archives, Chicago Regional Branch; Sarah Scott Diary, 2 January 1877, 2 April 1884, Brockway Family Collection, Michigan Technological University Archives, Houghton, MI; Lucena Harris Brockway, Diary, final pages of 1866, 11–13 February and 10–11 August 1869, and 16 May 1878, Brockway Family Collection, Michigan Technological University Archives, Houghton, MI. Mrs. Brockway wrote: "After breakfast Mrs. Williams came for me. I went over and her little boy was dying. Died on my lap. Mrs. Francis and I laid him out and I staid there all day with them at Mrs. Thomas's," and the next day, "Mrs. Williams' little Homer was buried to day at Eagle Harbor" (18 and 19 September 1879).

70. U.S. Census, 1880, Franklin Township, Houghton County, microfilm, T9-581, National Archives, Chicago Regional Branch.

71. Austrian, "Autobiographical and Historical Sketches," 65–66; "Eagle River Cemetery Recalls Pioneer Days," unidentified newspaper clipping, 12 September 1916, Keweenaw Historical Society Collection, B2, no. 139, Michigan Technological University Archives, Houghton, MI.

72. John H. Forster, fragment of letter, 1860s, Mullett Family Papers, Correspondence, Family, 1860–62, idem to wife Martha Mullett Forster, 11 July 1861 and 8 and 15 October 1871; Catherine Mullett Hall to sister Martha Mullett Forster, prob. 1862, all in Michigan Historical Collections, Bentley Historical Library, Ann Arbor; liaison reported in letter of Thomas Buzzo to James Cooper, 27 April 1859, quoted in Neph, *Adventure Story*, 18, 20.

73. Lucena Harris Brockway, Diary, 30 November and 6 December 1874, 31 August 1882, 27 July 1884, Brockway Family Collection, Michigan Technological University Archives, Houghton, MI.

74. Ibid., 13 September 1882, 28 May and 29 July 1884 (horse sold), and 6–7, 9, 11–12 December 1887.

75. Forster, "Lake Superior Country," 145.

76. Mid-1930s criticism of DSS&A is from the personal recollection of the author. For rail and road transportation see Bliss, "Federal Land Grants," 66–67; Theodore J. Karamanski, *Deep Woods Frontier: A History of Logging in Northern Michigan* (Detroit: Wayne State University Press, 1989), 60; *Houghton Centennial*, 5, 7, 9; Jamison, *This Ontonagon Country*, 129, 134; Jamison, *Rockland–Greenland–Mass*, 15; *Portage Lake Mining Gazette* (Houghton), 31 January and 21 February 1884; *Lake Superior Miner* (Ontonagon), 5 February 1870; *Evening Copper Journal* (Hancock), 9 April 1924.

77. *Portage Lake Mining Gazette* (Houghton), 6 July 1876 and 25 June and 2 July 1885.

78. Michigan Writers' Project *Michigan*, 129–30.

79. Austrian, "Autobiographical and Historical Sketches," 45, 95, Michigan Technological University Archives, Houghton, MI; for ship canal and its impact, see Edwin Henwood, manuscript, read 16 August 1917 Keweenaw Historical Society Collection, B2, no. 137, Michigan Technological University Archives, Houghton, MI; Utley and Cutcheon, *Michigan*, 4:158–59; Alexander, *East Hancock*, 2; *History Upper Peninsula*, 253.

80. *History Upper Peninsula*, 286, 514–15.

81. John H. Forster to Martha Mullett Forster, August 1860, Mullett Family Papers, Correspondence–Family, 1860–62, Michigan Historical Collections, Bentley Historical Library, Ann Arbor; *Portage Lake Mining Gazette* (Houghton), 20 October 1870; John Scott, Diary, 19 January and 8 February 1869, Brockway Family Collection, B2—all in Michigan Technological University Archives, Houghton, MI.

82. Forster, "Finance of Mining," 345–47.

83. "Daniel D. Brockway Wedding Anniversary" file, Michigan Historical Collections, Bentley Historical Library, Ann Arbor.

CHAPTER 5

1. John H. Forster, "Life in the Copper Mines of Lake Superior," *Michigan Pioneer Collections* 11(1887): 182.

2. For paternalism, see Gates, *Michigan Copper*, 94, 103–12; William H. McGuffey, *McGuffey's New Sixth Eclectic Reader* (Cincinnati: Wilson, Hinkle, 1857), 103, 113–17, 175–78, 180, 285–86, 398–400.

3. Robert L. Heilbroner, *The Economic Transformation of America* (New York: Harcourt Brace Jovanovich, 1977), 53.

4. Samuel S. Robinson to directors, 30 January 1864, Letterbook, pt. 1, no. 90; idem to unidentified correspondent, 14 June 1865, Letterbook, pt. 2, no. 408; idem to recruiting agent Chris. Taftjon(?), 7 March 1865, Letterbook, pt. 2, no. 366ff.—all in Robinson Papers, Michigan Historical Collections, Bentley Historical Library, Ann Arbor.

5. Romig, *Michigan Place Names*, 290; undated clipping, *Torch Lake Times* (Lake Linden), Keweenaw Historical Society Collection, B8, no. 316, Michigan Technological University Archives, Houghton, MI, p. 28.

6. *Memorial Record of the Northern Peninsula*, 340–42.

7. Gates, *Michigan Copper*, 44–45; Matthew 26:11, Zechariah 7:10; *Portage Lake Mining Gazette* (Houghton), 4 January 1872.

8. *Portage Lake Mining Gazette* (Houghton), 21 March, 2 May 1872; *History Upper Peninsula*, 47; Verwyst, *Life and Labors*, 338.

9. McKenney, *Sketches of a Tour*, 255; U.S. Census, 1860, Houghton County (microfilm) M653-544.

10. *History Upper Peninsula*, 255–56; undated newspaper clipping, Francis Jacker Scrapbook, Keweenaw Historical Society Collection, B8, no. 316, Michigan Technological University Archives, Houghton, MI; *Daily Mining Gazette* (Houghton), 26 April 1950.

11. *Portage Lake Mining Gazette* (Houghton), 25 April, 2 May 1872; McKenney, *Sketches of a Tour*, 251–52.

12. U.S. Census, 1860, Houghton County (microfilm) M653-544; McKenney, *Sketches of a Tour*, 250; F. Jacker story (dated 28 April 1888) in *Torch Lake Times* (Lake Linden), n.d., Keweenaw Historical Society Collection, B8, no. 316, Michigan Technological University Archives, Houghton, MI, p. 37.

13. Armas K. E. Holmio, *History of the Finns in Michigan*, trans. Elin Rynamon (Hancock, MI: Michigan Suomalaisten Historia–Seura); Patrick H. O'Brien, interview, Detroit, 16 October 1957, Michigan Historical Collections, Bentley Historical Library, Ann Arbor; *Portage Lake Mining Gazette* (Houghton), 18 June 1874; *Copper Country Evening News* (Calumet), 22 June 1896.

14. U.S. Census, 1900, Houghton County (microfilm) T623-714; *Memorial Record of the Northern Peninsula*, 425–26; *Native Copper Times* (Lake Linden), 7 May 1895; *Copper Country Evening News* (Calumet), 1 October 1896; *Calumet News*, 4 November 1907.

15. *Guide Francais des Etats-Unis* (Lowell, MA: *La Société de Publications Francaises des Etats-Unis*, 1891), Michigan Technological University Archives, Houghton, MI.

16. *Portage Lake Mining Gazette* (Houghton), 25 June 1885; *Copper Country Evening News* (Calumet), 30 March 1908; *Calumet News*, 2 June 1914, 26 December 1928; *Le Courrier du Michigan* (Lake Linden), June 1919, pp, 4, 10.

17. U.S., Census, esp. 1870:170, 313, 359; ibid., 1880:513; *Calumet News* 10 January 1908; Arthur W. Thurner, *Calumet Copper and People* (Hancock, 1974), 25.

18. *Memorial Record of the Northern Peninsula*, 460–61, 565–69; Patrick H. O'Brien, interview, Detroit, 16 October 1957, Michigan Historical Collections, Bentley Historical Library, Ann Arbor.

19. *Portage Lake Mining Gazette* (Houghton) 21 March 1863, 18 March 1886; *Copper Country Evening News* (Calumet), 17 March 1896; U.S. Census, 1890, Houghton County (microfilm) T623-714.

20. Samuel S. Robinson to unnamed correspondent, 3 March 1865, Letter-book, pt. 2, no. 355ff. Robinson Papers, Michigan Historical Collections, Bentley Historical Library, Ann Arbor; for Frimodig family information, see *Memorial Record of the Northern Peninsula*, 364–65; *Copper Country Evening News* (Calumet), 18 May and 2 September 1896; *Daily Mining Gazette* (Houghton), 30 April 1908.

21. *Copper Country Evening News* (Calumet), 26 April 1904; *Calumet News*, 11 September 1912, 3 January 1914, 23 December 1915.

22. Patrick H. O'Brien, interview, Detroit, 16 October 1957, Michigan Historical Collections, Bentley Historical Library, Ann Arbor, p. 3; Forster, "Life in the Copper Mines," 185; Alexander, *East Hancock*, 48; *Daily Mining Gazette* (Houghton), 29 December 1899; *Copper Country Evening News* (Calumet), 10 February 1898.

23. W. E. Maas, *Diamond Jubilee, 1879–1954, Saint Paul's Evangelical Lutheran Church* (Laurium, MI, 1954); *Calumet News*, 17 December 1932; the 1930s bakery, end of German preaching, Holy Week services, and lead soldiers are personal recollections of author.

24. Leslie Chapman, interview, prob. 1950s, Suomi College Oral History Project, Finnish–American Heritage Center, Hancock, MI, p. 9.

25. *Sunday Mining Gazette* (Houghton), 12 April 1908, 11 December 1914; *Calumet News*, 7 and 22 April 1914; Moyer, *Ke-Wee-Naw*, 143.

26. *Copper Country Evening News* (Calumet), 16 January 1896, 16 August 1904; *History Upper Peninsula*, esp. 276–320; Forster, "Life in Copper Mines," 184.

27. James Fisher, "Michigan's Cornish People," *Michigan History* 29 (1945): 379, 384. *Adit* is an opening to a mine at surface level, *shaft*, the opening through which ore was hoisted; *kibble* meant bucket, *collar*, the mouth of a shaft, *burrow*, a heap of refuse rock; *pass* indicated a chute, *gob* was waste rock, and the vibrating machine used to separate crushed ore from rock was called *jig*. See James E. Jopling, "Cornish Miners of the Upper Peninsula," *Michigan History* 12(1928): 560, 566-67.

28. Fisher, "Michigan's Cornish People," 384; Jopling, "Cornish Miners," 554–55; Mason, *Copper Country Journal*, 177–78.

29. Derisive use of "Cousin Jack" and 1937 schoolboy note are from personal recollections of the author; Fisher, "Michigan's Cornish People," 377, 381, 383–84; Mrs. Robert Grierson related stories of patronage and caroling in *Sunday Mining Gazette* (Houghton), 27 March 1932; *Copper Country Evening News* (Calumet), 26 December 1900.

30. Fisher, "Michigan's Cornish People," 378–80; Jopling, "Cornish Miners," 554; Penhale poetry, Keweenaw Historical Society Collection, B3, no. 156, Michigan Technological University Archives, Houghton, MI; newspaper clipping (prob. *Portage Lake Mining Gazette*), 30 January 1886, "Daniel Brockway Golden Wedding Anniversary" file, Michigan Historical Collections, Bentley Historical Library, Ann Arbor.

31. *Amerikan Suomalainen*, circa 1876, at Hancock, was the first of many Finnish-language newspapers, among which several later played important roles: *Amer-*

ikan Suometar, Työmies (Hancock), *Päivälehti, Walwoja, Opas* (Calumet). See David T. Halkola, "Finnish-Language Newspapers in the United States," in *The Finns in North America,* ed. Ralph J. Jalkanen (Lansing: Michigan State University Press for Suomi College, Hancock, MI, 1969), 74–85; T. A. Rickard, *The Copper Mines of Lake Superior* (New York: Engineering and Mining Journal, 1905), 158–59; Fisher, "Michigan's Cornish People," 380; for authentic pasty recipe, see Calumet Woman's Club, *Copper Country 101 All Time Favorites, Recipes* 11th ed. (Calumet, MI: Calumet Women's Club, 1981), 77–78; Lorraine Uitto Richards, *The Pasty of the Copper Country of Keweenaw: Everything You Always Needed To Know about Pasties!* (Hancock, MI: Timber Floating, 1990); *Daily Mining Gazette* (Houghton), 28 December 1899 and 2, 4, and 7 August 1934.

32. Fisher, "Michigan's Cornish People," 383; Margaret B. Macmillan, *The Methodist Church in Michigan: The Nineteenth Century* (Grand Rapids, MI: Michigan Area Methodist Historical Society and William B. Eerdmans, 1967), 386; Clarence Bennetts Collection, F10, Michigan Technological University Archives, Houghton, MI.

33. Fisher, "Michigan's Cornish People," 385; Nute, *Lake Superior,* 252; Central Mine Reunion Service Program, 1991, Collection of Charles Stetter, Laurium, MI; Moyer, *Ke-Wee-Naw,* 169.

34. Macmillan, *Methodist Church,* 338–40; *Calumet News,* 23 December 1913; for names of district superintendents, see *History Upper Peninsula,* 178; for Methodist pastors, 1872–1968 at L'Anse, see *Baraga County Historical Pageant, Souvenir Book,* p. 46; Moyer, *Ke-Wee-Naw,* 141.

35. U.S. Census 1870: 38–39; ibid., 1880:395 (Table V).

36. U.S. Census, 1860, Houghton County (microfilm) M683-544; ibid., 1870 (microfilm) M593-674; ibid., 1910:944.

37. Jamison, *This Ontonagon Country,* 247; for Finnish migration from mines to farms, see Elsie Collins, *From Keweenaw to Abbaye* (Ishpeming, MI, 1975). Among the most prominent entrepreneurs was J. H. Jasberg, born in 1861 in Finland, whose meteoric rise from 1880 to 1895 in Copper Country business and civil life impressed all. See *Biographical Record, Houghton, Baraga, Marquette Counties* (Chicago: Biographical, 1903).

38. *Memorial Record of the Northern Peninsula,* 366–67; Norman T. Moline, "Finnish Settlement in Upper Michigan," masters' thesis, University of Chicago, 1966, p. 24; Holmio, *History of the Finns,* 128–30, 133, 141–43.

39. Cotton Mather and Matti Kaups, "The Finnish Sauna: A Cultural Index to Settlement," *Annals of the Association of American Geographers* 53(1963): 499; Utley and Cutcheon, *Michigan* 4:262–63.

40. Holmio, *History of the Finns,* 119–24.

41. Ibid., 167–69; Romig, *Michigan Place Names,* 399, 549–50, 556, 577–78.

42. Holmio, *History of the Finns,* 160–63.

43. Karamanski, *Deep Woods Frontier,* 158–59; Clemens Niemi, *The Americanization of the Finnish People in Houghton County, Michigan* (Duluth: Finnish Daily Publishing, 1921), 19.

44. Holmio, *History of the Finns,* 177–82; for Jaakko Ojanperä as leader of settlers at Oskar's founding, see 177–78.

45. Ibid., 150–51, 153–55; *Copper Country Evening News* (Calumet), 3 May 1904.

46. Niemi, *Americanization of the Finnish People,* 20; Karamanski, *Deep Woods Frontier,* 159; Holmio, *History of the Finns,* 118; Michigan Writers' Project, *Michigan,* 106. As of 1901, a listing of local Finnish-language newspapers included three

weeklies: *American Untiset* (Calumet), *Suometar* (Calumet), and *Amerikan Suometar* (Hancock). See *Michigan Official Directory and Legislative Manual*, 1901:228.

47. Holmio, *History of the Finns*, 168.

48. Ibid., 143, 147, 152, 170–72; other Finnish settlements at various range towns described by Holmio paraphrased in Copper Range Historical Society newsletter, October 1991, p. 4; Niemi, *Americanization of the Finnish People*, 18; for maids, see Anna Isola, interview, 1121–22, Suomi College Oral History Project, Finnish–American Heritage Center, Hancock, MI.

49. Niemi, *Americanization of the Finnish People*, 24–25, 27.

50. Ibid., 29–31. By June 1907, the several Houghton County temperance societies held their twelfth annual picnic; see *Daily Mining Gazette* (Houghton), 20 June 1907. *Hyvä Toivo*, one of the oldest temperance societies in the Upper Peninsula, announced that after being inactive during the copper strike, regular meetings would resume at Red Jacket with hopes to launch a "big membership campaign"; see *Calumet News*, 22 April 1914. A physician who refused to obey a summons to attend a man stabbed in a Finnish saloon fracas was first threatened, then shot to death by a Finn who argued, "We pay him 60 cents a month to attend us [at the Portage Entry sandstone quarries] and he dare not refuse"; see *L'Anse Sentinel*, 14 January 1893; *Kalevala*, trans. W. F. Kirby (London: J. M. Dent, 1907), 1.1.165–66, 259–60.

51. Michael G. Karni, " 'Yhteishyva'; or, For the Common Good: Finnish Radicalism in the Western Great Lakes Region, 1900–1940," Ph.D. diss., University of Minnesota, 1975; Matti E. Kaups, "The Finns in the Copper and Iron Ore Mines of the Western Great Lakes Region, 1864–1905: Some Preliminary Observations," in *The Finnish Experience in the Western Great Lakes Region*, eds. Michael G. Karni, Matti E. Kaups, and Douglas J. Ollila, Jr. (Turku, Finland: Institute for Migration, 1975), 55–89; Arthur Puotinen, "Copper Country Finns and the Strike of 1913," in *The Finnish Experience* 143–53; Arthur Puotinen, "Early Labor Organization in the Copper Country," in *For the Common Good: Finnish Immigrants and the Radical Response to Industrial America*, eds. Michael G. Karni and Douglas J. Ollila, Jr. (Superior, WI: Työmies Society, 1977), 119–66.

52. Emily Greene Balch, *Our Slavic Fellow Citizens* (New York: Charities Publication Committee, 1910), 175–76, 307, 309; U.S. Census, 1910, Houghton County (microfilm), T623-714.

53. Frank Shaltz, interview by author, 29 July 1978, Calumet.

54. U.S. Census, 1910, 2:936, 938, 944.

55. Marie Prisland, *From Slovenia to America* (Chicago: Slovenian Women's Union of America and Bruce Publishing, 1968), 42, 110–15. Joseph Plautz, a Slovenian volunteer, traveled to Mexico in 1864 with Archduke Ferdinand Maximilian of Austria (whom the French installed as Mexican emperor) and later came from Mexico to Calumet, where he became a well-known veterinarian and his son, by the turn of the century, became editor of the Slovenian newspaper.

56. *Copper Country Evening News* (Calumet), 30 April and 30 November 1896, 4 March 1897, 5 May 1904; *Portage Lake Mining Gazette* (Houghton), 22 December 1887; *Daily Mining Gazette* (Houghton), 30 April 1908. The latter newspaper also described Poles as "a sturdy people, . . . among the best mine workers and business people." For additional information on Red Jacket's Polish church and school, including photograph, see *Daily Mining Gazette*, 14 February 1985; *Calumet News*, 23 December 1907, 1 January 1908, 11 April 1914.

57. *Calumet News*, 26 November 1907; Sacred Heart Church, catering to Irish and Germans, had 1,700 members in 1907; Saint Anne's (French) had 2,032; and Saint John the Baptist (Croatian) had 2,400 (ibid). The *Daily Mining Gazette* (Houghton), 31 July 1987, contains a brief history of Saint Joseph's Church. See

also *Copper Country Evening News* (Calumet), 5 August 1896; Russell M. Magnaghi, *Miners, Merchants, and Midwives: Michigan's Upper Peninsula Italians* (Marquette, MI: Belle Fontaine, 1987), 35–36, 39.

58. Magnaghi, *Miners, Merchants and Midwives*, 39, 43. The society continued until 1922, when national immigration restriction and emigration of Italians from the Keweenaw led to the merging of all Italian societies into the Christopher Columbus Society, (ibid., 44).

59. Ibid., 10, 29–30, 39.

60. Ibid., 47, 51–52, for boarders and women's lodges; *Daily Mining Gazette* (Houghton), 2 May 1908; *Copper Country Evening News* (Calumet), 1 September 1906; *Guida degli Italiani del Copper Country* (Laurium, MI: Minatore Italiano, 1910), Michigan Technological University Archives; *Calumet News*, 20 February 1922; Battista Bigando, interview, 1075–77, 1079, Suomi College Oral History Project, Finnish–American Heritage Center, Hancock, MI.

61. David Mac Frimodig, *Keweenaw Character: The Foundation of Michigan's Copper Country* (Lake Linden, MI: Forster, 1990), 66–73; quotation from p. 73; Barkell, *Hancock*, 65; *Daily Mining Gazette* (Houghton), 6–7 January 1915; for kosher meat preparation, see *Copper Country Evening News* (Calumet), 15 March 1898; *Calumet News*, 3 September 1913; young people in public schools from personal recollections of author.

62. *Calumet News*, 30 October 1907, 18 March 1914; *Daily Mining Gazette* (Houghton), 3 January 1915; Rickard, *Copper Mines*, 20.

63. Hubbard, *Memorials*, 7. A prize newspaper essay of 1928 written by Mrs. Robert Grierson and published in Detroit invited all to "come up to the top of the world," for "when you drink this clear, cold water, you come forever under [the] mystic spell" of the Keweenaw peninsula; see *Calumet News*, 12 December 1928. "Something catches men's imaginations and holds fast. . . . You can't identify . . . this . . . ultimate resource of the Ontonagon country—charm" (Jamison, *This Ontonagon Country*, 231, 233, 267); Hugh E. Boyer, "The Decline of the Progressive Party in Michigan's Upper Peninsula: The Case of Congressman William J. MacDonald in 1914," *Michigan Historical Review* 13 (Fall 1987): 92; *Daily Mining Gazette* (Houghton), 31 December 1913.

64. Clarence Bennetts Collection, F7, Michigan Technological University Archives, Houghton, MI; Niemi, *Americanization of the Finnish People*, 12–13, 35.

65. Annie Aldrich, interview, 1165–66, 1175, 1181, Suomi College Oral History Project, Finnish–American Heritage Center, Hancock, MI; quotation on pioneer women from Childs, "Reminiscences," 154–55; Thomas W. Buzzo to James Cooper, 20 May 1859, quoted in Neph, *Adventure Story*, 18.

66. Personal recollections of author. An Ontonagon newspaper, 13 April 1907, said the town had "one Chink and like most of his ilk he has an inquiring mind and a thirst for the coin of the realm. . . . He is not averse to turning a few cartwheels in other lines [although] washee washee is his regular vocation," quoted in Alma W. Swinton, *I Married a Doctor: Life in Ontonagon, Michigan from 1900 to 1919* (Marquette, MI, 1964), 393; interviews, Alice Isola, 1121–22, Frances Rozich, 17–18, Bertha Jacka, 7, Suomi College Oral History Project, Finnish–American Heritage Center, Hancock, MI; Holmio, *History of the Finns*, 140.

67. Lankton and Hyde, *Old Reliable*, 85; *Copper Country Evening News* (Calumet), 5 June 1896, 14 February 1898; Patrick H. O'Brien, interview, Detroit, 16 October 1957, Michigan Historical Collections, Bentley Historical Library, Ann Arbor, p. 3; quotation on Finns from P. B. McDonald, "The Michigan Copper Miners," *Outlook*, 7 February 1914, 298.

68. *Copper Country Evening News* (Calumet), 3 October 1896, 23 March

1898. Editors combined praise and slurs for various groups as, for example, in the call for Italians—who, in the past, "in the cause of good order, had taken the law into their own hands" and driven out of the community fellow Italians—to repeat such action and drive out a recent offender described by newspaper as "this thing . . . a disgrace to any nationality"; see *Portage Lake Mining Gazette* (Houghton), 9 February 1882. For ecumenical funeral service, see Swinton, *I Married a Doctor*, 331.

69. Ralph Paoli story is from Moyer, *Ke-Wee-Naw*, 96; information on John Gasparovich supplied by his granddaughters, Georgiana Delehanty (Park Forest, IL) and Anna Lynch (Laurium, MI); *Calumet News* (Calumet), 18–20 August 1910.

70. See chapter 7.

71. For earlier ethnic conflicts, see Rickard, *Copper Mines*, 18.

72. Author's recollections of events, 1932–46.

73. Jingo Viitala Vachon, *Tall Timber Tales*, (L'Anse, MI: L'Anse Sentinel, 1973), 14–15, 17.

74. *Portage Lake Mining Gazette* (Houghton), 22 June 1882.

75. Rickard, *Copper Mines*, 18–19.

76. U.S. Census, 1910, *Population*, 2:933, 937, 939, 945.

77. Ibid., 951.

78. Ibid., 951–52. Of thirty-seven African Americans, ages ten and over, in these three towns, only two were illiterate.

79. Ibid., 933, 937, 939, 945.

80. Quoted materials from Niemi, *Americanization of the Finnish People*, 7–8, 40. Libraries distributed large numbers of North American Civic League pamphlets entitled "Messages to New Comers to the United States"; see *Calumet News*, 1 November 1913. Lois A. Spencer of Menominee, Michigan, told a meeting of state librarians of a Croatian-language edition of James Bryce's *American Commonwealth* at the Calumet library, "It isn't so very old, but the first volume has been read so often that it has already been to the bindery," adding that very few books were stolen by immigrant readers; see *Calumet News*, 9 October 1913. For many people in the Copper Country, circa 1900–1940, to enter the libraries for hours of reading was closing "the doors to the outside world," a novel way to combine escape and erudition; see Moyer, *Ke-Wee-Naw*, 137; Thurner, *Calumet Copper and People*, 25.

CHAPTER 6

1. Gates, *Michigan Copper*, 204–5.

2. U.S. Census, 1890:183, 1910:933, 936–38, 944.

3. *Daily Mining Gazette* (Houghton), 22 June 1907; report of interview with Patrick Henry O'Brien, Detroit, 16 October 1957, Michigan Historical Collections, Bentley Historical Library, Ann Arbor; Gates, *Michigan Copper*, 225. "In our day [1897] copper is pre-eminently the electricians' metal, without which the wonderful inventions and discoveries in the field of electric science could not have been perfected" (Houston, *Copper Manual*, 6).

4. *Native Copper Times* (Lake Linden), 28 March 1893; *Engineering and Mining Journal*, 11 November 1893, pp. 495–97.

5. Gates, *Michigan Copper*, 16, 56; Houston, *Copper Manual*, 101; *History Upper Peninsula*, 537.

6. Karamanski, *Deep Woods Frontier*, 59–61.

7. Ibid., 217, for George Corrigan quotation.

8. George N. Fuller quoted in *Michigan History* 29(1945): 148; *Daily Mining Gazette* (Houghton), 4 August 1934.

9. Romig, *Michigan Place Names*, 43, 93, 115–16, 137, 189, 357, 411, 431; for Ewen's claim to 1893 log assembly, see Upper Peninsula Travel and Recreation Association, *Michigan's Upper Peninsula Travel Planner for All Seasons* (Iron Mountain, MI, 1991), 29; Karamanski, *Deep Woods Frontier*, 61.

10. Karamanski, *Deep Woods Frontier*, 61–64; *Portage Lake Mining Gazette* (Houghton), 3 September 1896.

11. *Portage Lake Mining Gazette* (Houghton), 24 September 1896; Karamanski, *Deep Woods Frontier*, 65.

12. Gates, *Michigan Copper*, 65–66, 71–72; Moyer, *Ke-Wee-Naw*, 152; J. R. Bennetts, manuscript autobiography, Clarence Bennetts Collection, F9, Michigan Technological University Archives, Houghton, MI.

13. Houston, *Copper Manual*, 70–71, 192; Holmio, *History of the Finns*, 188–91; Gates, *Michigan Copper*, 72, 218, 230.

14. Foster and Whitney, *Report 1850*, 153; Wax, "Calumet and Hecla Copper Mines," 32; Agassiz, *Letters and Recollections*, 87; Benedict, *Red Metal*, 111–14.

15. Neph, *Adventure Story*, 38.

16. Houston, *Copper Manual*, 46, 49–51.

17. Ibid., 50–51; see map depicting seventeen shafts, Benedict, *Red Metal*, 82; "Calumet & Hecla: Present Position and Assets," clipping, Boston News Bureau, 20 February 1907, Papers of and Relating to Alexander Agassiz, Agassiz Museum Archives, Library, Museum of Comparative Zoology, Harvard University, Cambridge; Gates, *Michigan Copper*, 209–10.

18. John H. Forster, "Life in the Copper Mines," 178–79.

19. *Daily Mining Gazette* (Houghton), 2 November and 13 and 15 December 1899 and 23 February 1940; Alexander, *East Hancock*, 2; Barkell, *Hancock*, 13.

20. *Daily Mining Gazette* (Houghton), 25 November 1899; Douglas House Register, 1881–1894, State Archives, Lansing.

21. U.S. Census, 1890:183, 186, 804; 1900:202, 206, 211; and 1910:904, 908–9, 915, 919–20, 952.

22. *Daily Mining Gazette* (Houghton), 23 February 1940.

23. Michigan Legislature, *Journal of the Senate, 1913*, 1:523, 608 and 2:1463, 1685, 1560–61, 1813, 2144; idem, *Journal of the House of Representatives, 1913* 2:1367 (Lansing: Wynkoop Hallenbeck Crawford, 1913).

24. Neph, *Adventure Story*, 35.

25. Barkell, *Hancock*, 35, 37; *Copper Country Evening News* (Calumet), 14 April 1904; *Calumet News*, 19 July 1921, 1 June 1929; *Daily Mining Gazette* (Houghton), 9 July 1966 (for history of Calumet hospital) and 29 March 1984 (for description of mining company hospital). A nurse who worked at the Calumet and Hecla Hospital in 1941–52, recalled working eight hours a day, seven days a week with sixteen-hour shifts when changing from night to afternoon shifts (Katherine Zimmerman Thurner, interview by author, Calumet, 1973); Lucena Harris Brockway, Diary, 20 September 1882, Brockway Family Collection, Michigan Technological University Archives, Houghton, MI. A Finnish hospital with twenty-five beds at East Hancock, begun "because the local Catholic institution did not meet the requirements of Protestants," operated from 1917 to 1931 (Holmio, *Finns in Michigan*, 132–33).

26. Arthur W. Thurner, "How a Library Came to the Copper Country: A Saga of Miners and Capitalists," *Wilson Library Bulletin* 50 (April 1976): 608–12; Marie F. Grierson, "Calumet and Hecla Library," *Mining Congress Journal* 17(October 1931): 561–62; *Calumet News*, 2 January, 8 October, and 1 November 1913 and

2 March 1914. In 1935, the Calumet Library housed more books than the Michigan College of Mining and Technology Library (40,989), the Houghton Public Library contained 15,311, Hancock, 12,000, and Painesdale, 9,985. Bertine E. Weston, ed., *The American Library Directory, 1935* (New York: Bowker, 1935), 190, 193, 196.

27. *Daily Mining Gazette* (Houghton), 28 November 1952; Paton, "History of Schools," 569.

28. School inspectors' reports, 1895, Reels 1198–1201; ibid., 1915, Reels 1266–69—both in State Archives, Lansing; *Daily Mining Gazette* (Houghton), 4 April 1907.

29. Paton, "History of the Schools," 567, 570; Jamison biographical sketch in Swinton, *I Married a Doctor*, 406–9; "Hennery" story related by the late Barbara Williams, Calumet, to author, circa 1976; David Mac Frimodig, *Keweenaw Character* (Lake Linden, MI: Forster, 1990), 66–69.

30. Anonymous biography of Frederick Jeffers, typescript, Howard Doolittle Papers, Michigan Historical Collections, Bentley Historical Library, Ann Arbor, pp. 12–18.

31. Newspaper clipping, *Galien River Gazette*, 1 September 1949; clipping, *Michigan Education Journal*, October 1949, p. 171; anonymous handwritten manuscript describing schools, pp. 2–3; Cora Jeffers autobiography, typescript, p. 3—all in Howard Doolittle Papers (hereafter Doolittle Papers), Michigan Historical Collections, Bentley Historical Library, Ann Arbor.

32. Cora Jeffers autobiography, typescript, pp. 2–3; anonymous handwritten manuscript describing schools, pp. 3, 15; Mrs. Mills to Howard Doolittle, 4 February 1964—all in Doolittle Papers, Michigan Historical Collections, Bentley Historical Library, Ann Arbor.

33. Newspaper clipping, *Mining Journal* (Marquette), 1 April 1949; Cora Jeffers autobiography, typescript, esp. (for her public speaking and suffrage activity) last page before Vita; J. Henry Dunstan to Howard Doolittle, 2 April 1951—all in Doolittle Papers, Michigan Historical Collections, Bentley Historical Library, Ann Arbor.

34. Frederick J. Cox to Cora and Frederick Jeffers, 19 March 1946, Doolittle Papers, Michigan Historical Collections, Bentley Historical Library, Ann Arbor.

35. Anonymous biography of Frederick Jeffers, typescript, Howard Doolittle Papers, Michigan Historical Collections, Bentley Historical Library, Ann Arbor, p. 26.

36. W. E. Trebilcock, "Calumet Schools," typescript, Calumet Public Library, p. 10; School inspectors' reports, 1895, Reel 1199; ibid., 1915, Reel 1267—all in State Archives, Lansing. See also Swinton, *I Married a Doctor*, 143.

37. Paton, "History of the Schools," 570–71; Verwyst, *Life and Labors*, 351–55; *Copper Country Evening News* (Calumet), 1 September 1906; School inspectors' reports, 1915, Reel 1267, State Archives, Lansing; information on 1930s at Sacred Heart and stern taskmasters at Saint Paul School supplied by various Calumet and Laurium residents to author in 1954 and 1992.

38. *Daily Mining Gazette* (Houghton), 3 October 1899; *Portage Lake Mining Gazette* (Houghton), 17 September and 17 December 1896; Michigan Department of State, *Michigan and Its Resources*, 4th ed. (Lansing: Smith, 1893), 144–48; David T. Halkola et al., *Michigan Tech Centennial, 1885–1985* (Houghton: Michigan Technological University, 1985), 47, 49, 51, 53, 65.

39. *Daily Mining Gazette* (Houghton), 18 and 23 December, 1899.

40. Ibid., 2 December 1899, 20 and 26 June 1907, and 13 July 1991; Barkell, *Hancock*, 85, 89.

41. *Daily Mining Gazette* (Houghton), 8 and 12 December 1899, 30 April

1908, 12 April 1969 (Green Sheet Supplement), 25 May 1991; Alexander, *East Hancock*, 2; Barkell, *Hancock*, 13, 87.

42. Calumet Light Guard and Houghton Light Infantry, *Our Boys in the Spanish–American War* (Houghton, MI: Gazette, 1900); *Daily Mining Gazette* (Houghton), 19 January 1915; *L'Anse Sentinel*, 21 September 1895, 2 July 1969; Danziger, *Chippewas of Lake Superior*, 107. For the plight of Native Americans at the end of the nineteenth century, see Francis Jacker, unidentified newspaper clipping, 7 March 1888, Keweenaw Historical Society Collection, B8, no. 316, Michigan Technological University Archives, Houghton.

43. *L'Union Franco–Américaine* (Lake Linden), 24 June 1890; Georges J. Joyaux, "French Press in Michigan: A Bibliography," *Michigan History* 36 (1952): 260–78.

44. *Daily Mining Gazette* (Houghton), 4 October and 8 November 1899 and 14 March 1991. Fire swept through the Bolman block in 1912; but after restoration and reoccupation, the edifice remained for thirty-eight years until a spectacular fire destroyed it (ibid., 3 March 1950); *Copper Country Evening News* (Calumet), 9 October 1907. For architecture, see Preservation Urban Design, *Calumet Downtown Historic District Plan* (Ann Arbor, 1979), 10–12, 14–15.

45. *Daily Mining Gazette* (Houghton), 4 April, 28 May and 14 and 19 June 1907 and 9 July 1966 (Souvenir Edition); *Welcome to the Village of Laurium's Eightieth Anniversary, 1889–1969—July 10, 11, 12, 13*; Clarence J. Monette, *Laurium, Michigan's Early Days* (Lake Linden: 1986).

46. Alexander, *East Hancock*, 5; *Daily Mining Gazette* (Houghton), 24 August 1991; Houston, *Copper Manual*, 64–66. For Tamarack Co-operative Association and Store, see *Daily Mining Journal* (Marquette), 5 June 1897 (Special Industrial Edition); U.S. Department of Labor, Bureau of Labor Statistics, *Michigan Copper District Strike*, Bulletin No. 139 (originally printed as S. Doc. 381) (Washington, 1914), 123–24; Forrest Crissey, "Every Man His Own Merchant," *Saturday Evening Post*, September 20, 1913, 16–17, 57–58.

47. Karamanski, *Deep Woods Frontier*, 216; *Copper Country Evening News*, 22 and 27 April and 17 August 1896, 2 January 1897; *Daily Mining Gazette* (Houghton) 12 December 1899, 2 May 1908, 1 and 2 December 1914; *Calumet News*, 26 and 28 October 1918; *L'Anse Sentinel*, 28 January 1893; Swinton, *I Married a Doctor*, 189.

48. James D. Horan, *The Pinkertons: The Detective Dynasty That Made History* (New York: Crown, 1967), 375–76; *Memorial Record of the Northern Peninsula*, 428. For moral crusades, see *Daily Mining Gazette* (Houghton), 8 November 1899, 12 April 1908, 1 August 1914.

49. Barkell, *Hancock*, 77; Mabel W. Oas, "A History of the Legitimate Drama in the Copper Country of Michigan from 1900–1910 with Special Study of the Calumet Theatre," typescript, Michigan Technological University Archives, Houghton, MI, pp. 19–20, 33–36, 40, 45–51, 68–72; *Copper Country Evening News* (Calumet), 24 October 1896, 1 November 1904, 1 September 1906; *Daily Mining Gazette* (Houghton), 30 April 1908, 30 January 1915, 30 May 1959.

50. For lecturers, see *Daily Mining Gazette* (Houghton), 27 March 1975. In 1907, at Red Jacket, the Grand Theatre offered "a full hour's entertainment," of short motion pictures for five cents in the afternoon and ten cents evenings (ibid., 4 April 1907; Alexander, *East Hancock*, 52), the schedule for the opening segment of *The Perils of Pauline* was Pastime Theater (Ontonagon) 14 April 1914, Crown (Calumet) 15 April, Lyric (Laurium) 16 April, Savoy (Hancock) 17 April, and Star (Houghton) 27 April. The advertisement depicted, in part, the beautiful heroine led astray by a scoundrel "who leads her into unthought of perils [with] pirates, aviators, scientists, Iceland peasants, highwaymen, society leaders, Chinamen and even Vikings

and Cyclops [crossing] her path" (*Calumet News*, 14 April 1914). For conversion to cinema and Finnish tenor, see *Calumet News* 15 and 18 April 1914.

51. *Portage Lake Mining Gazette* (Houghton), 9 July and 3 September 1896, 23 December 1899; *Daily Mining Gazette* (Houghton), 30 April 1908; Moyer, *Ke-Wee-Naw*, 79–80.

52. *Copper Country Evening News* (Calumet), 5 September 1906; *Daily Mining Gazette* (Houghton), 29 April 1908, 22 July 1914; *Evening Copper Journal* (Hancock), 14 July 1913; Swinton, *I Married a Doctor*, 332–35.

53. *Portage Lake Mining Gazette* (Houghton), 16 and 23 July and 10 and 24 September 1896; *Daily Mining Gazette* (Houghton), 2 and 20 June 1907, 30 July 1913. The round-trip railroad fare, Houghton to the Quebec shrine, was $25.00; see *Copper Country Evening News* (Calumet), 20 July 1896. One traveled via train from L'Anse to Mackinac Island and back on an excursion fare of $15.80 (*L'Anse Sentinel*, 21 September 1895).

54. *Copper Country Evening News* (Calumet), 1 and 3–4 September 1906; *L'Anse Sentinel*, 28 September 1895; *Portage Lake Mining Gazette* (Houghton), 16 July 1896.

55. For Electric Park, see Wilbert B. Maki, *Reminiscences of the Streetcar, 1900–1932* (Hancock, MI, n.d.) *Calumet News*, 9 October 1913, 28 May 1914; Bat Bigando interview, pp. 1078, 1080, and Bertha Jacka interview, p. 18—both in Suomi College Oral History Project, Finnish–American Heritage Center, Hancock, MI; David Mac Frimodig et al., *A Most Superior Land: Life in the Upper Peninsula of Michigan* (Lansing: Michigan Department of Natural Resources, 1983), 58; *Portage Lake Mining Gazette* (Houghton), 9 July 1896; *Daily Mining Gazette* (Houghton), 18 June 1907; Moyer, *Ke-Wee-Naw*, 113–14; Barkell, *Hancock*, 16.

56. *Daily Mining Gazette* (Houghton), 1 December 1914; *Calumet News*, 13 and 21 January 1914.

57. Clarence J. Monette, *Hancock, Michigan Remembered* (Lake Linden, MI, 1982); 1:100–102; *Daily Mining Gazette* (Houghton), 4 October 1899, 29 April 1908; *Calumet News*, 4 September 1913, 23 February 1914.

58. *L'Anse Sentinel* 21 September 1893; Frimodig, *Most Superior Land*, 177; *Portage Lake Mining Gazette* (Houghton), 3 and 10 September 1896; *Copper Country Evening News* (Calumet), 3 and 4 September 1906; *Daily Mining Gazette* (Houghton), 30 April 1908.

59. *Daily Mining Gazette* (Houghton), 16 December 1899; *Calumet News*, 26 December 1913 and 2 January and 6 March 1914; Moyer, *Ke-Wee-Naw*, 101–2; ibid., 151, for "moonlight nights" quotation; *Houghton Centennial*, 66; after games repast, Annie Aldrich interview, Suomi College Oral History Project, Finnish–American Heritage Center, Hancock, MI, pp. 1172–73. Lucena Harris Brockway, Diary, 12–13 February 1889, Brockway Family Collection, Michigan Technological University Archives, Houghton, MI.

60. The author particularly recalls a 1929–38 childhood hearing residents and former residents who returned on vacations speak at length and most eloquently of the "great days" before 1913.

CHAPTER 7

1. For detailed narrative, see Arthur W. Thurner, *Rebels on the Range: The Michigan Copper Miners' Strike of 1913–1914* (Lake Linden, MI: Forster, 1984).

2. Woodbridge N. Ferris Records Relating to Labor Strike in Copper Mining Industry, 1913–1914, (hereafter, Ferris Records), RG-46, B1, F3, State Archives, Lansing.

3. William Ellis's magazine story quoted in *Calumet News*, 16 December 1913.

4. For Miller's announcement, see *Calumet News*, 25 July 1913; Copper Country Commercial Club, *Strike Investigation* (Chicago: Donohue, 1913), 62; U.S. Congress, House, Committee on Mines and Mining, *Conditions in Copper Mines of Michigan: Hearings Before Subcommittee Pursuant to House Resolution 387*, 63d Cong., 2d sess. (Washington, 1914), 289, 602.

5. *Engineering and Mining Journal*, 3 September 1910, p. 440. Average pay per shift for year ending 30 June 1913 in Michigan Copper Country was about $2.98 for miners and $2.59 for trammers, while at Calumet and Hecla (May 1913), 86 percent of miners and 25 percent of trammers averaged more than three dollars a shift (Bureau of Labor Statistics, *Michigan Copper District Strike*, 11–21; Copper Country Commercial Club, *Strike Investigation*, 70–71).

6. Bureau of Labor Statistics, *Michigan Copper District Strike*, 11–12; House, *Conditions in Copper Mines*, 168–69.

7. *Engineering and Mining Journal*, 3 September 1910, p. 440. For the average number of days employed, see U.S. Department of the Interior, *Report on Mineral Industries in the United States*, Eleventh Census, 1890 (Washington: Government Printing Office, 1892), 156.

8. Gates, *Michigan Copper*, 128, 257, n. 64.

9. Lankton and Hyde, *Old Reliable*, 101.

10. *Engineering and Mining Journal*, 17 August 1912, p. 306.

11. Ibid., 30 December 1911, p. 1258.

12. U.S. Census, 1910, *Population*, 4:474.

13. *Engineering and Mining Journal*, 30 December 1911, p. 1258; ibid., 15 December 1906, p. 1127.

14. Western Federation of Miners, *Miners' Magazine*, 4 September 1913, 12.

15. F. W. Taussig, "The Copper Strike and Copper Dividends," *Survey*, 14 February 1914, 612–13.

16. Dwight E. Woodbridge, "The Lake Superior Copper Mines," *Engineering and Mining Journal*, 13 May 1911, 958.

17. *Engineering and Mining Journal*, 31 August 1912, 406; Lankton and Hyde, *Old Reliable*, 130; Gates, *Michigan Copper*, 131.

18. Angus Murdoch, *Boom Copper* (New York: Macmillan, 1943), 221. For parents' concerns that children work, Arthur W. Thurner, "Technology Old and New: The Copper Country Miner and the One-Man Drill, 1913–1914," presented at Michigan Technological University, 1983.

19. Gates, *Michigan Copper*, 131–32. The Copper Country middle-class fear of socialism paralleled that elsewhere in the United States during the Progressive period, 1900–1917 and influenced workers with expectations of upward mobility like Hancock Finnish laboring men who protested "recently arrived fellow countrymen" on the grounds that they were teaching anarchism/nihilism "under the guise of socialism"; see *Daily Mining Gazette* (Houghton), 14 April 1908. When the 1913–14 strike ended, William Rickard, socialist president of the Calumet local, blamed "red" socialism for the failure (Thurner, *Rebels on the Range*, 239).

20. John Ervin Brinley, Jr., *The Western Federation of Miners*, (Ann Arbor: University Microfilms International, 1981), 68–75 (for WFM as progressive, reform-minded, democratic), 80–94 (for leaders as socialists), and 202 (for 1908 Preamble).

21. *Daily Mining Gazette* (Houghton) 27 July 1913, for comprehensive listing

of militia arrivals and encampments; *Calumet News*, 25–26 and 28–29 July and 1 August 1913; House, *Conditions in Copper Mines*, 2166–67, 2173. Report of Brigadier General Pearley L. Abbey, 29 January 1914, Ferris Records, RG-46, B1, F3, gives troop total as 2,817; but his testimony before congressional committee, 9 March 1914, states peak figure as 2,765. See Michigan National Guard, Report of a Board of Officers Convened at Calumet, Michigan, 19 September 1913, State Archives, Lansing, p. 8 (hereafter, Officers' Report); Bureau of Labor Statistics, *Michigan Copper District Strike*, 43–44, for partial listing of injured workers; Thurner, *Rebels on the Range*, 1–6.

22. A 1914 report of the Social Service Commission of the Marquette, MI, diocese of the Protestant Episcopal Church concluded that 60 percent of the workers supported mine operators and less than 30 percent, the WFM, with 3,400 at Calumet and Hecla signing petitions "that the mine be reopened and they be allowed to earn their own living" *Survey*, 15 August 1914, 503.

23. Conclusions based on testimony of copper workers before congressional committee: House, *Conditions in Copper Mines*, 10–83, 109–22, 132–47, 162–93, 202–23, 236–37, 250–66, 289–90, 311–44, 372–84, 468, 482–85, 503–8, 521, 531, 550–55, 572, 583–87, 597–611, 2308.

24. For numbers employed, see Bureau of Labor Statistics, *Michigan Copper District Strike*, 42–43; House, *Conditions in Copper Mines*, 1456–57; John W. Black to Governor Ferris, 8 November 1913, Ferris Records RG-46, B1. For union's membership figures, see Western Federation of Miners Register of Local Union Assessments, April 1907–December 1933, Archives of the Western Federation of Miners and International Union of Mine, Mill, and Smelter Workers, Western Historical Collections, University of Colorado, Boulder (hereafter, WFM Assessment Register).

25. WFM Assessment Register.

26. Gates, *Michigan Copper*, 130–31, 258, n. 76.

27. *Calumet News*, 25 and 28 July and 1 August 1913; Michigan National Guard, Officers' Report, 8.

28. Bureau of Labor Statistics, *Michigan Copper District Strike*, 51–55, 58–59; House, *Conditions in Copper Mines*, 737, 1220–22, 1490, 1827, 2023–26, 2028; Ferris Records, RG-46, B1, F1; *Calumet News*, 10 and 29 July, 1 August, and 10 September 1913; Waddell's arrival reported, *Daily Mining Gazette* (Houghton), 29 July 1913.

29. Transcripts of a special hearing 15 August 1913 and the Houghton County coroner's inquest, 22–23 and 29–30 August and 3 September 1913, Ferris Records. Dan Sullivan (district union president) and Charles Hietala (secretary), on 15 August 1913, appealed to all organized labor, describing Waddell men as beating strikers, after forcing them into automobiles, halting parades, serving "purse-proud copper barons," concluding, "Bayonets do not scare us, and thugs won't mine copper" (*Miners' Magazine*, 4 September 1913); Waddell–Mahon circular, *Public*, 17 October 1913, pp. 996–97; Bureau of Labor Statistics, *Michigan Copper District Strike*, 59.

30. C.&H. Papers, B6, Michigan Technological University Archives, Houghton, MI.

31. *Daily Mining Gazette* (Houghton), 23 August and 16, 18, 21, and 30 December 1913; *Calumet News*, 15 and 16 December 1913.

32. Bureau of Labor Statistics, *Michigan Copper District Strike*, 38–41, 181–82; House, *Conditions in Copper Mines*, 93–94, 126–27, 129; Western Federation of Miners, Executive Board Minutes, 5 July 1909–24 March 1915, pp. 133, 135–36, 140–41; Western Federation of Miners, *Official Proceedings*, Annual Convention 1914, pp. 134, 277–79—both in WFM Archives, Western Historical Collections, University of Colorado, Boulder.

33. Claude T. Rice, "Labor Conditions at Calumet & Hecla," *Engineering and Mining Journal*, 23 December 1911, p. 1235.

34. WFM Assessment Register.

35. Bureau of Labor Statistics, *Michigan Copper District Strike*, 38.

36. In April 1914, Moyer said that the WFM's treasury in July 1913 made it impossible for the WFM to assume responsibility for such a strike, "yet, knowing their [Michigan workers'] demands were just, our federation came to their support" (*Chicago Record–Herald*, 14 April 1914).

37. Thurner, *Rebels on the Range*, 80–85.

38. Ibid., 84.

39. Ibid., 83–85.

40. U.S. Department of Labor, *Reports of the Department of Labor, 1914*, 99–101; Bureau of Labor Statistics, *Michigan Copper District Strike*, 170–83; House, *Conditions in Copper Mines*, 1527.

41. *Calumet News*, 2, 7, and 12 August 1913; *American Federation of Labor Weekly News Letter*, 16 August 1913.

42. In Washington, D.C., Moyer appealed to Senator William Borah (Republican, of Idaho) and others to investigate charges of peonage in the Michigan copper district (*Miners' Magazine*, 2 October 1913).

43. Western Federation of Miners Expenditure Summary, 1910–1933; Report of the Secretary–Treasurer of the WFM for Fiscal Year Ending 30 June 1914 (ibid., 1914); WFM, *Official Proceedings*, Annual Convention 1914, p. 279; and WFM Michigan Defense Fund Ledgers, books 1–2—all at WFM Archives, Western Historical Collections, University of Colorado, Boulder.

44. House, *Conditions in Copper Mines*, 1272–76, 1282–85, 1926–30; *Calumet News*, 11 September 1913; *People* v. *Annie Clements* [*sic*], Circuit Court, Houghton County Courthouse, File No. 4276 (in which record she signed her name as Ana Clemenc).

45. House, *Conditions in Copper Mines*, 817, 1276–77, 1829; *Calumet News*, 8, 13, and 15 November 1913.

46. House, *Conditions in Copper Mines*, 1153, 1248, 1829, 1834, 2046–52, 2178–80; Brigadier General Abbey to Governor Ferris, 3 September 1913, Ferris Records, RG-46, B1, F1; *Calumet News*, 28 August and 3, 5–6, 8, 11, and 24 September 1913; *Evening Copper Journal* (Hancock), 28 July and 28 August 1913; *Detroit Free Press*, 29 July 1913.

47. House, *Conditions in Copper Mines*, 1085–90, 1094, 2148–54, 2160–65, 2174–78; *Calumet News*, 12–13 and 16 September 1913; *Daily Mining Gazette* (Houghton), 4 November 1913; N. D. Cochran, *Miners' Magazine*, 23 October 1913, pp. 4–5; Major John S. Bersey, on duty in the Copper Country, wrote Governor Ferris on 13 October 1913, "'Big Annie' the female mob leader railed at the cavalry this morning thinking that they had overslept" (Ferris Records, RG-46, B1, F5).

48. House, *Conditions in Copper Mines*, 1555–69; Bureau of Labor Statistics, *Michigan Copper District Strike*, 9, 60–62; injunction text in *Daily Mining Gazette* (Houghton), 21 September 1913; Oberto statement, *Daily Mining Gazette*, 18 November 1914; Brigadier General Abbey to Governor Ferris, 22 September 1913, Ferris Records, RG-46, B1, F3; *Miners' Magazine*, 2 October 1913, pp. 8–9; *Calumet News*, 22, 24–27, and 29 September and 1 and 8 October 1913.

49. House, *Conditions in Copper Mines*, 1492–93, 1610–11; Bureau of Labor Statistics, *Michigan Copper District Strike*, 49, 62–64; Copper Country Commercial Club, *Strike Investigation*, 58; *Daily Mining Gazette* (Houghton), 1 October 1913; *Calumet News*, 19 September and 1 and 24–25 November 1913; *Detroit Free Press*, 29 July 1913.

50. Governor Ferris to Brigadier General Abbey, 9, 22, and 26 October and 26 November 1913; Abbe to Ferris, 1 and 25 October and 27 and 29 November

1913; Ferris to J. W. Black, 7 October 1913—all in Ferris Records, RG-46, B1, F3; House, *Conditions in Copper Mines*, 266–67, 1545–46, 1783–87, 1806–10; *Miners' Magazine*, 2 October 1913, p. 6; Thurner, *Rebels on the Range*, 269, nn. 33–34.

51. House, *Conditions in Copper Mines*, 1576–79; *Calumet News* 5–6 December 1913; *Sunday Mining Gazette* (Houghton), 7 December 1913.

52. Thurner, *Rebels on the Range*, 120–21.

53. Ibid., 121–23.

54. *Miners' Magazine*, 20 November 1913, p. 9.

55. Thurner, *Rebels on the Range*, 123–25.

56. Ibid., 125–27.

57. Ibid., 128–33.

58. Ibid., 133–35; for Dunnigan statement, see Timothy O'Brien affidavit, Ferris Records, RG-46, B3, F15.

59. Thurner, *Rebels on the Range*, 135.

60. Houghton County Coroner's inquest held at Red Jacket, Michigan 29–31 December 1913, into deaths in Italian Hall on 24 December 1913; copy of transcript in Michigan Technological University Archives, Houghton.

61. Thurner, *Rebels on the Range*, chap. 11.

62. Ibid., 154–65; *Chicago Record–Herald*, 11 March 1914 for Moyer's retraction as to Citizens Alliance being responsible for cry of fire at Italian Hall. Matt Saari, striker, who lost son in the panic, told reporter the the cry of fire came "from a group of men and women toward the front of the hall" (ibid., 26 December 1913); for Moyer as martyr, see *Chicago Tribune*, 28 December 1913. A Citizens Alliance member told reporter: "Moyer was told to get out of town because his record was bad. . . . This is a peaceful community and we want it to remain that way. The Cripple Creek [Colorado] and Coeur d'Alene [Idaho] records of the Western federation bar that organization forever from Calumet and the mining district here" (ibid., 30 December 1913).

63. House, *Conditions in Copper Mines* consists of seven parts and is an invaluable source for understanding labor in the Copper Country; *Calumet News*, 13 March 1914; *Chicago Record–Herald*, 13 March 1914. Taylor said, in effect, that the Copper Country resembled a kingdom dominated by MacNaughton as king (*Public* 20 March 1914, p. 277); but I have been unable to find a direct quotation.

64. Probably John J. Casey (Democrat) of Pennsylvania; see *Detroit Free Press*, 8 March 1914. More than a year after the end of the strike, Congressman Taylor was quoted as saying that "in the interest of harmony, and in view of the fact that the strike is ended," no report would be forthcoming—a situation that the WFM found intolerable. It accused Taylor of prejudice in favor of corporations and expressed astonishment at his reneging on a promise to report (*Miners' Magazine*, 6 May 1915, pp. 1, 3).

65. *Denver Post* of 13 April 1914 reported figures given here as official. I found no record of the figures in WFM Archives. The final issue of the strikers' newspaper *Miners' Bulletin*—14 April 1914—announced the end of the strike but supplied no figures. See also WFM Executive Board Minutes, Western Historical Collections, University of Colorado, Boulder, pp. 163–65; *Miners' Magazine*, 23 April 1914, pp. 7–8; *Calumet News*, 10 April 1914; *Detroit Free Press*, 14–15 April 1914; *Chicago Record–Herald*, 13 April 1914.

66. Thurner, *Rebels on the Range*, 236–37.

67. Ibid., 230–31. Failure in Michigan led directly to the rebellion of the WFM's strongest local at Butte, Montana, and to the WFM's eventual demise as an effective labor organization; see Arthur W. Thurner, "The Western Federation of Miners in Two Copper Camps: The Impact of the Michigan Copper Miners' Strike on Butte's Local No. 1," *Montana: The Magazine of Western History* 33(Spring 1983): 30–45.

68. Thurner, *Rebels on the Range*, 28–33, 35–38, 40–42.

69. Ibid., 26–27; Bureau of Labor Statistics, *Michigan Copper District Strike*, 136.

70. Graham R. Taylor, "The Clash in the Copper Country," *Survey*, 1 November 1913, p. 128; *Evening Copper Journal* (Hancock), 25 July 1913. A Finn armed with a club shouted at F. W. Denton, general manager of the Copper Range Consolidated, on the second day of the strike, "Stop you, I am the sheriff of Houghton County to-day" (Michigan National Guard, Officers' Report, p. 7).

71. *Engineering and Mining Journal*, 6 September 1913, 471; *Calumet News*, 22 October 1913; excerpts from a *Marquette Mining Journal* editorial on incredulity of foreign-born strikers expecting federal government takeover of mines, in *Calumet News*, 24 January 1914.

72. For one attempt to explain Moyer, see Arthur W. Thurner, "Charles H. Moyer and the Michigan Copper Strike, 1913–1914," *Michigan Historical Review* 17(Fall 1991): 1–19.

73. Quoted in Gates, *Michigan Copper*, 113–14.

74. Papers of and Relating to Alexander Agassiz, Agassiz Museum Archives, Library, Museum of Comparative Zoology, Harvard University.

75. Agassiz's early youth "was passed in a period of domestic confusion and sorrow which may have left its mark upon him throughout life, for his great self-reliance was a characteristic rarely developed in those whose early years have been free from care" (Alfred G. Mayer, "Alexander Agassiz, 1835–1910," *Popular Science Monthly* 77[November 1910]: 420); *Engineering and Mining Journal*, 16 April 1910, pp. 816–17. A salaried union official in the Michigan copper district said during the strike: "Them was the good old days when old Mr. Agassiz was at the head of C.&H. When he went the men lost their best friend. The men was always looked after then. A man knew that if he could get a job there, he was fixed for life" (Francis John Dyer, "The Truth About the Copper Strike," *National Magazine* 40[May 1914]: 235).

76. House, *Conditions in Copper Mines*, 1395–96, 1472–74, 1482–84, 1515, 1523.

77. Ibid., 1482.

78. Best material on "paternalism" in Claude T. Rice, "Labor Conditions at Calumet and Hecla," *Engineering and Mining Journal*, 23 December 1911, pp. 1235–39; idem, "Labor Conditions at Copper Range," *Engineering and Mining Journal*, 28 December 1912, pp. 1220–32. Also good is the Copper Country Commercial Club's *Strike Investigation*, with many illustrations of company housing; editorial, *Keweenaw Miner*, 22 August 1913; Lankton and Hyde, *Old Reliable*, 131; Curtis, "Calumet," 34. For an extremely negative view of corporate concern for workers, see Larry D. Lankton, *Cradle to Grave: Life, Work and Death at the Lake Superior Copper Mines* (New York: Oxford University Press, 1991).

79. *Daily Mining Gazette* (Houghton), 18 October 1899.

80. Peter Clark Macfarlane, "The Issues at Calumet," *Collier's*, 7 February 1914, pp. 5–6, 22–25; *Engineering and Mining Journal*, 13 December 1913, p. 1136.

81. Thurner, *Rebels on the Range*, 64.

82. Thomas Jefferson, *Writings* (New York: Library of America, 1984), 1024.

83. Gates, *Michigan Copper*, 138–41.

84. Ibid. for World War I profits; Lankton and Hyde, *Old Reliable*, 130–31.

85. Lankton and Hyde, *Old Reliable*, 136.

86. *Calumet and Hecla Mining Company Semi-Centennial Edition, 1866–1916, of "The Keweenaw Miner"* (Calumet, MI, 1916); *Boston Evening Transcript*, 28 June 1916.

87. Gates, *Michigan Copper*, 116; Lankton and Hyde, *Old Reliable*, 103; *Daily Mining Gazette* (Houghton), 5 December 1914.

88. Calumet Light Guard and Houghton Light Infantry, *Our Boys in the Spanish–American War*, 2–3, 5, 7, 9, 11, 13–14, 16, 19; *Houghton Centennial*, 47–49; *Calumet News*, 28 October 1918; for World War I casualties see *Daily Mining Gazette* (Houghton), 25 May 1991.

89. Gates, *Michigan Copper*, 204.

90. Utley and Cutcheon, *Michigan*, 2:372.

CHAPTER 8

1. Mrs. M. F. Turrell, "Journal Notes," *Michigan History* 12(1928): 397–98.

2. Gates, *Michigan Copper*, 155, 205, and 265, n. 52.

3. Lankton and Hyde, *Old Reliable*, 103, 106; Calumet and Hecla, *Annual Report, 1923*, 12; for days worked, mines idle, in 1924, see *Calumet News*, 14 October 1924; Benedict, *Red Metal*, 138; Edward LeGendre to Charles H. Moyer, 24 December 1925, B1, F1-12, Archives of the Western Federation of Miners and International Union of Mine, Mill, and Smelter Workers, Western Historical Collections, University of Colorado, Boulder.

4. Patrick H. O'Brien, interview, Detroit, 16 October 1957, Michigan Historical Collections, Bentley Historical Library, Ann Arbor, p. 24; Gates, *Michigan Copper*, 146, 154–55. Benedict refers to "the seven fat years of the roaring twenties, 1924 to 1930," followed by depression, 1930–1940, and the "false prosperity" of 1941–45 (*Red Metal*, 194).

5. Lankton and Hyde, *Old Reliable*, 106; Gates, *Michigan Copper*, 148–50, 154, 160; Alex Skelton quotation, ibid., 143; Frimodig, *Keweenaw Character*, 82–86.

6. *Calumet News*, 17 October 1924; Barkell, *Hancock*, 73; *Development Bureau News*, 1 December 1927, Upper Peninsula Travel and Recreation Association (hereafter UPTARA), B9, F1, State Archives, Lansing, p. 21.

7. Benedict, *Red Metal*, 196. Copper sold for 13 cents a pound in 1924, 14 in 1925, and 18 in 1929 (ibid.). See also *Development Bureau News*, 1 June 1930, UPTARA, B9, F3, State Archives, Lansing; U.S. Congress, Senate, Committee on Public Works, *Opportunities for Economic Development in Michigan's Upper Peninsula*, 87th Cong., 1st sess. (Washington, 1962), 18; Turrell, "Journal Notes," 398.

8. Calumet and Hecla, *Annual Report*, 1924:5; 1926:23; 1927:7; 1928:4, 7; 1929:2, 4–5, 16–17. Profitability at Quincy ceased in 1920, with no dividends paid 1921–48 (Lankton and Hyde, *Old Reliable*, 99); Benedict, *Red Metal*, 137–43, 198; *Development Bureau News*, 1 November 1926, UPTARA, B9, F1, State Archives, Lansing, p. 1; Keweenaw Bay and Arnheim Extension Study Group, *Trestles and Tracks: A History of Keweenaw Bay and Arnheim* (L'Anse, MI: L'Anse Sentinel, 1988), 2:23; Walter Crane, "Mining Methods and Practice in the Michigan Copper Mines," Bureau of Mines, Bulletin No. 306 (Washington: Department of Commerce, 1929), 29.

9. *Daily Mining Gazette* (Houghton), 23 December 1899 (Copper Range Railroad Supplement).

10. Collins, "Paine's Career," 140, 143.

11. Gates, *Michigan Copper*, 205, 220.

12. *Daily Mining Gazette* (Houghton), 1 December 1914; U.S. Congress, Senate, Committee on Public Works, *Opportunities for Economic Development in Michigan's Upper Peninsula*, 87th Cong., 1st sess. (Washington, 1962), 81. The average length of the growing season was 151 days at Houghton, 143 at Eagle Harbor, 89 at Bergland, and 78 at Ewen; see Dewey A. Seeley, "The Climate of Michigan," in *Michigan Agriculture*, (Lansing: Michigan Department of Agriculture, 1932), 26.

13. Karamanski, *Deep Woods Frontier*, 160; U.S. Census, 1860, Houghton County, Houghton Township, Clifton (microfilm) M653-544; Holmio, *Finns in Michigan*, 146; Michigan Department of Agriculture, *Our Responsibility* (Lansing, Department of Agriculture: 1921).

14. James L. Carter, *Superior: A State for the North Country* (Marquette, MI: Pilot Press, 1980), 37–43.

15. Turrell, "Journal Notes," 399; Michigan Writers' Project, *Michigan*, 567. A Lansing museum curator visiting Ontonagon County in 1928 expressed her "astonishment at the progress made in farming" and predicted that a "few more years will show our most fertile fields and our largest crops in this northern section" (Mrs. Ferrey, "Diary Notes," *Michigan History* 12[1928]: 621); Verne Church, *Crop Report for Michigan: Annual Summary, 1922* (Lansing: U.S. Department of Agriculture and Michigan Department of Agriculture, 1923).

16. *Development Bureau News*, 1 June 1926, 1 November and 1 December 1927, and 25 December 1928, UPTARA, B9, F1–2.

17. Ibid., 1 May 1931, November 1940, UPTARA, B9, F3–4; *Daily Mining Gazette* (Houghton), 31 August 1934.

18. *Development Bureau News*, 1 September 1929, UPTARA, B9, F2; President R. S. Shaw of Michigan State College, Lansing, promoted agriculture and acculturation and told those attending the Upper Peninsula Conservation Conference at Marquette (October 1930), that the state college was "desirous of cooperating with Upper Peninsula farming in every possible way," urging that the settler be assisted "to develop his property, his home and his family along the high standards of American living," (ibid., F3); Daniel D. Brockway to Barney Vasburg, 27 July 1884, Letterbook, 1883–85, Michigan Historical Collections, Bentley Historical Library, Ann Arbor.

19. For a brief history of the Development Bureau, see memorandum, 25 March 1954, UPTARA, F4; 1930s–1940s tourism and downstate remarks are from recollections of author; Michigan Writers' Project, *Michigan*, 87–88; *Development Bureau News*, 1 June 1926, 1 July 1929, UPTARA, B9, F1–2.

20. Raymond H. Torrey (secretary of the National Park Association, New York) and others from the Development Bureau coined the phrase "Hiawatha Land"; *Development Bureau News*, 1 July 1927; see also *Development Bureau News*, 1 February 1927, where passages appear from Longfellow's poem, VII, X, and XVI; ibid., 1 August, 1 September, and 1 October 1929 (for Manning) and 1 September 1929 (for Geismar and Stace)—all in UPTARA, B9, F1–2. Jay Shedd, Detroit, wrote, "The friendliness of upper peninsula people appeals to us. . . . Folks up here do not put on much dog or high hat the visitor," (*Development Bureau News*, 1 September 1929, UPTARA, B9, F1–2).

21. *Development Bureau News*, 1 June 1931, UPTARA, B9, F3.

22. Minutes of the twenty-first annual meeting of the Development Bureau, UPTARA, B9, F4. Note, especially Governor Wilbur M. Bruckner's reference to anticipated tourists in 1931 as economic depression settled over the state: "I am glad that army is coming," p. 8. George E. Bishop, on 13 June 1935, reported that a 40 percent rise in volume of tourist dollars in the Upper Peninsula (1934) seemed to have given birth to "a new faith in the future possibilities of the tourist and resort business" (UPTARA, B6, F2); Michigan Writers' Project, *Michigan*, 583–84; *Daily Mining Gazette* (Houghton), 28 December 1933 (Leon Lundmark), 9 July and 21 and 26 August 1934; *Calumet News*, 22 July 1933; *Evening News–Journal* (Calumet), 10 July 1939.

23. *Daily Mining Gazette* (Houghton), 21 July, 9 August 1934; *Evening News–Journal* (Calumet), 14 July 1939; Ontonagon advertisement, UPTARA, B9, F10; for Isle Royale, see *Development Bureau News*, 1 May 1931 and 1 April 1932, both in

UPTARA, B9, F3–4; for "ghost ships" on Lake Superior and Bible camp, see Michigan Writers' Project, *Michigan*, 121–22, 587.

24. Houghton County Treasurer's Office, Liquor License Tax Record, 1912–14, RG 77-105, B69, F11, Michigan Technological University Archives, Houghton, MI; Swinton, *I Married a Doctor*, 127, 133–36; *Copper Country Evening News* (Calumet), 12 March 1900; MacNaughton's remarks in House, *Conditions in Copper Mines*, 4:1460; Boyer, "Decline of the Progressive Party," 89; Raymbaultown information supplied by anonymous Calumet residents, March 1992; Leslie Chapman interview, Suomi College Oral History Project, Finnish–American Heritage Center, Hancock, MI, pp. 17–18. Every summer, grapes "by the ton" arrived at Red Jacket's Copper Range depot, below Pine Street; and "the authorities must have realized all these grapes weren't being manufactured into jelly"; see John E. Wilson letter in *Copper Island Sentinel* (Calumet), 25 July 1985. For raids in Houghton County, see *Calumet News*, 29 August 1921, 31 March 1927, and 31 August and 22 October 1929.

25. Calumet and Hecla, *Annual Report*, 1930:8; 1931:2–3, 7, 18; 1932:6; 1933:2–5; 1936:2–5; 1937:4–5, with inventories, 1928–37, on p. 11; 1948:4–5; Gates, *Michigan Copper*, 161–62.

26. *Calumet News*, 27 October and 5 November 1932; for earlier demand for tariff, see *Development Bureau News*, 1 December 1930, UPTARA, B9, F3.

27. *Calumet News*, 15 October 1924; Gates, *Michigan Copper*, 162.

28. Jess Gilbert and Craig Harris, "Unemployment, Primary Production, and Population in the Upper Peninsula of Michigan in the Great Depression," in *A Half Century Ago: Michigan in the Great Depression* (East Lansing: Michigan State University, 1980), 47.

29. Calumet and Hecla, *Annual Report*, 1932:8, 1933:2–5; for dividends paid, 1923–40, see 1940:12.

30. *Calumet News*, 28 December 1932; Bertha Jacka, interview, Suomi College Oral History Project, Finnish–American Heritage Center, Hancock, MI, p. 9. At Houghton–Hancock Atlantic and Pacific stores, sirloin steak sold for 23 cents a pound; fresh ground hamburger, four pounds for 25 cents, one dozen fresh corn, 16 cents, and three pounds of coffee, 99 cents; see *Daily Mining Gazette* (Houghton), 3 August 1934. Hancock's Kirkish Brothers store, celebrating twenty years since establishment, offered Imperial Valley head lettuce for 5 cents a head and four pounds of Maxwell House coffee for $1.05; see *Daily Mining Gazette*, 15 February 1933. Street scenes from 1931–35 are recollections of the author.

31. *Daily Mining Gazette* (Houghton), 19 February 1933; *Ontonagon Herald* (Ontonagon), 23 September 1933.

32. Edgar E. Robinson, *The Presidential Vote, 1896–1932* (Stanford: Stanford University Press, 1934), 91–92; *Calumet News*, 10 November 1932; *Copper Country Evening News* (Calumet), 13–14, 21, and 27 October and 4 November 1896; Boyer, "Decline of the Progressive Party," 77–79, 93. For Republican supremacy and challenge from Democrats, see David Halkola, "The Citadel Crumbles: Political Change in the Upper Peninsula of Michigan in the Great Depression," in *A Half Century Ago: Michigan in the Great Depression* (East Lansing: Michigan State University, 1980), 56–89; for earlier Republican dominance, see pp. 56–57.

33. Boyer, "Decline of the Progressive Party," 80; *Calumet News*, 10 October and 6 November 1912; Robinson, *Presidential Vote*, 91–92, 228, 230–31, 233; Michigan Department of State, *Michigan Official Directory and Legislative Manual, 1913* (Lansing, 1913), 483, 521, 532, 554–55 (hereafter, *Michigan Manual*); *Native Copper Times* (Lake Linden), 2 April 1895; *Copper Country Evening News* (Calumet), 14 August 1896; *Daily Mining Gazette* (Houghton), 27 June 1907; Leslie Chapman

interview, Suomi College Oral History Project, Finnish–American Heritage Center, Hancock, MI, p. 21.

34. *Calumet News*, 4 April 1933; *Michigan Manual*, 1937:246–48, 252–54, 274; 1941:269–71.

35. Halkola, "Citadel Crumbles," esp., 62, 81–82; map of twelfth congressional district in *Michigan Manual*, 1937: pl. 13.

36. *Michigan Manual*, 1949:128, 1951:120, 1961:119, 1965:148, 1971:113–14; Richard M. Scammon and Alice V. McGillivray, *America Votes* (Washington: Congressional Quarterly Elections Research Center, 1955), 1:161–62, 166; for contested election, see *New York Times*, 7 November and 4, 7, and 16 December 1948, 8 January and 28 July 1949; *Daily Mining Gazette* (Houghton), 9 February 1941; analysis made by Halkola, "Citadel Crumbles," 76–79.

37. *Ontonagon Herald*, 18 March 1933.

38. Ibid., 5 August and 23 September 1933; *Calumet News*, 4 April 1933.

39. Gilbert and Harris, "Michigan in the Great Depression," 37–38; Holmio, *History of the Finns*, 191; *Calumet News*, 4 April 1933.

40. Calumet and Hecla, *Annual Report*, 1932:16; *Calumet News*, 3 June and 20 July 1933; gardens and barter are recollections of the author.

41. *Daily Mining Gazette* (Houghton), 24 and 26 December 1933, 7 and 18 August 1934; Michigan Writers' Project, *Michigan* 583–84.

42. *Daily Mining Gazette* (Houghton), 3 July 1934; *Evening News–Journal* (Calumet), 10 and 20 July 1939; Works Projects Administration, Tabulation of Sponsor and Federal Participation in All Michigan Projects for Fiscal Years Ending 30 June 1936–39, State Archives, Lansing, pp. 256, 280–280A, 291, 315 (hereafter, WPA, Tabulation Michigan Projects, 1936–39).

43. Local Public Welfare Expenditures and Corresponding Tax Rates for Twenty Representative Counties for Year Ending 1936, Records of the Welfare and Relief Study Commission (Michigan), 1936–38, RG-35, B5, F12, Table 37 and material on Houghton County, State Archives, Lansing.

44. Lankton and Hyde, *Old Reliable*, 142; for Quincy's attempts to reopen with loans from federal government, see pp. 142–43.

45. "Accomplishments of the CCC in Michigan (under U.S. Department of Agriculture)" and covering letter, Vico C. Isola to Victor D. Clum, 14 March 1947, Natural Resources, Conservation Corps, 84-48, B1, State Archives, Lansing.

46. *Daily Mining Gazette* (Houghton), 17 August 1934, 12 July 1939, 2 February 1940, 11 February 1941; *Ontonagon Herald*, 19 August and 16 September 1933; fires listed, *L'Anse Sentinel*, 14 September 1933.

47. *Ontonagon Herald*, 19 August 1933; Hubbell youth's story ca. 1939 is a personal recollection of author.

48. *Daily Mining Gazette* (Houghton), 29 July 1934; Calumet and Hecla, *Annual Report*, 1933:4, 1934:3–4.

49. Calumet and Hecla, *Annual Report*, 1936:2–3 and 5, 1937:7, 1938:10.

50. Ibid., 1934:4–5, 1935:4–5, 1936:6, 1939:4–5; Gates, *Michigan Copper*, 165.

51. *Calumet News*, 29 April and 1 May 1933; *Ontonagon Herald*, 5 August 1933; in July 1935, Professor Sweet became director of WPA programs in Michigan's Upper Peninsula (Lankton and Hyde, *Old Reliable*, 143); George Weeks, *Stewards of the State* (Detroit and Ann Arbor: Detroit News and Historical Society of Michigan, 1987), 93; "tacks" and wheelbarrow anecdotes are personal recollections of the author.

52. Danziger, *Chippewas*, 114, 117, 124.

53. Ibid., 123, 127, 138–39.

54. Ibid., 132–36; Collier quoted, ibid., x. Ontonagon's 1854 reservation

consisted of 2,551 acres but was reduced to 724 acres by 1937 and was then occupied by a solitary Ojibwa male who received $96 annually in relief funds and $84 from a house he rented (ibid., 238, n. 30); for population, 1930, see "Historical Notes," *Michigan History* 16(1932): 362.

55. *Development Bureau News*, 1 December 1926, UPTARA, B9, F1; U.S. Census, 1920:232–34, 434, 459, 461, 463, 466; 1930:518, 522, 524, 529; 1940:505, 507–8, 510; *Daily Mining Gazette* (Houghton), 4 August 1934.

56. *Houghton Centennial*, 41; *Ontonagon Herald*, 2 September 1933; *Development Bureau News*, 1 September 1929, 1 April 1930, UPTARA, B9, F2, 3; Michigan Writers' Project *Michigan*, 594. Bus service three days per week via Northland Deluxe line, Calumet to Detroit in eighteen hours, began on 14 August 1934; see *Daily Mining Gazette* (Houghton), 12 August 1934 (Sunday ed.).

57. Moyer, *Ke-Wee-Naw*, 145; Wilbert B. Maki, *Hancock: A Mosaic of Memories* (Calumet, MI, 1984), 42; for Amphidrome in 1926 and 1933, see advertisement with photograph in *Development Bureau News*, 1 August 1926, UPTARA, B9, F1; *Daily Mining Gazette* (Houghton), 26 December 1991; Delia McCurdy letter, ibid., 2 January 1992.

58. *Calumet News*, 14–15 and 17 October 1924.

59. Raids to curb prostitution occurred perennially; see, e.g., *Calumet News*, 3 March 1930. The Onigaming was described as a "mecca" for higher strata of society during summer social season (ibid., 3 June 1933). The spectacular January 1929 fire that destroyed the landmark Washington School, Calumet, was believed to have been ignited by a student's dropping a cigarette behind broken plaster in a toilet room; see *Daily Mining Gazette*, 20 December 1952 (Green Sheet Supplement); John E. Wilson letter in *Copper Island Sentinel* (Calumet), 25 July 1985. Mrs. Wilcox had met Leopold when he was a boy visiting Ontonagon County in 1914; see Chris Chabot, *Tales of White Pine* (Ontonagon, MI: Ontonagon Herald, 1979), 36.

60. *Daily Mining Gazette* (Houghton), 3–4 August 1935; for Vairo story, see *Daily Mining Gazette*, prob. ca. 28 November 1952 (Green Sheet Supplement?); *Calumet News*, 7 October 1920.

61. For hockey, *Development Bureau News*, 1 April 1931, UPTARA, B9, F3; *Calumet News*, 7 December 1932; *Houghton Centennial*, 68; *Daily Mining Gazette* (Houghton), 2 September 1934, 7 October 1978 (Mishica story), 17 August 1991; Chabot, *Tales of White Pine*, 52–53.

62. *Daily Mining Gazette* (Houghton), 27 September 1923; *Calumet News*, 25 and 26 September 1923.

63. Niemi, *Americanization of the Finnish People*, 16; Swinton, *I Married a Doctor*, 423; *Calumet News*, 12 March 1929.

64. *Calumet News*, 10 November 1920; *Daily Mining Gazette* (Houghton), 10 October and 15 November 1921; for commemorative monuments, see *Development Bureau News*, 1 December 1931, UPTARA, B9, F3.

65. Paul Fromholz, Souvenirs and Letters, Keweenaw Historical Society Collection, B3, no. 154, Michigan Technological University Archives, Houghton, MI.

66. *Calumet News*, 14 October 1920, 16 October 1924, 11 February 1933; in 1921, enrollment on the first night of school was 370, an increase over 1920 but down from earlier years (*Calumet News*, 2 November 1921); Hilda Ruohoniemi, interview, Suomi College Oral History Project, Finnish–American Heritage Center, Hancock, MI, p. 3; 1918–19 Bulletin of Suomi College quoted in Niemi, *Americanization of the Finnish People*, 32.

67. Cynthia Beaudette story in *Daily Mining Gazette* (Houghton), 28 December 1991; Niemi, *Americanization of the Finnish People*, 27–28; Jingo Viitala Vachon, *Tall Timber Tales* (L'Anse, MI: L'Anse Sentinel, 1973), 9–11; *Houghton Centennial*,

25. Pioneer teacher at age sixteen, William Henry Bennetts, born in England in 1852, also worked as a drill boy in Cliff Mine (Clarence Bennetts Collection, F5 and 8, Michigan Technological University Archives, Houghton, MI. Excellence of schools as early as 1895 is mentioned, *Memorial Record of the Northern Peninsula*, 227; School inspectors' reports, 1928, Reel 1314, State Archives, Lansing; Chicago students in Copper Country are personal recollections of the author.

68. *Ontonagon Herald*, 30 September 1933; *Calumet News*, 31 May 1933; Baraga High School graduated forty, almost all of Finnish extraction (*Calumet News*, 1 June 1933); Robert Phillips of Purdue University, a former resident of the Copper Country gave the commencement addresses at both Hancock and Calumet (*Calumet News*, 1 June 1933). At the 12 November 1930 dedication ceremonies at Calumet's Washington School (elementary), Dr. Preston Bradley, popular Protestant clergyman of Chicago delivered the dedicatory address (*Development Bureau News*, 1 December 1930, UPTARA, B9, F3). See also School inspectors' reports, 1928, Reel 1314, and 1931, Reel 1324, State Archives, Lansing, MI. In Allouez Township, Keweenaw County, 147 out of the 333 ages 16–18 were not in school, while only 3 out of the 191 ages 14–15 did not attend school (School inspectors' reports 1931, Reel 1325, State Archives, Lansing).

69. *Calumet News*, 24 September 1923; Niemi, *Americanization of the Finish People*, 13–14; Finns celebrated the Fourth of July in "riotously American" fashion, calling it "Vortsulai," and showed their pride "in their adopted land" (Vachon, *Tall Timber Tales*, 102).

70. *Daily Mining Gazette* (Houghton), 4 July 1930; *Evening News–Journal* (Calumet), 18 July 1939; recent efforts by cultural pluralists tend to obscure the evidence of intermarriage that began early and accelerated after 1920.

71. *Daily Mining Gazette* (Houghton), 5 and 7 August 1934, 29 July 1935; *Ontonagon Herald*, 26 August 1933.

72. At the 1939 homecoming, the choir was directed by Alfred Nicholls, a choir member at Central Mine, 1880–90; see *Evening News–Journal* (Calumet), 17 July 1939. The story of Harry Vine is in *Daily Mining Gazette* (Houghton), 10 January 1992.

73. Holmio, *History of the Finns*, 165; *Daily Mining Gazette* (Houghton), 7 May and 7 July 1930; Halkola, "Finnish-Language Newspapers," 85–86. According to one scholar, a statement current ca. 1918 among some Finns was, "One must live according to the customs of the country [United States] or else he must go back to the old country" (Niemi, *Americanization of the Finnish People*, 42).

74. Gates, *Michigan Copper*, 167; *History Upper Peninsula*, 254.

75. Statement from first report of the state commissioner of mineral statistics, quoted in *History Upper Peninsula*, 159.

CHAPTER 9

1. *Evening News–Journal* (Calumet), 11 July 1939.

2. *Daily Mining Gazette* (Houghton), 3–4 January 1941.

3. Ibid., 9 and 12 February 1941.

4. Utley and Cutcheon, *Michigan*, 4:273.

5. *Daily Mining Gazette* (Houghton), 23 February 1940; Michigan Writers' Project, *Michigan*, 598.

6. Halkola, *Michigan Tech Centennial*, 82, 90–91, 94.

7. U.S. Census, 1940, *Agriculture*, 1:786, 789–90, 792; *Daily Mining Gazette* (Houghton), 11 February 1941.

8. Personal recollections of author; *Daily Mining Gazette* (Houghton), 4 January 1941.

9. Arthur W. Thurner, "Red Jacket/Calumet: The First Century," in *Calumet Village Centennial Souvenir Book* (Calumet, MI: Centennial Committee, 1975), 15; *Calumet News*, 1 June 1933.

10. Gates, *Michigan Copper*, 171–72; Thurner, *Rebels on the Range*, 252; CIO Proceedings, 1940, Gene Saari Collection, B14, pp. 200–202; for beginnings at Quincy, see Minute Book, Quincy Local 523, 1941, Gene Saari Collection, B12—both in Archives of Labor History and Urban Affairs, Wayne State University, Detroit.

11. Gates, *Michigan Copper*, 170; number of workers is calculated from p. 211, Table 10.

12. Eugene August Saari was born in Chisholm, Minnesota, on 21 June 1909, and his vita circa 1974 indicates that he was self-educated; additional biographical information was supplied by his wife Martha Jackson Saari in Saari's personal papers, Gene Saari Collection, box of photographs; for talks to seminary students, see note by Martha Saari, Gene Saari Collection, B14; for early history of unionization, 1938–41, see "We've Had Enough Nonsense," flyer, ca. 1950, issued by Quincy union and others, Gene Saari Collection, B19, file "C.&H. #4312"; clipping from *CIO News*, 7 April 1941 with Edward Laakaniemi letter: "Had it not been for the assistance and efforts of the International Woodworkers of America and especially those of Brother Saari, it is problematical whether we would be organized yet," Gene Saari Collection, B16; secretary's report, CIO Proceedings, 1940, Gene Saari Collection, B14, p. 36—all in Archives of Labor History and Urban Affairs, Wayne State University, Detroit.

13. "We've Had Enough Nonsense," Gene Saari Collection, B19, file "C.&H. #4312"; reference to 1913–14 from Scrapbook, Gene Saari Collection, B16—both in Archives of Labor History and Urban Affairs, Wayne State University, Detroit.

14. Gene Saari, typewritten speech prepared for radio, 26 February 1942, Gene Saari Collection, B12, file "C.&H. #584," p. 3, Archives of Labor History and Urban Affairs, Wayne State University, Detroit.

15. Ibid. p. 1; Langdon mentioned in 14 July 1942 letter to Witt, 2, Gene Saari Collection, B12, file "C.&H. #584; "Matters for C. & H. Employees To Think About," flyer, ibid.; Calumet and Hecla, *Annual Report*, 1942:5.

16. Gene Saari to Nathan Witt, 14 July 1942, p. 2; see also "Some Pertinent Facts for Calumet and Hecla Employees" and "What Is This 'Independent Union'?" flyer, Gene Saari radio script, 13 May 1942, Gene Saari Collection, B12, file "C.&H. #584," Archives of Labor History and Urban Affairs, Wayne State University, Detroit.

17. Calumet and Hecla, *Annual Report*, 1941:8–9, 1944:11; Patrick H. O'Brien, interview, Detroit, 16 October 1957, Michigan Historical Collections, Bentley Historical Library, Ann Arbor, p. 23. Endicott Lovell married Martha MacNaughton, James's daughter, before he went overseas during World War I (Moyer, *Ke-Wee-Naw*, 122–23), MacNaughton died 26 May 1949, at age 85, after a long illness, his obituary stating that he had "dominated the policies of Calumet & Hecla with the absoluteness of a dictator" (*New York Times*, 27 May 1949).

18. "Although this action involves a different procedure in employee dealings, . . . Management expects that the good will and pleasant employee relations of the past will continue" (Calumet and Hecla, *Annual Report*, 1942:5. An undated Independent Copper Workers Union flyer argued that eight tons of coal now cost the family at Calumet and Hecla $49.52 but a union victory would end company sales of coal, forcing workers to buy from the coal dealer for $96.00; see Gene Saari Collection, B12, file "C.&H. #584," Archives of Labor History and Urban Affairs,

Wayne State University, Detroit. See also union's counterattacks in "Independents Reach New High in Lying," flyer, and Finnish speech, translation, 3 November 1942, in the same file; printed agreement of union Local 584 with Calumet and Hecla, 13 July 1943, Gene Saari Collection, B6, Archives of Labor History and Urban Affairs, Wayne State University, Detroit.

19. Clippings in Scrapbook, Gene Saari Collection, B16; Quincy Mining Company Pay Roll Collection CIO Membership Dues, October 1943, lists names, Gene Saari Collection, B12, file "Quincy Mining Co."; for debates, see Minute Book, Quincy Local 523, Gene Saari Collection, B12—all in Archives of Labor History and Urban Affairs, Wayne State University, Detroit. See also *Daily Mining Gazette* (Houghton), 11 February 1941.

20. *Daily Mining Gazette* (Houghton), 20 August 1943 (Copper Rally Supplement); Benedict, *Red Metal*, 207; Calumet and Hecla, *Annual Report*, 1943:3; 1948:5.

21. Calumet and Hecla, *Annual Report*, 1943:3; Gates, *Michigan Copper*, 172.

22. *Daily Mining Gazette* (Houghton), 30 December 1939, 13–15 January and 2, 14–15, and 29 February and 16 March 1940.

23. Minute Book, Quincy Local 523, Gene Saari Collection, B12, Archives of Labor History and Urban Affairs, Wayne State University, Detroit.

24. *Daily Mining Gazette* (Houghton), 3 January and 17 March 1941, 21 March 1991; Halkola, *Michigan Tech Centennial*, 94–95.

25. Sixty-eight young women were in the June class of 1942 at Calumet High School; see *Daily Mining Gazette* (Houghton), 3 June 1942, 21 August 1943. For war deaths, see *Daily Mining Gazette*, 25 May 1991. The total graduated at Calumet High School (February and June 1942) was 175 (*Calumet High School Reunion, July 18, 1992*, 39–40).

26. For letters of servicemen, Gene Saari Collection, B17, Archives of Labor History and Urban Affairs, Wayne State University, Detroit. V-mail was a process of reducing letter size via microfilm and was sometimes referred to as "wee-mail"; see auxiliary's card, ibid., B18.

27. *Daily Mining Gazette* (Houghton), 8 July and 21 and 23 August 1943.

28. Four union locals ran advertisement calling for "More Copper! That is the Keynote of the Two-Day Copper Production for Victory Rally," *Daily Mining Gazette*, 20 and 23 August 1943; Landis quoted in *New York Times*, 5 March 1943.

29. *Daily Mining Gazette* (Houghton), 6 June 1942, 3 January 1944.

30. Ibid., 2 June 1942, 10 February 1944.

31. Ibid., 2 June 1942, 25 August 1943. Frederick Cox to Cora and Frederick Jeffers (no date), about Kenneth's air travel, in Howard Doolittle Papers, Michigan Historical Collections, Bentley Historical Library, Ann Arbor.

32. Gates, *Michigan Copper*, 173–80, 186–87; Patterson quoted in *Daily Mining Gazette* (Houghton), 20 August 1943 (Copper Rally Supplement); Calumet and Hecla, *Annual Report*, 1942:2, 1944:2.

33. Gates, *Michigan Copper*, 173, 177–80; Calumet and Hecla, *Annual Report*, 1941:3; Minute Book, Quincy Local 523, Gene Saari Collection, B12, Transcript of NLRB Conference, 18 December 1944, Gene Saari Collection, B17, pp. 68, 92, 94— both in Archives of Labor History and Urban Affairs, Wayne State University, Detroit.

34. Calumet and Hecla, *Annual Report*, 1941:2–3, 1944:9; *New York Times*, 31 October 1943, sec. 3.

35. Calumet and Hecla, *Annual Report*, 1941:3, 1943:9, 1944:8, 1945:10.

36. Ibid., 1942:3, 1948:5 (quotation); 1950:1 (Alabama).

37. Ibid., 1942:3, 1945:11.

38. Ibid., 1942:4, 7; 1944:4–5.

39. Ibid., 1945:11, 1946, 1952:7, 16; Senate bill discussed in Gene Saari letter to William Gates, 10 August 1949, and Gene Saari to Sidney Hillman, 25 April 1944—both in Gene Saari Collection, B16, Archives of Labor History and Urban Affairs, Wayne State University, Detroit. For an example of Copper Country businessmen citing federal subsidies for mines as "absolutely necessary" during war, Harry E. King to Gene Saari, 11 December 1944, Gene Saari Collection, B16, Archives of Labor History and Urban Affairs, Wayne State University, Detroit.

40. *Daily Mining Gazette* (Houghton), 17 April 1946; Calumet and Hecla, *Annual Report*, 1951:2–4.

41. Gates, *Michigan Copper*, 180; Lankton and Hyde, *Old Reliable*, 145–49, poem on 146; Copper Range suspension notice, 1945, reprinted in Moyer, *Ke-Wee-Naw*, 167.

42. For portal-to-portal pay, see Calumet and Hecla, *Annual Report*, 1946, 1948:14; for temporary closing of mine, see *Annual Report*, 1950:4; John Sitar to Allan L. Swim, 1 October 1949, Gene Saari Collection, B12, file "Calumet & Hecla," Archives of Labor History and Urban Affairs, Wayne State University, Detroit; Gene Saari, radio script, 4 August 1947, ibid.; "sacrifices for years" from Saari[?], "We have listened," anonymous ms., 1949, ibid. The company's Position in 1949 is outlined in Calumet and Hecla memorandum, 17 August 1949, ibid.

43. Ernst Modrok letter to *Daily Mining Gazette* (Houghton), 11 September 1949, Gene Saari Collection, B19, file "Calumet and Hecla, #4312"; Calumet and Hecla, *Annual Report*, 1949:3, 1950:1; for CIO criticism of IUMMSW, see Steel Workers advertisement in *Daily Mining Gazette* (Houghton), 25 April 1950, p. 9; for "Mine–Mill" criticism of CIO, citing April 1950 election as "bitter defeat" for workers, see "Report on Michigan," *Mine, Mill, and Smelter Workers Bulletin* (Butte), 19 August 1950, p. 3; for the scholar in 1950, see Gates, *Michigan Copper*, 187.

44. Calumet and Hecla, *Annual Report*, 1950:1; Benedict, *Red Metal*, 208; for government subsidies, see Elliot Bredhoff to Gene Saari, 2 April 1953, Gene Saari Collection, B15, file "Calumet & Hecla Correspondence," Archives of Labor History and Urban Affairs, Wayne State University, Detroit.

45. *Daily Mining Gazette* (Houghton), 9 July 1966 (Souvenir Edition); Calumet and Hecla, *Annual Report*, 1948:5; 1951:2–3, 16; 1952:6, 22; 1953:2; 1954:18–19; 1955:3, 10; 1958:11.

46. Calumet and Hecla, *Annual Report*, 1953:2, 1954:11; Elliot Bredhoff to Gene Saari, 2 April 1953, Gene Saari Collection, B15, file "Calumet & Hecla Correspondence," Archives of Labor History and Urban Affairs, Wayne State University, Detroit. For 1949 resolution by Local 4312, United Steel Workers of America, CIO, calling for federal legislation to subsidize copper companies' explorations, see "Resolution on Copper Conservation," Gene Saari Collection, B18, file "C.&H.," Archives of Labor History and Urban Affairs, Wayne State University, Detroit.

47. For endorsement of motion to form Women's Auxiliary, Minute Book, 20 December 1942, Quincy Local 523, IUMMSW, Gene Saari Collection, B12, Archives of Labor History and Urban Affairs, Wayne State University, Detroit; Martha Saari, Mae Grohman, and Miriam Tormala were officers of South Range Auxiliary in 1943, Gene Saari Collection, B16; Martha Saari's articles describing locals' Christmas celebrations at South Range and Hancock, 1943, in *the Union*, clippings in Scrapbook, Gene Saari Collection, B16; songbook, Gene Saari Collection, B18; poetry, Gene Saari Collection, B17; Minutes of Executive Board, South Range Local 494, Gene Saari Collection, B17; Minutes of Meetings, Gene Saari Collection, B17; Minute Book, Quincy Local 523, 1 and 26 July and 16 October 1942, Gene Saari Collection, B12; article on Local 4312, CIO–AFL, in Calumet Township Centennial Committee, *Calumet Township Centennial, 1866–1966*, Souvenir Program, 1966.

48. Gene Saari Collection, B12, Archives of Labor History and Urban Affairs, Wayne State University, Detroit.

49. Minutes of Meetings, South Range Local 494, 28 May, 9 and 23 July 1943, Gene Saari Collection, B17; *United Copper Workers Local 494, IUMMSW–CIO and Copper Range Company, April 10, 1943* (1943, Gene Saari Collection, B18), pp. 3, 17. For motions to purchase war bonds on 27 January, office incident on 24 August, and the union urging voter registration on 20 September 1944, see Minutes of South Range Local, Gene Saari Collection, B18—all in Archives of Labor History and Urban Affairs, Wayne State University, Detroit.

50. Gene Saari Collection, B17, Archives of Labor History and Urban Affairs, Wayne State University, Detroit.

51. Worker to Gene Saari, 5 January 1943, Gene Saari Collection, B12, file "C.&H. #584," Archives of Labor History and Urban Affairs, Wayne State University, Detroit.

52. John Clark, president of IUMMSW, to Gene Saari, terminating Saari's affiliation with union, 27 August 1949, Gene Saari Collection, B6, file "C.&H. Correspondence." For Saari's version of the episode describing his resignation 31 January 1950 and his depiction of IUMMSW as a "union which has lost respect, . . . more concerned with operating as a political front for the Communist Party than paying attention to the human needs" of workers, see radio script, 18 April 1950, Gene Saari Collection, B19, folder "C.&H. #4312," pp. 1, 6; Arthur J. Goldberg memorandum, 14 March 1950, ibid. The *Union Banner* (Norway, MI), March 1950, described local workers as astounded when they learned of Saari's switch from IUMMSW to Steel Workers.

53. John Sitar information from *Daily Mining Gazette* (Houghton), 7 February 1950; for historic links of "Mine–Mill" to Copper Country, attacks on Saari, and "Never had a muck stick," see "Mine–Mill" advertisements, *Daily Mining Gazette* 13, 15, and 17–19 April 1950; a clipping in Scrapbook indicated that Sitar as a child had been in Italian Hall, 24 December 1913, Gene Saari Collection, B16, Archives of Labor History and Urban Affairs, Wayne State University, Detroit; for "Mine–Mill" attack on Saari, Democrats, and Murray, see radio script, 15 April 1950, Gene Saari Collection, B19, folder "C.&H. #4312," esp. pp. 3, 6. In a conversation with Gene Saari, September 1981, at Marquette, the author was told that many of the most ardent men in the locals, 1939–69, had either participated in the 1913–14 strike or were descendants of such persons and sought to right the wrongs of the earlier time.

54. Ray Pasnick to Gene Saari, 17 April 1950, Gene Saari Collection, B19, file "C.&H. #4312"; radio scripts of 1950 by Gene Saari (10 April), L. M. Koski (12 April), and Harlow Wildman, (14 April), anonymous "Mine–Mill" script, "Local 584 Executive Board BEGS to get out of Mine Mill" (flyer), and Tally of Ballots, 20 April 1950, Gene Saari Collection, B19; for union plans after election victory, see Gene Saari to Nick Zonarich, 22 May 1950, Gene Saari Collection, B18, file "Zonarich"— all in Archives of Labor History and Urban Affairs, Wayne State University, Detroit. For results of both elections, see *Daily Mining Gazette* (Houghton), 21 and 28 April 1950.

55. Gene Saari to Noel Fox, 29 June 1950, and Gene Saari to Ray Pasnick, 16 June 1950—both in Gene Saari Collection, B18, Archives of Labor History and Urban Affairs, Wayne State University, Detroit.

56. Article by Martha Saari, ca. 1950, unidentified newspaper clipping, Scrapbook, Gene Saari Collection, B16. In 1952, a member of Local 4312 was invited to become a member of the Laurium Chamber of Commerce so businessmen could be informed of "future problems of the laborer"*Mining Gazette* clipping, 1952, Gene Saari Collection, B18; for statistics, see Marvin J. Miller to Gene Saari, 1 August 1950, Gene Saari Collection, B18, file "Research Department."

57. Calumet and Hecla, *Annual Report*, 1952:7, 10, 16; 1953:9; 1954:11–12.

58. Ibid., 1952:17; Earl T. Bester, form letter, 17 September 1952, Gene Saari Collection, B18, Archives of Labor History and Urban Affairs, Wayne State University, Detroit; *Daily Mining Gazette* (Houghton), 2 September and 11 October 1952.

59. *Daily Mining Gazette* (Houghton), 8–9, 13, and 20 September and 14 and 23–24 October and 8 November 1952; "To All Employees," Calumet and Hecla printed notice, Gene Saari Collection, B18, Earl T. Bester form letter to recording secretaries, 12 January 1953, Gene Saari Collection, B15, file "Earl Bester"—both in Archives of Labor History and Urban Affairs, Wayne State University, Detroit.

60. Local 4312 to Earl Bester, 5 January 1952 (actually 1953), Gene Saari Collection, file "Earl Bester"; Gene Saari notified H. Stott of Calumet and Hecla that dues were raised, effective 1 May 1953, Gene Saari Collection, B15; Gene Saari telegram and letter to director, U.S. Conciliation and Mediation Service, 16 April and 17 May 1955, Gene Saari Collection, B6, file "C.&H. Correspondence"; A. S. Kromer, "To All Members of the Calumet Division Organization," form letter, 2 May 1955, ibid.—all in Archives of Labor History and Urban Affairs, Wayne State University, Detroit. See also Calumet and Hecla, *Annual Report*, 1955:9; *Daily Mining Gazette* (Houghton), 8 November and 9 and 10 December 1952.

61. Copy of news story contained in 6:00 P.M. "Copper Country Newscast" over WHDF, 26 May 1955; Endicott Lovell to Governor G. Mennen Williams, 31 May 1955; Gene Saari to Carol Jacobson, 12 November 1955; all in Gene Saari Collection, B6, file "C.&H. Correspondence," Archives of Labor History and Urban Affairs, Wayne State University, Detroit.

62. Frank E. Hook to Gene Saari, 26 May 1955, ibid.

63. Information from "The Week That Was," *Daily Mining Gazette* (Houghton), 18 August 1988.

64. Strike relief figures, including list from District 33, Gene Saari Collection, B6, file "C.&H. Correspondence"; for the disciplinary episode, see correspondence between A. E. Petermann and Elliot Bredhoff and Earl T. Bester and Elliot Bredhoff, 24, 26, and 30 August 1955, ibid. Citizens thanked Saari in letters for helping end strike—one stating that "the long and costly strike . . . threatened to end the Copper Country as a wonderful place to live in" (Jessie M. Cameron to Gene Saari, 22 August 1955, ibid). See also Calumet and Hecla, *Annual Report*, 1955:2; *Daily Mining Gazette* (Houghton), 27 June 1957.

65. Calumet and Hecla, *Annual Report*, 1958:2, 16. Despite adverse business conditions in the United States in 1958, Calumet and Hecla earnings increased to $1.31 per share, up from $.87 in 1957, (*Annual Report*, 1958:2; 1959:1–3, 16. See also Michigan Department of Commerce, Resources Planning Division, *Michigan's Changing Population: A Historical Profile by Regions* (Lansing: 1967), 4, 6, 14.

66. Information is based on author's knowledge of experiences of relatives, friends, acquaintances, and longtime perusal of Copper Country newspaper stories of former residents.

67. U.S. Census, *Population*, 1940, 505, 507–8; 1950, 22:14, 16, 18, 20; 1960, 24:15, 17, 18, 20.

68. William Barkell, concluding that "nothing is so consistent as change," believed that the Copper Country by the 1960s was "finding a new place in the sun" in its striving "to transform the countryside and quaint little hamlets"; see Avery Color Studios, *Copper Country—God's Country* (Au Train, MI, 1973), 3.

69. The author, while observing workingmen and their families who benefited from union affiliation, at various times heard Gene Saari and associates described by nonunion people as "wreckers of the community" or "communists."

70. By the 1980s, although population continued to decline, a shift occurred

among those who remained, as they sought space, homes, lower taxes, and rural settings close to towns in all four counties of the Copper Country, a phenomenon not unlike urban/suburban developments at Detroit, Chicago, and Milwaukee; see *Daily Mining Gazette* (Houghton), 2 February 1988.

CHAPTER 10

1. *Daily Mining Gazette* (Houghton), 8 April 1969; *Milwaukee Journal,* 5 April 1969; T. S. Eliot, *Collected Poems 1902–1962* (London: Faber & Faber, 1963), 63.

2. *Daily Mining Gazette* (Houghton), 3–4 and 8 April 1969. In 1955, the union accepted fifteen cents less than its initial request; but the package that included an 8 percent increase on the current wages actually increased by fifteen cents an hour, while in 1949, the union took a real fifteen-cent cut from existing wages; see Gene Saari to Carol Jacobson, 12 November 1955, Gene Saari Collection, B6, file "C.&H. Correspondence," Archives of Labor History and Urban Affairs, Wayne State University, Detroit.

3. *Daily Mining Gazette* (Houghton), 4–5 and 15 April 1969.

4. Ibid, 10, 15, 26, and 29 April and 3 and 5–6 May 1969. Universal Oil Products announced that the shutdown was effective 9 April, (ibid., 10 April 1969); as of 4 May, some union men told reporters that Calumet and Hecla was bluffing; and Floyd Granroth of the local chamber of commerce said, "It's not like the old Calumet & Hecla, they never would close," *Milwaukee Journal,* 5 May 1969. Official notice of shutdown is given in a form letter from Cecil H. Suter: "As of this morning [9 April] your employment with the company has terminated"; see Gene Saari Collection, B14, Archives of Labor History and Urban Affairs, Wayne State University, Detroit; the complete text of the letter is also in *Daily Mining Gazette,* 12 April 1969. The company retained clerical/secretarial help until August.

5. Calumet and Hecla, *Annual Report,* 1962; *Detroit News,* 5 March 1969; Michigan Employment Security Commission, *Labor Market Letter—Upper Peninsula,* February 1967; for training, see C. H. Suter to Sylvio Guisfredi, 7 August 1968, Gene Saari Collection, B14, file "C.&H. News Clippings," Archives of Labor History and Urban Affairs, Wayne State University, Detroit.

6. In the early 1960s, the company described the mines as submarginal, with costs increasing and exhaustion of good ores approaching; see Calumet and Hecla, *Annual Report,* 1962:2–6; 1963:2, 5; 1964:2–3; 1967:3; *Engineering and Mining Journal* 167(1966): 14, 110, 152.

7. Calumet and Hecla, *Annual Report,* 1961: preceding p. 1; see also pp. 4–5; ibid., 1964:2, 1965:22. "An aggressive program to control operating costs and grade [of ore] is being followed to offset increased costs of materials, supplies and labor" (ibid., 1960:19).

8. United Steel Workers of America, *Nonferrous Report,* February 1969, p. 8; Gene Saari to Bob Christofferson, 31 [*sic*] April 1950, Gene Saari Collection, B18, file "Zonarich," Archives of Labor History and Urban Affairs, Wayne State University, Detroit; speech to Miami copper workers, 19 May 1951, ibid.

9. Calumet and Hecla, *Annual Report,* 1965:7–8; 1967:2–3, 10, 21; United Steel Workers of America, *Nonferrous Report,* August 1968, p. 3.

10. *Engineering and Mining Journal* 170(November 1969): 133; *Economic Development in Michigan's Upper Peninsula,* 50, 71; *New York Times,* 23 March 1968; Gates, *Michigan Copper,* 45.

11. *Daily Mining Gazette* (Houghton), 7 July 1966 (Souvenir Edition); Calumet and Hecla, *Annual Report*, 1967:1–2; *Wall Street Journal*, 22 December 1967, 23 February and 26 April 1968; *New York Times*, 22 December 1967.

12. Chabot, *Tales of White Pine*, 11, 14; Calumet and Hecla, *Annual Report*, 1925:21.

13. Chabot, *Tales of White Pine*, 16.

14. Ibid., 16, 18; *Science*, 12 March 1954, p. 354.

15. R. H. Ramsey, ed., "White Pine Copper," *Engineering and Mining Journal* 154(January 1953): 74, 76, 86–87.

16. *Economic Development in Michigan's Upper Peninsula*, 49 (Table 31); Chabot, *Tales of White Pine*, 18; *Daily Mining Gazette* (Houghton), 22 September 1988; Michigan Tourist Council, "Ghost Town Reborn," 1959, UPTARA, B1, F2.

17. Lillian Jackson to Gene Saari, 22 July 1953, organizer's "Report of New Local Union," October 1953, Gene Saari to Earl Bester, 22 December 1953, NLRB Tally of Ballots, 12 November 1953, and associated materials—all in Gene Saari Collection, B15, Archives of Labor History and Urban Affairs, Wayne State University, Detroit. On safety, see Gene Saari Collection, B16, Archives of Labor History and Urban Affairs, Wayne State University, Detroit, and *Ontonagon Herald*, 3 June 1965.

18. Chabot, *Tales of White Pine*, 81, 83.

19. Full-page advertisement by Copper Range Copper Company in *American Metal Market*, 17 September 1962, clipping, Gene Saari Collection, B14, Archives of Labor History and Urban Affairs, Wayne State University, Detroit.

20. *Milwaukee Journal*, 21 January 1968; *Wall Street Journal*, 5 January 1968; White Pine's production was actually 6.9 percent of nation's output according to the *Wall Street Journal*, 25 January 1968.

21. *Milwaukee Journal*, 21 January 1968.

22. *Wall Street Journal*, 2 February 1968; quotation from *Steel Labor*, August 1968.

23. *Wall Street Journal*, 5, 25, and 29 January and 2 February 1968; *Ontonagon Herald*, 2 February 1968; *Daily Mining Gazette* (Houghton), 26 January 1968, 6 February 1969.

24. *Milwaukee Journal*, 21 January 1968.

25. *Wall Street Journal*, 2 February 1968, 31 December 1969. Otis Brubaker, research director, USWA, argued in a letter that companies had for years successfully played off one union against another and that to stop this "divide-and-rule tactic," unions under Steel Workers and twenty-five associated unions sought to bring order out of that chaos (*Wall Street Journal*, 25 January 1968). Copper prices dropped drastically in 1969 (*New York Times*, 17 August 1969, pt. 3).

26. *Wall Street Journal*, 2 February 1968; association quoted in review of the strike, *Engineering and Mining Journal* 169(1968): 122; see also p. 21.

27. The company's offer is in Emerson P. Barrett to Gene Saari, 3 August 1968 and Sylvio Guisfredi to Carl Frankel, 7 October 1968—both in Gene Saari Collection, B14, file "C.&H. News Clippings," Archives of Labor History and Urban Affairs, Wayne State University, Detroit; for wage rates, see United Steel Workers of America, *Nonferrous Report*, December 1968, p. 3.

28. *Milwaukee Journal*, 24 November 1968; C. H. Suter to Sylvio Guisfredi, 7 August 1968, Gene Saari Collection, B14, file "C.&H. News Clippings," Archives of Labor History and Urban Affairs, Wayne State University, Detroit.

29. *Daily Mining Gazette* (Houghton), 16 March 1991.

30. United Steel Workers of America, *Nonferrous Report*, December 1968, p. 3; ibid., January 1969, pp. 1–2; "still 1913" quotation in *Steel Labor*, January 1969, p. 2; *Detroit Free Press*, 4 March 1969.

31. United Steel Workers of America, *Nonferrous Report*, December 1968, p. 3.

32. *Milwaukee Journal*, 24 November 1968.

33. Sylvio Guisfredi to Carl Frankel, 7 October 1968, Gene Saari Collection, B14, file "C.&H. News Clippings," Archives of Labor History and Urban Affairs, Wayne State University, Detroit; *Milwaukee Journal*, 26 February 1969.

34. United Steel Workers of America, *Nonferrous Report*, December 1968, p. 3; January 1969, pp. 1–2.

35. Chairman, Calumet and Hecla Trades Council to Guisfredi and Saari, 13 August 1968, Gene Saari Collection, B14, file "C.&H. News Clippings," Archives of Labor History and Urban Affairs, Wayne State University, Detroit.

36. *Press–Gazette* (Green Bay, WI), 10 November 1968, Gene Saari Collection, B14, file "C.&H. News Clippings," Archives of Labor History and Urban Affairs, Wayne State University, Detroit.

37. *Milwaukee Journal*, 24 November 1968.

38. Ibid.; correspondence of Gene Saari and Roy Johnson, 10 February 1969 and n.d., Gene Saari Collection, B14, Archives of Labor History and Urban Affairs, Wayne State University, Detroit.

39. *Milwaukee Journal*, 24 November 1968; *Daily Mining Gazette* (Houghton), 5 February 1969; *Detroit Free Press*, 4 March 1969.

40. For 26 February letter, see Gene Saari Collection, B14, Archives of Labor History and Urban Affairs, Wayne State University, Detroit; *Daily Mining Gazette* (Houghton), 22 March 1969.

41. Richard N. Speer to Local 4312, 1 April 1969, Gene Saari Collection, B14, file "C.&H. News Clippings," Archives of Labor History and Urban Affairs, Wayne State University, Detroit.

42. *Daily Mining Gazette*, 2 April 1969; for "bluffing," see *Daily Mining Gazette*, 4 April 1969 and *Milwaukee Journal*, 5 May 1969; for "pack up" remark, see *Detroit News*, 5 March 1969; John E. Wilson, letter to *Copper Island Sentinel* (Calumet), 25 July 1985.

43. T. S. Eliot's phrase is particularly apt, given the significance of 104 years of Calumet and Hecla in the Keweenaw Peninsula.

44. *New York Times*, 17 August 1969, pt. 3; undated, unidentified news clipping advertising Evanston building, Gene Saari Collection, B14, Archives of Labor History and Urban Affairs, Wayne State University, Detroit. Gene Saari was transferred to the Denver office of the union in May 1969, retired on 1 July 1974, and lived on Sugar Island (1974–86) near Sault Sainte Marie and at Evanston, Illinois, from 1986 until his death on 7 April 1990; see Gene Saari Collection, box of photographs and Martha Saari to author, 18 May 1993; for attempts to reopen mines, see *Daily Mining Gazette* (Houghton), 5 January 1971.

45. Karamanski, *Deep Woods Frontier*, 213; Michigan Writers' Project, *Michigan*, 595–96; Halkola, *Michigan Tech Centennial*, 99; by 1985, Michigan Tech's acreage at the Ford Center had expanded to approximately 4,000 acres (ibid). See also *L'Anse Sentinel*, 14 September 1933.

46. David L. Lewis, *The Public Image of Henry Ford* (Detroit: Wayne State University Press, 1976), 487, 489; Michigan Writers' Project, *Michigan*, 596; Karamanski, *Deep Woods Frontier*, 161–65. Growing up at Calumet in the 1930s, the author heard Ford lauded as demigod and cursed an antiunion reactionary.

47. Application for Technical Assistance Grant, 7 September 1977, duplicate, Gene Saari Collection, B14, Archives of Labor History and Urban Affairs, Wayne State University, Detroit.

48. Ibid.; see also Appendix to report made by Community Action Agency, Hancock, Gene Saari Collection, B14, Archives of Labor History and Urban Affairs, Wayne State University, Detroit.

49. Lankton and Hyde, *Old Reliable*, 147: *Daily Mining Gazette* (Houghton), 16 March 1991.

50. Walter S. White, *Guidebook for Field Conference Michigan Copper District, September 30–October 2, 1971* (Houghton: Michigan Technological University Press, 1971), 20–22, 25; *Engineering and Mining Journal* 191(January 1990): C47, C49.

51. For prices, 1925–1986, see *Engineering and Mining Journal* 188(March 1987): 26. For proposed mines, paper mills, and opposition, see, e.g. letters to editor, *Daily Mining Gazette* (Houghton), 29 August 1990, 7 March and 7 October 1991, 9–10 January and 1–3 and 17 June 1992, as well as articles in issues of 8 February, 4 June, 5 October, and 28 December 1991.

52. "Beyond the '80s," *Daily Mining Gazette* (Houghton), Supplement, 30 March 1989, sec. A, esp. pp. 2–3, 8–9; Dianne Trapp to Editor, *Daily Mining Gazette* (Houghton), 8 February 1991.

53. *Daily Mining Gazette* (Houghton), 19 April 1969.

54. "Beyond the '80s," sect. B, p. 2.

55. Halkola, *Michigan Tech Centennial*, 113–14, 135–37, 171, 174, 181; *Daily Mining Gazette* (Houghton), 3 April 1969.

56. *Daily Mining Gazette* (Houghton), 22 January 1985.

57. U.S. Department of Labor Women's Bureau, *Report [of the] Conference on Women in the Upper Peninsula Economy at University Center, Northern Michigan University, Marquette, Michigan, 16 May 1964*, i, vi, 3, 12–13, 15, 18, 21.

58. U.S. Census, 1990, Michigan, 24:2, 9–10, 14, 22; for Native Americans, Asians, and Hispanics, see pp. 60, 67–68, 72, 80. Under "Black," the 1990 census listed the following in the four counties: Baraga, 49; Houghton, 158; Keweenaw, 1; Ontonagon, 4. The median age in 1990 was Baraga, 36.7; Houghton, 31.7; Keweenaw, 46.4; Ontonagon, 40.2; see U.S. Census, 1990, Michigan, 24:2, 9–10, 14, 22.

CHAPTER 11

1. Quoted phrase used by David Mac Frimodig, *Keweenaw Character* (Lake Linden, MI: Forster, 1990), foreword.

2. Ibid.

3. *Development Bureau News*, 1 June 1926, UPTARA, B9, F1, State Archives, Lansing, p. 5.

4. John Bartlow Martin, *Call It North Country* (1944; reprint, Detroit: Wayne State University Press, 1986); Angus Murdoch, *Boom Copper* (New York: Macmillan, 1943); by the 1950s, the Copper Country Vacationist League greeted visitors approaching Houghton from the south with a huge sign: "Welcome to the Copper Country. You Are Now Breathing the Purest Most Vitalizing Air on Earth" (Putnam, *North to Adventure*, 4).

5. See, e.g., centennial booklets for Hancock, Houghton, Calumet, Lake Linden, Keweenaw County, and Calumet Township, Michigan Technological University Archives, Houghton.

6. Quoted material appeared on thousands of paper place mats used in restaurants and homes; for theater, see Calumet Theatre Rededication Program, 9–10 July 1974, copies in possession of author.

7. *Daily Mining Gazette* (Houghton), 15 February 1933, 13–15 February 1952, 30 January 1987, 31 January 1991 (Winter Carnival Supplement), and 30–31 January and 3 February 1992. Michigan Tech marketing students estimated that the

1992 winter carnival brought a half million dollars to the area (ibid., 15 April 1992; *Calumet News*, 15 February 1933).

8. *Daily Mining Gazette* (Houghton), 6 September 1990; 8 March and 20 August 1991, and 2 April 1992. A multicultural festival in 1991 involved students at Michigan Tech whose homes were in Panama, India, Switzerland, and many others (ibid., 21 August 1991).

9. Upper Peninsula Travel and Recreation Association and Michigan Travel Bureau, *Michigan's Upper Peninsula Travel Planner for All Seasons* (Lansing, 1991) 25, 31, 36, 74–75; *Daily Mining Gazette* (Houghton), 15 January 1992.

10. *Ontonagon Herald*, 29 July 1965. An estimated 5,000 attended the Baraga County history pageant at the lake shore, where sixty-eight Ojibwa and thirty-two whites enacted the story of Native Americans, missionaries, trappers, and settlers, 1650–1850 (*L'Anse Sentinel*, 30 July 1969).

11. *Daily Mining Gazette* (Houghton), 8 October 1984; *Copper Island Sentinel* (Calumet), 11 October 1984, where death toll at Italian Hall is shown erroneously as 73 (74 died as a result of panic). The lost labor cause again heralded, e.g., "The building was an embarrassment to capitalism; a reminder of the labor struggle" (ibid.)

12. Jamison, *This Ontonagon Country*, 115.

13. Holmio, *History of the Finns*, 144–45; *Daily Mining Gazette* (Houghton), 14 January 1903, 3 June 1975. For John Brevik story of how three women at Washington School, Calumet, helped him repair the ventilating system many years earlier, see *Daily Mining Gazette* (Houghton), 20 December 1952 (Green Sheet).

14. *Calumet News*, 10 January 1908.

15. Personal recollections of author.

16. Danziger, *Chippewas of Lake Superior*, 186; *Daily Mining Gazette* (Houghton), 18 February and 6 July 1991; Ojibwa Lanes, Lounge, and Casino at U.S. 41 and M-38 in Baraga opened at 3:00 P.M. and continued until 2:30 A.M. with "Las Vegas style entertainment," (advertisement in *Michigan's Upper Peninsula Travel Planner for All Seasons*, 23–24).

17. Rudolph J. Vecoli, "Return to the Melting Pot: Ethnicity in the United States in the Eighties," *Journal of American Ethnic History* 5(Fall 1985): 7–20, esp. 15–17.

18. William G. Lockwood and Yvonne R. Lockwood, "The Cornish Pasty in Northern Michigan," in *Michigan Folklore Reader*, ed. C. Kurt Dewhurst and Yvonne R. Lockwood, (East Lansing: Michigan State University, 1987), 363, 366–67, 371–72.

19. Niemi, *Americanization of the Finnish People*, 41; for excellent essays by recent scholars on successful Finnish adaptation to American culture, see Ralph J. Jalkanen, ed., *The Faith of the Finns* (East Lansing: Michigan State University Press, 1972).

20. Moline, "Finnish Settlements," 110.

21. Vachon, *Tall Timber Tales*, 100; *Daily Mining Gazette* (Houghton), 2 August 1938, 12 August 1992; Holmio, *History of the Finns*, 174.

22. *Daily Mining Gazette* (Houghton), 8 and 15 March 1991.

23. Ibid., 3 August 1938; at the 1950 Calumet–Laurium Homecoming, 900 attended the dance at the Calumet Armory (ibid., 7 August 1950).

24. United Steel Workers of America, *Nonferrous Report*, December 1968, p. 4.

25. Anecdote related by John Wilson, Calumet, in a letter to the author, 18 April 1992.

26. Rickard, *Copper Mines*, 19–20.

27. Halpa Jussi, is a personal recollection of the author, who remembers a classmate telling a teacher at M. M. Morrison School, Calumet, that the name meant "Help a Jew"; Austrian knights, *Copper Country Evening News* (Calumet), 24 December

1900; Mandan Hayseeds was a popular musical group that also broadcast over local
radio in 1930s, as related to the author on 25 November 1989 by one of the musicians,
Armando Zei; quotation from letter, *Daily Mining Gazette* (Houghton), 17 August
1992.

  28. Putnam, *North to Adventure*, 23.

  29. An extraordinary, relatively unused, source is Keweenaw Historical Society
Collection at Michigan Technological University Archives, Houghton.

  30. Central Mine's historian/archivist R. Charles Stetter, of Laurium, in a letter
to the author, 18 August 1991, supplied the quotation correctly stated here, which
differs slightly from statement found in 1991 Central Reunion program.

Bibliography

ARCHIVAL SOURCES

Agassiz, Alexander. Papers of and Relating to Alexander Agassiz. Agassiz Museum Archives. Museum of Comparative Zoology Library. Harvard University, Cambridge, MA.

Archives of the Western Federation of Miners and International Union of Mine, Mill, and Smelter Workers. Western Historical Collections. University of Colorado, Boulder.

Austrian, Joseph. "Autobiographical and Historical Sketches" Typescript. Michigan Technological University Archives, Houghton.

Bennetts, Clarence. Clarence Bennetts Collection. Michigan Technological University Archives, Houghton.

Brockway, Daniel D. Letterbooks and Wedding Anniversary Materials. Michigan Historical Collections. Bentley Historical Library. University of Michigan, Ann Arbor.

———. Diary, 1868. Brockway Family Collection. Michigan Technological University Archives, Houghton.

Brockway, Lucena Harris. Diaries, 1866–1897. Brockway Family Collection. Michigan Technological University Archives, Houghton.

Calumet and Hecla Papers. Michigan Technological University Archives, Houghton.

Calumet High School Reunion, July 18, 1992. Michigan Technological University Archives, Houghton.

Cowell, William George. William George Cowell Collection. Michigan Technological University Archives, Houghton.

Doolittle, Howard. Papers. Michigan Historical Collection. Bentley Historical Library. University of Michigan, Ann Arbor.

Douglass House Guest Register, 1863. Michigan Historical Collections. Bentley Historical Library. University of Michigan, Ann Arbor.

Bibliography   ———, 1881–94. State Archives, Lansing.

Edwards, James. "How We Crossed Portage Lake Before and After 1875." Typescript. Keweenaw Historical Society Collection. Michigan Technological University Archives, Houghton.

Ferris, Woodbridge N. Records Relating to Labor Strike in Copper Mining Industry, 1913–14. State Archives, Lansing.

Forster, John H. Papers and Letterpress Book. Michigan Historical Collections. Bentley Historical Library. University of Michigan, Ann Arbor. (Additional Forster letters in Mullet Family Papers.)

Fromholz, Paul. Souvenirs and Letters. Keweenaw Historical Society Collection. Michigan Technological University Archives, Houghton.

"The History of Otter Lake." Typescript by pupils of Askel School under direction of Elina Heikkinen. Keweenaw Historical Society Collection. Michigan Technological University Archives, Houghton.

Houghton Centennial Souvenir History and Program, 1961. Michigan Technological University Archives, Houghton.

Jacker, Francis. Scrapbook. Keweenaw Historical Society Collection. Michigan Technological University Archives, Houghton.

Jackson, Charles T. Letter to Honorable Robert J. Walker, 19 July 1848. Photocopy. Original at Marquette, Michigan, Historical Society. Michigan Historical Collections. Bentley Historical Library. University of Michigan, Ann Arbor.

Kausler, Fred. Memoir, ca. 1906. Typescript. Michigan Historical Collections. Bentley Historical Library. University of Michigan, Ann Arbor.

Mullett Family Papers. Correspondence–Family, 1860–62. Michigan Historical Collections. Bentley Historical Library. University of Michigan, Ann Arbor.

Oas, Mabel W. "A History of the Legitimate Drama in the Copper Country of Michigan from 1900–1910 with Special Study of the Calumet Theatre." Typescript. Michigan Technological University Archives, Houghton.

O'Brien, Patrick Henry. Interview, Detroit, 16 October 1957. Typescript. Michigan Historical Collections. Bentley Historical Library. University of Michigan, Ann Arbor.

Pitezel, John. "Fresh Breezes from Lake Superior." Autograph Manuscript. Clarke Historical Library. Central Michigan University. Mount Pleasant.

———. Journals and Letters, 1845–49. Clarke Historical Library. Central Michigan University. Mount Pleasant, MI.

Rawlings, Joseph W. V. "Recollections of a Long Life." Autograph Manuscript by son Samuel Rawlings, who copied and condensed from father's original manuscript. Keweenaw Historical Society Collection. Michigan Technological University Archives, Houghton.

———. "Reminiscences." Autograph manuscript, 27 August 1912. Keweenaw Historical Society Collection. Michigan Technological University Archives, Houghton.

Records of the Welfare and Relief Study Commission, 1936–38. Local Public Welfare Expenditures and Corresponding Tax Rates for Twenty Representative Counties for Year Ending 1936. State Archives, Lansing.

Robinson, Samuel S. Letterbooks (3 parts), Miscellaneous Letters, and Calendar to the Letterbooks. Michigan Historical Collections. Bentley Historical Library, Ann Arbor.

Saari, Gene. Gene Saari Collection. Archives of Labor History and Urban Affairs. Walter Reuther Library. Wayne State University, Detroit.

School Inspectors' Reports 1865, 1875, 1895, 1915, 1928, and 1931. Microfilm. State Archives, Lansing.

Scott, John. Diary, 1869. Brockway Family Collection. Michigan Technological University Archives, Houghton.

Shelden, Ransom. Scrapbook. Michigan Historical Collections. Bentley Historical Li-
brary, University of Michigan, Ann Arbor.
"Social Co-operation and Conservation in the Copper Country: Report for the Two
Years Ending October, 1910." Michigan Technological University Archives.
Suomi College Oral History Project. Finnish–American Heritage Center, Hancock,
MI.
Trebilcock, W.E. "Calumet Schools."Typescript, 1942. Calumet Public Library, Cal-
umet, MI.
Wagner, Moritz, and Carl Scherzer. Typescript Translation of Chapter 20 of *Reisen
in Nordamerika in den Jahren 1852 and 1853*. Keweenaw Historical Society
Collection. Michigan Technological University Archives, Houghton.
Willman, Charles. "Ontonagon County in the Civil War," Typescript. Clarke Historical
Library. Central Michigan University, Mount Pleasant.
Wright, Benjamin. Letters, 1858–60. Michigan Historical Collections. Bentley Histor-
ical Library, University of Michigan, Ann Arbor.

REPORTS

Calumet and Hecla, Annual Reports, 1923–69.
Houghton County. Coroner's Inquest held at Red Jacket, Michigan, December 29–
31, 1913, into deaths in Italian Hall on December 24. Copy of transcript at
Michigan Technological University Archives, Houghton.
———. Coroner's Inquest held August 22–23 and 29–30 and September 3, 1913, in
Portage Township, into death of Louis Tijan at Seeberville, Michigan, August
14, 1913. Transcript in State Archives, Lansing.
———. Hearing conducted at Seeberville, Michigan, August 15, 1913, by Houghton
County Prosecuting Attorney Anthony Lucas and Judge Alfred Murphy on ac-
tions of Copper Range Mining Company guards and Houghton County sheriff's
employees at Seeberville, August 14, 1913. Transcript in State Archives, Lansing.
Michigan National Guard. Report of a Board of Officers Convened at Calumet,
Michigan, September 19, 1913. In Compliance with Special Order No. 23.
Investigation of violence in opening days of 1913–1914 strike. Copy in State
Archives, Lansing.

SERIAL RECORDS OF WESTERN FEDERATION OF MINERS

Executive Board Minutes, 5 July 1909–24 March 1915.
Official Proceedings for annual conventions, 1901–8 and 1913 and biennial conventions 1914 and 1916.
Registers
Expenditure Summary, 1910–33. Local Unions (1894–1933), Defunct Unions,
and New Unions. Michigan Defense Fund Ledgers, Books 1–2. Quarterly Reports of Local Unions, March 1909–March 1911. Register of Local Union
Assessments, April 1907–December 1933.
Report of the Secretary–Treasurer of the Western Federation of Miners. For fiscal years
ending June 30 in 1913–16. The last two reports were combined and issued in
1916.

Church, Verne H. *Crop Report for Michigan: Annual Summary, 1922.* Lansing: U.S. Department of Agriculture and Michigan Department of Agriculture, 6 January 1923.

———. "Statistical Analysis." In *Michigan Agriculture.* Lansing: Department of Agriculture, 1 June 1922.

Foster J. W., and J. D. Whitney, *Report on the Geology and Topography of a Portion of the Lake Superior Land District in the State of Michigan.* Pt. 1, *Copper Lands.* 31st Cong., 1st sess., Exec. Doc. 69, 1850.

Hodge, Frederick Webb, ed. *Handbook of American Indians North of Mexico.* U.S. Bureau of American Ethnology, Bull. No. 30. Washington, 1907.

Michigan Department of Agriculture. *Our Responsibility.* Lansing: Department of Agriculture, 1921.

Michigan Department of Commerce, Resources Planning Division. *Michigan's Changing Population: A Historical Profile by Regions.* Lansing: Department of Commerce, 1967.

Michigan Department of State. *Michigan and Its Resources.* 4th ed. Lansing: Smith, 1893.

Michigan Employment Security Commission. *Labor Market Letter–Upper Peninsula.* Marquette, 1967–68.

Michigan Legislature. *Journal of the House of Representatives, 1913.* 2 vols. Lansing: Wynkoop Hallenbeck Crawford, 1913.

———. *Journal of the Senate, 1913.* 2 vols. Lansing: Wynkoop Hallenbeck Crawford, 1913.

Michigan Official Directory and Legislative Manual, 1901, 1913, 1937, 1949, 1951, 1961, 1965, 1971.

Records of the Welfare and Relief Study Commission, 1936–1938. State Archives, Lansing.

Seeley, Dewey A. "The Climate of Michigan." *Michigan Agriculture.* Lansing: Department of Agriculture, 1 June 1932.

U.S. Congress. House. Committee on Mines and Mining, *Conditions in Copper Mines of Michigan: Hearings Before Subcommittee Pursuant to House Resolution 387.* 63d Cong., 2d sess. Washington, 1914.

———. Senate. *Message from the President of the United States, to the Two Houses of Congress, at the Commencement of the First Session of the Thirty-First Congress, December 24, 1849.* Pt. 3. 31st Cong., 1st sess., Exec. Doc. 1. Washington, 1849. Contains reports of C. D. Jackson, S. Hill, et al.

———. Senate. Committee on Public Works. *Opportunities for Economic Development in Michigan's Upper Peninsula.* 87th Cong., 1st sess. Washington, 1962.

———. Senate. *Report to Accompany Joint Resolution S. 14, April 1, 1844.* 28th Cong., 1st sess. Washington, 1844.

U.S. Department of Agriculture. *Accomplishments of the CCC in Michigan (under U.S. Department of Agriculture)* (and covering letter, Vico C. Isola to Victor D. Clum, 14 March 1947). State Archives, Lansing.

U.S. Department of Commerce. Bureau of the Census. *Population,* 1860–1990. Washington: Bureau of the Census.

———. Bureau of Mines. "Mining Methods and Practice in the Michigan Copper Mines." Report by Walter Crane. Bulletin No. 306. Washington, 1929.

U.S. Department of the Interior. *Report on Mineral Industries in the United States.* Eleventh Census, 1890. Washington, 1892.

U.S. Department of Labor. Bureau of Labor Statistics. *Michigan Copper District Strike.*
   Bulletin No. 139. (Originally printed as S. Doc. 381.) Washington, 1914.
U.S. Department of Labor. Women's Bureau. *Report [of the] Conference on Women
   in the Upper Peninsula Economy held at University Center, Northern Michigan
   University, Marquette, Michigan, 16 May 1964.* Washington, 1964.
Work Projects Administration. *Tabulation of Sponsor and Federal Participation in all
   Michigan Projects for Fiscal Years Ending June 30, 1936–1939, Inclusive.* State
   Archives, Lansing.

NEWSPAPERS AND PERIODICALS

American Federation of Labor Weekly News Letter, 1913–14
Boston Evening Transcript, 1916
Boston Sunday Globe, 1885
Calumet News, 1907–38
Chicago Record–Herald, 1913–14
Chicago Tribune, 1913–14
Copper Country Evening News (Calumet), 1896, 1900, 1904, 1906–07
Copper Island Sentinel (Calumet), 1984–85
Daily Mining Gazette (Houghton), 1896–1992
Denver Post, 1902, 1914
Detroit Free Press, 1913–14, 1969
Detroit News, 1913–14, 1969
Engineering and Mining Journal, 1910–11, 1913–14, 1953, 1966, 1968, 1990
Evening Copper Journal (Hancock), 1913–14
Evening News–Journal (Calumet), 1939
Keweenaw Miner (Calumet), 1913, 1916
Lake Superior Miner (Ontonagon), 1870
L'Anse Sentinel (L'Anse), 1893, 1895, 1933, 1969
L'Union Franco–Américane (Lake Linden), 1890
Milwaukee Journal, 1968–69
Miners' Bulletin (Calumet), September 1913–April 1914
Miners' Magazine (Denver), 1907–15
Native Copper Times (Lake Linden), 1893, 1895
New York Times, 1913–14, 1943, 1949, 1968–69
Ontonagon Herald (Ontonagon), 1908, 1933, 1965, 1968
Portage Lake Mining Gazette (Houghton), 1870–71, 1876, 1882, 1896
Press–Gazette (Green Bay, WI), 10 November 1968
Science, 12 March 1954
Public, August 1913–May 1914
Truth (Houghton), November 1913–January 1914
Wall Street Journal, 1967–69

BOOKS, PAMPHLETS, ARTICLES, AND UNPUBLISHED MATERIALS

Agassiz, George R., editor. *Letters and Recollections of Alexander Agassiz.* Boston:
   Houghton Mifflin, 1913.

Bibliography   Alexander, Eleanor. *East Hancock Revisited: History of a Neighborhood Circa 1880–1920*. Hancock, MI, 1984.

Avery Color Studios, *Copper Country–God's Country*. Au Train, MI: Avery Color Studios, 1973.

Balch, Emily Greene. *Our Slavic Fellow Citizens*. New York: Charities Publication Committee, 1910.

Bald, F. Clever. "The Treaty of Greenville." *Michigan History* 29(1945): 209–23.

Baraga, Frederic. *A Theoretical and Practical Grammar of the Otchipwe Language for the Use of Missionaries and Other Persons Living Among the Indians*. 2d ed. Montreal: Beauchemin & Valois, 1878.

Baraga County Historical Society. *Baraga County Historical Pageant, Souvenir Book*. Baraga, MI: Baraga County Historical Society, 1969.

Barkell, Gordon G., ed. *Hancock, Michigan Centennial*. Hancock, MI: Hancock Centennial Committee, 1963.

Barnett, Leroy. "Lac La Belle, Keweenaw's First Ship Canal." *Michigan History* 69(January/February 1985): 41–46.

Benedict, C. Harry. *Red Metal: The Calumet and Hecla Story*. Ann Arbor: University of Michigan Press, 1952.

Bingham, Stephen D., ed. *Early History of Michigan with Biographies of State Officers, Member of Congress, Judges, and Legislators*. Lansing, Thorp, & Godfrey, 1888.

Biographical Record, Houghton, Baraga, Marquette Counties. Chicago: Biographical, 1903.

Bliss, A. N. "Federal Land Grants for Internal Improvements in the State of Michigan." *Michigan Pioneer Collections* 7(1884): 52–68.

Boyer, Hugh E. "The Decline of the Progressive Party in Michigan's Upper Peninsula: The Case of Congressman William J. MacDonald in 1914." *Michigan Historical Review* 13(Fall 1987): 75–94.

Brinley, John Ervin, Jr. *The Western Federation of Miners*. Ann Arbor: University Microfilms International, 1981.

Calumet and Hecla Mining Company Semi-Centennial Edition, 1866–1916. Calumet, MI: *Keweenaw Miner*, 1916.

Calumet Light Guard and Houghton Light Infantry. *Our Boys in the Spanish–American War . . . Company E, Third Regiment, Company G., Third Regiment, Michigan National Guard*. Houghton, MI: Gazette, 1900.

Calumet, Michigan, Village Centennial Committee. *Village of Calumet, Michigan, 1875–1975, Souvenir Centennial Book*. Calumet: Village of Calumet, 1975.

Calumet Township Centennial Committee. *Calumet Township Centennial, 1866–1966*. Souvenir Program. Calumet: Calumet Township Centennial Committee, 1966.

Carter, James L. *Superior: A State for the North Country*. Marquette, MI: Pilot, 1980.

Carter, James L., and Ernest H. Rankin, ed. *North to Lake Superior: The Journal of Charles W. Penny, 1840*. Marquette, MI: John M. Longyear Research Library, 1970.

Central Mine Reunion Service Program, 1991. Michigan Technological University Archives, Houghton.

Chabot, Chris. *Tales of White Pine*. Ontonagon, MI: Ontonagon Herald, 1979.

Chaput, Donald. *Hubbell: A Copper Country Village*. 1969. Reprint. Lake Linden, MI: Forster, 1986.

Chase, Lew Allen. "Early Copper Mining in Michigan." *Michigan History* 29(1945): 22–30.

———. "Early Days of Michigan Mining: Pioneering Land Sales and Surveys." *Michigan History* 29(1945): 166–79.

————. "Edwin James Hulbert, Copper Hunter." *Michigan History* 16(1932): 406–12.

————. "Michigan Copper Mines." *Michigan History* 29(1945): 479–88.

Childs, Mrs. W. A. "Reminiscences of Old Keweenaw." *Michigan Pioneer Collections* 30(1905): 150–55.

Clarke, Robert E. "Notes from the Copper Region." *Harper's New Monthly Magazine* 6(1853): 433–48, 577–88.

Collins, Elsie, *From Keweenaw to Abbaye*. Ishpeming, MI, 1975.

Collins, Frederick L. "Paine's Career Is a Triumph of Early American Virtues." *American Magazine* 105(June 1928): 40–41, 139–43.

Copper Country Commercial Club. *Strike Investigation*. Chicago: Donohue, 1913.

Copway, George [Kah-Ge-Ga-Gah-Bowh]. *Indian Life and Indian History by an Indian Author*. Boston: Colby, 1860.

"Cost of Producing Lake Superior Copper." *Engineering and Mining Journal*, 17 August 1912, p. 306.

Crissey, Forrest. "Every Man His Own Merchant." *Saturday Evening Post*, 20 September 1913, pp. 16–17, 57–58.

Curtis, William E. "Calumet, a Unique Municipality." *Chautauquan* 29(April 1899): 33-37.

Danziger, Edmund J. *The Chippewas of Lake Superior*. Norman: University of Oklahoma Press, 1978.

Densmore, Frances. *Chippewa Customs*. Washington: GPO, 1929.

————. *How Indians Use Wild Plants for Food, Medicine, and Crafts*. New York: Dover, 1974.

Distuenell, John. "The Upper Peninsula: Historical Events in Chronological Order." *Michigan Pioneer Collections* 7(1884): 152–53.

"Douglass Houghton Monument." *Michigan History* 29(1945): 579–84.

Drier, Roy Ward, and Octave Joseph Du Temple. *Prehistoric Copper Mining in the Lake Superior Region*. Calumet, MI, 1961.

Dyer, Francis J. "The Truth About the Copper Strike." *National Magazine* 40(May 1914): 235–51.

Ely, S. P. "Historical Address." *Michigan Pioneer Collections* 7(1884): 165–80.

Emery, B. Frank. "Fort Wilkins, 1844–46: A Frontier Stockaded Post Built To Protect Michigan's First Copper Mines." Old Forts and Historical Memorial Association, Detroit, 1932. Typescript.

Engineering Study of the Economic Resources of the Michigan Upper Peninsula. New York: Ebasco Services, 1953.

Fadner, Lawrence T. *Fort Wilkins 1844 and the U.S. Mineral Land Agency 1843*. New York: Vantage, 1966.

Ferrey, Mrs. "Diary Notes." *Michigan History* 12(1928): 621.

"The First Man of Marquette." *Michigan Pioneer Collections* 30(1903–4): 602–23.

Fisher, James. "Fort Wilkins." *Michigan History* 29 (1945): 155–65.

————. "Michigan's Cornish People." *Michigan History* 29(1945): 377–85.

Forster, John H. "Early Settlement of the Copper Regions of Lake Superior." *Michigan Pioneer Collections* 7(1884): 181–93.

————. "Finance of Mining—Lake Superior Mines." *Michigan Pioneer Collections* 13(1888): 342–50.

————. "Lake Superior Country." *Michigan Pioneer Collections* 8(1885): 136–45.

————. "Life in the Copper Mines of Lake Superior." *Michigan Pioneer Collections* 11(1887): 175–86.

————. "War Times in the Copper Mines." *Michigan Pioneer Collections* 18(1892): 375–82.

Frimodig, David Mac. *Keweenaw Character: The Foundation of Michigan's Copper Country.* Lake Linden, MI: Forster, 1990.

Frimodig, David Mac et al. *A Most Superior Land: Life in the Upper Peninsula of Michigan.* Lansing: Michigan Department of Natural Resources, 1983.

Fuller, George N., ed. *Geological Reports of Douglass Houghton, First State Geologist of Michigan, 1837–1845.* Lansing: Michigan Historical Commission, 1928.

Gabriel, Ralph H. *The Course of American Democratic Thought.* New York: Ronald, 1940.

Gagnieur, William F. "Indian Place Names in the Upper Peninsula, and Their Interpretation." *Michigan History* 2(1918): 526–55.

Gates, William B., Jr. *Michigan Copper and Boston Dollars: An Economic History of the Michigan Copper Mining Industry.* 1951. Reprint. New York: Russell & Russell, 1969.

Geismar, Leo M. *The Otter Lake Agricultural School for Boys and Girls.* Houghton, MI: n.d., Keweenaw Historical Society Collection. Michigan Technological University, Houghton.

Gilbert, Jess, and Craig Harris. "Unemployment, Primary Production, and Population in the Upper Peninsula of Michigan in the Great Depression." In *A Half Century Ago: Michigan in the Great Depression.* East Lansing: Michigan State University, 1980.

Glazer, Sidney. "The Michigan Labor Movement." *Michigan History* 29(1945): 73–82.

Goodrich, Samuel Griswold. "Lake Superior." *Michigan Pioneer Collections* 7(1884): 154–55.

Greenman, Emerson F. *The Indians of Michigan.* Lansing: Michigan Historical Commission, 1961.

Gregorich, Joseph. *The Apostle of the Chippewas.* Chicago: Bishop Baraga Association, 1932.

Grierson, Mary F. "Calumet and Hecla Library." *Mining Congress Journal* 17(October 1931): 561–62.

Griffin, James B., ed. *Lake Superior Copper and the Indians: Miscellaneous Studies of Great Lakes Pre-History.* Anthropological Papers, no. 17. Ann Arbor: University of Michigan, Museum of Anthropology, 1961.

Guida degli Italiani del Copper Country. Laurium, MI: Minatore Italiano, 1910.

Guide Francais des Etats–Unis. Lowell, MA: La Société de Publications Francaises des Etats–Unis, 1891.

Halkola, David T. "Finnish-Language Newspapers in the United States." In *The Finns in North America,* ed. Ralph J. Jalkanen. Lansing: Michigan State University Press for Suomi College, 1969.

———. "The Citadel Crumbles: Political Change in the Upper Peninsula of Michigan in the Great Depression." In *A Half Century Ago: Michigan in the Great Depression.* East Lansing: Michigan State University, 1980.

Halkola, David T. et al. *Michigan Tech Centennial, 1885–1985.* Houghton, MI: Michigan Technological University, 1985.

Halsey, John R. "Miskwabik—Red Metal: Lake Superior Copper and the Indians of Eastern North America." *Michigan History* 67(September/October 1983): 32–41

Hathaway, William H. "County Organization in Michigan." *Michigan History* 2(1918): 573–629.

Heilbroner, Robert L. *The Economic Transformation of America.* New York: Harcourt Brace Jovanovich, 1977.

Heino, Jack K. "Finnish Influence on the Cooperative Movement in America." *Michigan Academician* 3(Winter 1971): 55–60.

Henry, Alexander. *Travels and Adventures in Canada and the Indian Territories*
    Between the Years 1760 and 1776. Edmonton: Hurtig, 1969.
Hickerson, Harold. *Ethnohistory of Chippewa of Lake Superior.* New York: Garland
    1974.
————. *The Chippewa and Their Neighbors.* Prospect Heights, IL: Waveland, 1970.
Hinsdale, W. B. *Primitive Man in Michigan.* Ann Arbor: University of Michigan,
    1925.
Historic American Engineering Record. *The Upper Peninsula of Michigan: An Inven-
    tory of Historic Engineering and Industrial Sites.* Washington: Department of the
    Interior, 1978.
History of the Upper Peninsula of Michigan. Chicago: Western Historical, 1883.
Holmio, Armas K. E., *History of the Finns in Michigan.* Trans. by Elin Rynaman.
    Hancock, MI: Michigan Suomalaisten Historia–Seura, 1967.
Horan, James D. *The Pinkertons: The Detective Dynasty That Made History.* New York:
    Crown, 1967.
Houston, D. et al, *Copper Manual: Copper Mines, Copper Statistics, and a Summary
    of Information on Copper.* New York: Pratt, 1897.
Hubbard, Bela. *Memorials of a Half-Century in Michigan and the Lake Region.* New
    York: Putnam's Sons, 1888.
Hulbert, Edwin J. *Calumet-Conglomerate.* Ontonagon, MI: Ontonagon–Miner, 1893.
Hybels, Robert J. "The Lake Superior Copper Fever, 1841–47." *Michigan History*
    34(1950): 97–119, 224–44, 309–26.
Hyde, Charles K. "Undercover and Underground: Labor Spies and Mine Management
    in the Early Twentieth Century." *Business History Review* 60(Spring 1986): 1–27.
Jalkanen, Ralph J., editor. *The Faith of the Finns.* East Lansing: Michigan State Uni-
    versity Press, 1972.
Jamison, James K. *This Ontonagon Country.* Ontonagon, MI: Ontonagon Herald,
    1939.
Jamison, Knox. *A History of Ewen and Other Towns in the Southern Part of Ontonagon
    County, Michigan.* Ontonagon, MI, 1967.
————. *A History of Rockland–Greenland–Mass.* Ontonagon, MI, 1969.
————. *A History of Silver City: Ontonagon County, Michigan.* Ontonagon, MI, 1963.
Janke, Ronald A. *The Development and Persistence of U.S. Indian Land Problems as
    Shown by a Detailed Study of the Chippewa Indians.* Ann Arbor: Xerox University
    Microfilms, 1976.
Jenks, Albert E. "The Wild Rice Gatherers of the Upper Great Lakes." *Annual Report
    of the Bureau of American Ethnology* 19(1901): 1013–1160.
Jopling, James E. "Cornish Miners of the Upper Peninsula." *Michigan History*
    12(1928): 554–67.
Joralemon, Ira B. *Romantic Copper: Its Lure and Lore.* New York: Appleton–Century,
    1936.
Joyaux, Georges J. "French Press in Michigan: A Bibliography." *Michigan History*
    36(1952): 260–78.
Kalevala. Trans. W. F. Kirby. 2 vols. London: Dent, 1912.
Karamanski, Theodore J. *Deep Woods Frontier: A History of Logging in Northern
    Michigan.* Detroit: Wayne State University Press, 1989.
Karamanski, Theodore J., and Richard Zeitlin. *Narrative History of Isle Royale Na-
    tional Park.* Chicago: Loyola University Mid-American Research Center, 1988.
Karni, Michael G. " 'Yhteishyva'; or, For the Common Good: Finnish Radicalism in the
    Western Great Lakes Region, 1900–1940." Ph.D. diss. University of Minnesota,
    1975.
Karpiak, Steven. "The Establishment of the Porcupine Mountains State Park." *Michi-
    gan Academician* 11 (1978–79): 75–83.

Bibliography Kaups, Matti. "Patterns of Finnish Settlement in the Lake Superior Region." *Michigan Academician* 3(Winter 1971): 77–91.

————. "The Finns in the Copper and Iron Ore Mines of the Western Great Lakes Region, 1864–1905: Some Preliminary Observations." In *The Finnish Experience in the Western Great Lakes Region.* Turku, Finland: Institute for Migration, 1975.

Keller, Mark. *The Chippewa Land of Keweenaw Bay: An Allotment History.* Baraga, MI: Keweenaw Bay Tribal Council, 1981.

Kellogg, Louise Phelps. *The French Régime in Wisconsin and the Northwest.* Madison: State Historical Society of Wisconsin, 1925.

Keweenaw Bay and Arnheim Extension Study Group. *Trestles and Tracks: A History of Keweenaw Bay and Arnheim.* 2 vols. L'Anse, MI: L'Anse Sentinel, 1983–88.

Kirchhoff, C. "The State of the Copper Industry," *Nation,* 27 November 1884, pp. 454–55.

Knuth, Helen E. *Economic and Historical Background of Northeastern Minnesota Lands: Chippewa Indians of Lake Superior.* New York: Garland, 1974.

Kohl, Johann Georg. *Kitchi-Gami: Life Among the Lake Superior Ojibway.* Trans. Lascelles Wraxall. Saint Paul: Minnesota Historical Society Press, 1985.

Kolehmainen, John I. "The Inimitable Marxists: The Finnish Immigrant Socialists." *Michigan History* 36(1952): 395–405.

Krause, David J. *The Making of a Mining District: Keweenaw Native Copper, 1500–1870.* Detroit: Wayne State University Press, 1992.

Laitala, E. M. "Finnish Language Publications in the Lake Superior Region." *Michigan Academician* 3(Winter 1971): 41–44.

Lankton, Larry D. *Cradle to Grave: Life, Work, and Death at the Lake Superior Copper Mines.* New York: Oxford University Press, 1991.

Lankton, Larry D., and Charles K. Hyde. *Old Reliable: An Illustrated History of the Quincy Mining Company.* Hancock, MI: Quincy Mine Hoist Association, 1982.

Lanman, Charles. *A Canoe Voyage up the Mississippi and Around Lake Superior.* 1847. Reprint. Grand Rapids, MI: Black Letter, 1978. Originally titled *A Summer in the Wilderness.*

Larzelere. Claude S. "The Boundaries of Michigan." *Michigan Pioneer Collections* 30(1905): 1–27.

Lawrence, Charles B. "Keweena Portage." *Michigan History* 38(1954): 45–64.

Lemmer, John A. "Claude Jean Allouez, S.J. (1613–1689)." *Michigan History* 2(1918): 781–94.

Lewis, David L. *The Public Image of Henry Ford.* Detroit: Wayne State University Press, 1976.

Lewis, Ferris. *State and Local Government in Michigan.* Hillsdale, MI: Hillsdale Educational, 1979.

Lockwood, William G., and Yvonne R. Lockwood. "The Cornish Pasty in Northern Michigan." In *Michigan Folklife Reader,* ed. C. Kurt Dewhurst and Yvonne R. Lockwood, East Lansing: Michigan State University, 1987.

Lurie, Edward. *Louis Agassiz: A Life in Science.* Chicago: University of Chicago Press, 1960.

Maas, W. E. *Diamond Jubilee, 1879–1954, Saint Paul's Evangelical Lutheran Church.* Laurium, MI, 1954.

McDonald, P. B. "The Michigan Copper Miners." *Outlook,* 7 February 1914, pp. 297–98.

Macfarlane, Peter Clark. "The Issues at Calumet." *Collier's,* 7 February 1914, 5–6, 22–25.

McGuffey, William H. *McGuffey's New Sixth Eclectic Reader.* Cincinnati: Wilson, Henkle, 1857.

McKenney, Thomas L. *Sketches of a Tour to the Lakes, of the Character and Customs of*
the Chippeway Indians and of Incidents connected with the Treaty of Fond du Lac.
1827. Reprint. Barre, MA: Imprint Society, 1972.

McLaughlin, Andrew C. *Lewis Cass.* 1891. Reprint. New York: Chelsea House, 1980.

Macmillan, Margaret B. *The Methodist Church in Michigan: The Nineteenth Century.*
Grand Rapids: Michigan Area Methodist Historical Society and Eerdmans, 1967.

Magnaghi, Russell M. *Miners, Merchants, and Midwives: Michigan's Upper Peninsula*
Italians. Marquette, MI: Belle Fontaine, 1987.

Mahaffey, Charles G., and Felice R. Bassuk. *Images of the Cutover: A Historical Geog-*
raphy of Resource Utilization in the Lake Superior Region, 1845–1930. Madison:
University of Wisconsin Institute for Environmental Studies.

Maki, Wilbert. *Hancock: A Mosaic of Memories.* Calumet, MI, 1984.

———. *Reminiscences of the Streetcar, 1900–1932.* Hancock, MI, n.d.

Martin, John Bartlow. *Call It North Country: The Story of Upper Michigan.* 1944.
Reprint. Detroit: Wayne State University Press, 1986.

Martin, Patrick E. "Mining on Minong: Copper Mining on Isle Royale." *Michigan*
History 74(May/June 1990): 19–25.

Mason, Philip P., ed. *Copper Country Journal: The Diary of Schoolmaster Henry Hobart,*
1863–1864. Detroit: Wayne State University Press, 1991.

Mather, Cotton, and Matti Kaups. "The Finnish Sauna: A Cultural Index to Settlement." *Annals of the Association of American Geographers* 53(1963): 494–504.

Mayer, Alfred G. "Alexander Agassiz, 1835–1910." *Popular Science Monthly* 77(November 1910): 418–46.

Meads, Alfred. "History of Ascension Church at Ontonagon." *Michigan Pioneer*
Collections 30(1905): 495–506.

Memorial Record of the Northern Peninsula of Michigan. Chicago: Lewis, 1895.

Michigan Copper Mining District Historic Resources Management Plan. Houghton:
Western Upper Peninsula Planning and Development Regional Commission,
1990.

Michigan State Gazetteer and Business Directory for 1863–64. Detroit: Clark, 1863.

Michigan State Gazetteer and Business Directory, 1889–1890. Detroit: Polk, 1889.

Michigan Writers' Program of the Works Projects Administration. *Michigan: A Guide*
to the Wolverine State. American Guide Series, no. 46–5682. New York: Oxford
University Press, 1949.

Moffett, S. E. "Romances of the World's Great Mines, Part III—Calumet and Hecla."
Cosmopolitan 34(April 1903): 679–84.

Moline, Norman T. "Finnish Settlement in Upper Michigan." Masters' thesis, University of Chicago, 1966.

Monette, Clarence J. *Hancock, Michigan Remembered.* Vol. 1. Lake Linden, MI, 1982.

———. *Laurium, Michigan's Early Days.* Lake Linden, MI, 1986.

Moyer, Claire B. *Ke-Wee-Naw (The Crossing Place).* Denver: Big Mountain, 1966.

Neph, John R. *The Adventure Story.* Greenland, MI, 1976.

Niemi, Clemens. *Americanization of the Finnish People in Houghton County, Michigan.*
Duluth: Finnish Daily Publishing, 1921.

Niemi, Leslie. "Religious History of Finns in America." *Michigan Academician* 3(Winter 1971): 65–73.

Nute, Grace Lee. *Lake Superior.* Indianapolis: Bobbs–Merrill, 1944.

———. *The Voyageur.* Saint Paul: Minnesota Historical Society, 1955.

Opas, Pauli. "The Image of Finland and Finns in the Minds of Americans." *Michigan*
Academician 3(Winter 1971): 13–21.

Parker, Captain John G. "Autobiography." *Michigan Pioneer Collections* 30(1905):
582–85.

Parkman, Francis. *France and England in North America.* Vol. 1. New York: Library of America, 1983.

Paton, Florence. "History of the Schools of Portage Township in the Copper Country." *Michigan History* 2(1918): 556–72.

Paton, Lucy Allen. *Elizabeth Cary Agassiz: A Biography.* Boston: Houghton Mifflin, 1919.

Paul, Mrs. Carroll. "The Exhibit in the Officers Quarters at Fort Wilkins." *Michigan History* 36(1952): 415–19.

Peters, Bernard C. "The Origin and Meaning of Chippewa and French Place Names Along the Shoreline of the Keweenaw Peninsula." *Michigan Academician* 17(1984–85): 195–211.

———. "Wa-bish-kee-pe-nas and the Chippewa Reverence for Copper." *Michigan Historical Review* 15(Fall 1989): 47–60.

———. ed. *Lake Superior Journal: Bela Hubbard's Account of the 1840 Houghton Expedition.* Marquette: Northern Michigan University Press, 1983.

Platt, Robert S. "South Range, Keweenaw Copper Country: A Mining Pattern of Land Occupancy." *Economic Geography* 8(October 1932): 386–89.

Preservation Urban Design and John R. Johansen, *Calumet Downtown Historic District Plan.* Ann Arbor, 1979.

Prisland, Marie. *From Slovenia to America.* Chicago: Slovenian Women's Union of America and Bruce Publishing, 1968.

Puotinen, Arthur. "Copper Country Finns and the Strike of 1913." In Michael G. Karni, Matti E. Kaups, Douglas J. Ollila, Jr., eds. *The Finnish Experience in the Western Great Lakes Region.* Turku, Finland: Institute for Migration, 1975.

———. "Early Labor Organization in the Copper Country." In *For the Common Good: Finnish Immigrants and the Radical Response to Industrial America,* ed. Michael G. Karni and Douglas J. Ollila, Jr. Superior, WI: Työmies Society, 1977.

Puotinen, Heino A. "Development of Finnish Dialect." *Michigan Academician* 3(Winter 1971): 93–100.

Putnam, Beatrice M. *North to Adventure.* Detroit: Putnam Feature Services, 1960.

Quimby, George I. *Indian Culture and European Trade Goods.* Madison: University of Wisconsin Press, 1966.

———. *Indian Life in the Upper Great Lakes, 11,000 B.C. to A.D. 1800.* Chicago: University of Chicago Press, 1960.

Quimby, George I., and Albert C. Spaulding. *The Old Copper Culture and the Keweenaw Waterway.* Chicago: Field Museum of Natural History, 1963.

Rakestraw, Lawrence. *Historic Mining on Isle Royale.* U.S. National Park Service and Isle Royale Natural History Association, 1965.

Rankin, Ernest H. *Indians of Gitchee Gumee.* Marquette, MI: Marquette County Historical Society, 1966.

Ranta, Taimi. "Finnish Folklore." *Michigan Academician* 3(Winter 1971): 23–39.

Reeder, John T. "Evidences of Prehistoric Man on Lake Superior." *Michigan Pioneer Collections* 30(1905): 110–18.

"Report on Michigan." *Mine, Mill, and Smelter Workers Bulletin* (Butte), 19 August 1950.

Rice, Claude T. "Labor Conditions at Calumet and Hecla." *Engineering and Mining Journal,* 23 December 1911, pp. 1235–39.

———. "Labor Conditions at Copper Range." *Engineering and Mining Journal,* 28 December 1912, pp. 1229–32.

Rickard, T. A. *The Copper Mines of Lake Superior.* New York: Engineering and Mining Journal, 1905.

Robinson, Edgar E. *The Presidential Vote, 1896–1932.* Stanford: Stanford University Press, 1934.

Romig, Walter. *Michigan Place Names*. N.d. Reprint. Detroit: Wayne State University Press, 1986.

Saint John, John R. *A True Description of the Lake Superior Country*. 1846. Reprint. Iron Mountain, MI: Secord, 1988.

Saltonstall, Brayton. "An Early Visitor to Michigan." *Michigan History* 12(1928): 252–66.

Scammon, Richard M. *America Votes, 1*. New York: MacMillan, 1956.

Scammon, Richard M., and Alice V. McGillivray. *America Votes, 16*. Washington: Congressional Quarterly Elections Research Center, 1985.

Schoolcraft, Henry R. *The Hiawatha Legends*. Au Train, MI: Avery Color Studios, 1984.

Shea, John G. *History of the Catholic Missions Among the Indian Tribes of the United States, 1529–1854*. New York: Dunigan and Brother, 1855.

Sherzer, W. H. "An Unpublished Episode in Early Michigan History." *Michigan History* 16(1932): 214–17.

Stadius, Arnold. "Suomi College and Seminary." In *The Finns in North America*, ed. Ralph J. Jalkanen. Lansing: Michigan State University Press for Suomi College, 1969.

Starbuck, James C. "Ben Franklin and Isle Royale." *Michigan History* 46(1962): 157–66.

Stevens, Wayne E. "The Michigan Fur Trade." *Michigan History* 29(1945): 489–505.

Strassman, W. Paul. *Economic Growth in Northern Michigan*. East Lansing: Michigan Board of Agriculture, 1946.

Swinton, Alma W. *I Married a Doctor: Life in Ontonagon, Michigan, from 1900 to 1919*. Marquette, MI: 1964.

Taussig, F. W. "The Copper Strike and Copper Dividends." 14 February 1914, 612–13.

Taylor, Graham R. "The Clash in the Copper Country." *Survey*, 1 November 1913, 127–35, 145–49.

Ten Broeck, Joseph A. "Old Keweenaw." *Michigan Pioneer Collections* 30(1903–4): 139–49.

———. "A Sketch of John Senter of Houghton." *Michigan Pioneer Collections* 30(1903–4): 156–62.

Tharp, Louise Hall. "Professor of the World's Wonders." *American Heritage* 12(February 1961): 56–63.

Thayer, George W. "From Vermont to Lake Superior in 1845." *Michigan Pioneer Collections* 30(1903–4): 549–66.

Thurner, Arthur W. *Calumet Copper and People*. Hancock, MI: 1974.

———. "Charles H. Moyer and the Michigan Copper Strike, 1913–1914." *Michigan Historical Review* 17(Fall 1991): 1–19.

———. "How a Library Came to the Copper Country: A Saga of Miners and Capitalists." *Wilson Library Bulletin* 50(April 1976): 608–12.

———. *Rebels on the Range: The Michigan Copper Miners' Strike of 1913–1914*. Lake Linden, MI: Forster, 1984.

———. "Red Jacket/Calumet: The First Century." In *Calumet Village Centennial Souvenir Book*. Calumet, MI, 1975.

———. "Technology Old and New: The Copper Country Miner and the One-Man Drill, 1913–1914." Presented at Michigan Technological University, Houghton, 1983.

———. "The Western Federation of Miners in Two Copper Camps: The Impact of the Michigan Copper Miners' Strike on Butte's Local No. 1." *Montana: The Magazine of Western History* 33(Spring 1983): 30–45.

Bibliography   Thwaites, Reuben Gold, ed. *The Jesuit Relations and Allied Documents: Travels and Explorations of the Jesuit Missionaries in New France, 1610–1791.* Vols. 50–51. Cleveland: Burrows Brothers, 1899.

Tocqueville, Alexis de. *Democracy in America*, ed. J. P. Mayer. Trans. George Lawrence. Garden City: Doubleday, 1969.

Turrell, Mrs. M. F. "Journal Notes." *Michigan History* 12(1928): 397–98.

United Steel Workers of America. *Nonferrous Report.* Pittsburgh: USWA, 1968–69.

Upper Peninsula Travel and Recreation Association, *Development Bureau News.* Marquette, MI: Upper Peninsula Travel and Recreation Association, 1926–31.

Upper Peninsula Travel and Recreation Association and Michigan Travel Bureau. *Michigan's Upper Peninsula Travel Planner for All Seasons.* Lansing, 1991.

Utley, Henry M., and Byron M. Cutcheon. *Michigan as a Province, Territory, and State, the Twenty-Sixth Member of the Federal Union.* 4 Vols. New York: Publishing Society of Michigan, 1906.

Vachon, Jingo Viitala. *Tall Timber Tales.* L'Anse, MI: L'Anse Sentinel, 1973.

Vandercook, Roy C. "Michigan in the Great War." *Michigan History* 2(1918): 259–69.

Vecoli, Rudolph J. "Return to the Melting Pot: Ethnicity in the United States in the Eighties." *Journal of American Ethnic History* 5(Fall 1985): 7–20.

Verwyst, P. Chrysostomus, O.F.M. *Life and Labors of Right Reverend Frederic Baraga.* Milwaukee: Wiltzius, 1900.

Wagner, Moritz, and Carl Scherzer. *Reisen in Nordamerika in den Jahren 1852 und 1853.* 3 vols. Leipzig: Arnoldische Buchhandlung, 1857.

Wallin, Helen. *Douglass Houghton, Michigan's First State Geologist, 1837–1845.* Rev. ed. Lansing: Michigan Department of Natural Resources, 1970.

Walling, Regis M., and N. Daniel Rupp, *The Diary of Bishop Frederic Baraga.* Detroit: Wayne State University Press, 1990.

Warren, William W. *History of the Ojibway People.* 1885. Reprint. Saint Paul: Minnesota Historical Society, 1984.

Waters, Theodore. "Calumet and Hecla: The Deepest Copper Mine in the World." *Everybody's Magazine* 11(September 1904): 336–47.

Wax, Anthony S. "Calumet and Hecla Copper Mines: An Episode in the Economic Development of Michigan." *Michigan History* 16(1932): 5–41.

Weeks, George. *Stewards of the State.* Detroit and Ann Arbor: Detroit News and Historical Society of Michigan, 1987.

Welcome to the Village of Laurium's Eightieth Anniversary, 1889–1969—July 10, 11, 12, 13. Laurium, MI: Village of Laurium, 1969.

Western Upper Peninsula Planning and Development Regional Commission. *Michigan Copper Mining District Historical Resources Management Plan.* Houghton, MI: The Commission, 1990.

White, Walter S., ed. *Guidebook for Field Conference Michigan Copper District, September 30–October 2, 1971.* Houghton: Michigan Technological University Press, 1971.

Whittier, John Greenleaf. *The Poetical Works of Whittier.* Boston: Houghton Mifflin, 1975.

Wolf, Eric R. *Europe and the People Without History.* Berkeley: University of California Press, 1982.

Woodbridge, Dwight E. "The Lake Superior Copper Mines." *Engineering and Mining Journal*, 13 May 1911, 957–58.

Woodwell, Roland H. *John Greenleaf Whittier: A Biography.* Haverhill, MA: Trustees of the John Greenleaf Whittier Homestead, 1985.

Index

Abbey, General Pearley L., 192, 204, 208, 341–42 n.21

Abel, I., 150

Acculturation, 125, 138, 144, 151, 154–55, 157, 254; Catholics encourage, 59–60; creates new cultures, 142; dim view of, 65; education potent in process of, 155–56; entertainment and, 182; ethnic groups promote, 151; Methodists encourage, 57; peculiar nature of, 156–57; and popular culture, 256; power of, 257; pressures to bring about, 36–37, 53, 62, 85, 107, 124, 149, 155, 222, 255, 321–22 n.10; World War I and, 254

Adams, John Quincy, 41

Adams, Maude, 181

Adams, Russell, 253

Adams, S. E., and school curriculum, 86

Adams Express Company, and 1893 robbery, 180

Addams, Jane, 182

Adventure Mine, 113, 153

A. E. Seaman Mineralogical Museum, 73

African Americans, 48, 63–64, 65, 94, 98–99, 139–40, 251, 256, 310, 336 n.78; Civil War service of, 84; and discovery of copper, 114; at Eagle River, 139–40; experiences of, vis-à-vis other ethnic groups, 140; at Hancock, 140; at Houghton, 140; and intermarriage, 140; occupations of, 140; original homes of, 140; population figures, 139, 140, 360 n.58; work songs of, 118–19

Agassiz, Alexander, 92, 95–96, 110, 126, 185, 218, 224, 263–64, 313; as community builder, 91–92, 168; death of, 91; early life of, 90–91; managerial policies of, 162, 220–21; memorial of, at Calumet, 253; as mine superintendent, 91–92; paternalism of, 211, 327 n.17, 345 n.75; as president of Calumet and Hecla, 90; psychological portrait of, 91–92, 221, 327 n.17, 345 n.75; as scientist, 92

Agassiz, Anna Russell, wife of Alexander, 91, 95

Agassiz, Cécile Braun, mother of Alexander, 90–91

Agassiz, Elizabeth Cary, wife of Louis, 91

Agassiz, Louis, 90–91

Agassiz family, 126, 224

Agassiz Park, 224, 253

Agate Harbor, 52

Aggarto, Maggie, 204

Agriculture: in Baraga County, 106–7; at Cliff Mine, 52; copper companies and, 75, 113; expansion of, in 1930–40, 233, 260; farms and acreage in

Hancock Grove, 185
Hancock Rotary Club, 228
Hancock Township, 76
Hanna, Jason, 71
Harris, John, 83
Harris, William, 76
Hartman's Hall, 185
Harvard University, and Keweenaw copper, 88
Hays, John, and discovery of copper at Cliff Mine, 44
Hays' Point lighthouse, 58
Hebard, Charles, 299
Hecla Mine, 63, 86–87; calls for assessments, 92; dividends paid by, 92; and Edwin J. Hulbert, 92; exploration of its properties, 229
Hecla Stamp Mill, 111
Heinola, farming at, 144
Hennes, Louis and Joseph, pioneer merchants at Houghton, 102
Henry Alexander, 29–31
Henshaw, David, 45
Herbert Hoover Finnish Relief Fund, 265–66
Hersey, Lynn, 270
Hevesh, Rabbi Jacob, 151
Heywood, William, 84
Hiawatha (Longfellow), 94–95, 234–35
Hiawatha Land, as promotional device, 234–35
Hibernian Rifles Society, 148, 184
Hibernians, Ancient Order of, 101, 148
Higginson family, 126, 224
Hill, Captain Robert G., 205
Hill, Samuel W., plats Hancock, 76
Hills Creek Project, and expectations to mine copper, 286
Hillman, Sidney, 272
Hiltunen family, 145
Hirsch, J., pioneer merchant, 97
Hoar, Captain John, 80
Hoar Brothers, 102
Hoatson, John, 109, 120
Hoatson, Mr. and Mrs. Thomas, 121
Hobart, Henry, 67, 105, 136
Hocking, John E., 100–101
Hodges, Olive, 309
Hoffenbacher, Hannah, 102
Hoffenberg family, 151
Holliday, John, 31–32
Holmio, Armas K. E., 144
Holso, Isaac, 260
Holt, Brother, 55
Holy Cross Sisters, 111
Home Dramatic Club, 183
Homestake Copper Company, 300
Homier, Treffele, 129

Honkala, Elsie, 266
Hook, Representative Frank E., 241–42, 281
Hooper, Thomas, at White Pine, 289
Hospitals, 96, 167–68, 274, 337 n.25
Hotchkiss, W. O., 229
Hotels: at Calumet, 98; at Copper Harbor, 49; at Eagle Harbor, 69, 235–36; at Eagle River, 139; at Hancock, 101, 129, 176; at Houghton, 77–78, 149; at Lake Linden, 111; at L'Anse, 106, 177; at Ontonagon, 71, 87, 112; at Portage Lake, 140; at Red Jacket, 98, 189. See also Douglass House; Hotel Scott
Hotel Scott, 176, 313; Moyer deportation initiated at, 214
Houghton, Douglass: at Copper Harbor, 40; death of, 43; description of, 43; foresees exploitation of Keweenaw mineral wealth, 39; early life of, 37; monument at Eagle River, 43; confronts Native Americans at Ontonagon, 40–41; survey of 1840, 34, 37–39; surveys of 1842 and 1844, 39
Houghton, Jacob, 46
Houghton, Mich., 93, 127, 156; active moral citizenry at, 103; boosterism in 1926 at, 250; and Civil War, 83; development of, in 1871–90, 102–5; as economic center, 103; expansion circa 1907 at, 176; library at, 169; origins of, 76; plans to compete as major tourist center, 302; population, 77, 102, 166; as port, 80–82, 250–51; and rivalry with Hancock, 98, 102, 182; soirées at, 104–5; traveling shows at, 103–4; urban renewal at, 302–3. See also Michigan Technological University
Houghton Candle Factory, 103
Houghton Cigar Factory, 103
Houghton Club building, 177
Houghton conglomerate, 265
Houghton County, Mich., 43, 71; and agriculture, 231–33, 250, 260; and assistance for strikers' families, 279, 296; in Civil War, 83–84; copper production in 1874, 108; courthouse, 77, 102, 105; and demise of Calumet and Hecla in 1969, 298; growth of service industries in, 282; high cost of assisting poor in 1933, 244; jail, 77, 102; as mining center circa 1888, 121; mining in 1923–24, 226–27; New Deal provides work in, 246–47; and 1930s depression,

Titles in the Great Lakes Books Series

Kids Catalog of Michigan Adventures, by Ellyce Field, 1993

Henry's Lieutenants, by Ford R. Bryan, 1993

Historic Highway Bridges of Michigan, by Charles K. Hyde, 1993

Lake Erie and Lake St. Clair Handbook, by Stanley J. Bolsenga and Charles E. Herndendorf, 1993

Turkey Stearnes and the Detroit Stars: The Negro Leagues in Detroit, 1919-1933, by Richard Bak, 1994

Pontiac and the Indian Uprising, by Howard H. Peckham, 1994 (reprint)

Iron Fleet: The Great Lakes in World War II, by George J. Joachim, 1994

Queen of the Lakes, by Mark Thompson, 1994

Charting the Inland Seas: A History of the U.S. Lake Survey, by Arthur M. Woodford, 1994 (reprint)

Ojibwa Narratives of Charles and Charlotte Kawbawgam and Jacques LePique, 1893–1895. Recorded with Notes by Homer H. Kidder, edited by Arthur P. Bourgeois, 1994, co-published with the Marquette County Historical Society

Strangers and Sojourners: A History of Michigan's Keweenaw Peninsula, by Arthur W. Thurner, 1994